THE CONCISE HISTORY
OF WOMAN SUFFRAGE

The Concise History of Woman Suffrage

Selections from *History of Woman Suffrage,*
edited by Elizabeth Cady Stanton,
Susan B. Anthony, Matilda Joslyn Gage,
and The National American
Woman Suffrage Association

Edited and with an introduction by
MARI JO BUHLE
AND PAUL BUHLE

UNIVERSITY OF ILLINOIS PRESS
URBANA AND CHICAGO

The selections from the *History of Woman Suffrage* reprinted in
this book were drawn from Volume 1, © 1881 by Elizabeth Cady
Stanton, Susan B. Anthony, and Matilda Joslyn Gage, second
edition (1889) © 1887 by Susan B. Anthony, Elizabeth Cady
Stanton, and Matilda Joslyn Gage; Volume 3, © 1886 by
Susan B. Anthony; Volume 4, © 1902 by Susan B. Anthony;
Volumes 5 and 6, © 1922 by the National American
Woman Suffrage Association.
P 5 4 3 2 1

The Library of Congress cataloged the original
paperback edition as follows:
Main entry under title:

The Concise history of woman suffrage.
Includes index.
1. Women—Suffrage—United States—History—Sources.
I. Buhle, Paul, 1944– II. Buhle, Mari Jo, 1943– III. Stanton,
Elizabeth Cady, 1815–1902, ed. History of woman suffrage.
JK1896.C58   322.4'4   78-1733
ISBN 0-252-00669-0
ISBN 0-252-00691-7 pbk.

Revised paperback ISBN 0-252-07276-6

CONTENTS

ACKNOWLEDGMENTS

We wish to express our gratitude to William L. O'Neill and to Kerry Hoover, who jointly suggested this project, and to Frank O. Williams and Carole S. Appel who oversaw the production of the first edition. Anne Firor Scott has kindly given us her attention and encouragement, as she has other historians following her path-breaking work in women's history. We have benefited from the research of, and from discussions with, Ellen C. Du Bois, a pioneering scholar of the woman suffrage movement. Ann D. Gordon, Judith E. Smith, and Nancy A. Hewitt were kind enough to read the manuscript at various stages. Karen Inouye helped with the preparation of citations. We are indebted to the librarians at the Arthur and Elizabeth Schlesinger Library on the History of Women in American, Radcliffe College. Finally, we wish to thank the staff a the University of Illinois Press, especially Jennifer Clark and Joan Catapano.

PREFACE

Scholarship on the history of woman suffrage remained for decades the work of suffragists themselves and their biographers, who first chronicled and then celebrated the triumph of the movement. The six-volume *History of Woman Suffrage* has been both the outstanding example and primary source of these labors. Fifty years after the passage of the Nineteenth Amendment, historians began to challenge the heroic interpretation by questioning the accomplishments and motivations of the suffrage leaders and by adding several layers of complexity to the grand old story. *The Concise History of Woman Suffrage,* which was first published in 1978, appeared as a preliminary response to those historians: a selection of materials illustrating the ideas and actions of the suffrage agitators themselves. Now, another quarter-century later, scholarship in the field has taken on a depth and breadth of purpose that the pioneering suffragists could scarcely have imagined and placed the documents collected here in new light.

* * *

The *Woman Citizen* proclaimed in 1919 that the *History of Woman Suffrage* offers "glowing records of as wonderful women as the world ever saw." The paper predicted, "Here are stories to thrill the souls of oncoming generations of girls to the end of time."[1] This claim overstated the appeal of work, which rapidly became merely a scholar's tool. In part, the six volumes were lost to public view because the history of woman suffrage seemed to succeeding generations distant from contemporary concerns, the enthusiasm of its advocates remote from our own way of thinking. Then, too, the style and internal logic of the volumes create difficulties for even the most engaged reader.

The *History of Woman Suffrage* is neither a comprehensive record of the struggle for women's enfranchisement nor a smooth narrative of the movement's course. Rather, the six volumes compiled over forty years by a series of editors offer a vast compendium of reminiscences, reports, arguments, and commentaries unevenly shaped by the logic of the suffrage cause and its leading proponents. In the

preface to the first volume, editors Elizabeth Cady Stanton and Susan B. Anthony noted that what had persuaded them to undertake
the task of preserving the memories of those campaigners who had
already "fallen asleep" and of gathering the recollections of those
still alive was the intrinsic importance of the movement. Believing,
too, that the next generation of suffrage agitators required the
information to carry the struggle forward, they set themselves to
creating a record. The making of the *History* was at once, therefore,
a profoundly personal and self-consciously political venture. Few social movements have been graced with leaders who could assemble,
organize, and comment on such a vast amount of information.

The prime mover for the *History* was Susan B. Anthony. For decades she had gathered records of all kinds, believing that one day
they would be required for just such a chronicle. In 1876 she and
Elizabeth Cady Stanton agreed to write that history. Anthony would
be "the collector of material, the searcher of statistics, the business
manager, the keen critic, the detector of omissions, chronological
flaws and discrepancies in statement." Stanton, aided by Matilda
Joslyn Gage, would be "the matchless writer."[2] Although the magnitude of the project grew well beyond the initial plan for one "small
volume," Anthony maintained her key role. She exhausted her own
savings in the project before receiving a bequest of nearly $25,000
in 1886 to continue the work. Because Stanton and Gage had written with the expectation of royalties from sales, Anthony purchased
their rights in order to donate the volumes to schools, libraries,
and individuals who might use them to promote the cause. Only
when Anthony had passed her eightieth birthday, in 1900, did she
relinquish primary responsibility for editing the new volumes and
then only to her biographer, Ida Husted Harper, who is listed with
Anthony on the title page of volume four and alone on volumes
five and six.

The first three volumes (published in 1881, 1882, and 1886 re-
spectively) bear the impress of the early woman's rights movement.
The editors' technique of compilation faithfully reflected the in-
tensely idealistic character and breadth of a struggle pursued by
a small band of zealots. Reprinted speeches, convention reports,
and reminiscences dominate the first two volumes. Stanton and
Anthony's treatment of their own roles was for the most part open
and unguarded. They viewed their particular activities within the
framework of antebellum reform: always a minority in champion-

ing woman's cause but nevertheless an important force among the heroic legions laboring for the abolition of slavery. In the middle of the second volume, their tone shifts, reflecting the growing isolation of the woman's rights from other reform endeavors and the division within the new movement organized specifically to secure women's right to vote.

The *History of Woman Suffrage,* under the guidance of Stanton and Anthony, presents a defensive and highly partisan portrait of their own National Woman Suffrage Association (NWSA), which had formed in 1869. Lucy Stone, leader of the rival organization, the American Woman Suffrage Association (AWSA), refused to contribute to any history written by "those ladies."[3] Her decision was unfortunate but understandable. Stanton and Anthony, envisioning NWSA at the center of the woman's rights movement, simply excluded alternative arguments and strategies. They largely ignored AWSA and the larger woman's movement emerging in the Gilded Age, from women's clubs and temperance, labor, farmer, and civic reform organizations. Amply represented instead were the many congressional hearings on woman suffrage that NWSA regarded as critical to the drive for a federal suffrage amendment. In addition, the documentation of NWSA activities served its need for self-perpetuation in difficult times. State and local activists found encouragement in the publication of their names and the description of their efforts as well as by repeated exhortations to sacrifice for a goal that grew more distant.

While Elizabeth Cady Stanton withdrew from steadfast participation in the increasingly conservative suffrage movement, Susan B. Anthony maintained a selfless dedication to NWSA and its records. Before resigning from the presidency of the combined National American Woman Suffrage Association (NAWSA) in 1900, Anthony had begun preparations for a fourth volume, which appeared in 1902 under the general editorship of Ida Husted Harper. She continued to bear the initial expenses herself and was reimbursed only by contributions from individual suffragists.

The fourth volume was a compilation most notable for its commentaries on state campaigns. National convention reports, a main feature in earlier volumes, were reduced to bare summations and quotations from a few illustrious speeches. Because conventions had now become carefully orchestrated affairs with little controversy or spontaneous discussion of any kind, there was not much of substance to report in any case. For these years, NAWSA published convention proceedings separately. But even the merger of the two associations in 1890 merited only a minimum of documentation and no references to the earlier rivalries or subsequent changes in the suffrage camp that allowed the union.

The final two volumes, published in 1922, appeared as a study in contrast to the first two. While the first clearly represented a labor of love, an arduous effort by Stanton and Anthony to compile and annotate thousands of documents without even the assistance of a typewriter, the last bore the stamp of professional researchers who for the most part tapped the bulging and convenient archives of NAWSA. Carrie Chapman Catt had dedicated a financial bequest to the creation of the Suffrage Commission and Bureau of Suffrage Education and incorporated this task into its agenda. But unlike Stanton and Anthony, Catt chose to minimize her own remarkable role. Few excerpts of her speeches appeared in the final volumes, and her personal life remained sheltered from this historical record. While the antebellum period had brought personal commitment and activism together, the early twentieth century guarded their separation. The convention reports and anecdotes that revealed so much about the pioneers gave way to reports of state and congressional campaigns and the politicians' responses, emphasizing primarily matters of strategy, tactics, and power.

This systematic channeling of energies nevertheless failed to produce a comprehensive review of the modern movement for woman suffrage. The new editors passed over important controversies within NAWSA, such as relationships with the Progressive party and Anna Howard Shaw's competence as president, and allowed only occasional hints of internal turmoil to surface. More important, the latter volumes slighted or ignored altogether the work of other organizations that added to the final campaigns. The Congressional Union and the National Woman's Party, chief rivals to NAWSA, received minimal attention. Similarly, although such groups as labor unions, the Socialist party, the Woman's Christian Temperance Union, and women's clubs continued to play a major role in widening the suffrage constituency, the editors only rarely credited their work. No less than the first volumes, the last were written with an eye to the historical record. While the chroniclers of the early movement sought to emphasize its idealism, those of the latter movement chose to demonstrate its efficiency in a society that similarly admired bureaucratic mechanisms.

* * *

The new scholarship in the field of women's history has added several dimensions to the events catalogued in the original *History of Woman Suffrage*. Although the topic of woman suffrage itself remains far from popular among scholars who, as a group, continue to favor social and cultural history, the revival and subsequent defeat of the Equal Rights Amendment has given political history a new urgency. Since the mid-1980s, much effort has gone into the sifting of archives and broad-based research on companion reform and political movements. Collectively, scholars have significantly revised the historical record bequeathed by the suffragists. Content with neither a hagiography of leaders nor a simple narrative of a long campaign that inexorably led to victory, they added layers of complexity. They also built upon the foundation laid by a handful of historians who broke new ground in the late 1950s and 1960s and asked hard questions concerning the ultimate significance of the passage of the Nineteenth Amendment.[4] Equally important, rather than adhering to the schema provided by the *History of Woman Suffrage*, an attempt to document a movement that spanned the nation, scholars since the mid-1980s have narrowed their focus to provide a more exacting as well as critical portrait of leaders, organizations, and events.

One subject, however, has retained its central place: women's activism before the Civil War. In designing the first volume of the *History of Woman Suffrage*, Stanton, Anthony, and Gage were determined to emphasize the importance of both antislavery and the broader woman's rights agitation as backdrop to the woman suffrage movement, which organized during the Reconstruction Era. The first section of this volume, "Part One: To the Civil War," illustrates their effort to trace their roots back to the antebellum campaigns. Historians since have affirmed and expanded this perspective, highlighting the political precedents established within antislavery societies and especially the role of Angelina Grimke, whom the original editors acknowledge as one "who, having lived in the midst of slavery all her life, could faithfully describe its cruelties and abominations" [Document 3].[5] In addition, they have fashioned new biographies of key individuals and have made this question central to their inquiry.[6]

The recent scholarship on the relationship of woman's rights to antislavery is not, however, of one piece. Ellen Carol DuBois became the first to challenge the early suffragists' contention that women came to recognize their own oppression through participation in the antislavery movement, as suggested by the editors' commentary on the World's Anti-Slavery Convention, London, England, June, 1840 [Document 4]. To the contrary, DuBois argued, the women who insisted on joining men to speak against slavery, such as Lucretia Stone and Stanton herself, were already keenly aware of the limitations placed on their sex. Rather than a catalyst for woman's rights, DuBois further contended, the long and hard campaign to abolish slavery actually tended to slow the development of an independent woman's rights movement.[7]

Since the publication of DuBois's path-breaking *Feminism and Suffrage: The Emergence of an Independent Woman's Rights Movement in America, 1848–1869* (1978), other historians have similarly revised or augmented the original narrative, situating woman's rights within a larger arena of moral reform. Interfacing with the scholarship in cultural and social history, these scholars argued that many suffragists, in addition to activists in a wide array of campaigns, justified their actions in terms of their domestic or familial roles, none being more instrumental than Republican Motherhood. By mapping the ideological legacy of the American Revolution and modernization, historians documented the new responsibility that antebellum white women embraced: to educate their sons for citizenship and to provide moral guidance to their husbands. With the expansion of their roles as mothers and as wives, these women, mainly in the North, pursued an increasingly wide range of religious, benevolent, and, in some cases, reform activities.[8]

Although historians at first imagined that activist women progressed through a series of stages, from religious to political campaigns, recent writers have made a point to distinguish among the various venues of public activism and, moreover, refuse to draw a straight line of development from moral reform to woman's rights agitation.[9] They have further demonstrated that antislavery women differed among themselves in terms of class, race, religious affiliation, and motivation for joining the struggle. Many African American women, for example, organized against slavery and for the welfare of their community without taking up the cause for woman's rights. Other activists, such as Catharine Beecher, also pursued their reformist goals while intently distancing themselves from the campaign for woman's rights.[10] As several of the selections here suggest, the antebellum woman's rights conventions provided activists with a forum for airing major differences among themselves, particularly on questions of marriage and divorce [Document 18]. Sharply attuned to these differences, recent historians have expanded the context for women's activism far beyond the antislavery, property rights, and temperance agitation emphasized in the documents here. They have also highlighted the importance of religion, particularly the positive influences of the Hicksite Quakers and the evangelical Protestants energized by the Second Great Awakening, that the avowed anti-clerics, Stanton and Gage, side-stepped in preparing the *History*.[11]

Altogether, recent scholars have created a far more complex version of antebellum women's activism and its relationship to woman's rights than the documents selected by Stanton, Anthony, and Gage indicate. Nancy Isenberg has asked a series of questions as a prelude to reformulating the relationship between woman's rights based on the principle of equality with men and broad claims to citizenship grounded on woman's unique potential. She asked why the editors of the *History of Woman Suffrage* privileged the 1848 meeting at Seneca Falls, thereby minimizing the significance of other conventions now lost to history. Isenberg further discounted the editors' own investment in the *Declaration of Sentiments* and resolutions presented at this first convention as "all the most radical friends of the movement have since claimed" [Document 5].[12] Nevertheless, despite these tough questions, the documents in "Part One: To The Civil War" continue to sustain the research of scholars. The speeches and declarations culled from the many conventions held before the Civil War provide apt illustrations of the various ways in which women activists wrestled with the pressing issues of the day, employed metaphors and analogies to widen the ideological parameters of "woman's sphere," and, ultimately, redefined the meaning of womanhood.[13]

Recent scholars have also restored the international context that was so important to the first generation of woman's rights activists. The Polish Jew Ernestine Rose began her address the Second National Convention, held in Worcester, Massachusetts, October 15–16, 1851, by saluting as sisters the women who fought valiantly in France during the Revolution of 1848 and suffered imprisonment in its aftermath [Document 8]. British suffragists in particular served for decades as eager hosts to leading American visitors, provided introductions to distinguished intellectuals and artists, and created a bridge to continental woman's rights movements. Indeed, the original *History of Woman Suffrage* contains proportionally far more documents illustrating the early suffragists' feelings of solidarity with activists abroad than the selection in this volume indicates.[14]

Standing firm in the new scholarship is a second major theme: the significance of the Civil War. "The labor women accomplished, the hardships they endured, the time and strength they sacrificed in the war that summoned three million men to arms," Gage wrote, "can never be fully appreciated" [Document 19]. Recently historians have been closing in on this claim. In a profusion of new monographs, they have verified Gage's contention by examining in close detail women's activities during the Civil War, on the battlefront as well as the homefront, North and South.[15] They have also explored the vast quantity of fictional literature on the subject that women writers produced.[16] In addition to filling these gaps, historians have followed the lead of Stanton and Anthony to examine in close detail the Woman's National Loyal League [Documents 20 and 21]. Unlike the original editors, who acknowledged foremost its purpose of promoting the Emancipation Proclamation, recent scholars have stressed the role of the Loyal League in transforming the woman's rights movement into a national enterprise with a cadre of well-trained leaders.[17] In summary, the Civil War continues to mark a turning point in the history of the woman's rights movement.

Recent scholars, however, have ventured further into the history of race relations during Reconstruction and after than the original editors of the *History of Woman Suffrage* were prepared to do. The selections collected here in "Part Two: The Civil War to 1885" highlight the controversies provoked by the introduction of the words "race" and "sex" into the Constitution with the passage of the Fourteenth and Fifteenth Amendments. Since the mid-1980s, historians have focused on the significance of the suffragists' response to this event, particularly the realignments that took place as a consequence. They have reassessed the significance of the division of ranks in terms of strategy and the rise of overt racism within the larger movement.[18] Nevertheless, despite the attention given to the 1869 suffrage schism, most historians have sustained the partisan politics of Stanton and Anthony and illustrated in this volume. Like the original editors of the *History of Woman Suffrage,* they have continued to exclude AWSA from serious consideration while agreeing with Stanton and Anthony's judgment that the faction led by Lucy Stone and followers promoted an essentially conservative strategy. Yet, while acknowledging the radical implications of NWSA's federal initiative, recent scholars have underscored the increasing racism of its leaders, including Stanton herself. Several documents in "Part Three: 1885–1920" support this emphasis, perhaps none so clearly as the frequently cited address by Henry B. Blackwell to the 1895 NAWSA Convention held in Atlanta wherein he outlines the "statistical argument" for woman suffrage as "one solution of the negro problem" [Document 47].[19]

For several historians, especially those focused on regional aspects, race has emerged as the key factor in their studies while at the same time producing no consensus. Majorie Spruill Wheeler provided a highly influential study of the emerging Southern woman suffrage movement at the end of the nineteenth century, acknowledging its radical edge, especially for its cultural context, yet insisting that racism determined both strategy and arguments that fed the ongoing campaign for white supremacy.[20] Other historians have taken a different line, affirming Anne Firor Scott and Andrew Scott's earlier rejection of racism as the prime motivating factor in the Southern suffrage movement. They envision the South as akin to the North in generating a wide range of convictions on race relations. States' rights as well as rabid racism played important roles within the Southern movement, they acknowledge, but did not singularly determine the course of suffrage history in the region.[21]

If unsettling in scholarship concerning the South, the consideration of race relations has virtually transformed scholarship on the Western suffrage movement. The suffrage pioneers themselves had celebrated the western states and territories as the seedbed of democracy as well as credited the hard campaigning of women [Document 46]. Recently, historians have fashioned a far more complex picture of politics in the West. Some have emphasized expedient reasons for granting women the right to vote, such as an attempt to attract settlers or to offset the enfranchisement of African American or Mexican American men. They have widened the context to place woman suffrage within a larger discussion of the political status of Native Americans and Mormons within territories seeking admission to the union. Most shocking of all, they have envisioned the accession of the right to vote in the Western states less a victory for women than a strategic setback for the national movement for woman suffrage. The success in Western states, it now seems, actually undermined the strategy focused on change at the federal level, that is, as an amendment to the Constitution, by making woman suffrage an issue to be settled by individual states.[22]

The attention to race has pushed forward a wave of scholarship on the participation of African American women in the woman suffrage movement. Stanton and Anthony had limited their coverage to the dramatic, oft-quoted speeches of Sojourner Truth, who allied with NWSA after the Civil War [Documents 7 and 26]. The larger story of Truth and her legacy awaited the publication of Nell Irwin Painter's stunning biography in 1996.[23] Rosalyn Terborg-Penn followed with a major study rescuing black suffragists from obscurity by combing the *History of Woman Suffrage* to identify 135 African Americans whom previous historians had overlooked. The racism of the mainstream woman suffrage movement kept many of these women at a distance, she explained, yet did not quash their desire for political enfranchisement. To the contrary, women like Frances Ellen Watkins Harper, Ida B. Wells, Anna Julia Cooper, and Mary Church Terrell agitated steadfastly for not only woman suffrage but universal suffrage. From the 1860s through the 1880s, Terborg-Penn pointed out, African American women were more likely to affiliate with AWSA than with NWSA but conducted most of their work under the auspices of black women's clubs or through their churches.[24]

In addition to underscoring the significance of race relations and racism within campaigns for the ballot, Terborg-Penn joined a group of other historians who explored venues for suffrage agitation outside the mainstream movement. Since the publication in 1981 of Ruth Bordin's stellar history of the Woman's Christian Temperance Union [WCTU], historians have acknowledged the important role various organizations had played in the historic struggle for the vote. Not only the WCTU but, after the turn of the twentieth century, the National Federation of Women's Clubs, the College Settlement Association, and the National Association for the Advancement of Colored People in particular mobilized their troops in large numbers. Reformers like Frances Willard and Jane Addams have recently achieved a place of prominence in the suffrage campaign that the original editors of the *History of Woman Suffrage* denied them.[25]

Historians have made similar cases for the People's, Socialist, and Progressive parties. In the most persuasive argument, put forward with great care by Rebecca Edwards, the People's party in particular offered a way out of the dilemmas facing the suffrage movement in an Imperial age. Among the two major parties, Republicans offered the manliness of the conqueror, Democrats the supposed defense of white Southern womanhood. After the practical collapse of the People's party into the William Jennings Bryan "fusion" campaign in 1896, and despite the efforts of socialists subsequently to enlist their sympathies, suffragists felt that they had nowhere to go to forge an alliance necessary for victory.[26]

In addition to suffragists' relationships with political parties, historians have also provided new insights into the role of the antisuffragists. Susan E. Marshall, for example, argued that self-interest rather than traditional mores prompted many professional or well-to-do women to mobilize against the woman suffrage movement at the end of the nineteenth century and to fashion a form of public activism that was ultimately more similar than different from the styles of suffragists.[27]

If recent scholars have tended to emphasize the conservatism of the late nineteenth-century woman suffrage movement, associating its leading activists with an increasingly nationalist and imperialist political agenda, scholars of the next two decades of the campaign have sounded a more upbeat note. Indeed, the Progressive Era (1900–1920) has now been recast as a high point of women's political activism, both within and beyond the formal political area. Women's efforts to reshape government's responsibilities for social welfare at city, state and national levels has come to be seen as setting the stage for what would become one of the major reforms of the twentieth century, the development of public-funded welfare programs.[28]

A large volume of scholarship now provides a useful supplement to the documents collected here in "Part Three: 1885–1920." Whereas the original *History of Woman Suffrage* held a steady light on NAWSA and the state campaigns it sponsored during the final push toward victory, recent scholars have emphasized the energy and militancy flowing from the National Woman's Party [NWP]. Carrie Chapman Catt, the architect of the "winning plan," has continued to earn the respect of historians, but she now has genuine rivals in the realm of tactics and strategy.[29] Recent historians, Christine A. Lunardini in the lead, have given principal credit to Alice Paul and the NWP, attributing a large part of the credit for the final victory to their unwavering focus on the initiative for a federal amendment and willingness to adopt the partisan politics that ultimately converted President Woodrow Wilson [Document 76].[30] Ellen Carol DuBois, in discussing the career of Stanton's daughter, Harriot Stanton Blatch, traced the roots of the militant tactics to England and then followed them out to the United States and the subsequent flowering in the Equality League and the NWP.[31] Although the majority of these scholars highlighted suffrage tactics in the northeast, several pursued both the rise of militant suffrage tactics and the greater diversity of groups and individuals in other regions of the country.[32]

This expanded venue has offered innovative approaches to the decreasing boundaries between commercial and political culture in the twentieth century, showing that suffragists were taking crucial cues from the expanding consumer culture. By recounting how activists helped to create a popular culture symbolizing themselves and their cause—such as the suffrage parade outfit, including hats, sash, buttons and pennant sold by Macy's for a total $1.68—Margaret Finnegan takes the scholarship in this new direction. Suffrage associations filled budget gaps by selling a wide variety of memorabilia, ranging from postcards to statuettes, and sponsoring suffrage plays and dramatic performances. The editors of suffrage journals and newspapers redesigned their formats to encourage advertisers, and leaders suggested ways for campaigners to present themselves to the public and even starred occasionally in silent films.[33] Recent scholars have also identified, with prolific examples, the images created by talented illustrators of the suffrage movement, from the first woman's rights papers to the Progressive era press by turns dramatizing the cause, urging activists onward through fallow times, and ridiculing the powerful opposition movement to women's enfranchisement. In a variety of ways, NAWSA's contribution takes on new meaning as an example of modern pressure group politics.[34]

In 1920, at the celebration sponsored jointly by NAWSA and the League of Women Voters, the victors paid honor to the pioneering suffragists, rejoiced that the struggle was finally over, and then asked how they could best serve their "beloved nation" [Document 83]. Recently historians have responded to this query, jettisoning a claim by William L. O'Neill that the campaign for woman suffrage failed because so little changed politically or socially in its

aftermath.[35] They have studied in great detail the political involve-
ments of women in the wake of the suffrage victory as well as the
realignments within the movement forced by the new initiative for
the Equal Rights Amendment, the political mobilization to achieve
its passage during the 1970s-80s, and the subsequent bitter defeat
(along with the racially-tinged "welfare reform" and growing challenges to women's abortion rights) in the face of a rising political
conservatism.[36] They have also examined the legacy of nonparti-
sanship, which NAWSA promoted, as well as the significance of
the ideology grounded exclusively in the affinity of gender. Other
studies have deepened the sense that if women's desire to participate
remained strong, the doors that opened to their full participation
in the political process remained only slightly ajar, their impact on
the two-party system minimal.[37]

New documentary collections and anthologies of essays have
provided fuller representation of the suffrage movement, as have
a small spate of biographies of its leaders. None is more relevant
than the volumes edited by Ann D. Gordon, who directs the Elizabeth Cady Stanton-Susan B. Anthony Papers Project. Scrupulous
attention has been given to the details of correspondence, public
appearances, private reflections, and contemporary responses.[38]
Several collections of essays offer a wide variety of detailed coverage,
some entries summarizing research in monographs, but like the
continuing proliferation of state studies treating the specific cru-
sades, individuals, and local or regional activity in unprecedented
depth.[39] Finally, several historians, notably Julie des Jardins, have
begun to study the history of women's history itself, emphatically
including the construction and publication of *The History of Woman
Suffrage*.[40] This scholarship promises a further development in our
understanding of the issues raised here.

* * *

The Concise History of Woman Suffrage now enters its second edition as a small effort to promote the revival of scholarship begun
in the mid-1980s. The selections here, retained in whole from the
first edition, reflect, for better or worse, our process of evaluation.
Constraints of space and other editorial considerations caused us
to choose sparingly from certain categories of materials. Personal
reminiscences of individuals such as Emily Collins and Clarina Howard Nichols seemed distant from the general narrative. The many

newspaper articles and letters reprinted in the volumes reflected upon the suffrage movement only indirectly. Congressional debates from the 1880s to the suffrage victory largely concerned the opposition rather than major events in the movement's own history. We have chosen only a small fraction of the state studies because most were overburdened with details gathered for the sake of inclusiveness. And, finally, international materials, despite their importance to suffrage leaders and future historians, demanded more context than this one volume could provide.

In the main we have tried to provide a selection both readable for today's audience and true to the spirit of the original volumes. The pioneers of woman suffrage emphasized the politics of both principle and strategy as well as the organizational apparatus that served them. Whenever possible we have allowed them and their successors to speak for themselves, through texts of speeches, proceedings, and resolutions from major conventions. We hope the readers of this edition will come to share our conviction, that the richness and variety of material left by the suffrage movement, the spark of great personalities, and the flare of grand events both heroic and tragic give this history a rightful place of importance long denied it.

NOTES

1. "A Gigantic Task," *Woman Citizen* (New York, December 6, 1919.

2. *History of Woman Suffrage*, I: 7–8. The remainder of the information on the production of the volumes is drawn from IV: v-vi, and V: iv-v. Ellen Carol DuBois, *Woman Suffrage and Women's Rights* (New York, 1998), Chapter 11.

3. Lucy Stone to Harriet Robinson, March 4, 1879, Harriet Robinson Collection, The Arthur and Elizabeth Schlesinger Library, Radcliffe College.

4. Eleanor Flexner, *Century of Struggle: The Woman's Rights Movement in the United States* (Cambridge, Mass.: 1959); Aileen Kraditor, *Ideas of the Woman Suffrage Movement* (New York, 1965); Gerda Lerner, *The Grimke Sisters of North Carolina: Pioneers for Women's Rights and Abolitionism* (New York, 1967).

5. Katherine DePre Lumpkin, *The Emancipation of Angelina Grimke* (Chapel Hill, 1974); Blanche Glassman Hersh, *The Slavery of Sex: Feminist-Abolitionists in America* (Urbana, 1978); Jean Fagan Yellin, *Women and Sisters: The Antislavery Feminists in American Culture* (New Haven, 1989); Jean Fagan Yellin and John C. Van Horne, eds., *The Abolitionist Sisterhood: Women's Political Culture in Antebellum America* (Ithaca, 1994); Kathryn Kish Sklar, *Women's Rights Emerges Within the Antislavery Movement, 1850–1870: A Brief History with Documents* (Boston and New York, 2000).

6. Lois Banner, *Elizabeth Cady Stanton: A Radical for Woman's Rights* (Boston, 1980); Elisabeth Griffith, *In Her Own Right: The Life of Elizabeth Cady Stanton* (New York,

1984); Dorothy Sterling, *Ahead of Her Time: Abby Kelley and the Politics of Antislavery* (New York, 1991); Ira V. Brown, *Mary Grew: Abolitionist and Feminist (1813–1896)* (Selinsgrove, 1991); Andrew Moor Kerr, *Lucy Stone: Speaking Out for Equality* (New Brunswick, N.J., 1996); Carol Kolmerton, *The American Life of Ernestine Rose* (Syracuse, 1999).

7. Ellen Carol DuBois, *Feminism and Suffrage: The Emergence of an Independent Women's Movement in America, 1848–1869* (Ithaca, 1978).

8. Nancy F. Cott, *The Bonds of Womanhood: "Woman's Sphere" in New England, 1780–1835* (New Haven, 1978); Linda Kerber, *Women of the Republic: Intellect and Ideology in Revolutionary America* (Chapel Hill, 1980).

9. Keith E. Melder, *The Beginnings of Sisterhood: The American Women's Rights Movement, 1800–1850* (New York, 1977); Nancy A. Hewitt, *Women's Activism and Social Change: Rochester, New York, 1822–1872* (Ithaca, 1984); Lori D. Ginzberg, *Women and the Work of Benevolence: Morality, Politics, and Class in Nineteenth-Century United States* (New Haven, 1990); Anne M. Boylan, *The Origins of Women's Activism, New York and Boston, 1797–1840* (Chapel Hill, 2002); Bruce Dorsey, *Reforming Men and Women: Gender in the Antebellum City* (Ithaca, 2002).

10. Kathryn Kish Sklar, *Catharine Beecher: A Study in American Domesticity* (New Haven, 1973); Shirley J. Yee, *Black Women Abolitionists: A Study in Activism, 1828–1860* (Knoxville, Tenn., 1989); Debra Gold Hansen, *Strained Sisterhood: Gender and Class in the Boston Female Anti-Slavery Society* (Amherst, 1993).

11. Nancy A. Hardesty, *Your Daughters Shall Prophesy: Revivalism and Feminism in the Age of Finney* (Brooklyn, 1991); Julie Roy Jeffrey, *The Great Army of Abolitionism: Ordinary Women in the Antislavery Movement* (Chapel Hill, 2000); Lori D. Ginzberg, *Women and Antebellum Reform* (Wheeling, Ill., 2002).

12. Nancy Isenberg, *Sex and Citizenship in Antebellum America* (Chapel Hill, 1998). A further exploration of citizenship is Linda J. Kerber, *No Constitutional Right to Be Ladies: Women and the Obligations of Citizenship* (New York, 1998).

13. Karen Sanchez-Eppler, *Touching Liberty: Abolitionism, Feminism, and the Politics of the Body* (Berkeley, 1993); Sylvia D. Hoffert, *When Hens Crow: The Women's Rights Movement in Antebellum America* (Bloomington, Indiana, 1995); Carla L. Peterson, *"Doers of the Word": African American Women Speakers and Writers in the North (1830–1880)* (New York, 1995); Jean V. Matthews, *Women's Struggle for Equality: The First Phase, 1828–1876* (Chicago, 1997); Gerda Lerner, *The Feminist Thought of Sarah Grimke* (New York, 1998); Frances Smith Foster, ed., *A Brighter Day Coming: A Frances Ellen Watkins Harper Reader* (New York, 1990).

14. Caroline Daley and Melanie Nolan, eds., *Suffrage and Beyond: International Feminist Perspectives* (New York, 1994); Margaret H. McFadden, *Golden Cables of Sympathy: The Transatlantic Sources of Nineteenth-century Feminism* (Lexington, Kentucky, 1999); Bonnie S. Anderson, *Joyous Greetings: The First International Women's Movement, 1830–1860* (Oxford, England, 2000).

15. George Rable, *Civil Wars: Women and the Crisis of Southern Nationalism* (Urbana, 1989); Richard Hall, *Patriots in Disguise: Women Warriors of the Civil War* (New York, 1993); Elizabeth D. Leonard, *Yankee Women: Gender Battles in the Civil War* (New York, 1994); Ella Forbes, *African American Women During the Civil War* (New York, 1998); Norralee Frankel, *Freedom's Women: Black Women and Families in Civil War Era Mississippi* (Bloomington, Ind., 1999); Elizabeth D. Leonard, *All the Daring of the Solider: Women of the Civil War Armies* (New York, 1999); Judith Ann Giesberg,

Civil War Sisterhood: The U.S. Sanitary Commission and Women's Politics in Transition (Boston, 2000); DeAnne Blanton and Lauren M. Cook, *They Fought Like Demons: Women Soldiers in the American Civil War* (Baton Rouge, 2002).

16. Elizabeth Young, *Disarming the Nation: Women's Writing and the American Civil War* (Chicago, 1999); Lyda Cullen Sizer, *The Political Work of Northern Women Writers and the Civil War, 1850–1872* (Chapel Hill, 2000).

17. Wendy Hamand Venet, *Neither Ballots nor Bullets: Women Abolitionists and the Civil War* (Charlottesville and London, 1991).

18. Nell Painter, *Sojourner Truth, a Life, a Symbol* (New York, 1996); Rosalyn Terborn-Penn, *African American Women and the Struggle for the Vote, 1850–1920* (Bloomington, Ind., 1998).

19. Nancie Caraway, *Segregated Sisterhood: Racism and the Politics of American Feminism* (Knoxville, Tenn., 1991); Louise Michele Newman, *White Women's Rights: The Racial Origins of Feminism in the United States* (New York, 1999), Chapter 2.

20. Marjorie Spruill Wheeler, *New Women of the New South: The Leaders of the Woman Suffrage Movement in the Southern States* (New York, 1993).

21. Anne F. Scott and Andrew Scott, eds., *One Half the People: The Fight for Woman Suffrage* (Philadelphia, 1975); Elna C. Green, *Southern Strategies: Southern Women and the Woman Suffrage Question* (Chapel Hill, 1997); Sarah Barringer Gordon, *The Mormon Question: Polygamy and Constitutional Conflict in Nineteenth Century America* (Chapel Hill, 2002).

22. Beverly Beeton, *Women Vote in the West: The Woman Suffrage Movement, 1869–1896* (New York, 1986).

23. Nell Irwin Painter, *Sojourner Truth, A Life, A Symbol.* (New York, 1996).

24. Rosalyn Terborg-Penn, *African American Women in the Struggle for the Vote, 1850–1920*; Evelyn Brooks Higginbotham, *Righteous Discontent: The Women's Movement in the Black Baptist Church, 1880–1920* (Cambridge, Mass., 1992); Ann D. Gordon, ed., *African American Women and the Vote, 1837–1965* (Amherst, Mass., 1997).

25. Ruth Bordin, *Woman and Temperance: The Quest for Power and Liberty, 1873–1900* (Chapel Hill, 1981); Karen J. Blair, *The Clubwoman as Feminism: True Womanhood Redefined, 1868–1914* (New York, 1980); Suzanne M. Marilley, *Woman Suffrage and the Origins of Liberal Feminism in the United States, 1820–1920* (Cambridge, Mass., 1996); Melanie Gustafson, *Women and the Republic Party* (Urbana, 2001).

26. Michael Goldberg, *An Army of Women: Gender and Politics in Gilded Age Kansas* (Baltimore, 1997); Mari Jo Buhle, *Women and American Socialism, 1870–1920* (Urbana, Ill., 1981); Rebecca Edwards, *Angels in the Machinery: Gender in American Party Politics from the Civil War to the Progressive Era* (New York, 1997).

27. Susan E. Marshall, *Splintered Sisterhood: Gender and Class in the Campaign against Woman Suffrage* (Madison, 1997); Jane Camhi, *Women Against Women: American Anti-Suffrage, 1880–1920* (Brooklyn, N.Y., 1994); Thomas J. Jablonsky, *The Home, Heaven and the Mother Party: Female Antisuffrage in the United States, 1868–1920* (Brooklyn, 1924).

28. See, for instance, Anne Firor Scott, *Natural Allies* (Urbana, 1991); Melanie Gustafson, *Women and the Republican Party* (Urbana, 2001), and Robyn Muncy, *Creating a Female Dominion in American Reform, 1880–1935* (New York, 1991).

29. Robert Booth Fowler, *Carrie Catt: Feminist Politican* (Boston, 1986).

30. Christine A. Lunardini, *From Equal Suffrage to Equal Rights: Alice Paul and the National Woman's Party, 1910–1928* (1986); Linda G. Ford, *Iron-Jawed Angels: The Suf-*

frage Militancy of the National Woman's Party 1912–1920 (Landham, Maryland, 1991); Linda J. Lumsden, *Rampant Women: Suffragists and the Rights of Assembly* (Knoxville, Tenn., 1997)

31. Ellen Carol DuBois, *Harriott Stanton Blatch and the Winning of the Suffrage Battle* (New Haven, 1997).

32. Steven Buechler, *The Transformation of the Woman Suffrage Movement: The Case of Illinois, 1850–1920* (New Brunswick, N.J., 1986); Gaye Gullett, *Becoming Citizens: The Emergence and Development of the California Women's Movement, 1880–1911* (Urbana, Ill., 2000)

33. Margaret Finnegan, *Selling Suffrage: Consumer Culture and Votes for Women* (New York, 1999); Alice Sheppard, *Cartooning for Suffrage* (Albuquerque, N.M., 1994); Katharine Cockin, *Women and Theatre in the Age of Suffrage: The Pioneer Players, 1911–1925* (New York, 2001).

34. Sarah Graham Hunter, *Woman Suffrage and the New Democracy* (New Haven, 1996).

35. William L. O'Neill, *Everyone Was Brave* (Chicago, 1969).

36. J. Stanley Lemons, *The Woman Citizen: Social Feminism in the 1920s* (Chicago, 1975); Susan Becker, *The Origins of the ERA: American Feminism Between the Wars* (Westport, Conn., 1981); Nancy F. Cott, *The Grounding of American Feminism* (New Haven, 1987)

37. Carole Nichols, *Votes and More for Women: Suffrage and After in Connecticut* (New York, 1983); Felice D. Gordon, *After Winning: The Legacy of the New Jersey Suffragists, 1920–1947* (New Brunswick, N.J., 1986); Anna L. Harvey, *Votes Without Leverage: Women in American Electoral Politics, 1920–1970* (Cambridge, England and New York, 1998); Beverly Palmer, ed., *The Selected Letters of Lucretia Coffin Mott* (Urbana, 2002).

38. To the time of this writing, three volumes have appeared: Ann D. Gordon, ed., *The Selected Papers of Elizabeth Cady Stanton and Susan B. Anthony, Vol I: In the School of Anti-Slavery, 1840–1866* (New Brunswick, N.J., 1997); *Vol. II: Against the Aristocracy of Sex, 1866–1873* (New Brunswick, N.J., 2000); and *Vol.III: National Protection for National Citizens, 1873–1880* (New Brunswick, N.J., 2003).

39. Marjorie Spruill Wheeler, ed., *Votes for Women! The Woman Suffrage Movement in Tennessee, the South, and the Nation* (Knoxville, Tenn., 1995); Ellen Carol DuBois, *Woman Suffrage and Woman's Rights* (New York, 1998); Jean H. Baker, ed., *Votes for Women: The Struggle for Suffrage Revisited* (New York, 2002). Among the state studies, Carole Nichols's *Votes and More for Women: Suffrage and After in Connecticut* (New York, 1983) is illustrative for its attention to the complexities of suffrage alliances and strategies and its considerations of the consequences for women's participation in politics after the passage of the Nineteenth Amendment.

40. Julie des Jardins, *Women and the Historical Enterprise in America: Gender, Race and the Politics of Memory, 1880–1970* (Chapel Hill, 2003).

INTRODUCTION: WOMAN SUFFRAGE AND AMERICAN REFORM

THE HISTORY OF THE WOMAN suffrage movement represents a little-understood but vital phase of American reform. The simple faith underlying the movement's key demand, the ballot, was the belief in republican citizenship passed down from the American Revolution. Women tested the limits of that doctrine in practice, just as blacks did in contesting for their emancipation and enfranchisement. Women's expectation of an unfolding, ultimately universal freedom was compelling if sanguine, and in time, the definitions of emancipation changed. The champions of woman suffrage were bypassed by other reformers and new causes. But behind the strategic changes remained fundamental strengths that outlasted political confusion and the dilution of idealism: women's capacity to grow beyond their present limitations and women's ability to organize so as to enforce their demands.

Three distinct stages mark the evolution of woman suffrage agitation. Before the Civil War, the woman's rights movement was part of a larger force aiming at universal reform. During the Reconstruction era, the reform community disintegrated into scattered, independent forces. After 1885 the suffrage movement grew into a tightly coordinated national organization. Throughout these stages, woman suffrage shared the larger problems of American reform, was spiritually uplifted by its early faith and finally confronted by the difficulties of the narrowed potential to change fundamentally the nature of American society. What the suffrage advocates did, how their efforts linked up with other reform causes, how alliances shaped their decisions, how victories and defeats successively remolded them on the way to their final goal, and how their consciousness and composition changed over the century—these are the byways we seek to explore in the following pages.

1

Before the war

Antebellum reformers encouraged two distinct but complementary interpretations of the national heritage. They celebrated the American Revolution as the victory of natural rights over the artificial restraints of church and crown. The eighteenth-century revolutionists had believed that the finite mind of man could touch the Infinite and discover for itself immutable laws governing human behavior. Their nineteenth-century descendants followed the interpretation sanctioned by Jefferson, Paine, and others that each generation had the duty to free itself of the dead hand of the past, to search anew for the proper forms of government.[1] Faith in the power of self-government brought reformers to glorify the ideal of the American Republic even in the face of undemocratic processes and to exhort their fellow citizens to achieve the immanent possibilities of the nation. Young America would be the showplace of world progress. At the same time, many reformers took up the supremely moral responsibility to guard republican institutions and thus refurbish the revolutionary legacy. The evangelical enthusiasms of the New World, held in check in New England by theocracy and federalism until the early decades of the nineteenth century, burst out with the expansion of the new nation.[2] Frontier violence, widespread drunkenness, and reported licentiousness were fervently attacked as violations of America's sacred trust. Only the extirpation of sin could block the greed of planters and other social parasites and turn aside the impiety of the emerging urban life. For reformers, republicanism and moralism ultimately combined: the ideal portrayed by the first required the protection of the second.

By the 1820s, woman's rights pioneer Frances Wright drew on the republican tradition to extend the principles of the Declaration of Independence, which she called her "Holy Bible" of reform. Wright and her collaborators promoted

NOTE: Much of the material discussed in this Introduction refers to our selection of documents from the *History of Woman Suffrage,* and we have not cited these sources specifically.

1. See Carl Becker, *The Declaration of Independence* (New York, 1942), 26, 39.
2. Avery O. Craven, "The Northern Attack on Slavery," in David Brion Davis, ed., *Antebellum Reform* (New York, 1967), 25.

sweeping changes in public and personal life. Through a program of universal education, Americans would collectively realize the promise of a democracy that knew neither sex, color, nor class and that enshrined the individual conscience as the highest human authority. Wright railed against the submergence of woman in marriage as a violation of natural rights and challenged the institution of marriage on the ground that it circumscribed woman's individualism, placing her outside true citizenship. Through lecture tours from the eastern seaboard to the northwest frontier, Wright attracted a sympathetic though hesitant female audience.[3]

The next generation of woman's rights supporters came to parallel conclusions about woman's place in the Republic but drew the lessons more cautiously. In effect, Elizabeth Cady Stanton and her colleagues recognized that the American Revolution had cut the nexus of feudal customs treating the state as a network of patriarchal families. Civil society was to be the link between the individual and the state. The founding fathers had been more concerned with their sons than with their wives or daughters in the definitions of citizenship. Yet women paid taxes and were bound by most of the same laws as their husbands, fathers, and sons. Equality, they averred, meant only the extension of principle inherent in the revolutionary legacy. Unlike Frances Wright, most of the women in the mainstream woman's rights movement made no direct challenge to the institution of marriage, but they did protest the idealization of woman's domestic role while her individual prerogatives were denied.

Wright's messianic faith in the American Republic had been shaken by its rapid descent from virtue. The fruit of individualistic democracy, ripened by the economic boom and bust in the early decades of the century, had been poverty alongside wealth, avarice, and cupidity in economic affairs and in government.[4] Moral reformers, too, were moved

3. Frances Wright, "Miss Wright's Parting Address," *The Free Enquirer* (New York), June 19, 1830.
4. Frances Wright, *An Address on the State of the Public Mind and the Measures Which It Calls for, As Delivered in New York and Philadelphia, Autumn, 1829* (New York, 1829).

by the apparent desecration of the Republic. The "Empire of Philanthropy" flourished from the 1810s to the 1830s in an essentially conservative defense of institutions. Temperance organizations, Bible societies, and missionary movements spread to attack the vice that accompanied godlessness. But democratic theology and frontier expansion also opened up moral reform to perfectionism. Social evils were viewed as the sins of individual selfishness multiplied and condoned by existing institutions. The religious fervor of the new movement was intellectually distant from Wright's rationalism. But moral reform scarcely less than natural rights pointed toward a future ideal society and suggested public agitation as the only possible route.[5]

As Wright had noted during her speaking tours against insurgent Protestantism, women were the principal constituency of moral reform. The prayer meetings of the revivalist waves in the 1820s and 1830s, particularly in the West, drew an audience overwhelmingly female. Women were the main force, if not the leadership, in the campaigns for temperance and Christian virtues. Charles Grandison Finney's evangelical crusade of the 1830s and 1840s sanctioned their participation and local initiative. Eventually, women took over the *Advocate of Moral Reform*, a leading paper inspired by Finney, not only writing but typesetting the text. Crusading women were also among the first of their sex to travel about the country without chaperones, to challenge female passivity in practice, to assert the active potentialities of woman's purported moral superiority and the corollary right to reshape male behavior—in short, to convene a sisterhood against the vices of man's world.[6]

The climate of moral reform was the background for women's participation in the antislavery struggle. Abolitionism had deep historical roots in the aversion of a

[handwritten margin note: Moral reform]

5. John L. Thomas, "Romantic Reform in America," in Davis, ed., *Antebellum Reform*, 154–59.

6. Alice Rossi, "Introduction: Social Roots of the Woman's Movement in America," in Rossi, ed., *The Feminist Papers* (New York, 1974 ed.), 277. See also Nancy F. Cott, "Young Women in the Second Great Awakening in New England," *Feminist Studies*, III (Fall, 1975).

minority of Americans to the "peculiar institution." But anti-slavery sentiment grew into a political movement only in the 1830s when northern Blacks and women enthusiastically responded to the Garrisonian agitation for immediate emancipation. Abolitionism crystallized one side of American reform, for it named slavery as a personal sin, with the entire nation the guilty accomplice, and sought redemption for individual and society alike through massive moral agitation. Individual women became leading journalists and lecturers. Elizabeth Chandler conducted a "women's section" of the *Genius of Universal Emancipation* as early as 1829; Lydia Maria Child's 1833 tract, *An Appeal in Favor of that Class of Americans Called Africans*, reputedly converted Wendell Phillips, Thomas Wentworth Higginson, and Charles Sumner; fiery speakers like Abby Kelley Foster stirred public sentiment in sympathetic districts. A mass of anonymous women conducted the fund-raising bazaars, supplied the pennies and nickels to keep antislavery agents (including a few women, like Susan B. Anthony) operating when philanthropic funds dried up, and played a dominant role as collectors and signers in the great petitions to Congress in the 1830s and 1840s.[7]

The participation of women in abolitionism raised new controversies. Southern congressmen railed at their intrusion into men's affairs. Conservative churchmen issued official warnings against indelicacy. Most of the leading women in public life shied away from such open self-assertion, preferring the path of individual advancement. Catharine Beecher, prominent educator, chastised Angelina and Sarah Grimké for presuming to lead public agitation by speaking to mixed audiences. Even among abolitionists, women's power rapidly emerged as a divisive issue. In 1836, the executive committee of the American Anti-Slavery Society proposed

7. Alma Lutz, *Crusade for Freedom* (Boston, 1968), 10–17, 25–26; Keith Melder, "Beginning of the Woman's Rights Movement in the United States, 1800–1840," Ph.D. dissertation, Yale University, 1965, 186–87; Gerda Lerner, "The Grimké Sisters and the Struggle against Race Prejudice," *Journal of Negro History*, XLVIII (Oct., 1963), 285; Jane H. Pease and William H. Pease, "The Role of Women in the Antislavery Movement," *Canadian Historical Association: Historical Papers Presented at Annual Meeting, 1967.*

that women be taken on as antislavery agents. Following the Grimké sisters' tour the following year, state and local antislavery organizations vigorously debated woman's role. By 1840, the question of "woman's place" had precipitated a crisis in the American and international antislavery movement. Extreme reformers like Garrison, committed to any number of "ultra" causes like nonresistance, were converted by women's grievances and encouraged their advancement in the abolitionist movement. Others like the more moderate wing associated with Arthur Tappan wanted to unburden the antislavery cause from other demands and therefore drew back from the spectre of women's leadership. When Abby Kelley Foster was elected to office in the Anti-Slavery Society, anti-Garrisonian dissidents bowed out to form their own, more single-minded movement. Woman's rights, in its first years, had already hastened a momentous division of American reform forces. The dispute forced many women to articulate their position.[8]

Women active in both wings of the antislavery movement gained a new self-confidence from the testing of their moral courage. Threatened, mobbed, their reputations tarnished by a hostile press, they drew a parallel between the oppression of Blacks and of themselves. They, too, experienced what Sarah Grimké called the "irrepressible desire for mental and spiritual freedom which glows in the breast of many who hardly dare speak the sentiments. . . ."[9] In turn, their sense of oppression gave them an insight into the lethargic response of most Americans to the antislavery herald. "Can we expect any earnest anti-slavery effort," Frances Gage asked, "while nearly every man in the country over twenty-five years of age owns one pair of hands. . . ?"[10] True progress, then, demanded as its goal universal freedom. Man, like the slaveholder, could not perceive the injustice of his acts; only the snapping of the fetters on the most humble could show the meaning of democracy.

8. Melder, "Beginning of the Woman's Rights Movement," 186–87, 270, 339–41.

9. Sarah Grimké, "Human Rights," *The Liberator*, Oct. 6, 1837.

10. Frances D. Gage, "Letter," *ibid.*, Dec. 28, 1860.

The heated political climate of the 1840s and 1850s further encouraged a particular group of women to seize the opportunity for claiming their rights. The mass participation in politics sparked in the Jacksonian era had created a climate for the sectional agitator and the challenge to entrenched political elites. The breakdown of the major party system in the late forties and fifties freed new energies and gave reformers important roles in the newer political movements that outstripped the abolitionist forces. The Republican party, born of an amalgam of tendencies in 1856, significantly publicized the campaign activities of its presidential candidate's wife, Jessie Benton Frémont.[11] In some ways its rise summed up the optimistic entrepreneurialism training its guns upon the southern economic and political system. "Only a movement which viewed society as a collection of individuals, which viewed freedom as the property of every man, which believed every individual had the right to seek advancement as a unit in competitive society," writes historian Eric Foner, "could condemn slavery as utterly and completely as, in their own ways, abolitionists and Republicans did."[12] In the political triumph of individualism, why should women be excluded? The first woman's rights advocates were model candidates for such a response. Mostly from Whig-linked, comfortable middle-class families in western New York, they were in an ideal position to feel the intense optimism about the potential economic and social opportunities for the individual in the advancing nation. Many of these women had proved that despite the limited opportunities of their sex they could themselves enter the competitive economic world and gain their own sustenance.[13]

For these women and the larger movement that grew around them, natural rights and moral reform, individ-

11. Anne F. Scott and Andrew M. Scott, "Consent of the Governed," in Scott and Scott, eds., *One Half the People*, 7.

12. Eric Foner, "Causes of the Civil War," *Civil War History*, XX (Sept., 1974), 205.

13. Ross Evans Paulson, *Women's Suffrage and Prohibition: A Comparative Study of Equality and Social Control* (Glenview, Ill., 1973), 35–43; Rossi, "Social Roots of the Woman's Movement in America," 65–74.

ualism and moral responsibility were always concurrent. Natural rights became the advanced ideology of the leaders, including Lucretia Mott, Elizabeth Cady Stanton, Paulina Wright Davis, Matilda Joslyn Gage and Ernestine Rose, women with a cosmopolitan sensibility, broad education, and a fundamental mistrust of human institutions. They believed so little in the efficacy of "artificial" union that they constantly announced their freedom of action and until the Civil War barely tolerated even a standing committee to prepare for conventions. Moral reform was by and large the perspective of the followers, women of more limited circumstances, pietistic, seeking to sanctify all institutions save those most heinous like slavery. As historians of the nineteenth-century labor movement have emphasized, reformers combined "emergent" and "residual" values. Labor insurgents frequently drew upon their republican heritage to define a place in society, charging the capitalist with the usurper's role. The Declaration of Independence was reinterpreted as a timely document: the welfare of the masses had stood above the king's property and now stood above the would-be "monarchs" and "tyrants" of the factories and mills.[14] In similar fashion, women argued that men's "property," whether slaves or wives, was by nature a usurpation. Men had failed to fulfill the promise of the republican heritage. Women's answer was a leap to freedom—a leap they defined in the traditional terms of the Constitution, the "naturalness" of God-given functions and social relations unconstrained by man-made laws and customs. They suggested for themselves a historic role that stretched back to the formation of the Republic, through the brave dissent of worldly wives and unworldly Shakers, and reached forward toward a destiny for woman that the founders would not live to see.

This synthetic view had practically no limits. Claims the leaders made in the 1840s preceded public sentiment by decades. They denounced woman's oppression by the Church and called upon their sex to refuse to pay taxes to the state.

14. Leon Fink, "Class Conflict in the Gilded Age: The Figure and the Phantom," *Radical History Review*, III (Fall-Winter, 1975), 60-62.

They were avid in their internationalism as few Americans were at the time. The *Liberator* quoted a London paper as early as 1838 suggesting that while abolitionism was essentially an American affair, "the direct and energetic influence of women upon the moral character of laws and institutions is a matter which concerns the whole civilized world."[15] Women were to be a new element in the introduction of global republicanism. Hence, women's rights advocates celebrated the French events of 1848 and praised their socialist counterparts, decried the rise of the second Napoleon, and looked toward the day when monarchy would be abolished everywhere. No less were woman's rights advocates concerned with the ostensibly private aspects of life. Married women among them were determined to be called by their own first names and sometimes by their entire maiden names. They introduced one of the most shocking, but also characteristic, innovations of the era, the "Bloomer" costume. The Reverend Samuel J. May justified the revolutionary style in terms of absolute piety: "The structure of our bodies, each limb, each member, is undoubtedly the best that He could devise. Is it not impious folly, then, to corrupt, abuse, or prevent the development and right action of the body? . . . The Bloomer may not be the best dress that can be devised. Let it then be improved. . . ." With this optimism about the prospects for reform, women could look to temperance, love, and mutual respect, even cooperative labor as "natural" because existing practices seemed merely irrational and atavistic. What had the American Revolution meant if it had not been the starting point for further perfection? Samuel May signed his letter, "Yours for Improvement in Everything," summing up the expectation that all would be improved as part of the unfolding process of human enlightenment and regeneration.[16]

The promise of a movement sustained by this optimistic temperament was already apparent in the Seneca Falls Decla-

15. "Women in the Field," from *London True Sun*, quoted in *The Liberator*, Mar. 16, 1838.

16. Samuel J. May, "Dress Reform Association," *The Liberator*, June 26, 1857.

ration of 1848. "It might be said of this platform," Colonel
Thomas Wentworth Higginson recalled later, "as Frederick
Douglass once said of another platform, 'This is the deck; all
else is open sea.'"[17] Laden with all the essential demands that
women in America and abroad would make for decades, the
statement was a fundamental social document modeled on
the Declaration of Independence. Brief and abstract, it carried the meaning of freedom to the very limits established by
bourgeois revolution. The entire "history of Mankind" was
one of "repeated injuries and usurpations on the part of man
toward woman." Nor was this a mere matter of legal sanctions, since man had "endeavored . . . to destroy her confidence in her own powers, to lessen her self-respect," in short
to deprive her of subjectivity. Justice, and her sense of grievance, demanded that she be given "immediate admission to
all rights and privileges."

Woman's rights had advanced beyond abolitionism in
identifying the proximity of the oppressive agent. In a sense,
the discontent of the 1830s between employer and craftsman,
city and country, East and West had been displaced into a
clash between northern and southern civilization.[18] The anti-
slavery effort had helped create the northern indictment of
southern paternalism and languor as a cause of national
distress. Women reformers shared this view, but also acceler-
ated their own demands. Even in the midst of sectional controversy in the 1850s they insisted that oppression existed in
every northern city and home. Men in particular, male-
founded institutions in general, had to be confronted.

Not surprisingly, woman's rights advocates had greater
difficulty than abolitionists in creating an audience. They had
some access to small-town newspapers, the major reform
sheets, the *Liberator* and *National Anti-Slavery Standard*, and
they founded their own short-lived press of a few papers.
They had an advantage in the public readiness for the reform

17. "Address of Col. T. W. Higginson," *Woman's Journal* (Boston), Feb. 14, 1891.
18. Raimondo Luraghi, "The Civil War and the Modernization of American
Society: Social Structure and Industrial Revolution in the Old South before and
during the War," *Civil War History*, XVIII (Sept., 1972), 242.

message in New England, New York, and the Old Northwest, where audiences had been prepared by abolitionist speakers, often the same women orators. Woman's rights "conventions" were held in dozens of towns, large and small. Reform meetings not only raised pressing issues of the day but were also rudimentary forms of public entertainment like the contemporary traveling dioramas, simultaneously educational and a pleasant escape from day-to-day routines. Thus an initial public sensation against women speakers faded in many places into semi-tolerant amusement. The reformers spread and consolidated their movement by publishing tracts and accounts of conventions, appointing unpaid "agents" to keep areas astir, and developing new spellbinders. But unlike the antislavery movement, their issues precipitated no national crisis. They could not form a political party of their own nor set larger forces into motion. Thus woman's rights advocates had to demonstrate the power behind their demands in different ways.

Temperance agitation provided an arena for women's political self-assertion. Long the numerical majority in temperance societies, women had always been relegated to secondary roles. By the 1850s, woman's rights advocates pointed to women as the true victims of alcohol. "What rights do the wives and children of drunkards have?" Amelia Bloomer's *Lily* had asked.[19] Woman could defend her home and the future of the race only by changes in laws and customs that would allow her honorably to leave an intolerable domestic situation and still retain custody over her children. Only the victim, woman's rights leaders argued, could understand fully the necessity for these reforms. Therefore only a temperance movement guided by women could achieve the domestic tranquillity idealized by the society. Thus Susan Anthony led the female temperance movement briefly in New York and was among the women who demanded full rights to participate in the World Temperance Convention of 1853. The defense of woman's rights during their expulsion from the convention served, as an observer commented, "as a

19. "Woman's Rights," *Lily* (Seneca Falls, N.Y.), Oct. 1, 1849.

lens to concentrate the rays of truth."[20] As antislavery and other questions pressed reformers, the significance of temperance fell away. Woman's rights leaders had not been able to make the movement their own, and they now deprecated local-option laws and similar measures as superficial, touching the result but not the cause of the evil. No matter. Their point had been made.

The woman's rights movement first succeeded in influencing legislation in the campaigns for a Married Woman's Property Act in New York. A change in the state constitution in 1856 brought a long-standing issue of woman's property into public debate. Wealthy families were concerned with the protection of legacies in women's names, since the colonial equity laws had been successively narrowed, leaving the wife few privileges. Stanton and Anthony stepped into the situation, raising larger principles of women's power over their own property and person. Anthony orchestrated a petition campaign, gaining signatures and spreading natural rights propaganda for women across the state. Stanton delivered to the state legislature the first theoretical document on jurisprudence as applied to women. Even the limited victory for women's property rights was sweet, for the reformers could claim independent influence in its passage.

By 1860, this advance was one of many that woman's rights leaders could proclaim as a sign of momentum in the movement. Women across the North had pierced the walls of their confinement. Educational opportunities had multiplied. A few outstanding women had been able to enter medicine, the ministry, and a scattering of other professions. Other states had extended women's property rights. And most important, the issue of woman's rights had been exposed to public scrutiny and serious discussion.

Yet the movement itself remained both small and fragile. Far more women believed in their own individual economic advance than in the importance of collective agitation. Compared to temperance and abolitionism, the scale of woman's rights activities was small. Full-time crusaders were agonized by the apparent indifference of the vast majority of women.

20. "Dear Una," *Una* (Providence, R.I.), Oct., 1853.

Paulina Wright Davis surveyed the financial collapse of her own paper, the *Una*, and dolefully concluded in 1854 that "we have come to feel, mortifying as is the truth, that woman's freedom must first be proclaimed by man, that her own hand will never 'strike the blow' or her heart pulsate to freedom's note till her oppressor wakens her from the dreamless sleep of her present life. . . ."[21] In this light, the heroic convention phase had been not only a sign of moral strength but a measure of organizational weakness. More substantial forms were disdained, in part, because women knew they lacked the influence to build a powerful political movement.

Internal unity was, moreover, constantly threatened by principled disagreements. Natural rights advocates treasured above all the individual autonomy of woman in all her social relations. Moral reformers, on the other hand, considered woman to be the natural guardian of the family and by virtue of this position the agent of a purified civilization. Hence, the institution of marriage was for some reformers a mere civil contract, for others a holy sacrament. In these opposite perspectives, divorce was either woman's right or a violation of a higher law. Similarly, the sanction for women's rights was disputed: did they need to find justification in the Bible or could the Word be treated as a mere historical metaphor describing a stage of human events long since passed? The feeling was widespread among the more cautious supporters that public disagreement on such questions detracted from the movement's image and slowed the acceptance of woman's rights. Some Boston women even went so far as to organize in 1858-60 a "narrow platform" movement, designed to free the woman's cause from controversial subjects of personal morality. The platform was to be closed except to recognized speakers, only the "respectable" class of women invited to attend, and special care taken not to raise such sensitive matters as marriage reform.[22]

The burgeoning of a united woman's rights movement therefore required a continued compromise among varying

21. "To Our Readers," ibid., Dec., 1854.

22. *Report of Woman's Rights Meeting at Mercantile Hall,* May 22, 1859 (Boston, 1859).

elements and a public respectability. Reform women needed the sanction of more powerful forces than their own. And most of all, they needed to find the means to touch American women's inclination to support a virtuous national cause.

The Civil War provided all three. With the shots fired at Fort Sumter, an era of American reform passed forever. Reformers had done much to set into motion political forces that would culminate in Radical Republicanism. But now their old forms of patient agitation and education seemed irrelevant for the massive mobilization required to defeat the South and banish slavery from the land. For the first time, they found themselves within the governing coalition. They had a unique opportunity to use mainstream political sanction for their own purposes but also had the corresponding difficulty of voicing their most far-reaching demands. They felt vindicated when Lincoln's administration was forced to accept one after another of the claims they had made for Black freedom. For their part, woman's rights advocates found they could use these war efforts to reach new masses and to gain a hearing for their arguments at the highest levels of government.

Woman's rights leaders suspended conventions for the duration but looked for other means to establish their presence as an autonomous force in the war effort. Above all, they wanted to remind the thousands of women engaged in volunteer work that the issues of the day demanded not only enthusiastic participation but also discussion and debate. The Emancipation Proclamation gave them the opportunity to act independently. They called a meeting of the "Loyal Women of the Nation" in 1863 to support Sumner's demands in Congress for the enlistment of Blacks in the army and for the conversion of the war into a battle for freedom. Angelina Grimké's address, "Soldiers of our Second Revolution," given at this meeting, indicates the stress laid upon total democracy: "In this War, the Black man was the first victim, the workingman of whatever color the next; and now *all* who contend for the rights of labor, for free speech, free schools, and a free government. . . . The nation is in a death struggle. It must become either one vast slavocracy of petty tyrants, or wholly the land of the free. . . ."[23] Only a minority of the woman's rights veterans were willing to express their positions openly in such dramatic terms. But Stanton and Anthony, at the helm of the Woman's National Loyal League, put forward a program for vigorous action. They called for a critical support of the union and exerted a constant pressure upon the government to expand the national commitment to democracy.

The Woman's National Loyal League rapidly gained a public sanction the prewar woman's movement had lacked. By enlisting thousands of women into political activities around the war effort, woman's rights advocates became important allies to the Radical Republicans. Generals upheld the women's esteem, congressmen franked their tracts for national distribution, and sympathizers aided their circulation of petitions for the extension and permanence of the Emancipation Proclamation.

The wartime campaign for Black rights also had a subtle effect upon the nature of woman's rights demands. Before the war, suffrage had only been the central principle in a constellation of desired revisions in laws and customs. Now, the hope for a democratic renewal of national life rested upon the increased participation in the political process. Citizenship seemed to count for more than moral power in the titanic political struggles expected to lie ahead. While women reformers had previously disdained organization for its own sake and often emphasized their distrust of any institutions, their more recent experience with the government gave them a lesson in the realities of political power. Not only for Blacks and for the nation, but for themselves as well, they narrowed woman's rights to woman suffrage.

"The War for the Union," Henry Blackwell wrote in 1869, "will seem to Posterity a stern and terrible prelude to a beneficent and comprehensive Reformation."[24] The enfranchisement of Blacks would, it was believed, lead to the rebuild-

23. Quoted in Gerda Lerner, *The Grimké Sisters from South Carolina* (New York, 1967), 354.

24. Henry Blackwell, "The Era of Reconstruction," *Woman's Advocate* (New York), I (Jan., 1869), 7.

ing of a southern society open to the political and economic energies of the North, and the enfranchisement of women could imbue the whole order with a universal democratic ethos. Woman's rights activists pictured themselves as the cutting edge of a new reform movement, universal as in antebellum days, but armed with the political allies and the expanded influence they had won in wartime. They would sweep away archaic and harmful social institutions with the aid of a new addition to the reform coalition—Labor.

Supporters of woman suffrage shared with other reformers a sense of the deepest problems on the political horizon. They recognized what historians later confirmed, that the Thermidor had grown strong within the Second American Revolution. Wartime business expansion presaged the development of an "aristocracy of gold" on a scale unknown to prewar America. Reform women feared that the subordination of the working class, long regarded by Americans as a temporary inconvenience of birth, was evidently permanent so long as the existing order prevailed. But they staked their hopes in the victory of natural rights principles restated in economic terms. As Elizabeth Cady Stanton phrased her faith, a "government based on caste and class privilege cannot stand."[25] The laborer would be the "coming man," whose recognition of woman as his natural ally, as one suffrage supporter suggested, would "grace his triumphal advance and fill his era with glory."[26] A "glorious, bloodless, millennial revolution" would follow, claimed Stanton and Anthony's collaborator Parker Pillsbury: the promise of American democracy would be fulfilled.[27]

The first stage of strategy was to maintain the universality of reform in the Woman's National Loyal League by binding together Black and woman suffrage. An American Equal Rights Association, founded in 1866 by reform veterans,

25. Elizabeth Cady Stanton, "Anniversary of the Equal Rights Association," *The Revolution* (New York), May 18, 1869.

26. Mrs. E. L. G. Willard, "The Labor Question," *Woman's Advocate* (Dayton, Ohio), Aug. 21, 1869. This newspaper is distinct from the New York journal of the same name.

27. Parker Pillsbury, "Call to All Hands," *The Revolution*, Aug. 26, 1869.

sought to coordinate energies. But the demands on women's behalf were hamstrung for lack of Radical Republican support. Only a few of the outstanding congressional Radicals like Ben Wade, George Julian, and later Ben Butler were ever seriously committed to the issue of woman's rights as such.[28] As the Republicans made clear that woman suffrage would have to stand aside during the "Negro's hour" and was by no means assured support afterward, AERA was thrown onto the horns of a dilemma. To demand woman suffrage at the expense of failing to support the Radical Reconstruction program was considered a betrayal of abolitionism. To support Blacks' rights over women's was to countenance the completion of Reconstruction at women's expense.

Woman's rights leaders hoped to redress Republican indifference by generating momentum from the state level upward. In the spring of 1867, the New York State constitution was to be revised and updated. Woman's rights advocates were not wholly surprised to be defeated in their effort to gain suffrage through constitutional revision, but they were stung by the opposition of prominent reform editor Horace Greeley. In the fall, a state referendum in Kansas held simultaneously on Black and woman suffrage proved crucial to the subsequent history of the women's movement. Over the course of the campaign, the state Republican party shifted from a chilly neutrality to outright opposition. The women's abolitionist allies in the East who might have had some impact on Western Republicanism withheld their support until late in the campaign out of fear of endangering Black suffrage. Henry Blackwell, Lucy Stone, Stanton, Anthony, and a handful of others practically conducted the canvass alone.

Reform forces were thrown into conflict over the implications of Republican actions. Many veterans, including most of the powerful woman's rights figures in New England, felt that women could not withhold this final sacrifice for the freedom of Blacks. Stanton and Anthony disagreed. They accepted as fellow speaker in Kansas the notorious George Francis Train, Democratic financier and Negrophobe. Train

28. Hans L. Trefousse, *The Radical Republicans, Lincoln's Vanguard for Racial Justice* (New York, 1969), 27.

dramatically called upon Kansas voters to place the "Woman first, and the Negro last." Local suffrage societies in some parts of the state fused with Democrats against the Republican program. The defeat of both suffrage measures in the referendum brought mutual recriminations about poor strategy and doubtful principles. Stanton and Anthony had circulated petitions against the Fourteenth Amendment for excluding women from the addition of enfranchised citizens and thereby inserting the word "male" into the Constitution. With Train's financial support, they published a new, strident paper, *The Revolution*, which voiced disapproval of the proposed Fifteenth Amendment as a further degradation of women. The New Englanders meanwhile convened a regional suffrage organization. Political leaders of Massachusetts Republicanism, abolitionist veterans like Frederick Douglass and Abby Kelley Foster, and cultural figures like Julia Ward Howe and Louisa May Alcott rallied behind the Fifteenth Amendment in the name of woman's rights. While Stanton conducted a major national suffrage meeting in Washington, D. C., to focus attention upon the responsibility of Congress to discharge its duties to female citizens, New Englanders worked separately behind the Congressional scene in support of Radical Republicans.[29]

This mounting disagreement was no clear-cut issue of principles, despite the participants' opposing claims to the heritage of antebellum reform. Race was not the issue. Both sides had been valiant fighters for Black rights, and in both camps could be heard warnings that southern Blacks were too "ignorant" to rule while women were excluded from democratic participation. Neither was faith in the Republican party the overriding concern. Both sides appealed for nonpartisan support of woman suffrage and believed that the idealism necessary for the passage of the measure would be generated outside the major parties.[30]

29. Ellen C. DuBois, "Origins of the Woman Suffrage Movement, 1865–1869," Ph.D. dissertation, Northwestern University, 1975, chap. 3; "Home Intelligence," *Woman's Advocate* (New York), I (Jan., 1869), 54–56.

30. Stanton and Anthony's position is apparent from our selection of documents; for the other side, see Henry Blackwell, "The Era of Reconstuction," 12; and Henry Blackwell, "Principles and Parties," *Woman's Advocate* (New York), I (March, 1869), 157.

The differences were rather of milieu and style. The New Englanders were part of a vital, almost cohesive regional reform movement with contacts that reached from the labor movement to the elite of the state Republican parties. Stanton and Anthony in New York State were far more isolated and had to rely largely upon their own resources to build an agitational movement. New England reformism had the stamp of gentility, the abiding moral commitment of the crusaders for the rights of the oppressed. Stanton and Anthony bridled at the prospect of the subordination of woman suffrage to any moral claim and insisted upon a forthright defense of woman's rights before all else. In that spirit, they frequently went further than their New England counterparts, in the open radicalism of their claims and in their associations with flamboyant reformers like Train. *The Woman's Advocate*, a New England–style organ published in 1869 from the same office as the *National Anti-Slavery Standard*, was formal, almost literary in its format and editorial restraint. *The Revolution* was one of the most vociferous journals of the century, proclaiming demands of equal pay for equal work, eight-hour workdays, abolition of standing armies, "Science not Superstition" in religious thought, temperance, greenbacks, and a progressive national economics. Even if the New Englanders leaned in the same direction, they would test the winds of the political climate and hold woman suffrage distant from other reforms so that more conservative elements might join them on that issue alone; Stanton and Anthony's group proclaimed the necessity for a new "People's Party" to sweep past Republicanism and linked woman suffrage to a grand reform victory.[31]

The passage of the Fifteenth Amendment and the congressional discussion of a possible Sixteenth Amendment specifically for women's enfranchisement provided the two sides a last opportunity to coalesce. A spring meeting of the American Equal Rights Association in 1869 found both factions in attendance, with some mutual goodwill. But the differences were already too great. Henry Blackwell, Lucy Stone, Frederick Douglass, and their allies could not forgive

31. E. C. DuBois, "Origins of the Woman Suffrage Movement," chaps. 3–5; "The Revolution," *The Revolution*, Jan. 8, 1869.

Stanton and Anthony for publicizing Train's racist slurs or for opposing the Fourteenth and Fifteenth Amendments. "Tried at the tribunal of public opinion . . . in the light of its creed and its history," the *Woman's Advocate* concluded, "its fame is tarnished."[32] The AERA was a dead letter.

On the other hand, a new constituency for woman suffrage had appeared. With their experience mostly in the Civil War, the new recruits lacked the spirit of universal reformism. They were more single-minded in their support of women's enfranchisement, less likely to look upon the fate of Blacks and the conditions of labor as foremost questions. And they seemingly disdained discussions of marriage and free love as distractions from their goal. In short, they were part of a new generation with its sight limited to specific measures.[33] Similar activists in working-class organizations and temperance and Black movements would convey corresponding desires for self-reliance rather than dependence upon a general reform climate.

Stanton and Anthony caucused with the supporters they could muster after the New Englanders left the last meeting of the AERA, and formed a National Woman Suffrage Association. Their rivals complained of this backstreet method and argued that NWSA was little more than a clique. They issued a call for a national movement, as if NWSA did not exist, and in the fall of 1869 formed the American Woman Suffrage Association.[34]

Neither side could escape the fate of the larger reform community. Despite all efforts, neither could extend its ranks beyond the middle class. Both wings attempted a limited labor agitation. The New Englanders, characteristically philanthropic, worked in Boston to establish welfare institutions for downtrodden laborers. They also cooperated with

32. "Shall There Be Unity?" *Woman's Advocate* (New York), I (June, 1869), 323.

33. See Mrs. E. L. G. Willard, "Free-Love-Ism," *The Agitator* (Chicago), Apr. 17, 1869.

34. The AWSA side of the controversy is related in Henry Blackwell, "The American Woman Suffrage Association," *Woman's Journal* (Boston), Jan. 8, 1870; the NWSA side in [Laura Curtis Bullard,] "The Cleveland Meeting," *The Revolution*, Dec. 1, 1870; and an independent observer's position in "A Woman's View of the Two Societies," *ibid.*, Dec. 8, 1870.

the New England Labor Reform Association, an umbrella organizing group at whose 1869 convention a prominent banner read, "To reduce the hours of household drudgery and increase woman's wages is the 'better half' of labor reform."[35] But these efforts had few long-term benefits. The New England Labor Reform Association declined into insignificance in the early 1870s, while charity work proved a poor means for gaining recruits to the suffrage cause.

Stanton and Anthony chose more dramatic means to make the connection between working women's exploitation and their lack of political rights. *The Revolution* led a public defense campaign for Hester Vaughan, an impoverished servant on trial for allegedly killing her illegitimate child, and drew prominent reformers and even New York City officials to a mass protest rally in her behalf. Susan Anthony also joined with discharged female compositors to form a Working Woman's Association in New York in 1868. *The Revolution* gained no political advantage through Vaughan's release. And more important, Anthony's labor-organizing initiatives were rebuffed. Her attempts to open the skilled labor market for women and to organize the unskilled seamstresses of New York were fruitless. Only a small professional class of women, such as journalists, seemed amenable to *The Revolution's* emphasis upon the vote as working women's first priority. Within two years of its formation, the Working Woman's Association drifted toward philanthropy. Meanwhile, the 1869 convention of the National Labor Union excluded Anthony for sending *The Revolution* to a "rat" or scab printing shop and for advising women to take the place of striking workers in the book trade.[36] Suffrage advocates continued to give moral support to working women's groups that sprang up sporadically around the country but could construct no grand alliance with them.

As W. E. B. Du Bois remarked about the fiasco of Recon-

35. "New England Labor Convention," *The Revolution*, Feb. 11, 1869.

36. E. C. DuBois, "Origins of the Woman Suffrage Movement," chap. 5; Alma Lutz, "Susan B. Anthony for the Working Woman," *Boston Public Library Quarterly*, VII (Jan., 1959), 41; Israel Kugler, "The Trade Union Career of Susan B. Anthony," *Labor History*, II (Winter, 1961), 90–100.

struction, reformers were not yet economic-minded enough. Suffrage supporters naïvely assumed that political revolution in the South guaranteed the freedman's future participation in government.[37] And they blanched at the prospect of a permanent laboring class as "the knell of republican institutions" even while the most advanced hailed industrial cooperation as "the great question of the future . . . to which we must come, sooner or later."[38] NWSA increasingly ignored the economics of reform, in the name of natural rights; AWSA took an idealistic position that allowed it to patronize the poor without coming to grips with the momentum of lower-class discontent. But it is doubtful whether deeper knowledge would have greatly benefited the two suffrage organizations in the generation or so after their formation. As Matilda Joslyn Gage noted at the end of the seventies, too few of the dozens of local and regional labor parties that had sprung up bothered to include woman suffrage planks, and "so long as it has not been done," women could view male-dominated reform movements only "with distrust."[39] The woman suffrage movement had little choice but to accept the divisions among reformers. It could take no other position and still defend its own principles.

The choices made by suffrage activists, therefore, were essentially different roads to isolation. The AWSA, with its abolitionist belief in the individual conscience, harkened back to the glory days of American reform; the NWSA, with its all-female list of officers, suggested that woman's conscience could trust only woman's experience. AWSA began publication of its own weekly paper, the *Woman's Journal*, with the financial and political backing of prominent New England reformers. "Devoted to the Interests of Woman, to her Education, Industrial, Legal and Political Equality and especially her right to Suffrage," as its masthead declared, the *Journal* built a moral case against the abandonment of woman suffrage by the Radical Reconstruction coalition. *The Revolution*,

37. W. E. B. Du Bois, *Black Reconstruction* (Cleveland, 1964 ed.), 591–97.

38. *The Agitator*, Apr. 17, 1869.

39. [Matilda Joslyn Gage,] Editorial, *National Citizen and Ballot Box* (Syracuse, N.Y.), Oct., 1878.

meanwhile, failed financially after a last-minute effort by Anthony to merge the two wings and save her paper as their combined organ.[40]

For a brief period, Stanton and Anthony answered these setbacks with yet more dramatic moves. They were drawn to Victoria Woodhull, co-publisher of *Woodhull & Claflin's Weekly* and foremost exponent of the creation of a People's Party for the 1872 electoral campaign. According to the New York *Times*, an Apollo Hall convention "which was decorated with a number of peculiarly-worded banners, was nearly filled with ladies, wearing eye-glasses and short hair in general." Addresses made "on the subject of marriage" were "of such a nature as to be unfit for publication." In short, freedom of divorce was openly advocated.[41] In 1871, Stanton had followed Woodhull's lead in holding public discussions on birth control. In Iowa, for instance, Stanton had gained a few followers through these discussions. But the time was not ripe for such bold notions of woman's personal and sexual rights. Woodhull's People's Party immediately collapsed, and her erratic politics ended in a free-love scandal. Suffrage societies in Iowa repudiated Stanton's efforts and insisted upon the sanctity of marriage and the impropriety of women's raising such daring questions. The AWSA treated Woodhull as the organization had treated George Francis Train, a political freak to whom Stanton and Anthony had irresponsibly attached themselves and the suffrage cause.[42]

The last card belonged to AWSA. Ulysses Grant, a close friend of reform notable Mary Livermore, was reported generally favorable to woman suffrage. Henry Blackwell was allowed to write the mildly pro-suffrage plank in the Republican platform of 1872, and AWSA enthusiastically swung

40. The unity maneuvers are discussed from a hostile viewpoint in "Mr. Tilton's Meeting," *Woman's Journal*, Apr. 9, 1870. Stanton and Anthony temporarily merged NWSA into a Union Woman Suffrage Association, placing *The Revolution* into the hands of Laura Curtis Bullard of UWSA and Tilton at the head of UWSA—Tilton an obvious parallel figure to Henry Blackwell as president of the AWSA.

41. "Convention of the Equal Rights Association," *New York Times*, May 12, 1872.

42. Lucy Stone to Harriet Robinson, Mar. 4, 1879, Harriet Robinson Collection, Schlesinger Library, Radcliffe College. This reference was provided by Ellen DuBois. Louise R. Noun, *Strong-Minded Women: The Emergence of the Woman-Suffrage Movement in Iowa* (Ames, 1969), 182–97.

into support work, even deserting Wendell Phillips's independent Labor-Temperance campaign for Congress in order to stay on the party bandwagon. Mammoth rallies in Boston, Worcester, and Springfield heralding the link of woman's cause to Republicanism briefly recalled the optimism of antislavery days. Even Anthony and other NWSA leaders followed AWSA's initiative in speaking for Grant.[43]

But Grant's victory was an empty one for women. Republicans held that they were not bound by a promise that could not, in any case, be pushed through Congress. The last hopes for early enfranchisement faded away. The Radical Republicans, heart of the reform movement in national government, divided among themselves and dwindled in number over the following years. The economic downturn in 1873 ended the era of expectations. Plans by Phillips and others to supersede the Republican party died in a pessimism about the functioning of political democracy. Both *The Revolution* and Phillips's *National Standard* were taken over by Christian temperance sheets indifferent to woman's rights and other reform issues.[44] The woman suffrage movement would rise again but never with the same confidence in the efficacy of agitation to stir the populace and expose society to the power of Truth.

Legal challenges remained a slim hope for woman suffrage. Victoria Woodhull made an eloquent plea to Congress, arguing that the Reconstruction amendments had already enfranchised women, and confidants of Grant privately allowed that he had been impressed by her views.[45] Susan Anthony attempted to test the law but was prevented by legal technicalities from doing so. The definitive ruling came when Virginia Minor brought a case against Missouri to the Supreme Court. Her argument, by now familiar, was that vot-

43. "Women in Politics," *Woman's Journal*, Aug. 3, 1872; Henry Blackwell, "Attitudes toward Political Parties," *Woman's Tribune* (Beatrice, Nebr.), May 1, 1890; A[ntoinette] B[rown] B[lackwell], "The Fourteenth Amendment and the Tribune," *Woman's Journal*, Aug. 24, 1872; and "The Women in Council," *ibid.*, Oct. 12, 1872.

44. "The National Standard—the Future," *National Standard* (New York), Dec., 1872; Elizabeth Cady Stanton, *Eighty Years and More, Reminiscences, 1815–1897* (New York, 1971 ed.), 257.

45. [Aaron M. Powell,] "Editorial Comments," *National Standard*, Jan. 21, 1871.

ing was either a right and a privilege of citizenship, in which case women necessarily possessed the right, or it was not, in which case Blacks had not been enfranchised by the amendments. The negative decision on her plea, rendered in 1876, left suffrage advocates only a political route, one which now appeared far less promising than it had in 1865.

Susan Anthony later recalled that in these difficult years all the possible arguments had already been made both for and against woman suffrage. Women simply lacked the power and influence to force the issue. NWSA's congressional lobbying and the introduction of the "Susan B. Anthony Amendment" in 1878 consequently produced no memorable political debate. Suffrage supporters generally argued in the name of abstract justice; the opposition was summed up by a southern senator who, some years later, complained that he was "second fiddle now at home, so at the ballot box I am determined to be the whole brass band."[46] AWSA's strategy of supporting partial suffrage at the local level and referenda at the state level was scarcely more successful. School suffrage and similar reforms advanced incrementally. The Wyoming territorial legislature granted women's vote in 1869, and the progressive Mormon hierarchy similarly obliged Utah territory in 1870. But both of these victories could be essentially attributed to local conditions, and neither served as a precedent for any further successful legislative action. Washington Territory, which granted women's vote in 1883, had its own act abrogated by the Supreme Court, after complicated legal maneuvering, and women actually lost the vote there in 1889. The deadlock for a real state victory continued until the nineties.

As the scale of women's involvement in charity, church, temperance, and self-education societies enlarged, both suffrage organizations grew. For the first time, recruitment was based singularly upon the support of woman suffrage by women. NWSA leaned toward the most literal interpretation of this position as an emerging consciousness of the female sex, while AWSA continued to stress woman suffrage as

46. A. Elizabeth Taylor, "Woman Suffrage Movement in Arkansas," *Arkansas Historical Quarterly* (Spring, 1951), 12, quoting an Arkansas politician in 1890.

part of a greater moral principle.[47] But the results were similar. Drawing upon the "new women" of the professions and the ranks of independent-minded, middle-class house-wives, membership expanded from the hundreds to the thousands. The suffrage press kept the issue burning for members and sympathizers. The *Woman's Journal* was joined by several less important, unofficial NWSA organs, most notably the monthly *Woman's Tribune* published by Clara Colby in Beatrice, Nebraska. Here and there the suffrage workers took part in political campaigns, as in the guber-natorial election of former Radical Republican Ben Butler on the Massachusetts Democratic ticket in 1882. The reneging of the Massachusetts Democrats on their election promises was the disappointing outcome. Even western Republicans, from whom the suffrage supporters had expected better, remained lukewarm and occasionally blocked women's en-franchisement during the few opportunities for the measure to pass. Henry Blackwell again drew the lesson: "to hold to Woman Suffrage and know no party."[48] As so often, principle was the crusaders' protection against despair. But the veteran's comment also characterized a political indepen-dence adopted in the last days of Reconstruction and never wholly deserted.

The main dynamic in women's reform activities of the Gilded Age lay outside the woman suffrage movement. The war had fostered among thousands of woman a sense of their capacity for organization. But only a few carried that impulse beyond the traditional notion of women's service to society. Far more important than suffrage was a second great wave of movements for temperance, social purity, and the suppres-sion of vice. These activities repeated women's experiences in temperance and church groups from 1810 through the 1830s but involved far greater numbers and more female direction. Thousands of women gained a new sense of confi-dence denied them in male-dominated society. The Woman's

47. See, for instance, the differences indicated over Anthony's public support of a New York woman who had admittedly bribed voters in order to defeat a candidate for the state legislature: while AWSA attacked the immorality of such a gesture, Anthony defended it in "Corresponding Editor," *National Citizen and Ballot Box*, Aug., 1880.

48. Henry Blackwell, "Attitudes toward Political Parties."

Christian Temperance Union was the great proof of women's capacity, as it developed under Frances Willard from a Crusade Against Drink to a social movement whose primary concern was female self-reliance. The WCTU demonstrated the potential in women's friendship for one another, their intellectual scope, their moral strength in public and private spheres, and even their talent for successful business management.[49]

Far more than their antebellum predecessors, the modern moral reformers placed the blame for social chaos, poverty, exploitation, and unhappiness upon men. Temperance advocates lashed out at men as the drunkards ruining the home and as the brewers and distillers polluting society. Social purity and moral education supporters demanded enlightenment to erase the double standard. As railroad speculation, urban sprawl, labor rioting, and the growth of "new" immigration from southern and eastern Europe changed the face of America and challenged many existing values, some women reformers drew the conclusion that a society ruled by men was doomed. Elizabeth Stuart Phelps, author of the best-selling sentimental novel *The Gates Ajar*, was quoted as remarking, "It is not a figure of speech to say that the 'Woman Question' is the most tremendous question God has ever asked the world, since he asked, 'What think ye of Christ?' on Calvary."[50]

Through this moral power even the lion and the lamb, Capital and Labor, Wall Street and the poor, might be brought to lie down together. At the end of the eighties, WCTU, women's clubs, and AWSA leaders joined in endorsing the ethical socialism of Edward Bellamy's novel, *Looking Backward*. Bellamy had sanctioned the belief that women were "wardens of the world to come, to whose keeping the keys of the future are confided."[51] Throughout the 1870s and 1880s, women had been active in forming study circles for their own information and clubs and boarding houses for the "alien class" of female factory employees. By raising pub-

---

49. See Mary T. Lathrop, "The National Women's Christian Temperance Union," *National Council of Women, Transactions* (Philadelphia, 1891), 150.

50. Jesse H. Jones, "A Proposal," *Woman's Journal*, Nov. 4, 1871.

51. Edward Bellamy, *Looking Backward* (New York, 1969 ed.), 80.

lic concern about poverty, this handful of leaders helped prepare a vast constituency for a political awakening.

Now a new constituency of reform-minded women raised suffrage as a national issue. The familiar moral-reform claim to the ballot was reasserted in the Midwest, plains states, and far West as part of the agrarian attack on monopolists and mainstream politicians. Women had flocked into the Granges and Farmers Alliances, where support of woman suffrage was proclaimed to be the "bright light whose rays have carried equality, happiness and good cheer to thousands of rural homes."[52] Women's participation encouraged agrarians to stand up against liquor and even tobacco while they took on Wall Street and the railroads. Only calculating "caucus" politics at the national level, women claimed, had prevented reform coalition parties from endorsing suffrage.[53] The growing prestige of suffrage and the outspoken support by such a figure as Frances Willard for the Knights of Labor encouraged expectations for an all-around reform alliance. By 1886, Henry Blackwell could suggest that "the explicit and unsolicited endorsement of woman suffrage by so many state conventions of Third Party, prohibitionists and by the Knights of Labor, when contrasted with the silence and stolid indifference of the old parties on the subject, is a confirmation of Wendell Phillips' prediction that the three burning questions of Woman Suffrage, Temperance, and Labor will become the great political issues of our immediate future, and will be natural allies."[54]

The St. Louis Conference of the People's Party in 1892 marked the apogee of the coalition dream. Women in the Farmers Alliance had formed a National Woman's Alliance to urge unqualified endorsement of suffrage by the national political movement. The Knights of Labor and independent

---

52. "The Grange and Woman Suffrage," *Woman's Column* (Boston), Feb. 20, 1892.

53. Solon J. Buck, *The Granger Movement* (Lincoln, 2d ed., undated), 297–98; "Greenbackism Again" (letter from Lucinda Chandler), *National Citizen and Ballot Box*, July, 1880.

54. Henry Blackwell, "Woman Suffrage, Temperance, and Labor," *Woman's Journal*, Sept. 18, 1886.

trade unions, the Prohibition party under the leadership of Frances Willard, and an amalgam of other reformers pledged their support for a comprehensive program of woman suffrage, temperance, and labor and agrarian reforms. But this grand attempt at union faltered due to political maneuvering at the conference. The Prohibitionists continued to field their own candidates. The Knights of Labor waned and populism itself neared the disastrous fusion with the Bryan Democracy in 1896. The net result of this reform upsurge was minimal for the suffrage goal. In some localities, Populists backed state referenda, and women actually won the vote in Colorado and Idaho, where liquor forces put up little resistance. But elsewhere dozens of suffrage referenda were defeated, due in part to local Populist indifference.[55]

Moral reformers felt a deepening sense of betrayal as the larger society moved onward, still selfish, competitive, reckless toward woman's special needs and sensitivities. Never again would rural women be able to summon the traditions of American reform idealism into a crusade of womanhood against the Money Power. Suffrage veterans expressed their bitterness by asserting their Yankee moral superiority over the masses. Like their old ally Thomas Wentworth Higginson, they could remain active in reform movements for decades, even end their illustrious careers supporting some brand of socialism, without relinquishing the notion that few people were capable of the reformers' own nobility of character.[56] They had lost faith in a unitary, sweeping reform movement after the failure of Radical Reconstruction. They had nevertheless pursued an alliance of mighty forces in the 1880s and 1890s. But many had also come to fear a lower class that refused to listen to their pleas. They suspected the organization of labor as a selfish special interest, a threat to class

55. "The National Woman's Alliance Incorporated," *Farmer's Wife* (Topeka, Kans.), Jan., 1892; "The St. Louis Conference and the Women's Demand," *ibid.*, Feb., 1892; Mary Earhart, *Frances Willard, From Prayers to Politics* (Chicago, 1944), 231–43.
56. "In Memoriam" (to T. W. Higginson), *Woman's Journal*, May 20, 1911; Tilden G. Edelstein, *Strange Enthusiasms, a Life of Thomas Wentworth Higginson* (New Haven, 1968), 379–80.

reconciliation based upon principles of social harmony.[57] Observing for themselves the vote of immigrants in California, North Dakota, Kansas, and elsewhere against woman suffrage, they made the "ignorant classes" the scapegoat for the limits of their movement's progress.[58]

This reaction reinforced their growing isolation from the eastern, urban masses of poor and working people. The suffragists' alliance with the temperance movement had so alienated those masses that a leader estimated the linkage had set back suffrage for a generation. They failed to make any headway with Catholic opponents who feared, with some justification, that women's vote would be used as a weapon of nativism.[59] Encouraged by the growth of women's clubs and a small suffrage movement in the South, the national movement publicized the claim that white women's votes would guarantee control over the Negro population. In many regions, and especially in the Midwest and West, where workers and farmers were mainly old-stock Protestants, the suffrage movement remained democratic and open. But elsewhere, and notably among the leaders, NAWSA became by the late 1890s a self-consciously elite movement.

Concurrently, suffrage leaders adapted the structure of their movement to a more narrow political philosophy. The amalgamation of NWSA and AWSA in 1890 entailed a tightening up of delegate representation at national conventions and eliminated the spontaneity of discussions once typical of

57. See Sarah Williams, Editorial, "Where Are We Drifting?" *Ballot Box* (Toledo, Ohio), Aug., 1877, on the Great Strikes of that year (the *Ballot Box* was predecessor to the *National Citizen and Ballot Box*); Lucy Stone, "One Solution to the Labor Question in Light of Homestead," *Woman's Column*, July 16, 1892, advising workers to save their wages and abandon strikes.

58. See Henry Blackwell, "Unconditional Suffrage," *Woman's Journal*, Oct. 20, 1894, and Elizabeth Cady Stanton, "Educated Suffrage Again," *ibid.*, Dec. 22, 1894. In a study of the Colorado referendum campaign of 1876, one scholar has discovered the suffrage leaders' exaggeration of the importance of the "ignorant vote" in defeating the measure. Probably elsewhere as well, the "prosperous" vote against suffrage outweighed the ballots of the poor and foreign-born. See Billie Barnes Jensen, "Colorado Woman Suffrage Campaigns of the 1870s," *Journal of the West*, XII (Apr., 1973), 268–69.

59. Carrie Chapman Catt and Nettie Rogers Shuler, *Woman Suffrage and Politics* (Seattle, 1969 ed.), 134–35, 158–59; James J. Kenneally, "Catholicism and Woman Suffrage in Massachusetts," *Catholic Historical Review*, LIII (Apr., 1967), 47–48.

NWSA meetings. The emerging functionaries likewise more
eagerly pursued public respectability. In an unprecedented
move, NAWSA's new ruling council used its authority to
repudiate the *Woman's Bible* compiled at the behest of
Elizabeth Cady Stanton, so as to guard the organization's
standing with ministers and others sensitive to moral
heterodoxy.[60]

Strategically, these moves were largely self-defeating. If, as
the most conservative suffragist supporters argued, women's
vote meant mere preservation of existing institutions, then
women's energies could more easily be turned to their traditional causes like temperance and social purity, while men
continued to conduct politics.[61] Southern men, at any rate,
did not need southern white women's vote to maintain their
predominance over Blacks, any more than northern industrial elites needed women's moral contribution to hold sway
over the foreign-born working class. Attempts to draw on
public fears of "race suicide" were merely self-contradictory
for a movement making claims for a wider democracy.

A few younger women spoke against this drift. Harriot
Stanton Blatch and Alice Stone Blackwell, respective daughters of the NWSA and AWSA founders, sought to articulate
an alternative worldview. Blackwell, soon to become editor of
the *Woman's Journal*, espoused the Fabian ideal that lower
classes could be led forward by reformers. Against her

60. See report on Susan B. Anthony's last-minute defense of platform inclusiveness in "National Executive Session," *Woman's Tribune*, Feb. 22, 1890; the summary
of negotiations, showing concessions from each side, in "The Negotiations for
Union," *Woman's Journal*, May 5, 1888; and the implicit denunciation of the concessions to conservative, theocratic tendencies in Matilda Joslyn Gage's formation of a
Woman's National Liberal Union, in *Woman's National Liberal Union, a Report of the
Convention for Organization, February 24-25, 1890* (Syracuse, N. Y., 1890). Another
suffrage pioneer, Olympia Brown, concurrently launched an unsuccessful, inde-
pendent suffrage association to maintain emphasis upon a national amendment: see
Charles E. Neu, "Olympia Brown and the Woman's Suffrage Movement," *Wisconsin
Magazine of History*, XLIII (Summer, 1960), 283.

61. See the claims for woman's nurture and woman's self-assertion—the first
stated in traditional, the second in modern terms—in contemporary articles:
"Editorial Notes," *Woman's Journal*, Sept. 6, 1894, and Annie E. Tomlinson, "The
New Woman and the Marriage Problem," *ibid.*, Sept. 5, 1896. On the conservative
conclusion to the drive for prohibition, see Paulson, *Woman's Suffrage and Prohibition*,
167.

mother's support of "educated suffrage," Blatch similarly argued that democracy could grow only through wider participation in the process of self-government. "We are ever trying to get morals and character out of intellect," Blatch warned, "but they grow on quite other soil . . . the spirit of democracy is not a treasure hidden in America, but is everywhere throbbing in the heart of Democracy."[62] Yet neither good will nor abstract democratic affirmations could extricate the suffrage movement from its dilemma.

Organization became the dominant logic of the emerging leadership. A suffrage writer complained in 1895, "All that is vulgar, grotesque, commonplace and prosaic had, in the popular imagination, centered in the 'woman movement.'"[63] This was no great exaggeration. Carrie Chapman Catt rose from the ranks in this period as a prophet and architect of a new movement predicated upon tight organization and finely coordinated strategy. She was no sentimental moralist. She made calculated appeals to labor and political radicals, and for a time she even took hair treatments from Emma Goldman in order to discuss anarchist philosophy.[64] But while Elizabeth Cady Stanton had regarded the whole world as her province, Catt's vision was purposefully narrow, her nervous energies concentrated on the immediate tactical implications of any situation.[65] Although she made few ideological statements, her respect for power may be inferred from remarks in a journal of a state movement directed by Catt, a decade later: "Knight Errantry is not dead, nor is it useless, but it is not the dominant note of our age. . . . [The] big organization is the genius of modern life. Until women, who from lack of training and experience are impatient of or

62. Harriot Stanton Blatch, "An Open Letter to Mrs. Stanton," *Woman's Journal*, Dec. 22, 1894. Alice Stone Blackwell's defensive explanation of her own non-party socialism is found in "Suffrage and Socialism," *ibid.*, Jan. 8, 1916. After the passage of the Suffrage Amendment, Blatch joined the Socialist party and Blackwell played auxiliary roles to it, as a member of a board of sponsors of the labor and socialist journal, *The Labor Age*.

63. Lida Calvert, "Charlotte Perkins Stetson, a Poet of Two Reforms," *Woman's Tribune*, June 22, 1895.

64. Peck, *Carrie Chapman Catt*, 120.

65. Harriet Taylor Upton, "Random Recollections" (mimeographed, unpaged, Ohio [1927?]), on deposit at Schlesinger Library, Radcliffe.

awed by big combination, are educated up to such standards of work and business, they are not vital factors in the world life of today. This . . . is not something artificial that we have evolved as a basis of suffrage activity, but it is an American institution wrought into the very fibre of our political life."[66] This hard-headed view disguised a political philosophy. Like all great modern reform organizations, the twentieth-century suffrage movement counterbalanced commitment with the drive for perfect coordination and control of its ranks. Catt succeeded in drawing upon diverse energies at the local level and forged them into a disciplined political organization.

By the turn of the century, the new reform stirrings soon to culminate in progressivism pushed thousands of women's club members to the peripheries of suffrage. Club activities focused on the urban problems that women could resolve only through participation in the political process. And the social respectability of the suffrage movement was now almost beyond question.[67] This tendency was paralleled by the reform inclinations of younger college women. In 1900, Maud Wood Park and Inez Haynes directed the formation of a College Equal Suffrage League in Boston. Park and Haynes were among the first Americans to respond to the dramatic "suffragette" campaigns in Britain, where militants took to direct action and went to jail for the cause. New York women, led by younger groups, staged a mass parade that quickly inspired imitators in other major cities. The NAWSA equivalent to "militancy" was to sponsor, on the state level, the first open-air meetings held in thirty years. Massachusetts women toured the state in automobiles, holding impromptu rallies.[68] The national movement, meanwhile, was placed in a better position to help its chapters. Millionaire Alva Belmont financed a transfer of headquarters from Warren, Ohio, to

66. "The Woman Suffrage Party," *Woman Voter* (New York), Jan., 1912.

67. This tendency is described in "Women's Clubs and Woman Suffrage," *Woman's Column*, May 14, 1904, and by Mrs. O. H. P. Belmont, "Woman Suffrage as It Looks To-Day," *Forum*, XLIII (Mar., 1910), 267.

68. Sharon Hartman Strom, "Leadership and Tactics in the American Woman Suffrage Movement: A New Perspective from Massachusetts," *Journal of American History*, LXII (Sept., 1976), 308–10.

New York City. Literature distribution grew tenfold, expanding the outreach of the movement considerably.[69]

Suffragists inside and outside NAWSA took the next step by creating campaign "fronts" among the various sympathetic forces. The WCTU and women's clubs were part of these joint efforts. But the participation of socialist and labor groups also strengthened the appeal for working-class support. Harriot Stanton Blatch returned from England to launch the Equality League of Self-Supporting Women in New York, drawing such notables as Charlotte Perkins Gilman and Florence Kelley, and rank-and-file leaders among wage-earning women. New York's Inter-Urban Council, reorganized by Carrie Chapman Catt in 1907, consolidated suffrage energies conducting the first rigorous agitation along district lines. Out of this proliferation of diverse activities grew the Woman Suffrage party, the most coordinated suffrage organization to grace New York, or for that matter the nation. More than a thousand district captains put steady pressure upon the New York political machines to accept women's demands.[70] The odds in Manhattan were too great to be overcome immediately, but the coalition set the pattern for breakthroughs elsewhere. In Washington in 1910 and California in 1911, suffrage referenda triumphed. Unity, organization, and mass publicity held the promise for the future.[71]

But the influx of a new, vastly enlarged constituency after 1910 reinforced the earlier conservative turn in the suffrage leadership. Thousands of middle-class urbanites who had hung back in the first spurt of the movement growth now joined. They looked to the men of the "better classes" to promote their victory and interpreted events in the suffrage

69. On the expansion of the *Woman's Journal*, see "Publisher's Department," *Woman's Journal*, May 27, 1911.

70. Eleanor Flexner, *Century of Struggle* (Cambridge, 1960), 250–54.

71. For the important socialist contribution to these and other state suffrage campaigns, see James Weinstein, *The Decline of Socialism in America, 1912-1925* (New York, 1967), 60–61; and Agnes Downing, "Woman Suffrage in California," *Progressive Woman*, V (Sept., 1911), 3.

struggle according to this view. Women gained the electoral vote in 1913 in Illinois through an elite coalition of NAWSA lobbyists and Progressive party officials in the state legislature. The following municipal elections in Illinois, when women's votes padlocked more than a thousand saloons in local-option measures, multiplied the difficulties of future referenda. In Michigan, Ohio, and Wisconsin, vigorous and deep-rooted suffrage organizations were defeated by what were termed the "invisible forces" of liquor dealers and machine politicians—but also, no doubt, by thousands of voters who elevated their right to drink over woman's right to vote. Suffrage leaders again gave vent to the "humiliation" they felt at the continued polling of recent immigrants and Blacks.[72]

A straw in the wind was the public criticism and state suffrage organizations' resolutions of censure against Jessie Ashley, a former national treasurer of NAWSA. Ashley had written a series of essays in the *Woman's Journal* discussing the plight of working women and advocating suffrage cooperation with socialists. In a "Swan Song" to her series, Ashley warned,

> O, you Great Genteel Ones, you who resent the words of such as I, could you but feel the scorn in which our class is held by the class you fear so much! Could you but sit one hour in the midst of real wage-earning girls, as one of them, and read their souls through their clear, fierce young eyes; could you but understand what they think of us and all our privileges, you would not perhaps respect quite so much of the opinions of our politicians, of our sleek Respectables, of our kid-glove gentlemen from whom we beg the ballot on bended, trembling knees. . . . If I could but reach their ears! But they judge us by our deeds. . . .[73]

72. See Carrie Chapman Catt's own recounting of the Illinois victory, the following defeats, and the lessons the suffrage leadership drew, in Catt and Shuler, *Woman Suffrage and Politics*, chaps. 13–15.

73. Jessie Ashley, "A Swan Song," *Woman's Journal*, Jan. 20, 1912; see the earlier praise poured upon Ashley as NAWSA treasurer, in "Jessie Ashley," *Progress* (New York), June, 1910.

This search for respectability was not a simple or comprehensive process. Particularly in the small towns of the Middle West and West where suffrage had not yet been won, the common labors continued. The NAWSA leadership itself had by no means lost all its idealism. In the *Woman's Journal*, Alice Stone Blackwell continued to attack Wall Street as the main enemy of woman suffrage and the rich woman as the least interested in the vote. The New York organ, the *Woman Voter*, displayed particularly close ties to the Women's Trade Union League and appealed for a female solidarity across class lines.[74] Even Carrie Chapman Catt ardently defended a "feminism" the public still feared.[75] But the movement could no longer promote any single, coherent vision of social freedom for women.

In the nineteenth century, suffrage activists had shared the faith of other reformers that woman's vote would be achieved amidst the transformation of the entire social order. The model of natural rights was a republic of hard-working but happy citizens, laboring together for a better world; the model of moral reform was the society as the great, sanctified family bound by love and mutual respect. The ideal of the Progressive era was far less sanguine. For modern reformers, competition and relative inequality were permanent features of the social order, but expanding abundance, comprehensive education, and efficient government would allow opportunities for all citizens. Through such a compromise, social stability could be guaranteed. For the long run, reformers looked to the model of the corporation to balance differing social interests: farmers, workers, businessmen, and consumers would each form a "bloc" to secure their share of the commonwealth.[76]

Sometimes genteel reform, as in the case of the Progressive

74. See Alice Stone Blackwell, "Wall Street Our Enemy," *Woman's Journal*, Dec. 9, 1911, or her analysis of the Oregon elite opposition to suffrage in 1906 in "An Object Lesson," *Independent*, LXI (July 26, 1906), 198–99; "Wage Earners' Equal Suffrage League," *Woman Voter*, Dec., 1911.

75. See "Mrs. Catt on Feminism," *Woman's Journal*, Jan. 9, 1915.

76. William A. Williams, *The Contours of American History* (Cleveland, 1961), 358–59. Robert H. Wiebe, *The Search for Order, 1877-1920* (New York, 1967), 156–70.

party in 1912, seemed to promise more. Theodore Roosevelt salvaged democratic slogans from the nineteenth-century social movements and helped popularize an antimonopoly, anticorruption rhetoric. Suffrage leaders responded more enthusiastically than they had to any movement since Radical Republicanism. Jane Addams, Mary Dreier, and other figures unofficially represented the sentiments of many NAWSA activists in the Progressive campaign.[77] But how were the historic goals of woman's rights to be realized in Progressive-styled movements that aimed at adjustment more than transformation of the existing order? Suffragists followed the mainstream and demanded the political inclusion of women into American society as one great estate among the plural powers. Their moral strength remained in the nature of their goal, a democratic participation that suggested at least remnants of natural rights ideology however stripped of its once-revolutionary implications.

Within the suffrage movement, this political orientation was never seriously challenged. Some socialists who had cooperated with NAWSA launched their own, independent campaigns after 1910, protesting the political timidity of the mainstream movement. The most substantial threat to NAWSA, however, was not ideological but rather tactical. The national leadership failed, before 1916, to coordinate statewide efforts into a great strategy for victory. Goaded by the prospect of success, younger women set out their own plans for a renewed emphasis on the national suffrage amendment. Alice Paul, Lucy Burns, and a handful of other women, most fresh from college, gained the backing of Alva Belmont to sustain a movement outside NAWSA. They were vivacious and dramatic, like their heroine Inez Mulholland, who had been described as "a beauty but she doesn't care; she is rich but she means to 'earn her living'; she is a student, but she does everything rather than be a blue-stocking. She is

77. See the lauding of California Progressives in "Drawing the Lines," *Woman's Journal*, Oct. 21, 1911; Jane Addams, "Why I Seconded Roosevelt's Nomination," *ibid.*, Aug. 17, 1912; and "Women Active at Convention," *ibid.*, Aug. 10, 1912. The best overall analysis of this commitment is in Kraditor, *The Ideas of the Woman Suffrage Movement*, 213–14.

frank and democratic. . . . She was known to all at Vassar as the great 'radical,' a suffragist, a Socialist, every kind of 'ist' that the faculty wished to abolish."[78] Like all activists who lack a substantial organizational base, they depended on publicity to put their ideas across. They made their task easier by proclaiming no ideology and expressing "but one plank, the enfranchisement of the women of America through a federal amendment."[79] They distributed their own lively magazine, *The Suffragist*, and in 1916 formed a National Woman's Party of women in the states with full suffrage, in order to defeat the Democrats as the responsible "party in office." To the horror of NAWSA, these younger women responded to American entry in World War I by picketing the White House. Assaulted by crowds, arrested, confined to dingy prisons, they kept up a vigil in the spirit of moral resistance. They succeeded in generating constant public interest in women's vote and perhaps in frightening Democrats to bring reluctant party members into line.[80] They claimed the mantle of the nineteenth-century movement and earned their place in tradition by unrelenting militance. But like NAWSA leaders, they were already far from the reform moods of the past: they set out to win, not to bring the public a deep education, and they envisioned as their goal a single act, not a transformation of laws, morals, and manners.

The National American Woman Suffrage Association regained the initiative in 1915, with the reinstatement of Carrie Chapman Catt as president. Once more showing her powers of adaptation, Catt followed Paul in demanding from her lieutenants absolute personal loyalty and full-time commitment to suffrage work. She ran roughshod over the last elements of states' rights resistance, the southern suffrage leaders, most of whom now bolted to form their own ineffec-

78. "Prominent Paraders," *Woman's Journal*, May 6, 1911.

79. See the sympathetic treatment of the NWP's importance in influencing congressmen, in Charles A. Beard, "The Woman's Party," *New Republic*, VII (July 29, 1916), 329–31; and Alice Paul's oral reminiscence, edited and introduced by Robert S. Gallagher, "I Was Arrested, of Course," *American Heritage*, XXV (Feb., 1974), 16–24.

80. Inez Haynes Irwin, *The Story of the Woman's Party* (New York, 1921), 157.

tual organization. Catt could bring the entire resources of the movement to bear upon individual, critical campaigns; and she could use the growing state strength of suffrage forces to improve the chance of congressional approval of a constitutional amendment. After the Emergency Convention, which she called in 1916, she later reminisced, "there were no defections, no doubts, no differences in the Association. A great army in perfect discipline moved forward toward its goal."[81]

The New York State campaigns of 1915–17 showed that the national scale had tipped toward suffrage. Home of the Seneca Falls convention, site of the first great struggles for women's property rights, New York had always been considered by suffragists to be divided between its progressive Yankee western sector and ignorant, immigrant Manhattan. In 1917, the Manhattan vote won the state against upcounty balloting, and hostile news accounts credited socialists with supplying the margin of victory. History had thrust the metropolis to the center of modern democracy. With the passage of the Volstead Act the same year, many urban bosses recognized the worst had already happened and bowed to the inevitable.

American entry into World War I solidified the evolving suffrage strategy. In 1914, the *Woman's Journal* publicized the call for peace of suffragists from twenty-six nations. The Americans appealed for a movement "to show war-crazed men that between contending armies there stand thousands of women and children who are innocent victims of men's unbridled ambitions; that under the heels of each advancing army are crushed the lives, the hopes, the happiness of countless women whose rights have been ignored."[82] But by 1917, NAWSA took a patriotic stand for national victory, even while claiming that when women were free, wars would cease. The *Woman's Journal* became the *Woman Citizen* and declared that "No jockeying with the pacifist past can save the world

81. Catt and Shuler, *Woman Suffrage and Politics*, 263.

82. "An Appeal to Women," *Woman's Journal*, Aug. 15, 1914. A "front" was re-created for the purpose of forming a National Women's Peace Party; it included Addams, Catt, Charlotte Perkins Gilman, Anna Howard Shaw, and Harriot Stanton Blatch. "Women's Peace Society Forms in Washington," *ibid.*, Jan. 16, 1915.

now. . . . However the War may have been intrigued in the beginning, by capital, by secret diplomacy, war is here. And superior to all the intrigue . . . is an ideal that is sustaining the world today—the ideal of democracy."[83]

NAWSA vigorously adapted itself to the organizational opportunities of wartime. The familiar women's volunteer efforts of bandage-rolling and part-time farm labor were supplemented by a twentieth-century "Americanization" campaign conducted under government auspices. The obvious aim of the government campaign, parallel to that of the old Sanitary Commission, was the efficient use of human resources for war. But from the volunteers' perspective, it was no less the opportunity to use government agencies to defend working standards of blue-collar women, to distribute information about venereal disease, and to teach English and other practical skills to foreign-born slum dwellers.[84]

Yet the most striking difference between these missions and the Civil War woman's rights activities was that NAWSA women made no effort to organize themselves independently of the government for advanced democratic demands.[85] The government was espoused as the true expression of their interests, "an intimate part of ourselves . . . whether its administration wholly satisfied us or not, it stands for our own effort to hold ourselves coherently to group action, group control, group progress. . . ."[86] Suffrage leaders themselves

83. "This War to End War," *Woman Citizen* (Boston), June 16, 1917. In 1917, Catt refused to join a delegation of prosuffrage socialists, prohibitionists and NWP members; see David Morgan, *Suffragists and Democrats: The Politics of Woman Suffrage in America* (East Lansing, 1972), 118.

84. See "America and the Immigrant: A Suffragist Strikes a Balance," *Woman Citizen*, June 2, 1917; Ethel M. Smith, "Safeguarding Industrial Standards," *ibid.*, June 9, 1917; "What Shocks Women," *ibid.*, Jan. 26, 1918; and Alice Stone Blackwell, "Social Hygiene," *ibid.*, Jan. 17, 1920.

85. At the onset of the European war, National Woman's Party journalists had pointed out that the lesson of the Civil War was suffrage movement independence and not acquiescence to government policies: "Women and the War," *Suffragist* (Washington, D. C.), May 2, 1914. NWP locals attempting to form "fronts" with NAWSA units for the final suffrage push were rebuffed; see Caroline Katzenstein, *Lifting the Curtain* (Philadelphia, 1955), 294–95.

86. "Our, Not The," *Woman Citizen*, Sept. 28, 1918.

were transformed into federal functionaries. Anna Howard Shaw became director of women's auxiliary work and on approaching death during wartime, asked to be buried with her quasi-military medals.[87] These combined sacrifices allowed Catt to claim the fruits of victory, asserting that the suffragists' role in aiding the assimilation of immigrants "results in uninterrupted industry, [and] stands next in importance to the men in the trenches and usefulness to success in the war."[88]

Antiwar dissidents threatening industrial production were singled out as enemies. Catt blamed the Industrial Workers of the World, then facing unprecedented government harrassment and mass arrests, for intended "destruction, in order to block the progress of the war. . . ."[89] The *Woman Citizen* proudly defended woman suffrage by contrast as a "bourgeois movement" with "nothing radical about it in this twentieth century life of ours," the "representative of the most coherent, tightest-welded, farthest reaching section of society—the middle."[90]

With Woodrow Wilson's belated support, woman suffrage at last passed through Congress as a war measure. Yet the final stages of gaining the vote were wreathed in tradition. Suffrage leaders at their greatest moment of triumph could not refrain from looking backward at the long road that three generations of reform-minded women had trod.[91] The decisive vote in the state ratification campaign was cast in the Tennessee legislature by a twenty-four-year old Representative who concluded: "I know that a mother's advice is always safest for her boy to follow and my mother wanted me to vote for ratification. I desired that my party in both State and Nation might say it was a Republican from the mountains of East Tennessee, purest Anglo-Saxon section in the world,

87. William A. Linkugel and Kim Griffin, "The Distinguished War Service of Dr. Anna Howard Shaw," *Pennsylvania History*, XXVIII (Oct., 1961), 384.

88. NAWSA *Proceedings, 1917* (Washington, 1917), 165; see also Morgan's analysis of the war's effect upon the suffrage movement, *Suffrage Politics*, 185.

89. "John Hay, Mrs. Catt, and Patriotism," *Woman Citizen*, Nov. 10, 1917.

90. "A Bourgeois Movement," *ibid.*, July 7, 1917.

91. "A Gigantic Task," *Woman Citizen*, Dec. 6, 1919.

who made woman suffrage possible. . . ."[92] These echoes of sanctified motherhood and race pride were an ironic, almost mocking statement about the history of the woman suffrage movement. When the substance of the vibrant, universal reformism had passed, only the shadows of its vision remained.

The triple victory in world war, prohibition, and woman suffrage seemed to point the way to a new era of American history. At the final NAWSA convention, Carrie Chapman Catt suggested that the dangers and enemies of true democracy would be overcome by the middling spirit:

> Wherever there is a cause of justice, of common national welfare of national progress, here in America we "tell it to the people," and from mountain and valley, city and farm, this great middle class rally to its support.
>
> Were all our population like these, our democracy would be safe for the nation and safe for the world. But at one end of our national life is the mass of illiteracy which knows not America nor her ideals . . . [and] at the other extreme hurried men, busy with big risks and thrilled with the prospect of accomplishing some super task, knowing commercial America only . . . furnish the spirit, the funds, and the motive whereby American Democracy has become endangered.[93]

The convention expressed its approval in a resolution noting that "revolution is rife in Europe and may spread to America," but "prompt redress of legitimate grievances, . . . the removal of the sense of injustice is the surest safeguard against revolution by violence."[94]

The "legitimate grievances" were obviously demands that could be made and accepted without drastic social change. Shortly after the ratification, the *Nation* polled leaders of the National Woman's Party on the rights of Black women in the

92. *History of Woman Suffrage*, VI, 624.
93. *Handbook of the N.A.W.S.A. and Proceedings of the Jubilee Convention* (New York, 1919), 80.
94. *Ibid.*, 250. In the same vein, but somewhat to the left of the mainstream position, were the editorials of Alice Stone Blackwell. See "Declaration of Indignation," against war profiteering, and "For Freedom of the Press," against the Wilson administration's censorship policies, both in *Woman Citizen*, Oct. 4, 1919.

South. Most responses reflected indifference, and Alva Belmont, herself a native southerner, was surprised that anyone should suggest interference into a "Southern problem."[95] Women who had gone to jail to gain the vote would not necessarily challenge the basis of other inequities. Similarly, Catt suggested at the first League of Women Voters meeting in 1920 a deceptively easy route to women's share of political power. Once in whatever organization they chose, women should "make . . . connections" with the "progressive elements," drive to the center of the party power, and find the "engine that moves the wheels of your party machinery."[96] Surely this was Catt's own experience as an agitator. But it revealed a poor estimation of the alterations required in American society for women to claim the actual power to which their formal political rights entitled them.

But this shortsightedness was no personal failure on the part of the leaders. They had continued, as best they understood it, a world-view that their predecessors in broad fields of reform, and not only suffragists, had handed down to them. American conditions and the American spirit had made possible the formation of a woman's rights movement that spoke new truths to the world. Americans had led the agitation against slavery, creating a citizenry at least formally universal. No less a revolutionary figure than Wendell Phillips had lionized this genius for democracy, the individual rights of the humblest worker to reach farther than his or her foreign cousins could. And the most visionary followers of woman suffrage toward the end of the nineteenth century, like the free-love advocate Lucinda Chandler, had called for "Americanism, in its original purity, genuineness and grandeur" as the panacea for social ills.[97] The step beyond this *idée fixe* was one that few of the reformers could take.

Yet for all the late disappointments in the outcome of woman suffrage, something elusive and far more important

95. "White Woman's Burden," *Nation*, CXII (Feb. 16, 1921), 257–58.
96. *Handbook and First National Convention of the League of Women Voters*, 1920 (New York, 1920), 82, 84.
97. Lucinda Chandler, "What Is Americanism: The Labor Problem," *Woman's Tribune*, Aug. 22, 1888.

than the ballot itself had been gained. No contemporary observer saw this more clearly than the young Walter Lippmann, who in 1915 reflected that "while the winning of the vote will itself change nothing very radically, it will register one of the greatest changes in the world." He saw that the demand for the right to vote was, in a larger sense, the insistence upon public recognition that women no longer lived (if they ever had lived) in the sheltered existence of sentimental nineteenth-century romance:

> In the old-fashioned relationship of men and women sex is pervasive. It dictates dress, speech, opinions, interests; if there is a common interest, it is a flirtation, a duel, a chase, full of double meanings and half-communicated intentions. It never travels far from its sexual base. Much gaiety and finesse are associated with it, and I suppose the greater part of the happiness which men have snatched from a disorganized world. But at the same time it has thwarted and stunted and impoverished human relationships, and it is extolled only because people have not had the imagination to see what life might be in a ventilated society.
>
> At bottom, the struggle might almost be described as an effort to alter the tone of people's voices and the look in their eyes. But that means an infinitely greater change, a change in the initial prejudice with which men and women react towards each other and the world. In some ways the change is too subtle for expression, but modern men and women recognize it, and know that in this spiritual emancipation lies the hope of finding answers to the more obvious problems of women's position. . . . It is a matter of reacting in a fresher way, of fingering the issues directly instead of leering and smirking and giggling over them. . . . [Women] have to take part in the wider affairs of life. Their demand for the vote expresses that aspiration. Their winning of it would be a sign that men were civilized enough to understand the aspiration.[98]

The leering and smirking and giggling continue sixty-odd years after these words were written; the modern American woman is neither a fully equal citizen nor Honored Mother of the Race. Still, and in the midst of confusion at the outcome

98. Walter Lippmann, "The Vote as Symbol," *New Republic*, VI (Oct. 9, 1915), 4–5.

of political democracy, she is in practice centuries beyond the woman of 1919. The right to vote could not in itself have meant all that nineteenth-century pioneers expected; individual reforms, once granted, become part of a larger system of institutions. But woman's right to vote is an inescapable and, by now, historic form of self-assertion.

PART ONE: TO THE CIVIL WAR

I. PROLOGUE

"PRECEDING CAUSES," WRITTEN BY Matilda Joslyn Gage in 1881, places the nineteenth-century woman's rights movement within a larger history of Western civilization. The central themes indicate the editors' views on their own accomplishments and those of their more distant predecessors. Within this context, the major figures of the antebellum agitation are introduced.

Behind the details, Gage presents a characteristic nineteenth-century version of historical development, an objective process unraveling itself through human events as universal progress toward a rational order. The twin barriers to human rights, Gage contends, are the Church and the State. Both conspire to limit freedom. The Church stifles free inquiry and the State maintains artificial order through a temporal sanction. Woman is the greatest victim in this tyranny because she is more socially helpless than man and more subject to the sway of superstition. Gage's analysis here is also typical of her life-long commitment to the separation of Church and State and to the diminishment of their combined powers.

Progress, in Gage's view, was signified by rational thinking and individual self-sufficiency. Thus, her historical narrative focuses on the standard milestones of the West: the Renaissance and Reformation as the first stage, the Enlightenment and American Revolution as the immediate precursors to the final advance toward perfection in the nineteenth century. Gage's "great women" are individuals who excelled in free thinking, education, or professional work and those women who inaugurated the drive for progressive reform.

DOCUMENT 1 (I: 25–42): Preceding Causes, written by Matilda Joslyn Gage in 1881

As civilization advances there is a continual change in the standard of human rights. In barbarous ages the right of the strongest was the only one recognized ; but as mankind progressed in the arts and sciences intellect began to triumph over brute force. Change is a law of life, and the development of society a natural growth. Although to this law we owe the discoveries of unknown worlds, the inventions of machinery, swifter modes of travel, and clearer ideas as to the value of human life and thought, yet each successive change has met with the most determined opposition. Fortunately, progress is not the result of pre-arranged plans of individuals, but is born of a fortuitous combination of circumstances that compel certain results, overcoming the natural inertia of mankind. There is a certain enjoyment in habitual sluggishness ; in rising each morning with the same ideas as the night before ; in retiring each night with the thoughts of the morning. This inertia of mind and body has ever held the multitude in chains. Thousands have thus surrendered their most sacred rights of conscience. In all periods of human development, thinking has been punished as a crime, which is reason sufficient to account for the general passive resignation of the masses to their conditions and evironments.

Again, " subjection to the powers that be " has been the lesson of both Church and State, throttling science, checking invention, crushing free thought, persecuting and torturing those who have dared to speak or act outside of established authority. Anathemas and the stake have upheld the Church, banishment and the scaffold the throne, and the freedom of mankind has ever been sacrificed to the idea of protection. So entirely has the human will been enslaved in all classes of society in the past, that monarchs have humbled themselves to popes, nations have knelt at the feet of monarchs, and individuals have sold themselves to others under the subtle promise of " protection "—a word that simply means release from all responsibility, all use of one's own faculties—a word that has ever blinded people to its true significance. Under authority and

EDITORS' NOTE: The numbers in parentheses in the document headings refer to volumes and pages of the original edition. The centered row of asterisks found in a few documents indicates material deleted from within a portion of the original document. M.J.B., P.B.

this false promise of " protection," self-reliance, the first incentive
to freedom, has not only been lost, but the aversion of mankind
for responsibility has been fostered by the few, whose greater bodily
strength, superior intellect, or the inherent law of self-development
has impelled to active exertion.   Obedience and self-sacrifice—the
virtues prescribed for subordinate classes, and which naturally grow
out of their condition—are alike opposed to the theory of individual
rights and self-government.   But as even the inertia of mankind is
not proof against the internal law of progress, certain beliefs have
been inculcated, certain crimes invented, in order to intimidate the
masses.   Hence, the Church made free thought the worst of sins,
and the spirit of inquiry the worst of blasphemies ; while the State
proclaimed her temporal power of divine origin, and all rebellion
high treason alike to God and the king, to be speedily and severely
punished.   In this union of Church and State mankind touched the
lowest depth of degradation.   As late as the time of Bunyan the
chief doctrine inculcated from the pulpit was obedience to the temporal power.

All these influences fell with crushing weight on woman ;
more sensitive, helpless, and imaginative, she suffered a thousand
fears and wrongs where man did one.   Lecky, in his " History of
Rationalism in Europe," shows that the vast majority of the victims
of fanaticism and witchcraft, burned, drowned, and tortured, were
women.   Guizot, in his " History of Civilization," while decrying
the influence of caste in India, and deploring it as the result of barbarism, thanks God there is no system of caste in Europe ; ignoring
the fact that in all its dire and baneful effects, the caste of sex everywhere exists, creating diverse codes of morals for men and women,
diverse penalties for crime, diverse industries, diverse religions and
educational rights, and diverse relations to the Government.   Men
are the Brahmins, women the Pariahs, under our existing civilization.   Herbert Spencer's " Descriptive Sociology of England," an
epitome of English history, says : " Our laws are based on the all-
sufficiency of man's rights, and society exists to-day for woman only
in so far as she is in the keeping of some man."   Thus society, including our systems of jurisprudence, civil and political theories,
trade, commerce, education, religion, friendships, and family life,
have all been framed on the sole idea of man's rights.   Hence, he
takes upon himself the responsibility of directing and controlling
the powers of woman, under that all-sufficient excuse of tyranny,
" divine right."   This same cry of divine authority created the
castes of India ; has for ages separated its people into bodies, with dif-

ferent industrial, educational, civil, religious, and political rights; has maintained this separation for the benefit of the superior class, and sedulously taught the doctrine that any change in existing conditions would be a sin of most direful magnitude.

The opposition of theologians, though first to be exhibited when any change is proposed, for reason that change not only takes power from them, but lessens the reverence of mankind for them, is not in its final result so much to be feared as the opposition of those holding political power. The Church, knowing this, has in all ages aimed to connect itself with the State. Political freedom guarantees religious liberty, freedom to worship God according to the dictates of one's own conscience, fosters a spirit of inquiry, creates self-reliance, induces a feeling of responsibility.

The people who demand authority for every thought and action, who look to others for wisdom and protection, are those who perpetuate tyranny. The thinkers and actors who find their authority within, are those who inaugurate freedom. Obedience to outside authority to which woman has everywhere been trained, has not only dwarfed her capacity, but made her a retarding force in civilization, recognized at last by statesmen as a dangerous element to free institutions. A recent writer, speaking of Turkey, says: " All attempts for the improvement of that nation must prove futile, owing to the degradation of its women ; and their elevation is hopeless so long as they are taught by their religion that their condition is ordained of heaven." Gladstone, in one of his pamphlets on the revival of Catholicism in England, says: " The spread of this religion is due, as might be expected, to woman ; " thus conceding in both cases her power to block the wheels of progress. Hence, in the scientific education of woman, in the training of her faculties to independent thought and logical reasoning, lies the hope of the future.

The two great sources of progress are intellect and wealth. Both represent power, and are the elements of success in life. Education frees the mind from the bondage of authority and makes the individual self-asserting. Remunerative industry is the means of securing to its possessor wealth and education, transforming the laborer to the capitalist. Work in itself is not power; it is but the means to an end. The slave is not benefited by his industry ; he does not receive the results of his toil ; his labor enriches another— adds to the power of his master to bind his chain still closer. Although woman has performed much of the labor of the world, her industry and economy have been the very means of increasing her degradation. Not being free, the results of her labor have gone to build up and sustain the very class that has perpetuated this injustice. Even in the family, where we should naturally look for the truest conditions, woman has always been robbed of the fruits of her own toil. The influence the Catholic Church has had on religious free thought, that monarchies have had on political free thought, that serfdom has had upon free labor, have all been cumulative in the family upon woman. Taught that father and husband stood to her in the place of God, she has been denied liberty of conscience, and held in obedience to masculine will. Taught that the fruits of her industry belonged to others, she has seen man enter into every avocation most suitable to her, while she, the uncomplaining drudge of the household, condemned to the severest labor, has been systematically robbed of her earnings, which have gone to build up her master's power, and she has found herself in the condition of the slave, deprived of the results of her own labor. Taught that education for her was indelicate and irreligious, she has been kept in such gross ignorance as to fall a prey to superstition, and to glory in her own degradation. Taught that a low voice is an excellent thing in woman, she has been trained to a subjugation of the vocal organs, and thus lost the benefit of loud tones and their well-known invigoration of the system. Forbidden to run, climb, or jump, her muscles have been weakened, and her strength deteriorated. Confined most of the time to the house, she has neither as strong lungs nor as vigorous a digestion as her brother. Forbidden to enter the pulpit, she has been trained to an unquestioning reverence for theological authority and false belief upon the most vital interests of religion. Forbidden the medical profession, she has at the most sacred times of her life been left to the ignorant supervision of male physicians, and seen her young children die by thousands. Forbidden to enter the courts, she has seen her sex unjustly tried and condemned for crimes men were incapable of judging.

Woman has been the great unpaid laborer of the world, and although within the last two decades a vast number of new employments have been opened to her, statistics prove that in the great majority of these, she is not paid according to the value of the work done, but according to sex. The opening of all industries to woman, and the wage question as connected with her, are most subtle and profound questions of political economy, closely interwoven with the rights of self-government.

The revival of learning had its influence upon woman, and we find in the early part of the fourteenth century a decided tendency toward a recognition of her equality. Christine of Pisa, the most eminent woman of this period, supported a family of six persons by her pen, taking high ground on the conservation of morals in opposition to the general licentious spirit of the age. Margaret of Angoulême, the brilliant Queen of Navarre, was a voluminous writer, her Heptaméron rising to the dignity of a French classic. A paper in the *Revue des Deux Mondes*, a few years since, by M. Henri Baudrillart, upon the " Emancipation of Woman," recalls the fact that for nearly four hundred years, men, too, have been ardent believers in equal rights for woman.

In 1509, Cornelius Agrippa, a great literary authority of his time, published a work of this character. Agrippa was not content with claiming woman's equality, but in a work of thirty chapters devoted himself to proving " the superiority of woman." In less than fifty years (1552) Ruscelli brought out a similar work based on the Platonic Philosophy. In 1599, Anthony Gibson wrote a book which in the prolix phraseology of the times was called, " A Woman's Worth defended against all the Men in the World, proving to be more Perfect, Excellent. and Absolute, in all Virtuous Actions, than any man of What Quality Soever." While these sturdy male defenders of the rights of woman met with many opponents, some going so far as to assert that women were beings not endowed with reason, they were sustained by many vigorous writers among women. Italy, then the foremost literary country of Europe, possessed many women of learning, one of whom, Lucrezia Morinella, a Venetian lady, wrote a work entitled, " The Nobleness and Excellence of Women, together with the Faults and Imperfections of Men."

The seventeenth century gave birth to many essays and books of a like character, not confined to the laity, as several friars wrote upon the same subject. In 1696, Daniel De Foe wished to have an institute founded for the better education of young women. He said : " We reproach the sex every day for folly and impertinence, while I am confident had they the advantages of education equal to us, they would be guilty of less than ourselves." Alexander's History of Women, John Paul Ribera's work upon Women, the two huge quartos of De Costa upon the same subject, Count Ségur's " Women : Their Condition and Influence," and many other works showed the drift of the new age.

The Reformation, that great revolution in religious thought, loosened the grasp of the Church upon woman, and is to be looked upon as one of the most important steps in this reform. In the reign of Elizabeth, England was called the Paradise of Women When Elizabeth ascended the throne, it was not only as queen, but she succeeded her father as the head of the newly-formed rebellious Church, and she held firm grasp on both Church and State during the long years of her reign, bending alike priest and prelate to her fiery will. The reign of Queen Anne, called the Golden Age of English Literature, is especially noticeable on account of Mary Astell and Elizabeth Elstob. The latter, speaking nine languages, was most famous for her skill in the Saxon tongue. She also replied to current objections made to woman's learning. Mary Astell elaborated a plan for a Woman's College, which was favorably received by Queen Anne, and would have been carried out, but for the opposition of Bishop Burnett.

During the latter part of the eighteenth century, there were public discussions by women in England, under the general head of Female Parliament. These discussions took wide range, touching upon the entrance of men into those industries usually assigned to women, and demanding for themselves higher educational advantages, and the right to vote at elections, and to be returned members of Parliament.

The American Revolution, that great political rebellion of the ages, was based upon the inherent rights of the individual. Perhaps in none but English Colonies, by descendants of English parents, could such a revolution have been consummated. England had never felt the bonds of feudalism to the extent of many countries; its people had defied its monarchs and wrested from them many civil rights, rights which protected women as well as men, and although its common law, warped by ecclesiasticism, expended its chief rigors upon women, yet at an early day they enjoyed certain ecclesiastical and political powers unknown to women elsewhere. Before the Conquest, abbesses sat in councils of the Church and signed its decrees; while kings were even dependent upon their consent in granting certain charters. The synod of Whitby, in the ninth century, was held in the convent of the Abbess Hilda, she herself presiding over its deliberations. The famous prophetess of Kent at one period communicated the orders of Heaven to the Pope himself. Ladies of birth and quality sat in council with the Saxon Witas—*i. e.*, wise men—taking part in the Witenagemot, the great National Council of our Saxon ancestors in England. In the seventh century this National Council met at Baghamstead to enact a new code of laws, the queen, abbesses, and many ladies of quality taking part and signing the decrees. Passing by other similar instances, we find in the reign of Henry III. that four women took seats in Parliament, and in the reign of Edward I. ten ladies were called to Parliament, while in the thirteenth century, Queen Elinor became keeper of the Great Seal, sitting as Lord Chancellor in the *Aula Regia*, the highest court of the Kingdom. Running back two or three centuries before the Christian era, we find Martia, her seat of power in London, holding the reins of government so wisely as to receive the surname of Proba, the Just. She especially devoted herself to the enactment of just laws for her subjects, the first principles of the common law tracing back to her; the celebrated laws of Alfred, and of Edward the Confessor, being in great degree restorations and compilations from the laws of Martia, which were known as the "Martian Statutes."

When the American colonies began their resistance to English tyranny, the women—all this inherited tendency to freedom surging in their veins—were as active, earnest, determined, and self-sacrificing as the men, and although, as Mrs. Ellet in her "Women of the Revolution" remarks, "political history says but little, and that vaguely and incidentally, of the women who bore their part in the revolution," yet that little shows woman to have been endowed with as lofty a patriotism as man, and to have as fully understood the principles upon which the struggle was based. Among the women who manifested deep political insight, were Mercy Otis Warren, Abigail Smith Adams, and Hannah Lee Corbin; all closely related to the foremost men of the Revolution. Mrs. Warren was a sister of James Otis, whose fiery words did so much to arouse and intensify the feelings of the colonists against British aggression. This brother and sister were united to the end of their lives in a friendship rendered firm and enduring by the similarity of their intellects and political views. The home of Mrs. Warren was the resort of patriotic spirits and the headquarters of the rebellion. She herself wrote, "By the Plymouth fireside were many political plans organized, discussed, and digested." Her correspondence with eminent men of the Revolution was extensive and belongs to the history of the country. She was the first one who based the struggle upon "inherent rights," a phrase afterward made the corner-stone of political authority. Mrs. Warren asserted that "'inherent rights' belonged to all mankind, and had been conferred on all by the God of nations." She numbered Jefferson among her correspondents, and the Declaration of Independence shows the influence of her mind. Among others who sought her counsel upon political matters were Samuel and John Adams, Dickinson, that pure patriot of Pennsylvania, Jefferson, Gerry, and Knox. She was the first person who counseled separation and pressed those views upon John Adams, when

he sought her advice before the opening of the first Congress. At
that time even Washington had no thought of the final independence
of the colonies, emphatically denying such intention or desire on
their part, and John Adams was shunned in the streets of Philadelphia for having dared to hint such a possibility. Mrs. Warren sustained his sinking courage and urged him to bolder steps. Her advice was not only sought in every emergency, but political parties
found their arguments in her conversation. Mrs. Warren looked
not to the freedom of man alone, but to that of her own sex also.

England itself had at least one woman who watched the struggle
of America with lively interest, and whose writings aided in the dis-
semination of republican ideas. This was the celebrated Catharine
Sawbridge Macaulay, one of the greatest minds England has ever
produced—a woman so noted for her republican ideas that after her
death a statue was erected to her as the "Patroness of Liberty."
During the whole of the Revolutionary period, Washington was in
correspondence with Mrs. Macaulay, who did much to sustain him
during those days of trial. She and Mrs. Warren were also correspondents at that time. She wrote several works of a republican
character, for home influence; among these, in 1775, "An Address to the people of England, Scotland, and Ireland, on the present
Important Crisis of Affairs," designed to show the justice of the
American cause. The gratitude Americans feel toward Edmund
Burke for his aid, might well be extended to Mrs. Macaulay.

Abigail Smith Adams, the wife of John Adams, was an American
woman whose political insight was worthy of remark. She early
protested against the formation of a new government in which woman should be unrecognized, demanding for her a voice and representation. She was the first American woman who threatened rebellion
unless the rights of her sex were secured. In March, 1776, she
wrote to her husband, then in the Continental Congress, "I long to
hear you have declared an independency, and, by the way, in the
new code of laws which I suppose it will be necessary for you to
make, I desire you would remember the ladies, and be more generous and favorable to them than your ancestors. Do not put such
unlimited power into the hands of husbands. Remember, all men
would be tyrants if they could. If particular care and attention are
not paid to the ladies, we are determined to foment a rebellion, and
will not hold ourselves bound to obey any laws in which we have no
voice or representation." Again and again did Mrs. Adams urge the
establishment of an independency and the limitation of man's power
over woman, declaring all arbitrary power dangerous and tending to

revolution. Nor was she less mindful of equal advantages of education. " If you complain of education in sons, what shall I say in regard to daughters, who every day experience the want of it ? " She expressed a strong wish that the new Constitution might be distinguished for its encouragement of learning and virtue. Nothing more fully shows the dependent condition of a class than the methods used to secure their wishes. Mrs. Adams felt herself obliged to appeal to masculine selfishness in showing the reflex action woman's education would have upon man. "If," said she, " we mean to have heroes, statesmen, and philosophers, we should have learned women." Thus did the Revolutionary Mothers urge the recognition of equal rights when the Government was in the process of formation. Although the first plot of ground in the United States for a public school had been given by a woman (Bridget Graffort), in 1700, her sex were denied admission. Mrs. Adams, as well as her friend Mrs. Warren, had in their own persons felt the deprivations of early educational advantages. The boasted public school system of Massachusetts, created for boys only, opened at last its doors to girls, merely to secure its share of public money. The women of the South, too, early demanded political equality. The counties of Mecklenberg and Rowan, North Carolina, were famous for the patriotism of their women. Mecklenberg claims to have issued the first declaration of independence, and, at the centennial celebration of this event in May, 1875, proudly accepted for itself the derisive name given this region by Tarleton's officers, " The Hornet's Nest of America." This name—first bestowed by British officers upon Mrs. Brevard's mansion, then Tarleton's headquarters, where that lady's fiery patriotism and stinging wit discomfited this General in many a sally— was at last held to include the whole county. In 1778, only two years after the Declaration of Independence was adopted, and while the flames of war were still spreading over the country, Hannah Lee Corbin, of Virginia, the sister of General Richard Henry Lee, wrote him, protesting against the taxation of women unless they were allowed to vote. He replied that " women were already possessed of that right," thus recognizing the fact of woman's enfranchisement as one of the results of the new government, and it is on record that women in Virginia did at an early day exercise the right of voting. New Jersey also specifically secured this right to women on the 2d of July, 1776—a right exercised by them for more than a third of a century. Thus our country started into governmental life freighted with the protests of the Revolutionary Mothers against being ruled without their consent. From that hour to the present, women have been con-

tinually raising their voices against political tyranny, and demanding
for themselves equality of opportunity in every department of life.

In 1790, Mary Wollstonecraft's "Vindication of the Rights of
Women," published in London, attracted much attention from liberal minds. She examined the position of woman in the light of
existing civilizations, and demanded for her the widest opportunities
of education, industry, political knowledge, and the right of representation. Although her work is filled with maxims of the highest
morality and purest wisdom, it called forth such violent abuse, that
her husband appealed for her from the judgment of her contempo-
raries to that of mankind. So exalted were her ideas of woman, so
comprehensive her view of life, that Margaret Fuller, in referring to
her, said : " Mary Wollstonecraft—a woman whose existence proved
the need of some new interpretation of woman's rights, belonging
to that class who by birth find themselves in places so narrow that,
by breaking bonds, they become outlaws." Following her, came
Jane Marcet, Eliza Lynn, and Harriet Martineau—each of whom in
the early part of the nineteenth century, exerted a decided influence
upon the political thought of England. Mrs. Marcet was one of the
most scientific and highly cultivated persons of the age. Her "Conversations on Chemistry," familiarized that science both in England
and America, and from it various male writers filched their ideas.
It was a text-book in this country for many years. Over one hundred and sixty thousand copies were sold, though the fact that this
work emanated from the brain of a woman was carefully withheld.
Mrs. Marcet also wrote upon political economy, and was the first person who made the subject comprehensive to the popular mind. Her
manner of treating it was so clear and vivid, that the public, to whom
it had been a hidden science, were able to grasp the subject. Her
writings were the inspiration of Harriet Martineau, who followed
her in the same department of thought at a later period. Miss
Martineau was a remarkable woman. Besides her numerous books
on political economy, she was a regular contributor to the London
Daily News, the second paper in circulation in England, for many
years writing five long articles weekly, also to Dickens' *Household
Words*, and the *Westminster Review*. She saw clearly the spirit and
purpose of the Anti-Slavery Movement in this country, and was a
regular contributor to the *National Anti-Slavery Standard*, published in New York. Eliza Lynn, an Irish lady, was at this time writing leading editorials for political papers. In Russia, Catharine II.,
the absolute and irresponsible ruler of that vast nation, gave utterance to views, of which, says La Harpe, the revolutionists of France

and America fondly thought themselves the originators. She caused her grandchildren to be educated into the most liberal ideas, and Russia was at one time the only country in Europe where political refugees could find safety. To Catharine, Russia is indebted for the first proposition to enfranchise the serfs, but meeting strong opposition she was obliged to relinquish this idea, which was carried to fruition by her great-grandson, Alexander.

This period of the eighteenth century was famous for the executions of women on account of their radical political opinions, Madame Roland, the leader of the liberal party in France, going to the guillotine with the now famous words upon her lips, " Oh, Liberty, what crimes are committed in thy name ! " The beautiful Charlotte Corday sealed with her life her belief in liberty, while Sophia Lapiérre barely escaped the same fate ; though two men, Siéyes and Condorcét, in the midst of the French Revolution, proposed the recognition of woman's political rights.

Frances Wright, a person of extraordinary powers of mind, born in Dundee, Scotland, in 1797, was the first woman who gave lectures on political subjects in America. When sixteen years of age she heard of the existence of a country in which freedom for the people had been proclaimed; she was filled with joy and a determination to visit the American Republic where the foundations of justice, liberty, and equality had been so securely laid. In 1820 she came here, traveling extensively North and South. She was at that time but twenty-two years of age. Her letters gave Europeans the first true knowledge of America, and secured for her the friendship of LaFayette. Upon her second visit she made this country her home for several years. Her radical ideas on theology, slavery, and the social degradation of woman, now generally accepted by the best minds of the age, were then denounced by both press and pulpit, and maintained by her at the risk of her life. Although the Government of the United States was framed on the basis of entire separation of Church and State, yet from an early day the theological spirit had striven to unite the two, in order to strengthen the Church by its union with the civil power. As early as 1828, the standard of " The Christian Party in Politics " was openly unfurled. Frances Wright had long been aware of its insidious efforts, and its reliance upon women for its support. Ignorant, superstitious, devout, woman's general lack of education made her a fitting instrument for the work of thus undermining the republic. Having deprived her of her just rights, the country was now to find in woman its most dangerous foe. Frances Wright lectured that winter in the

large cities of the West and Middle States, striving to rouse the
nation to the new danger which threatened it. The clergy at once
became her most bitter opponents. The cry of "infidel" was started
on every side, though her work was of vital importance to the country and undertaken from the purest philanthropy. In speaking of
her persecutions she said: " The injury and inconvenience of every
kind and every hour to which, in these days, a really consistent reformer stands exposed, none can conceive but those who experience
them. Such become, as it were, excommunicated after the fashion of
the old Catholic Mother Church, removed even from the protection
of law, such as it is, and from the sympathy of society, for whose
sake they consent to be crucified."

Among those who were advocating the higher education of
women, Mrs. Emma Willard became noted at this period. Born
with a strong desire for learning, she keenly felt the educational
disadvantages of her sex. She began teaching at an early day, introducing new studies and new methods in her school, striving to
secure public interest in promoting woman's education. Governor
Clinton, of New York, impressed with the wisdom of her plans, invited her to move her school from Connecticut to New York. She
accepted, and in 1819 established a school in Watervleit, which soon
moved to Troy, and in time built up a great reputation. Through
the influence of Governor Clinton, the Legislature granted a portion
of the educational fund to endow this institution, which was the
first instance in the United States of Government aid for the education of women. Amos B. Eaton, Professor of the Natural Sciences in the Rensselaer Institute, Troy, at this time, was Mrs. Willard's faithful friend and teacher. In the early days it was her
custom, in introducing a new branch of learning into her seminary,
to study it herself, reciting to Professor Eaton every evening the
lesson of the next day. Thus she went through botany, chemistry,
mineralogy, astronomy, and the higher mathematics. As she could
not afford teachers for these branches, with faithful study she fitted
herself. Mrs. Willard's was the first girls' school in which the higher
mathematics formed part of the course, but such was the prejudice
against a liberal education for woman, that the first public examination of a girl in geometry (1829) created as bitter a storm of ridicule as has since assailed women who have entered the law, the pulpit, or the medical profession. The derision attendant upon the
experiment of advancing woman's education, led Governor Clinton
to say in his message to the Legislature: " I trust you will not be
deterred by commonplace ridicule from extending your munificence

to this meritorious institution." At a school convention in Syracuse, 1845, Mrs. Willard suggested the employment of women as superintendents of public schools, a measure since adopted in many States. She also projected the system of normal schools for the higher education of teachers. A scientific explorer as well as student, she wrote a work on the " Motive Power in the Circulation of the Blood," in contradiction to Harvey's theory, which at once attracted the attention of medical men. This work was one of the then accumulating evidences of woman's adaptation to medical study.

In Ancient Egypt the medical profession was in the hands of women, to which we may attribute that country's almost entire exemption from infantile diseases, a fact which recent discoveries fully authenticate. The enormous death-rate of young children in modern civilized countries may be traced to woman's general enforced ignorance of the laws of life, and to the fact that the profession of medicine has been too exclusively in the hands of men. Though through the dim past we find women still making discoveries, and in the feudal ages possessing knowledge of both medicine and surgery, it is but recently that they have been welcomed as practitioners into the medical profession. Looking back scarcely a hundred years, we find science much indebted to woman for some of its most brilliant discoveries. In 1736, the first medical botany was given to the world by Elizabeth Blackwell, a woman physician, whom the persecutions of her male compeers had cast into jail for debt. As Bunyan prepared his "Pilgrim's Progress" between prison walls, so did Elizabeth Blackwell, no-wise disheartened, prepare her valuable aid to medical science under the same conditions. Lady Montague's discovery of a check to the small-pox, Madam Boivin's discovery of the hidden cause of certain hemorrhages, Madam de Coudray's invention of the manikin, are among the notable steps which opened the way to the modern Elizabeth Blackwell, Harriot K. Hunt, Clemence S. Lozier, Ann Preston, Hannah Longshore, Marie Jackson, Laura Ross Wolcott, Marie Zakrzewska, and Mary Putnam Jacobi, who are some of the earlier distinguished American examples of woman's skill in the healing art.

Mary Gove Nichols gave public lectures upon anatomy in the United States in 1838. Paulina Wright (Davis) followed her upon physiology in 1844, using a manikin in her illustrations.* Mari-

---

* As showing woman's ignorance and prejudice, Mrs. Davis used to relate that when she uncovered her manikin some ladies would drop their veils because of its indelicacy, and others would run from the room ; sometimes ladies even fainted.

ana Johnson followed Mrs. Davis, but it was 1848 before Elizabeth Blackwell—the first woman to pass through the regular course of medical study—received her diploma at Geneva.* In 1845–6, preceding Miss Blackwell's course of study, Dr. Samuel Gregory and his brother George issued pamphlets advocating the education and employment of women-physicians, and, in 1847, Dr. Gregory delivered a series of lectures in Boston upon that subject, followed in 1848 by a school numbering twelve ladies, and an association entitled the "American Female Medical Education Society." In 1832, Lydia Maria Child published her "History of Woman," which was the first American storehouse of information upon the whole question, and undoubtedly increased the agitation. In 1836, Ernestine L. Rose, a Polish lady—banished from her native country by the Austrian tyrant, Francis Joseph, for her love of liberty—came to America, lecturing in the large cities North and South upon the "Science of Government." She advocated the enfranchisement of woman. Her beauty, wit, and eloquence drew crowded houses. About this period Judge Hurlbut, of New York, a leading member of the Bar, wrote a vigorous work on "Human Rights,"† in which he advocated political equality for women. This work attracted the attention of many legal minds throughout that State. In the winter of 1836, a bill was introduced into the New York Legislature by Judge Hertell, to secure to married women their rights of property. This bill was drawn up under the direction of Hon. John Savage, Chief-Justice of the Supreme Court, and Hon. John C. Spencer, one of the revisers of the statutes of New York. It was in furtherance of this bill that Ernestine L. Rose and Paulina Wright at that early day circulated petitions. The very few names they secured show the hopeless apathy and ignorance of the women as to their own rights. As similar bills were pending in New York until finally passed in 1848, a great educational work was accomplished in the constant discussion of the topics involved. During the winters of 1844–5–6, Elizabeth Cady Stan-.

---

* The writer's father, a physician, as early as 1843–4, canvassed the subject of giving his daughter (Matilda Joslyn Gage) a medical education, looking to Geneva—then presided over by his old instructor—to open its doors to her. But this bold idea was dropped, and Miss Blackwell was the first and only lady who was graduated from that institution until its incorporation with the Syracuse University and the removal of the college to that city.

† Judge Hurlbut, with a lawyer's prejudice, first prepared a paper against the rights of woman. Looking it over, he saw himself able to answer every argument, which he proceeded to do—the result being his "Human Rights."

ton, living in Albany, made the acquaintance of Judge Hurlbut and a large circle of lawyers and legislators, and, while exerting herself to strengthen their convictions in favor of the pending bill, she resolved at no distant day to call a convention for a full and free discussion of woman's rights and wrongs.

In 1828, Sarah and Angelina Grimke, daughters of a wealthy planter of Charleston, South Carolina, emancipated their slaves and came North to lecture on the evils of slavery, leaving their home and native place forever because of their hatred of this wrong. Angelina was a natural orator. Fresh from the land of bondage, there was a fervor in her speech that electrified her hearers and drew crowds wherever she went. Sarah published a book reviewing the Bible arguments the clergy were then making in their pulpits to prove that the degradation of the slave and woman were alike in harmony with the expressed will of God. Thus women from the beginning took an active part in the Anti-Slavery struggle. They circulated petitions, raised large sums of money by fairs, held prayer-meetings and conventions. In 1835, Angelina wrote an able letter to William Lloyd Garrison, immediately after the Boston mob. These letters and appeals were considered very effective abolition documents.

In May, 1837, a National Woman's Anti-Slavery Convention was held in New York, in which eight States were represented by seventy-one delegates. The meetings were ably sustained through two days. The different sessions were opened by prayer and reading of the Scriptures by the women themselves. A devout, earnest spirit prevailed. The debates, resolutions, speeches, and appeals were fully equal to those in any Convention held by men of that period. Angelina Grimke was appointed by this Convention to prepare an appeal for the slaves to the people of the free States, and a letter to John Quincy Adams thanking him for his services in defending the right of petition for women and slaves, qualified with the regret that by expressing himself " adverse to the abolition of slavery in the District of Columbia," he did not sustain the cause of freedom and of God. She wrote a stirring appeal to the Christian women of the South, urging them to use their influence against slavery. Sarah also wrote an appeal to the clergy of the South, conjuring them to use their power for freedom.

Among those who took part in these conventions we find the names of Lydia Maria Child, Mary Grove, Henrietta Sargent, Sarah Pugh, Abby Kelley, Mary S. Parker, of Boston, who was president of the Convention; Anne Webster, Deborah Shaw, Martha Storrs,

Mrs. A. L. Cox, Rebecca B. Spring, and Abigail Hopper Gibbons, a daughter of that noble Quaker philanthropist, Isaac T. Hopper.

Abby Kelley was the most untiring and the most persecuted of all the women who labored throughout the Anti-Slavery struggle. She traveled up and down, alike in winter's cold and summer's heat, with scorn, ridicule, violence, and mobs accompanying her, suffering all kinds of persecutions, still speaking whenever and wherever she gained an audience; in the open air, in school-house, barn, depot, church, or public hall; on week-day or Sunday, as she found opportunity. For listening to her, on Sunday, many men and women were expelled from their churches. Thus through continued persecution was woman's self-assertion and self-respect sufficiently developed to prompt her at last to demand justice, liberty, and equality for herself.

In 1840, Margaret Fuller published an essay in the *Dial*, entitled "The Great Lawsuit, or Man *vs.* Woman: Woman *vs.* Man." In this essay she demanded perfect equality for woman, in education, industry, and politics. It attracted great attention and was afterward expanded into a work entitled "Woman in the Nineteenth Century." This, with her parlor conversations, on art, science, religion, politics, philosophy, and social life, gave a new impulse to woman's education as a thinker.

"Woman and her Era," by Eliza Woodson Farnham, was another work that called out a general discussion on the status of the sexes, Mrs. Farnham taking the ground of woman's superiority. The great social and educational work done by her in California, when society there was chiefly male, and rapidly tending to savagism, and her humane experiment in the Sing Sing (N. Y.), State Prison, assisted by Georgiana Bruce Kirby and Mariana Johnson, are worthy of mention.

In the State of New York, in 1845, Rev. Samuel J. May preached a sermon at Syracuse, upon "The Rights and Conditions of Women," in which he sustained their right to take part in political life, saying women need not expect "to have their wrongs fully redressed, until they themselves have a voice and a hand in the enactment and administration of the laws."

In 1847, Clarina Howard Nichols, in her husband's paper, addressed to the voters of the State of Vermont a series of editorials, setting forth the injustice of the property disabilities of married women.

In 1849, Lucretia Mott published a discourse on woman, delivered in the Assembly Building, Philadelphia, in answer to a Lyceum lecture which Richard H. Dana, of Boston, was giving in many of the chief cities, ridiculing the idea of political equality for woman. Elizabeth Wilson, of Ohio, published a scriptural view of woman's rights and duties far in advance of the generally received opinions. At even an earlier day, Martha Bradstreet, of Utica, plead her own case in the courts of New York, continuing her contest for many years. The temperance reform and the deep interest taken in it by women; the effective appeals they made, setting forth their wrongs as mother, wife, sister, and daughter of the drunkard, with a power beyond that of man, early gave them a local place on this platform as a favor, though denied as a right. Delegates from woman's societies to State and National conventions invariably found themselves rejected. It was her early labors in the temperance cause that first roused Susan B. Anthony to a realizing sense of woman's social, civil, and political degradation, and thus secured her life-long labors for the enfranchisement of woman. In 1847 she made her first speech at a public meeting of the Daughters of Temperance in Canajoharie, N. Y. The same year Antoinette L. Brown, then a student at Oberlin College, Ohio, the first institution that made the experiment of co-education, delivered her first speech on temperance in several places in Ohio, and on Woman's Rights, in the Baptist church at Henrietta, N. Y. Lucy Stone, a graduate of Oberlin, made her first speech on Woman's Rights the same year in her brother's church at Brookfield, Mass.

Nor were the women of Europe inactive during these years. In 1824 Elizabeth Heyrick, a Quaker woman, cut the gordian knot of difficulty in the anti-slavery struggle in England, by an able essay in favor of immediate, unconditional emancipation. At Leipsic, in 1844, Helene Marie Weber—her father a Prussian officer, and her mother an English woman—wrote a series of ten tracts on " Woman's Rights and Wrongs," covering the whole question and making a volume of over twelve hundred pages. The first of these treated of the intellectual faculties; the second, woman's rights of property; the third, wedlock—deprecating the custom of woman merging her civil existence in that of her husband; the fourth claimed woman's right to all political emoluments; the fifth, on ecclesiasticism, demanded for woman an entrance to the pulpit; the sixth, upon suffrage, declared it to be woman's right and duty to vote. These essays were strong, vigorous, and convincing. Miss Weber also lectured in Vienna, Berlin, and several of the large German cities. In England, Lady Morgan's " Woman and her Master " appeared ;—a work filled with philosophical reflections, and of the same general bearing as Miss Weber's. Also an "Appeal of Women," the joint work of Mrs. Wheeler and William Thomson—a strong and vigorous essay, in which woman's limitations under the law were tersely and pungently set forth and her political rights demanded. The active part women took in the Polish and German revolutions and in favor of the abolition of slavery in the British West Indies, all taught their lessons of woman's rights. Madam Mathilde Anneke, on the staff of her husband, with Hon. Carl Schurz, carried messages to and fro in the midst of danger on the battle-fields of Germany.

Thus over the civilized world we find the same impelling forces, and general development of society, without any individual concert of action, tending to the same general result; alike rousing the minds of men and women to the aggregated wrongs of centuries and inciting to an effort for their overthrow.

The works of George Sand, Frederika Bremer, Charlotte Brontë, George Eliot, Catharine Sedgwick, and Harriet Beecher Stowe, in literature; Mrs. Hemans, Mrs. Sigourney, Elizabeth Barrett Browning, in poetry; Angelica Kauffman, Rosa Bonheur, Harriet Hosmer, in art; Mary Somerville, Caroline Herschell, Maria Mitchell, in science; Elizabeth Fry, Dorothea Dix, Mary Carpenter, in prison reform; Florence Nightingale and Clara Barton in the camp—are all parts of the great uprising of women out of the lethargy of the past, and are among the forces of the complete revolution a thousand pens and voices herald at this hour.

II. Antislavery Origins

THE EDITORS OF THE *History of Woman Suffrage* traced the origins of their movement to women's engagement from the 1830s through the 1850s in the antislavery cause. Women organized antislavery societies, took a public role in the movement, and ultimately demanded equality of participation in the worldwide effort.

The formation of the American Anti-Slavery Society in 1833 marked a new period in abolitionism, unifying several diverse strains in opposition to colonization schemes and inadvertently raising the question of women's participation to a new level. For a temporary solution, Lucretia Mott moved to create the Philadelphia Female Anti-Slavery Society a few days after the national organization was founded. In the next several years, as antislavery forces swelled, women dramatically increased their agitation. The southern-born Grimké sisters rapidly became leading figures in this rising movement. As speakers and pamphleteers they were unexcelled. Angelina's *Letters to Catharine Beecher* was one of the most powerful tracts against the colonization-oriented moderates. Sarah's *Letters on the Equality of the Sexes*, published in 1837 and foreshadowing many of the demands that the later woman's rights movement would bring into open debate, drew an analogy between the condition of the woman and the slave and insisted on equality for all under the law. A barnstorming lecture tour across New England drew crowds that were themselves a precedent in their "promiscuity," the mixing of men and women in the same audience.

Pennsylvania Hall was the physical symbol of the reform constituency. By the same token it was the natural target for anti-reform mobs. Angelina Grimké, who in speaking two days after her marriage to Theodore Weld dramatized her own continuing commitment to both antislavery and woman's rights, typified the reformer's courage under pressure. Sarah Smith underlined women's specific responsibility to put an end to the depravity of slavery. At the end of the third day, these voices were temporarily silenced: crowds broke through the doors of the unguarded building and set fire to it, destroying the hall. Prominent abolitionists of both sexes had to be spirited away for their own safety. Yet the women had made their point. Angelina Grimké in particular had roused women beyond sympathy to action. As she articulated the implications of a moral commitment, women would educate themselves and their neighbors, conduct discussions, and by circulating petitions use their own potential link with the highest offices in the land. That done, there would be no turning back.

After nearly a decade marked by women's continued participation in virtually all aspects of antislavery agitation, the women's rights issue surfaced at the London Convention of 1840. Confronted with exclusion from the meetings, women experienced a deepened consciousness of their common cause. In particular, as Lucretia Mott's biographer suggested, Elizabeth Cady Stanton was profoundly encouraged by the elder advocate, who personally demonstrated a willingness to "question the opinions of popes, kings, and parliamentarians . . . maintaining no higher authority than her own judgment as a pure-minded woman of education."[1]

1. Lloyd D. M. Hare, *Lucretia Mott, the Greatest American Woman* (New York, 1937), 193.

DOCUMENT 2 (I: 339–41): Sarah T. Smith, Address to Anti-Slavery Societies, Second National Anti-Slavery Convention of American Women, Philadelphia, Pennsylvania, May 15, 1838

DEAR FRIENDS:—In that love for our cause which knows not the fear of man, we address you in confidence that our motives will be understood and regarded. We fear not censure from you for going beyond the circle which has been drawn around us by physical force, by mental usurpation, by the usages of ages; not any one of which can we admit gives the right to prescribe it; else might the monarchs of the old world sit firmly on their thrones, the nobility of Europe lord it over the man of low degree, and the chains we are now seeking to break, continue riveted on the neck of the slave. Our faith goes not back to the wigwam of the savage, or the castle of the feudal chief, but would rather soar with hope to that period when "right alone shall make might"; when the truncheon and the sword shall lie useless; when the intellect and heart shall speak and be obeyed; when "He alone whose right it is shall rule and reign in the hearts of the children of men."

We are told that it is not within "the province of woman" to discuss the subject of slavery; that it is a "political question," and that we are "stepping out of our sphere" when we take part in its discussion. It is not true that it is merely a political question; it is likewise a question of justice, of humanity, of morality, of religion; a question which, while it involves considerations of immense importance to the welfare and prosperity of our country, enters deeply into the home—concerns the every-day feelings of millions of our fellow beings. Whether the laborer shall receive the reward of his labor, or be driven daily to unrequited toil; whether he shall walk erect in the dignity of conscious manhood, or be reckoned among the beasts which perish; whether his bones and sinews shall be his own, or another's; whether his child shall receive the protection of its natural guardian, or be ranked among the live-stock of the estate, to be disposed of as the caprice or interest of the master may dictate; whether the sun of knowledge shall irradiate the hut of the peasant, or the murky cloud of ignorance brood darkly over it; whether "every one shall have the liberty to worship God according to the dictates of his own conscience," or man assume the prerogative of Jehovah and impiously seek to plant himself upon the throne of the Almighty. These considerations are all involved in the question of liberty or slavery.

And is a subject comprehending interests of such magnitude, merely a "political question," and one in which woman "can take no part without losing something of the modesty and gentleness which are her most appropriate ornaments"? May not the "ornament of a meek and quiet spirit" exist with an upright mind and enlightened intellect?

Must woman necessarily be less gentle because her heart is open to the claims of humanity, or less modest because she feels for the degradation of her enslaved sisters, and would stretch forth her hand for their rescue?

By the Constitution of the United States, the whole physical power of the North is pledged for the suppression of domestic insurrections; and should the slaves maddened by oppression endeavor to shake off the yoke of the task-master, the men of the North are bound to make common cause with the tyrant, to put down at the point of the bayonet every effort on the part of the slave for the attainment of his freedom. And when the father, husband, son, and brother shall have left their homes to mingle in the unholy warfare; "to become the executioners of their brethren, or to fall themselves by their hands," will the mother, wife, daughter, and sister feel that they have no interest in this subject? Will it be easy to convince them that it is no concern of theirs, that their homes are rendered desolate and their habitations the abodes of wretchedness? Surely this consideration is of itself sufficient to arouse the slumbering energies of woman, for the overthrow of a system which thus threatens to lay in ruins the fabric of her domestic happiness; and she will not be deterred from the performance of her duty to herself, her family, and her country, by the cry of "political question."

But, admitting it to be a political question, have we no interest in the welfare of our country? May we not permit a thought to stray beyond the narrow limits of our own family circle and of the present hour? May we not breathe a sigh over the miseries of our countrywomen nor utter a word of remonstrance against the unjust laws that are crushing them to the earth? Must we witness "the headlong rage of heedless folly" with which our nation is rushing onward to destruction, and not seek to arrest its downward course? Shall we silently behold the land which we love with all the heart-warm affection of children, rendered a hissing and a reproach throughout the world by the system which is already "tolling the death-knell of her decease among the nations"?

No; the events of the last two years have "cast their dark shadows before," overclouding the bright prospects of the future, and shrouding our country in more than midnight gloom; and we can not remain inactive. Our country is as dear to us as to the proudest statesman; and the more closely our hearts cling to "our altars and our homes," the more fervent are our aspirations, that every inhabitant of our land may be protected in his fireside enjoyments by just and equal laws; that the foot of the tyrant may no longer invade the domestic sanctuary, nor his hand tear asunder those whom God himself has united by the most holy ties.

Let our course then still be onward! Justice, humanity, patriotism; every high and every holy motive urge us forward, and we dare not refuse to obey. The way of duty lies open before us, and though no pillar of fire be visible to the outward sense, yet an unerring light shall illumine our pathway, guiding us through the sea of persecution and the wilderness of prejudice and error, to the promised land of freedom, where "every man shall sit under his own vine and fig-tree, and none shall make him afraid."

DOCUMENT 3 (I: 333–37): Angelina Grimké's Address, with comments by Abby Kelley and Lucretia Mott, National Anti-Slavery Convention, Philadelphia, Pennsylvania, May 16, 1838

Pennsylvania Hall was one of the most commodious and splendid buildings in the city, scientifically ventilated and brilliantly lighted with gas. It cost upward of $40,000. Over the forum, in large gold letters, was the motto, " Virtue, Liberty, Independence." On the platform were superb chairs, sofas, and desk covered with blue silk damask; everything throughout the hall was artistic and complete. Abolitionists from all parts of the country hastened to be present at the dedication; and among the rest came representatives of the Woman's National Convention, held in New York one year before.

Notices had been posted about the city threatening the speedy destruction of this temple of liberty. During this three days' Convention, the enemy was slowly organizing the destructive mob that finally burned that grand edifice to the ground. There were a large number of strangers in the city from the South, and many Southern students attending the medical college, who were all active in the riot. The crowds of women and colored people who had attended the Convention intensified the exasperation of the mob. Black men and white women walking side by side in and out of the hall, was too much for the foreign plebeian and the Southern patrician.

As it was announced that on the evening of the third day some ladies were to speak, a howling mob surrounded the building. In the midst of the tumult Mr. Garrison introduced Maria Chapman,* of Boston, who rose, and waving her hand to the audience to become quiet, tried in a few eloquent and appropriate remarks to bespeak a hearing for Angelina E. Grimké, the gifted orator from South Carolina, who, having lived in the midst of slavery all her life, could faithfully describe its cruelties and abominations. But the indescribable uproar outside, cries of fire, and yells of defiance, were a constant interruption, and stones thrown against the windows a warning of coming danger. But through it all this brave Southern woman stood unmoved, except by the intense earnestness of her own great theme.

ANGELINA GRIMKÉ'S ADDRESS.

Do you ask, " What has the North to do with slavery ? " Hear it, hear it! Those voices without tell us that the spirit of slavery is *here*, and has been roused to wrath by our Conventions; for surely liberty would not foam and tear herself with rage, because her friends are multiplied daily, and meetings are held in quick succession to set forth her virtues and extend her peaceful kingdom. This opposition shows that slavery has done its deadliest work in the hearts of our citizens. Do you ask, then, " What has the North to do ? " I answer, cast out first the spirit of slavery from your own hearts, and then lend your aid to convert the South. Each one present has a work to do, be his or her situation what it may, however limited their means or insignificant their supposed influence. The great men of this country will not do this work; the Church will never do it. A desire to please the world, to keep the favor of all parties and of all conditions, makes them dumb on this and every other unpopular subject.

As a Southerner, I feel that it is my duty to stand up here to-night and bear testimony against slavery. I have seen it! I have seen it! I know it has horrors that can never be described. I was brought up under its wing. I witnessed for many years its demoralizing influences and its destructiveness to human happiness. I have never seen a happy slave. I have seen him dance in his chains, it is true, but he was not happy. There is a wide difference between happiness and mirth. Man can not enjoy happiness while his manhood is destroyed. Slaves, however, may be, and sometimes are mirthful. When hope is extinguished, they say,

---

* She was the positive power of so much anti-slavery work, that James Russell Lowell spoke of her as " the coiled-up mainspring of the movement."

"Let us eat and drink, for to-morrow we die." [Here stones were thrown at the windows—a great noise without and commotion within].

What is a mob ? what would the breaking of every window be ? What would the levelling of this hall be ? Any evidence that we are wrong, or that slavery is a good and wholesome institution ? What if the mob should now burst in upon us, break up our meeting, and commit violence upon our persons, would that be anything compared with what the slaves endure ? No, no; and we do not remember them, "as bound with them," if we shrink in the time of peril, or feel unwilling to sacrifice ourselves, if need be, for their sake. [Great noise]. I thank the Lord that there is yet life enough left to feel the truth, even though it rages at it; that conscience is not so completely seared as to be unmoved by the truth of the living God. [Another outbreak of the mob and confusion in the house].

How wonderfully constituted is the human mind! How it resists, as long as it can, all efforts to reclaim it from error! I feel that all this disturbance is but an evidence that our efforts are the best that could have been adopted, or else the friends of slavery would not care for what we say and do. The South know what we do. I am thankful that they are reached by our efforts. Many times have I wept in the land of my birth over the system of slavery. I knew of none who sympathized in my feelings; I was unaware that any efforts were made to deliver the oppressed; no voice in the wilderness was heard calling on the people to repent and do works meet for repentance, and my heart sickened within me. Oh, how should I have rejoiced to know that such efforts as these were being made. I only wonder that I had such feelings. But in the midst of temptation I was preserved, and my sympathy grew warmer, and my hatred of slavery more inveterate, until at last I have exiled myself from my native land, because I could no longer endure to hear the wailing of the slave.

I fled to the land of Penn; for here, thought I, sympathy for the slave will surely be found. But I found it not. The people were kind and hospitable, but the slave had no place in their thoughts. I therefore shut up my grief in my own heart. I remembered that I was a Carolinian, from a State which framed this iniquity by law. Every Southern breeze wafted to me the discordant tones of weeping and wailing, shrieks and groans, mingled with prayers and blasphemous curses. My heart sank within me at the abominations in the midst of which I had been born and educated. What will it avail, cried I, in bitterness of spirit, to expose to the gaze of strangers the horrors and pollutions of slavery, when there is no ear to hear nor heart to feel and pray for the slave ? But how different do I feel now! Animated with hope, nay, with an assurance of the triumph of liberty and good-will to man, I will lift up my voice like a trumpet, and show this people what they can do to influence the Southern mind and overthrow slavery. [Shouting, and stones against the windows].

We often hear the question asked, "What shall we do ?" Here is an opportunity. Every man and every woman present may do something, by showing that we fear not a mob, and in the midst of revilings and threatenings, pleading the cause of those who are ready to perish. Let me urge every one to buy the books written on this subject; read them, and lend them to your neighbors. Give your money no longer for things which pander to pride and lust, but aid in scattering "the living coals of truth upon the naked heart of the nation"; in circulating appeals to the sympathies of Christians in behalf of the outraged slave.

But it is said by some, our "books and papers do not speak the truth"; why, then, do they not contradict what we say? They can not. Moreover, the South has entreated, nay, commanded us, to be silent; and what greater evidence of the truth of our publications could be desired?

Women of Philadelphia! allow me as a Southern woman, with much attachment to the land of my birth, to entreat you to come up to this work. Especially, let me urge you to petition. Men may settle this and other questions at the ballot-box, but you have no such right. It is only through petitions that you can reach the Legislature. It is, therefore, peculiarly your duty to petition. Do you say, "It does no good!" The South already turns pale at the number sent. They have read the reports of the proceedings of Congress, and there have seen that among other petitions were very many from the women of the North on the subject of slavery. Men who hold the rod over slaves rule in the councils of the nation; and they deny our right to petition and remonstrate against abuses of our sex and our kind. We have these rights, however, from our God. Only let us exercise them, and, though often turned away unanswered, let us remember the influence of importunity upon the unjust judge, and act accordingly. The fact that the South looks jealously upon our measures shows that they are effectual. There is, therefore, no cause for doubting or despair.

It was remarked in England that women did much to abolish slavery in her colonies. Nor are they now idle. Numerous petitions from them have recently been presented to the Queen to abolish apprenticeship, with its cruelties, nearly equal to those of the system whose place it supplies. One petition, two miles and a quarter long, has been presented. And do you think these labors will be in vain? Let the history of the past answer. When the women of these States send up to Congress such a petition our legislators will arise, as did those of England, and say: "When all the maids and matrons of the land are knocking at our doors we must legislate." Let the zeal and love, the faith and works of our English sisters quicken ours; that while the slaves continue to suffer, and when they shout for deliverance, we may feel the satisfaction of "having done what we could."

ABBY KELLY, of Lynn, Massachusetts, rose, and said: I ask permission to say a few words. I have never before addressed a promiscuous assembly; nor is it now the maddening rush of those voices, which is the indication of a moral whirlwind; nor is it the crashing of those windows, which is the indication of a moral earthquake, that calls me before you. No, these pass unheeded by me. But it is the "still small voice within," which may not be withstood, that bids me open my mouth for the dumb · that bids me plead the cause of God's perishing poor; aye, *God's* poor.

The parable of Lazarus and the rich man we may well bring home to ourselves. The North is that rich man. How he is clothed in purple and fine linen, and fares sumptuously! *Yonder,* YONDER, at a little distance, is the gate where lies the Lazarus of the South, full of sores and desiring to be fed with the crumbs that fall from our luxurious table. Look! see him there! even the dogs are more merciful than we. Oh, see him where he lies! We have long, very long, passed by with averted eyes. Ought not we to raise him up; and is there one in this Hall who sees nothing for himself to do ?

LUCRETIA MOTT, of Philadelphia, then stated that the present was not a meeting of the Anti-Slavery Convention of American women, as was supposed by some, and explained the reason why their meetings were confined to females; namely, that many of the members considered it improper for women to address promiscuous assemblies. She hoped that such false notions of delicacy and propriety would not long obtain in this enlightened country.

DOCUMENT 4 (I: 53–62): World's Anti-Slavery Convention, London, England, June 1840

The call for that Convention invited delegates from all Anti-Slavery organizations. Accordingly several American societies saw fit to send women, as delegates, to represent them in that august assembly. But after going three thousand miles to attend a World's Convention, it was discovered that women formed no part of the constituent elements of the moral world. In summoning the friends of the slave from all parts of the two hemispheres to meet in London, John Bull never dreamed that woman, too, would answer to his call. Imagine then the commotion in the conservative anti-slavery circles in England, when it was known that half a dozen of those terrible women who had spoken to promiscuous assemblies, voted on men and measures, prayed and petitioned against slavery, women who had been mobbed, ridiculed by the press, and denounced by the pul-

pit, who had been the cause of setting all American Abolitionists by
the ears, and split their ranks asunder, were on their way to England. Their fears of these formidable and belligerent women must
have been somewhat appeased when Lucretia Mott, Sarah Pugh,
Abby Kimber, Elizabeth Neal, Mary Grew, of Philadelphia, in
modest Quaker costume, Ann Green Phillips, Emily Winslow, and
Abby Southwick, of Boston, all women of refinement and education,
and several, still in their twenties, landed at last on the soil of Great
Britain. Many who had awaited their coming with much trepida-
tion, gave a sigh of relief, on being introduced to Lucretia Mott,
learning that she represented the most dangerous elements in the
delegation. The American clergymen who had landed a few days
before, had been busily engaged in fanning the English prejudices
into active hostility against the admission of these women to the
Convention. In every circle of Abolitionists this was the theme,
and the discussion grew more bitter, personal, and exasperating
every hour.

The 12th of June dawned bright and beautiful on these discordant
elements, and at an early hour anti-slavery delegates from different
countries wended their way through the crooked streets of London
to Freemasons' Hall. Entering the vestibule, little groups might be
seen gathered here and there, earnestly discussing the best disposition
to make of those women delegates from America. The excitement
and vehemence of protest and denunciation could not have been
greater, if the news had come that the French were about to invade
England. In vain those obdurate women had been conjured to withhold their credentials, and not thrust a question that must produce
such discord on the Convention. Lucretia Mott, in her calm, firm
manner, insisted that the delegates had no discretionary power in
the proposed action, and the responsibility of accepting or rejecting
them must rest on the Convention.

At eleven o'clock, the spacious Hall being filled, the Convention
was called to order. The venerable Thomas Clarkson, who was to
be President, on entering, was received by the large audience standing; owing to his feeble health, the chairman requested that there
should be no other demonstrations. As soon as Thomas Clarkson
withdrew, Wendell Phillips made the following motion:

"That a Committee of five be appointed to prepare a correct list of the
members of this Convention, with instructions to include in such list,
all persons bearing credentials from any Anti-Slavery body."

This motion at once opened the debate on the admission of women
delegates.

Mr. Phillips: When the call reached America we found that it was an invitation to the friends of the slave of every nation and of every clime. Massachusetts has for several years acted on the principle of admitting women to an equal seat with men, in the deliberative bodies of anti-slavery societies. When the Massachusetts Anti-Slavery Society received that paper, it interpreted it, as it was its duty, in its broadest and most liberal sense. If there be any other paper, emanating from the Committee, limiting to one sex the qualification of membership, there is no proof; and, as an individual, I have no knowledge that such a paper ever reached Massachusetts. We stand here in consequence of your invitation, and knowing our custom, as it must be presumed you did, we had a right to interpret "friends of the slave," to include women as well as men. In such circumstances, we do not think it just or equitable to that State, nor to America in general, that, after the trouble, the sacrifice, the self-devotion of a part of those who leave their families and kindred and occupations in their own land, to come three thousand miles to attend this World's Convention, they should be refused a place in its deliberations.

One of the Committee who issued the call, said: As soon as we heard the liberal interpretation Americans had given to our first invitation, we issued another as early as Feb. 15, in which the description of those who are to form the Convention is set forth as consisting of " gentlemen."

Dr. Bowring: I think the custom of excluding females is more honored in its breach than in its observance. In this country sovereign rule is placed in the hands of a female, and one who has been exercising her great and benignant influence in opposing slavery by sanctioning, no doubt, the presence of her illustrious consort at an anti-slavery meeting. We are associated with a body of Christians (Quakers) who have given to their women a great, honorable, and religious prominence. I look upon this delegation from America as one of the most interesting, the most encouraging, and the most delightful symptoms of the times. I can not believe that we shall refuse to welcome gratefully the co-operation which is offered us.

The Rev. J. Burnet, an Englishman, made a most touching appeal to the American ladies, to conform to English prejudices and custom, so far as to withdraw their credentials, as it never did occur to the British and Foreign Anti-Slavery Society that they were inviting ladies. It is better, said he, that this Convention should be dissolved at this moment than this motion should be adopted.

The Rev. Henry Grew, of Philadelphia: The reception of women as a part of this Convention would, in the view of many, be not only a violation of the customs of England, but of the ordinance of Almighty God, who has a right to appoint our services to His sovereign will.

Rev. Eben Galusha, New York: In support of the other side of this question, reference has been made to your Sovereign. I most cordially approve of her policy and sound wisdom, and commend to the consideration of our American female friends who are so deeply interested in the subject, the example of your noble Queen, who by sanctioning her consort, His Royal Highness Prince Albert, in taking the chair on an occasion not dissimilar to this, showed her sense of propriety by putting her Head foremost in an assembly of gentlemen. I have no objection to woman's being the neck to turn the head aright, but do not wish to see her assume the place of the head.

George Bradburn, of Mass.: We are told that it would be outraging the customs of England to allow women to sit in this Convention. I have a great respect for the customs of old England. But I ask, gentlemen, if it be right to set up the customs and habits, not to say prejudices of Englishmen, as a standard for the government on this occasion of Americans, and of persons belonging to several other independent nations. I can see neither reason nor policy in so doing. Besides, I deprecate the principle of the objection. In America it would exclude from our conventions all persons of color, for there customs, habits, tastes, prejudices, would be outraged by *their* admission. And I do not wish to be deprived of the aid of those who have done so much for this cause, for the purpose of gratifying any mere custom or prejudice. Women have furnished most essential aid in accomplishing what has been done in the State of Massachusetts. If, in the Legislature of that State, I have been able to do anything in furtherance of that cause, by keeping on my legs eight or ten hours day after day, it was mainly owing to the valuable assistance I derived from the women. And shall such women be denied seats in this Convention? My friend George Thompson, yonder, can testify to the faithful services rendered to this cause by those same women. He can tell you that when "gentlemen of property and standing" in "broad day" and "broadcloth," undertook to drive him from Boston, putting his life in peril, it was our women who made their own persons a bulwark of protection around him. And shall such women be refused seats here in a Convention seeking the emancipation of slaves throughout the world? What a misnomer to call this a World's Convention of Abolitionists, when some of the oldest and most thorough-going Abolitionists in the world are denied the right to be represented in it by delegates of their own choice.

And thus for the space of half an hour did Mr. Bradburn, six feet high and well-proportioned, with vehement gesticulations and voice of thunder, bombard the prejudices of England and the hypocrisies of America.

George Thompson: I have listened to the arguments advanced on this side and on that side of this vexed question. I listened with profound attention to the arguments of Mr. Burnet, expecting that from him, as I was justified in expecting, I should hear the strongest arguments that could be adduced on this, or any other subject upon which he might be pleased to employ his talents, or which he might adorn with his eloquence. What are his arguments? Let it be premised, as I speak in the presence of American friends, that that gentleman is one of the best controversialists in the country, and one of the best authorities upon questions of business, points of order, and matters of principle. What are

the strongest arguments, which one of the greatest champions on any
question which he chooses to espouse, has brought forward? They are
these:

1st. That English phraseology should be construed according to English usage.
2d. That it was never contemplated by the anti-slavery committee that ladies should
occupy a seat in this Convention.
3d. That the ladies of England are not here as delegates.
4th. That he has no desire to offer an affront to the ladies now present.

Here I presume are the strongest arguments the gentleman has to
adduce, for he never fails to use to the best advantage the resources
within his reach. I look at these arguments, and I place on the other
side of the question, the fact that there are in this assembly ladies who
present themselves as delegates from the oldest societies in America.
I expected that Mr. Burnet would, as he was bound to do, if he intended
to offer a successful opposition to their introduction into this Convention, grapple with the constitutionality of their credentials. I thought
he would come to the question of title. I thought he would dispute
the right of a convention assembled in Philadelphia, for the abolition of slavery, consisting of delegates from different States in the
Union, and comprised of individuals of both sexes, to send one or
all of the ladies now in our presence. I thought he would grapple with
the fact, that those ladies came to us who have no slavery from a country in which they have slaves, as the representatives of two millions and
a half of captives. Let gentlemen, when they come to vote on this question, remember, that in receiving or rejecting these ladies, they acknowledge or despise [loud cries of No, no]. I ask gentlemen, who shout " no,"
if they know the application I am about to make. I did not mean to
say you would despise the ladies, but that you would, by your vote,
acknowledge or despise the parties whose cause they espouse. It appears
we are prepared to sanction ladies in the employment of all means, so
long as they are confessedly unequal with ourselves. It seems that the
grand objection to their appearance amongst us is this, that it would be
placing them on a footing of equality, and that would be contrary to
principle and custom. For years the women of America have carried
their banner in the van, while the men have humbly followed in the
rear. It is well known that the National Society solicited Angelina
Grimke to undertake a mission through New England, to rouse the
attention of the women to the wrongs of slavery, and that that distinguished woman displayed her talents not only in the drawing-room,
but before the Senate of Massachusetts. Let us contrast our conduct
with that of the Senators and Representatives of Massachusetts who did
not disdain to hear her. It was in consequence of her exertions, which
received the warmest approval of the National Society, that that interest
sprung up which has awakened such an intense feeling throughout
America. Then with reference to efficient management, the most vigorous anti-slavery societies are those which are managed by ladies.

If now, after the expression of opinion on various sides, the motion
should be withdrawn with the consent of all parties, I should be glad.

But when I look at the arguments against the title of these women to sit amongst us, I can not but consider them frivolous and groundless. The simple question before us is, whether these ladies, taking into account their credentials, the talent they have displayed, the sufferings they have endured, the journey they have undertaken, should be acknowledged by us, in virtue of these high titles, or should be shut out for the reasons stated.

Mr. Phillips, being urged on all sides to withdraw his motion, said: It has been hinted very respectfully by two or three speakers that the delegates from the State of Massachusetts should withdraw their credentials, or the motion before the meeting. The one appears to me to be equivalent to the other. If this motion be withdrawn we must have another. I would merely ask whether any man can suppose that the delegates from Massachusetts or Pennsylvania can take upon their shoulders the responsibility of withdrawing that list of delegates from your table, which their constituents told them to place there, and whom they sanctioned as their fit representatives, because this Convention tells us that it is not ready to meet the ridicule of the morning papers, and to stand up against the customs of England. In America we listen to no such arguments. If we had done so we had never been here as Abolitionists. It is the custom there not to admit colored men into respectable society, and we have been told again and again that we are outraging the decencies of humanity when we permit colored men to sit by our side. When we have submitted to brick-bats, and the tar tub and feathers in America, rather than yield to the custom prevalent there of not admitting colored brethren into our friendship, shall we yield to parallel custom or prejudice against women in Old England? We can not yield this question if we would; for it is a matter of conscience. But we would not yield it on the ground of expediency. In doing so we should feel that we were striking off the right arm of our enterprise. We could not go back to America to ask for any aid from the women of Massachusetts if we had deserted them, when they chose to send out their own sisters as their representatives here. We could not go back to Massachusetts and assert the unchangeableness of spirit on the question. We have argued it over and over again, and decided it time after time, in every society in the land, in favor of the women. We have not changed by crossing the water. We stand here the advocates of the same principle that we contend for in America. We think it right for women to sit by our side there, and we think it right for them to do the same here. We ask the Convention to admit them; if they do not choose to grant it, the responsibility rests on their shoulders. Massachusetts can not turn aside, or succumb to any prejudices or customs even in the land she looks upon with so much reverence as the land of Wilberforce, of Clarkson, and of O'Connell. It is a matter of conscience, and British virtue ought not to ask us to yield.

Mr. Ashurst: You are convened to influence society upon a subject connected with the kindliest feelings of our nature; and being the first assembly met to shake hands with other nations, and employ your combined efforts to annihilate slavery throughout the world, are you to commence by saying, you will take away the rights of one-half of creation ? This is the principle which you are putting forward.

The Rev. A. Harvey, of Glasgow: It was stated by a brother from America, that with him it is a matter of conscience, and it is a question of conscience with me too. I have certain views in relation to the teaching of the Word of God, and of the particular sphere in which woman is to act. I must say, whether I am right in my interpretations of the Word of God or not, that my own decided convictions are, if I were to give a vote in favor of females, sitting and deliberating in such an assembly as this, that I should be acting in opposition to the plain teaching of the Word of God. I may be wrong, but I have a conscience on the subject, and I am sure there are a number present of the same mind.

Captain Wanchope, R. N., delegate from Carlisle: I entreat the ladies not to push this question too far. I wish to know whether our friends from America are to cast off England altogether. Have we not given £20,000,000 of our money for the purpose of doing away with the abominations of slavery? Is not that proof that we are in earnest about it?

James C. Fuller: One friend said that this question should have been settled on the other side of the Atlantic. Why, it was there decided in favor of woman a year ago.

James Gillespie Birney: It has been stated that the right of women to sit and act in all respects as men in our anti-slavery associations, was decided in the affirmative at the annual meeting of the American Anti-Slavery Society in May, 1839. It is true the claim was so decided on that occasion, but not by a large majority; whilst it is also true that the majority was swelled by the votes of the women themselves. I have just received a letter from a gentleman in New York (Louis Tappan), communicating the fact, that the persistence of the friends of promiscuous female representation in pressing that practice on the American Anti-Slavery Society, at its annual meeting on the twelfth of last month, had caused such disagreement among the members present, that he and others who viewed the subject as he did, were then deliberating on measures for seceding from the old organization.

Rev. C. Stout: My vote is that we confirm the list of delegates, that we take votes on that as an amendment, and that we henceforth entertain this question no more. Are we not met here pledged to sacrifice all but everything, in order that we may do something against slavery, and shall we be divided on this *paltry question* and suffer the whole tide of benevolence to be stopped by *a straw* ? No ! You talk of being men, then be men ! Consider what is worthy of your attention.

Rev. Dr. Morrison: I feel, I believe, as our brethren from America and many English friends do at this moment, that we are treading on the brink of a precipice; and that precipice is the awaking in our bosoms by this discussion, feelings that will not only be averse to the great object for which we have assembled, but inconsistent, perhaps, in some degree, with the Christian spirit which, I trust, will pervade all meetings connected with the Anti-Slavery cause. We have been unanimous against the common foe, but we are this day in danger of creating division among heartfelt friends. Will our American brethren put us in this position!

Will they keep up a discussion in which the delicacy, the honor, the respectability of those excellent females who have come from the Western world are concerned? I tremble at the thought of discussing the question in the presence of these ladies—for whom I entertain the most profound respect—and I am bold to say, that but for the introduction of the question of woman's rights, it would be impossible for the shrinking nature of woman to subject itself to the infliction of such a discussion as this.

As the hour was late, and as the paltry arguments of the opposition were unworthy much consideration—as the reader will see from the specimens given—Mr. Phillips' reply was brief, consisting of the correction of a few mistakes made by different speakers. The vote was taken, and the women excluded as delegates of the Convention, by an overwhelming majority.

George Thompson: I hope, as the question is now decided, that Mr. Phillips will give us the assurance that we shall proceed with one heart and one mind.

Mr. Phillips replied: I have no doubt of it. There is no unpleasant feeling in our minds. I have no doubt the women will sit with as much interest behind the bar* as though the original proposition had been carried in the affirmative. All we asked was an expression of opinion, and, having obtained it, we shall now act with the utmost cordiality.

Would there have been no unpleasant feelings in Wendell Phillips' mind, had Frederick Douglass and Robert Purvis been refused their seats in a convention of reformers under similar circumstances? and, had *they* listened one entire day to debates on their peculiar fitness for plantation life, and unfitness for the forum and public assemblies, and been rejected as delegates on the ground of color, could Wendell Phillips have so far mistaken their real feelings, and been so insensible to the insults offered them, as to have told a Convention of men who had just trampled on their most sacred rights, that "they would no doubt sit with as much interest behind the bar, as in the Convention"? To stand in that august assembly and maintain the unpopular heresy of woman's equality was a severe ordeal for a young man to pass through, and Wendell Phillips, who accepted the odium of presenting this question to the Convention, and thus earned the sincere gratitude of all womankind, might be considered as above criticism, though he may have failed at one point to understand the feelings of woman. The fact is important to mention, however, to show that it is

---

* The ladies of the Convention were fenced off behind a bar and curtain, similar to those used in churches to screen the choir from the public gaze.

almost impossible for the most liberal of men to understand what
liberty means for woman. This sacrifice of human rights, by men
who had assembled from all quarters of the globe to proclaim universal emancipation, was offered up in the presence of such women
as Lady Byron, Anna Jameson, Amelia Opie, Mary Howitt,
Elizabeth Fry, and our own Lucretia Mott. The clergy with
few exceptions were bitter in their opposition. Although, as Abolitionists, they had been compelled to fight both Church and Bible
to prove the black man's right to liberty, conscience forbade them
to stretch those sacred limits far enough to give equal liberty to
woman.

The leading men who championed the cause of the measure
in the Convention and voted in the affirmative, were Wendell
Phillips, George Thompson, George Bradburn, Mr. Ashurst, Dr.
Bowring, and Henry B. Stanton. Though Daniel O'Connell was
not present during the discussion, having passed out with the
President, yet in his first speech, he referred to the rejected delegates, paying a beautiful tribute to woman's influence, and saying
he should have been happy to have added the right word in the
right place and to have recorded his vote in favor of human equality.

William Lloyd Garrison, having been delayed at sea, arrived
too late to take part in the debates. Learning on his arrival
that the women had been rejected as delegates, he declined
to take his seat in the Convention; and, through all those interesting discussions on a subject so near his heart, lasting ten days,
he remained a silent spectator in the gallery. What a sacrifice for
a principle so dimly seen by the few, and so ignorantly ridiculed by
the many! Brave, noble Garrison! May this one act keep his
memory fresh forever in the hearts of his countrywomen!

The one Abolitionist who sustained Mr. Garrison's position, and sat
with him in the gallery, was Nathaniel P. Rogers, editor of the *Herald
of Freedom*, in Concord, New Hampshire, who died in the midst of
the Anti-Slavery struggle. However, the debates in the Convention had the effect of rousing English minds to thought on the
tyranny of sex, and American minds to the importance of some
definite action toward woman's emancipation.

As Lucretia Mott and Elizabeth Cady Stanton wended their way
arm in arm down Great Queen Street that night, reviewing the exciting scenes of the day, they agreed to hold a woman's rights convention on their return to America, as the men to whom they had
just listened had manifested their great need of some education on
that question. Thus a missionary work for the emancipation of

woman in "the land of the free and the home of the brave" was then and there inaugurated. As the ladies were not allowed to speak in the Convention, they kept up a brisk fire morning, noon, and night at their hotel on the unfortunate gentlemen who were domiciled at the same house.

III. THE CONVENTION AS AGITATION

FROM 1848 TO THE BEGINNING of the Civil War, woman's rights advocates met in a growing number of local, state, and national conventions. Although participants did little more than pass resolutions, these meetings were extremely important. As the antislavery movement had created a public for reformers, the woman's movement separated and expanded a sector of that following for its own purposes. Conventions put the issues of woman's rights into the press and before the public eye almost continuously. Woman's place and woman's prerogative were raised as moral and political questions. Opponents of women's rights were forced to debate the movement's advocates, at least to the extent of acknowledging grudgingly the social presence of women who refused to be limited by domestic responsibilities. Most of the leading male and female orators of the antislavery cause appeared at these conventions or expressed in public letters their solidarity with woman's rights. During the period of conventions, leading women developed a sense of confidence and gained a public stature. Among these strong-minded women, initial hesitancy was replaced with a verve and audacity to question all matters that pertained to woman's condition.

The convention was the finest fruit of American democratic optimism. The belief that conversation among a group of powerless individuals could sway events stemmed from the expectation that democracy would inevitably grow to meet new conditions. The notable feature of the convention was the open platform: no ideas, no man or woman, were barred. In an era when individualism was the ideal, the reformer was the ultimate individual: eccentric, even crankish, but often brilliant and always lively. Rarely has any era of American reform been blessed with such extraordinary figures as Ernestine Rose, Sojourner Truth, and Elizabeth Cady Stanton. Woman's cause in the United States has never seen their like again.

Even more important than their exemplary character was the reformers' choice of issues. As the resolutions of the Second Worcester Convention made clear, by 1851 the judgment of the Seneca Falls meeting had become definitive: the ballot was the cornerstone of the movement. Differences on other matters would continue, most vividly in questions of marriage and religion, where some participants sought to realize the "true meanings" of institutions and faiths, while others disdained all artificial pieties. But all arguments, whether laying stress upon absolute equality or special privilege, addressed the emergence of woman as a person in her own right. Neither ridicule by the press nor the small size of the movement could obfuscate the significance of the demand for the ballot as symbol for woman's claim to self-determination.

DOCUMENT 5 (I: 67–74): Seneca Falls Convention,
Seneca Falls, New York, July 19-20, 1848, including the
Declaration of Sentiments and Resolutions

WOMAN'S RIGHTS CONVENTION.—A Convention to discuss the social,
civil, and religious condition and rights of woman, will be held in the
Wesleyan Chapel, at Seneca Falls, N. Y., on Wednesday and Thursday,
the 19th and 20th of July, current; commencing at 10 o'clock A.M. During the first day the meeting will be exclusively for women, who are earnestly invited to attend. The public generally are invited to be present
on the second day, when Lucretia Mott, of Philadelphia, and other ladies and gentlemen, will address the convention.

This call, without signature, was issued by Lucretia Mott, Martha
C. Wright, Elizabeth Cady Stanton, and Mary Ann McClintock.
At this time Mrs. Mott was visiting her sister Mrs. Wright, at Auburn, and attending the Yearly Meeting of Friends in Western New
York. Mrs. Stanton, having recently removed from Boston to Seneca Falls, finding the most congenial associations in Quaker families,
met Mrs. Mott incidentally for the first time since her residence
there. They at once returned to the topic they had so often

discussed, walking arm in arm in the streets of London, and Boston, "the propriety of holding a woman's convention." These four ladies, sitting round the tea-table of Richard Hunt, a prominent Friend near Waterloo, decided to put their long-talked-of resolution into action, and before the twilight deepened into night, the call was written, and sent to the *Seneca County Courier*. On Sunday morning they met in Mrs. McClintock's parlor to write their declaration, resolutions, and to consider subjects for speeches. As the convention was to assemble in three days, the time was short for such productions; but having no experience in the *modus operandi* of getting up conventions, nor in that kind of literature, they were quite innocent of the herculean labors they proposed. On the first attempt to frame a resolution; to crowd a complete thought, clearly and concisely, into three lines; they felt as helpless and hopeless as if they had been suddenly asked to construct a steam engine. And the humiliating fact may as well now be recorded that before taking the initiative step, those ladies resigned themselves to a faithful perusal of various masculine productions. The reports of Peace, Temperance, and Anti-Slavery conventions were examined, but all alike seemed too tame and pacific for the inauguration of a rebellion such as the world had never before seen. They knew women had wrongs, but how to state them was the difficulty, and this was increased from the fact that they themselves were fortunately organized and conditioned; they were neither "sour old maids," "childless women," nor "divorced wives," as the newspapers declared them to be. While they had felt the insults incident to sex, in many ways, as every proud, thinking woman must, in the laws, religion, and literature of the world, and in the invidious and degrading sentiments and customs of all nations, yet they had not in their own experience endured the coarser forms of tyranny resulting from unjust laws, or association with immoral and unscrupulous men, but they had souls large enough to feel the wrongs of others, without being scarified in their own flesh.

After much delay, one of the circle took up the Declaration of 1776, and read it aloud with much spirit and emphasis, and it was at once decided to adopt the historic document, with some slight changes such as substituting "all men" for "King George." Knowing that women must have more to complain of than men under any circumstances possibly could, and seeing the Fathers had eighteen grievances, a protracted search was made through statute

books, church usages, and the customs of society to find that exact
number.   Several well-disposed men assisted in collecting the
grievances, until, with the announcement of the eighteenth, the
women felt they had enough to go before the world with a good
case.   One youthful lord remarked, "Your grievances must be
grievous indeed, when you are obliged to go to books in order to
find them out."

The eventful day dawned at last, and crowds in carriages and on
foot, wended their way to the Wesleyan church.   When those having charge of the Declaration, the resolutions, and several volumes
of the Statutes of New York arrived on the scene, lo! the door was
locked.   However, an embryo Professor of Yale College was lifted
through an open window to unbar the door; that done, the church
was quickly filled.   It had been decided to have no men present, but
as they were already on the spot, and as the women who must take
the responsibility of organizing the meeting, and leading the discussions, shrank from doing either, it was decided, in a hasty council
round the altar, that this was an occasion when men might make
themselves pre-eminently useful.   It was agreed they should remain,
and take the laboring oar through the Convention.

James Mott, tall and dignified, in Quaker costume, was called to
the chair; Mary McClintock appointed Secretary, Frederick Douglass, Samuel Tillman, Ansel Bascom, E. W. Capron, and Thomas
McClintock took part throughout in the discussions.   Lucretia Mott,
accustomed to public speaking in the Society of Friends, stated the
objects of the Convention, and in taking a survey of the degraded
condition of woman the world over, showed the importance of in-
augurating some movement for her education and elevation.   Elizabeth and Mary McClintock, and Mrs. Stanton, each read a well-
written speech; Martha Wright read some satirical articles she had
published in the daily papers answering the diatribes on woman's
sphere.   Ansel Bascom, who had been a member of the Constitutional Convention recently held in Albany, spoke at length on the
property bill for married women, just passed the Legislature, and the
discussion on woman's rights in that Convention.   Samuel Tillman, a
young student of law, read a series of the most exasperating statutes
for women, from English and American jurists, all reflecting the
tender mercies of men toward their wives, in taking care of their
property and protecting them in their civil rights.

The Declaration having been freely discussed by many present,
was re-read by Mrs. Stanton, and with some slight amendments
adopted.

DECLARATION OF SENTIMENTS.

When, in the course of human events, it becomes necessary for one portion of the family of man to assume among the people of the earth a position different from that which they have hitherto occupied, but one to which the laws of nature and of nature's God entitle them, a decent respect to the opinions of mankind requires that they should declare the causes that impel them to such a course.

We hold these truths to be self-evident: that all men and women are created equal; that they are endowed by their Creator with certain inalienable rights; that among these are life, liberty, and the pursuit of happiness; that to secure these rights governments are instituted, deriving their just powers from the consent of the governed. Whenever any form of government becomes destructive of these ends, it is the right of those who suffer from it to refuse allegiance to it, and to insist upon the institution of a new government, laying its foundation on such principles, and organizing its powers in such form, as to them shall seem most likely to effect their safety and happiness. Prudence, indeed, will dictate that governments long established should not be changed for light and transient causes; and accordingly all experience hath shown that mankind are more disposed to suffer, while evils are sufferable, than to right themselves by abolishing the forms to which they were accustomed. But when a long train of abuses and usurpations, pursuing invariably the same object evinces a design to reduce them under absolute despotism, it is their duty to throw off such government, and to provide new guards for their future security. Such has been the patient sufferance of the women under this government, and such is now the necessity which constrains them to demand the equal station to which they are entitled.

The history of mankind is a history of repeated injuries and usurpations on the part of man toward woman, having in direct object the establishment of an absolute tyranny over her. To prove this, let facts be submitted to a candid world.

He has never permitted her to exercise her inalienable right to the elective franchise.

He has compelled her to submit to laws, in the formation of which she had no voice.

He has withheld from her rights which are given to the most ignorant and degraded men—both natives and foreigners.

Having deprived her of this first right of a citizen, the elective franchise, thereby leaving her without representation in the halls of legislation, he has oppressed her on all sides.

He has made her, if married, in the eye of the law, civilly dead.

He has taken from her all right in property, even to the wages she earns.

He has made her, morally, an irresponsible being, as she can commit many crimes with impunity, provided they be done in the presence of her husband. In the covenant of marriage, she is compelled to promise obedience to her husband, he becoming, to all intents and purposes, her master—the law giving him power to deprive her of her liberty, and to administer chastisement.

He has so framed the laws of divorce, as to what shall be the proper causes, and in case of separation, to whom the guardianship of the children shall be given, as to be wholly regardless of the happiness of women—the law, in all cases, going upon a false supposition of the supremacy of man, and giving all power into his hands.

After depriving her of all rights as a married woman, if single, and the owner of property, he has taxed her to support a government which recognizes her only when her property can be made profitable to it.

He has monopolized nearly all the profitable employments, and from those she is permitted to follow, she receives but a scanty remuneration. He closes against her all the avenues to wealth and distinction which he considers most honorable to himself. As a teacher of theology, medicine, or law, she is not known.

He has denied her the facilities for obtaining a thorough education, all colleges being closed against her.

He allows her in Church, as well as State, but a subordinate position, claiming Apostolic authority for her exclusion from the ministry, and, with some exceptions, from any public participation in the affairs of the Church.

He has created a false public sentiment by giving to the world a different code of morals for men and women, by which moral delinquencies which exclude women from society, are not only tolerated, but deemed of little account in man.

He has usurped the prerogative of Jehovah himself, claiming it as his right to assign for her a sphere of action, when that belongs to her conscience and to her God.

He has endeavored, in every way that he could, to destroy her confidence in her own powers, to lessen her self-respect, and to make her willing to lead a dependent and abject life.

Now, in view of this entire disfranchisement of one-half the people of this country, their social and religious degradation—in view of the unjust laws above mentioned, and because women do feel themselves aggrieved, oppressed, and fraudulently deprived of their most sacred rights, we insist that they have immediate admission to all the rights and privileges which belong to them as citizens of the United States.

In entering upon the great work before us, we anticipate no small amount of misconception, misrepresentation, and ridicule; but we shall use every instrumentality within our power to effect our object. We shall employ agents, circulate tracts, petition the State and National legislatures, and endeavor to enlist the pulpit and the press in our behalf. We hope this Convention will be followed by a series of Conventions embracing every part of the country.

The following resolutions were discussed by Lucretia Mott, Thomas and Mary Ann McClintock, Amy Post, Catharine A. F. Stebbins, and others, and were adopted:

WHEREAS, The great precept of nature is conceded to be, that "man shall pursue his own true and substantial happiness." Blackstone in his

Commentaries remarks, that this law of Nature being coeval with mankind, and dictated by God himself, is of course superior in obligation to any other. It is binding over all the globe, in all countries and at all times; no human laws are of any validity if contrary to this, and such of them as are valid, derive all their force, and all their validity, and all their authority, mediately and immediately, from this original; therefore,

Resolved, That such laws as conflict, in any way, with the true and substantial happiness of woman, are contrary to the great precept of nature and of no validity, for this is " superior in obligation to any other."

Resolved, That all laws which prevent woman from occupying such a station in society as her conscience shall dictate, or which place her in a position inferior to that of man, are contrary to the great precept of nature, and therefore of no force or authority.

Resolved, That woman is man's equal—was intended to be so by the Creator, and the highest good of the race demands that she should be recognized as such.

Resolved, That the women of this country ought to be enlightened in regard to the laws under which they live, that they may no longer publish their degradation by declaring themselves satisfied with their present position, nor their ignorance, by asserting that they have all the rights they want.

Resolved, That inasmuch as man, while claiming for himself intellectual superiority, does accord to woman moral superiority, it is pre-eminently his duty to encourage her to speak and teach, as she has an opportunity, in all religious assemblies.

Resolved, That the same amount of virtue, delicacy, and refinement of behavior that is required of woman in the social state, should also be required of man, and the same transgressions should be visited with equal severity on both man and woman.

Resolved, That the objection of indelicacy and impropriety, which is so often brought against woman when she addresses a public audience, comes with a very ill-grace from those who encourage, by their attendance, her appearance on the stage, in the concert, or in feats of the circus.

Resolved, That woman has too long rested satisfied in the circumscribed limits which corrupt customs and a perverted application of the Scriptures have marked out for her, and that it is time she should move in the enlarged sphere which her great Creator has assigned her.

Resolved, That it is the duty of the women of this country to secure to themselves their sacred right to the elective franchise.

Resolved, That the equality of human rights results necessarily from the fact of the identity of the race in capabilities and responsibilities.

Resolved, therefore, That, being invested by the Creator with the same capabilities, and the same consciousness of responsibility for their exercise, it is demonstrably the right and duty of woman, equally with man, to promote every righteous cause by every righteous means; and especially in regard to the great subjects of morals and religion, it is self-evidently her right to participate with her brother in teaching them, both in private and in public, by writing and by speaking, by any instrumentalities proper to be used, and in any assemblies proper to be held; and this

being a self-evident truth growing out of the divinely implanted principles of human nature, any custom or authority adverse to it, whether
modern or wearing the hoary sanction of antiquity, is to be regarded as
a self-evident falsehood, and at war with mankind.

At the last session Lucretia Mott offered and spoke to the following resolution :

Resolved, That the speedy success of our cause depends upon the
zealous and untiring efforts of both men and women, for the overthrow
of the monopoly of the pulpit, and for the securing to woman an equal
participation with men in the various trades, professions, and commerce.

The only resolution that was not unanimously adopted was the
ninth, urging the women of the country to secure to themselves the
elective franchise. Those who took part in the debate feared a demand for the right to vote would defeat others they deemed more
rational, and make the whole movement ridiculous.

But Mrs. Stanton and Frederick Douglass seeing that the power
to choose rulers and make laws, was the right by which all others
could be secured, persistently advocated the resolution, and at last
carried it by a small majority.

Thus it will be seen that the Declaration and resolutions in the very
first Convention, demanded all the most radical friends of the movement have since claimed—such as equal rights in the universities, in
the trades and professions ; the right to vote ; to share in all political
offices, honors, and emoluments ; to complete equality in marriage,
to personal freedom, property, wages, children ; to make contracts ;
to sue, and be sued ; and to testify in courts of justice. At this
time the condition of married women under the Common Law, was
nearly as degraded as that of the slave on the Southern plantation.
The Convention continued through two entire days, and late into
the evenings. The deepest interest was manifested to its close.

The proceedings were extensively published, unsparingly ridiculed by the press, and denounced by the pulpit, much to the surprise and chagrin of the leaders. Being deeply in earnest, and believing their demands pre-eminently wise and just, they were wholly
unprepared to find themselves the target for the jibes and jeers of
the nation. The Declaration was signed by one hundred men, and
women, many of whom withdrew their names as soon as the storm
of ridicule began to break. The comments of the press were carefully preserved, and it is curious to see that the same old arguments, and objections rife at the start, are reproduced by the press

of to-day. But the brave protests sent out from this Convention touched a responsive chord in the hearts of women all over the country.

Conventions were held soon after in Ohio, Massachusetts, Indiana, Pennsylvania, and at different points in New York.

DOCUMENT 6 (I: 75–78): Rochester Convention, Rochester, New York, August 2, 1848

Those who took part in the Convention at Seneca Falls, finding at the end of the two days, there were still so many new points for discussion, and that the gift of tongues had been vouchsafed to them, adjourned, to meet in Rochester in two weeks. Amy Post, Sarah D. Fish, Sarah C. Owen, and Mary H. Hallowell, were the Committee of Arrangements. This Convention was called for August 2d, and so well advertised in the daily papers, that at the appointed hour, the Unitarian Church was filled to overflowing.

Amy Post called the meeting to order, and stated that at a gathering the previous evening in Protection Hall, Rhoda De Garmo, Sarah Fish, and herself, were appointed a committee to nominate officers for the Convention, and they now proposed Abigail Bush, for President; Laura Murray, for Vice-President; Elizabeth McClintock, Sarah Hallowell, and Catherine A. F. Stebbins, for Secretaries. Mrs. Mott, Mrs. Stanton, and Mrs. McClintock, thought it a most hazardous experiment to have a woman President, and stoutly opposed it.

To write a Declaration and Resolutions, to make a speech, and debate, had taxed their powers to the uttermost; and now, with such feeble voices and timid manners, without the slightest knowledge of Cushing's Manual, or the least experience in public meetings, how could a woman preside? They were on the verge of leaving the Convention in disgust, but Amy Post and Rhoda De Garmo assured them that by the same power by which they had resolved, declared, discussed, debated, they could also preside at a public meeting, if they would but make the experiment. And as the vote of the majority settled the question on the side of woman, Abigail Bush took the chair, and the calm way she assumed the duties of the office, and the admirable manner in which she discharged them, soon reconciled the opposition to the seemingly ridiculous experiment.

The proceedings were opened with prayer, by the Rev. Mr. Wicher, of the Free-will Baptist Church. Even at that early day, there were many of the liberal clergymen in favor of equal rights for women. During the reading of the minutes of the preliminary meeting by the Secretary, much uneasiness was manifested concerning the low voices of women, and cries of "Louder, louder!" drowned every other sound, when the President, on rising, said:

Friends, we present ourselves here before you, as an oppressed class, with trembling frames and faltering tongues, and we do not expect to be able to speak so as to be heard by all at first, but we trust we shall have the sympathy of the audience, and that you will bear with our weakness now in the infancy of the movement. Our trust in the omnipotency of right is our only faith that we shall succeed.

As the appointed Secretaries could not be heard, Sarah Anthony Burtis, an experienced Quaker school-teacher, whose voice had been well trained in her profession, volunteered to fill the duties of that office, and she read the reports and documents of the Convention with a clear voice and confident manner, to the great satisfaction of her more timid coadjutors.

Several gentlemen took part in the debates of this Convention. Some in favor, some opposed, and others willing to make partial concessions to the demands as set forth in the Declaration and Resolutions. Frederick Douglass, William C. Nell, and William C. Bloss advocated the emancipation of women from all the artificial disabilities, imposed by false customs, creeds, and codes. Milo Codding, Mr. Sulley, Mr. Pickard, and a Mr. Colton, of Connecticut, thought "woman's sphere was home," and that she should remain in it; he would seriously deprecate her occupying the pulpit.

Lucretia Mott replied, that the gentleman from New Haven had objected to woman occupying the pulpit, and indeed she could scarcely see how any one educated in New Haven, Ct., could think otherwise than he did. She said, we had all got our notions too much from the clergy, instead of the Bible. The Bible, she contended, had none of the prohibitions in regard to women; and spoke of the "honorable women not a few," etc., and desired Mr. Colton to read his Bible over again, and see if there was anything there to prohibit woman from being a religious teacher. She then complimented the members of that church for opening their doors to a Woman's Rights Convention, and said that a few years ago, the Female Moral Reform Society of

Philadelphia applied for the use of a church in that city, in which to hold one of their meetings; they were only allowed the use of the basement, and on condition that none of the women should speak at the meeting.   Accordingly, a D.D. was called upon to preside. and another to read the ladies' report of the Society.

Near the close of the morning session, a young bride in traveling dress,* accompanied by her husband, slowly walked up the aisle, and asked the privilege of saying a few words, which was readily granted.   Being introduced to the audience, she said, on her way westward, hearing of the Convention, she had waited over a train, to add her mite in favor of the demand now made, by the true women of this generation :

It is with diffidence that I speak upon this question before us, not a diffidence resulting from any doubt of the worthiness of the cause, but from the fear that its depth and power can be but meagerly portrayed by me. . . . . Woman's rights—her civil rights—equal with man's—not an equality of moral and religious influence, for who dares to deny her that?—but an equality in the exercise of her own powers, and a right to use all the sources of erudition within the reach of man, to build unto herself a name for her talents, energy, and integrity. We do not positively say that our intellect is as capable as man's to assume, and at once to hold, these rights, or that our hearts are as willing to enter into his actions; for if we did not believe it, we would not contend for them, and if men did not believe it, they would not withhold them with a smothered silence. . . . . In closing, she said: There will be one effect, perhaps unlooked for, if we are raised to equal administration with man. It will classify intellect. The heterogeneous triflings which now, I am very sorry to say, occupy so much of our time, will be neglected; fashion's votaries will silently fall off; dishonest exertions for rank in society will be scorned; extravagance in toilet will be detested; that meager and worthless pride of station will be forgotten; the honest earnings of dependents will be paid; popular demagogues crushed; impostors unpatronized; true genius sincerely encouraged; and, above all, pawned integrity redeemed! And why? Because enfranchised woman then will feel the burdens of her responsibilities, and can strive for elevation, and will reach all knowledge within her grasp. . . . . If all this is accomplished, man need not fear pomposity, fickleness, or an unhealthy enthusiasm at his dear fireside; we can be as dutiful, submissive, endearing as daughters, wives, and mothers, even if we hang the wreath of domestic harmony upon the eagle's talons.

Thus for twenty minutes the young and beautiful stranger held her audience spell-bound with her eloquence, in a voice whose pathos thrilled every heart. Her husband, hat and cane in hand, remained standing, leaning against a pillar near the altar, and

---

* Rebecca Sanford, now Postmaster at Mt. Morris, N. Y.

seemed a most delighted, nay, reverential listener. It was a scene never to be forgotten, and one of the most pleasing incidents of the Convention.

Sarah Owen read an address on woman's place and pay in the world of work. In closing, she said:

An experienced cashier of this city remarked to me that women might be as good book-keepers as men; but men have monopolized every lucrative situation, from the dry-goods merchant down to whitewashing. Who does not feel, as she sees a stout, athletic man standing behind the counter measuring lace, ribbons, and tape, that he is monopolizing a woman's place, while thousands of rich acres in our western world await his coming ? This year, a woman, for the first time, has taken her place in one of our regular medical colleges. We rejoice to hear that by her dignity of manner, application to study, and devotion to the several branches of the profession she has chosen, she has secured the respect of her professors and class, and reflected lasting honor upon her whole sex. Thus we hail, in Elizabeth Blackwell, a pioneer for woman in this profession.

It is by this inverted order of society that woman is obliged to ply the needle by day and by night, to procure even a scanty pittance for her dependent family. Let men become producers, as nature has designed them, and women be educated to fill all those stations which require less physical strength, and we should soon modify many of our social evils. I am informed by the seamstresses of this city, that they get but thirty cents for making a satin vest, and from twelve to thirty for making pants, and coats in the same proportion. Man has such a contemptible idea of woman, that he thinks she can not even sew as well as he can; and he often goes to a tailor, and pays him double and even treble for making a suit, when it merely passes through his hands, after a woman has made every stitch of it so neatly that he discovers no difference. Who does not see gross injustice in this inequality of wages and violation of rights ? To prove that woman is capable of prosecuting the mercantile business, we have a noble example in this city in Mrs. Gifford, who has sustained herself with credit. She has bravely triumphed over all obloquy and discouragement attendant on such a novel experiment, and made for herself an independent living.

In the fields of benevolence, woman has done great and noble works for the safety and stability of the nation. When man shall see the wisdom of recognizing a co-worker in her, then may be looked for the dawning of a perfect day, when woman shall stand where God designed she should, on an even platform with man himself.

DOCUMENT 7 (I: 115–17): Akron Convention, Akron, Ohio, May 28-29, 1851. Reminiscences by Frances D. Gage of Sojourner Truth

The leaders of the movement trembled on seeing a tall, gaunt black woman in a gray dress and white turban, surmounted with an uncouth sun-bonnet, march deliberately into the church, walk with the air of a queen up the aisle, and take her seat upon the pulpit steps. A buzz of disapprobation was heard all over the house, and there fell on the listening ear, "An abolition affair!" "Woman's rights and niggers!" "I told you so!" "Go it, darkey!"

I chanced on that occasion to wear my first laurels in public life as president of the meeting. At my request order was restored, and the business of the Convention went on. Morning, afternoon, and evening exercises came and went. Through all these sessions old Sojourner, quiet and reticent as the "Lybian Statue," sat crouched against the wall on the corner of the pulpit stairs, her sun-bonnet shading her eyes, her elbows on her knees, her chin resting upon her broad, hard palms. At intermission she was busy selling the "Life of Sojourner Truth," a narrative of her own strange and adventurous life. Again and again, timorous and trembling ones came to me and said, with earnestness, "Don't let her speak, Mrs. Gage, it will ruin us. Every newspaper in the land will have our cause mixed up with abolition and niggers, and we shall be utterly denounced." My only answer was, "We shall see when the time comes."

The second day the work waxed warm. Methodist, Baptist, Episcopal, Presbyterian, and Universalist ministers came in to hear and discuss the resolutions presented. One claimed superior rights and privileges for man, on the ground of "superior intellect"; another, because of the "manhood of Christ; if God had desired the equality of woman, He would have given some token of His will through the birth, life, and death of the Saviour." Another gave us a theological view of the "sin of our first mother."

There were very few women in those days who dared to "speak in meeting"; and the august teachers of the people were seemingly getting the better of us, while the boys in the galleries, and the sneerers among the pews, were hugely enjoying the discomfiture, as they supposed, of the "strong-minded." Some of the tender-skinned friends were on the point of losing dignity, and the atmosphere betokened a storm. When, slowly from her seat in the corner rose Sojourner Truth, who, till now, had scarcely lifted her head. "Don't let her speak!" gasped half a dozen in my ear. She moved slowly and solemnly to the front, laid her old bonnet at her feet, and turned her great speaking eyes to me. There was a hissing sound of disapprobation above and below. I rose and announced " Sojourner Truth," and begged the audience to keep silence for a few moments.

The tumult subsided at once, and every eye was fixed on this almost Amazon form, which stood nearly six feet high, head erect, and eyes piercing the upper air like one in a dream. At her first word there was a profound hush. She spoke in deep tones, which, though not loud, reached every ear in the house, and away through the throng at the doors and windows.

" Wall, chilern, whar dar is so much racket dar must be somethin' out o' kil-ter. I tink dat 'twixt de niggers of de Souf and de womin at de Norf, all talkin' 'bout rights, de white men will be in a fix pretty soon. But what's all dis here talkin' 'bout ?

" Dat man ober dar say dat womin needs to be helped into carriages, and lifted ober ditches, and to hab de best place everywhar. Nobody eber helps me into carriages, or ober mud-puddles, or gibs me any best place !" And rais-ing herself to her full height, and her voice to a pitch like rolling thunder, she asked. " And a'n't I a woman ? Look at me ! Look at my arm ! (and she bared her right arm to the shoulder, showing her tremendous muscular power). I have ploughed, and planted, and gathered into barns. and no man could head me ! And a'n't I a woman ? I could work as much and eat as much as a man—when I could get it—and bear de lash as well ! And a'n't I a woman ? I have borne thirteen chilern, and seen 'em mos' all sold off to slav-ery, and when I cried out with my mother's grief, none but Jesus heard me ! And a'n't I a woman ?

" Den dey talks 'bout dis ting in de head ; what dis dey call it ? " (" Intel-lect," whispered some one near.) " Dat's it, honey. What's dat got to do wid womin's rights or nigger's rights ? If my cup won't hold but a pint, and yourn holds a quart, wouldn't ye be mean not to let me have my little half-measure full ? " And she pointed her significant finger, and sent a keen glance at the minister who had made the argument. The cheering was long and loud.

" Den dat little man in black dar, he say women can't have as much rights as men, 'cause Christ wan't a woman ! Whar did your Christ come from ? " Rolling thunder couldn't have stilled that crowd, as did those deep, wonderful tones, as she stood there with outstretched arms and eyes of fire. Raising her voice still louder, she repeated, " Whar did your Christ come from ? From God and a woman ! Man had nothin' to do wid Him." Oh, what a rebuke that was to that little man.

Turning again to another objector, she took up the defense of Mother Eve. I can not follow her through it all. It was pointed, and witty, and solemn ; eliciting at almost every sentence deafening applause ; and she ended by as-serting : " If de fust woman God ever made was strong enough to turn de world upside down all alone, dese women togedder (and she glanced her eye over the platform) ought to be able to turn it back, and get it right side up again ! And now dey is asking to do it, de men better let 'em." Long-contin-ued cheering greeted this. " 'Bleeged to ye for hearin' on me, and now ole So-journer han't got nothin' more to say."

Amid roars of applause, she returned to her corner, leaving more than one of us with streaming eyes, and hearts beating with gratitude. She had taken

us up in her strong arms and carried us safely over the slough of difficulty
turning the whole tide in our favor.   I have never in my life seen anything like
the magical influence that subdued the mobbish spirit of the day, and turned
the sneers and jeers of an excited crowd into notes of respect and admiration.
Hundreds rushed up to shake hands with her, and congratulate the glorious
old mother, and bid her God-speed on her mission of " testifyin' agin concerning the wickedness of this 'ere people."

DOCUMENT 8 (I: 237–42): Second National Convention, Worcester, Massachusetts, October 15-16, 1851. Address by Ernestine Rose

After having heard the letter read from our poor incarcerated sisters of France, well might we exclaim, Alas, poor France! where is thy glory? Where the glory of the Revolution of 1848, in which shone forth the pure and magnanimous spirit of an oppressed nation struggling for Freedom? Where the fruits of that victory that gave to the world the motto, "Liberty, Equality, and Fraternity"? A motto destined to hurl the tyranny of kings and priests into the dust, and give freedom to the enslaved millions of the earth. Where, I again ask, is the result of those noble achievements, when woman, ay, one-half of the nation, is deprived of her rights? Has woman then been idle during the contest between "right and might"? Has she been wanting in ardor and enthusiasm? Has she not mingled her blood with that of her husband, son, and sire? Or has she been recreant in hailing the motto of liberty floating on your banners as an omen of justice, peace, and freedom to man, that at the first step she takes practically to claim the recognition of her rights, she is rewarded with the doom of a martyr?

But right has not yet asserted her prerogative, for might rules the day; and as every good cause must have its martyrs, why should woman not be a martyr for her cause? But need we wonder that France, governed as she is by Russian and Austrian despotism, does not recognize the rights of humanity in the recognition of the rights of woman, when even here, in this far-famed land of freedom, under a Republic that has inscribed on its banner the great truth that "all men are created free and equal, and endowed with inalienable rights to life, liberty, and the pursuit of happiness"—a declaration borne, like the vision of hope, on wings of light to the remotest parts of the earth, an omen of freedom to the oppressed and down-trodden children of man—when, even here, in the very face of this eternal truth, woman, the mockingly so-called "better half" of man, has yet to plead for her rights, nay, for her life. For what is life without liberty, and what is liberty without equality of rights? And as for the pursuit of happiness, she is not allowed to choose any line of action that might promote it; she has only thankfully to accept what man in his magnanimity decides as best for her to do, and this is what he does not choose to do himself.

Is she then not included in that declaration? Answer, ye wise men of the nation, and answer truly; add not hypocrisy to oppression! Say that she is not created free and equal, and therefore (for the sequence follows on the premise) that she is not entitled to life, liberty, and the pursuit of happiness. But with all the audacity arising from an assumed superiority, you dare not so libel and insult humanity as to say, that she is not included in that declaration; and if she is, then what right has man, except that of might, to deprive woman of the rights and privileges he claims for himself? And why, in the name of reason and justice, why should she not have the same rights? Because she is woman? Humanity recognizes no sex; virtue recognizes no sex; mind recognizes no sex; life and death, pleasure and pain, happiness and misery, recognize no sex. Like man, woman comes involuntarily into existence; like him, she possesses physical and mental and moral powers, on the proper cultivation of which depends her happiness; like him she is subject to all the vicissitudes of life; like him she has to pay the penalty for disobeying nature's laws, and far greater penalties has she to suffer from ignorance of her more complicated nature; like him she enjoys or suffers with her country. Yet she is not recognized as his equal!

In the laws of the land she has no rights; in government she has no voice. And in spite of another principle, recognized in this Republic, namely, that "taxation without representation is tyranny," she is taxed without being represented. Her property may be consumed by taxes to defray the expenses of that unholy, unrighteous custom called war, yet she has no power to give her vote against it. From the cradle to the grave she is subject to the power and control of man. Father, guardian, or husband, one conveys her like some piece of merchandise over to the other.

At marriage she loses her entire identity, and her being is said to have become merged in her husband. Has nature thus merged it? Has she ceased to exist and feel pleasure and pain? When she violates the laws of her being, does her husband pay the penalty? When she breaks the moral laws, does he suffer the punishment? When he supplies his wants, is it enough to satisfy her nature? And when at his nightly orgies, in the grog-shop and the oyster-cellar, or at the gaming-table, he squanders the means she helped, by her co-operation and economy, to accumulate, and she awakens to penury and destitution, will it supply the wants of her children to tell them that, owing to the superiority of man she had no redress by law, and that as her being was merged in his, so also ought theirs to be? What an inconsistency, that from the moment she enters that compact, in which she assumes the high responsibility of wife and mother, she ceases legally to exist, and becomes a purely submissive being. Blind submission in woman is considered a virtue, while submission to wrong is itself wrong, and resistance to wrong is virtue, alike in woman as in man.

But it will be said that the husband provides for the wife, or in other words, he feeds, clothes, and shelters her! I wish I had the power to make every one before me fully realize the degradation contained in that idea. Yes! he *keeps* her, and so he does a favorite horse; by law they are both considered his property. Both may, when the cruelty of the owner compels them to, run away, be brought back by the strong arm of the law, and according to a still extant law of England, both may be led by the halter to the market-place, and sold. This is humiliating indeed, but nevertheless true; and the sooner these things are known and understood, the better for humanity. It is no fancy sketch. I know that some endeavor to throw the mantle of romance over the subject, and treat woman like some ideal existence, not liable to the ills of life. Let those deal in fancy, that have nothing better to deal in; we have to do with sober, sad realities, with stubborn facts.

Again, I shall be told that the law presumes the husband to be kind. affectionate, and ready to provide for and protect his wife. But what right, I ask, has the law to presume at all on the subject? What right has the law to intrust the interest and happiness of one being into the hands of another? And if the merging of the interest of one being into the other is a necessary consequence on marriage, why should woman always remain on the losing side? Turn the tables. Let the identity and interest of the husband be merged in the wife. Think you she would act less generously toward him, than he toward her? Think you she is not capable of as much justice, disinterested devotion, and abiding affection, as he is? Oh, how grossly you misunderstand and wrong her nature! But we desire no such undue power over man; it would be as wrong in her to exercise it as it now is in him. All we claim is an equal legal and social position. We have nothing to do with individual man, be he good or bad, but with the laws that oppress woman. We know that bad and unjust laws must in the nature of things make man so too. If he is kind, affectionate, and consistent, it is because the kindlier feelings, instilled by a mother, kept warm by a sister, and cherished by a wife, will not allow him to carry out these barbarous laws against woman.

But the estimation she is generally held in, is as degrading as it is foolish. Man forgets that woman can not be degraded without its reacting on himself. The impress of her mind is stamped on him by nature, and the early education of the mother, which no after-training can entirely efface; and therefore, the estimation she is held in falls back with double force upon him. Yet, from the force of prejudice against her, he knows it not. Not long ago, I saw an account of two offenders, brought before a Justice of New York. One was charged with stealing a pair of boots, for which offense he was sentenced to six months' imprisonment; the other crime was assault and battery upon his wife: he was let off with a reprimand from the judge! With my principles, I am entirely opposed to punishment, and hold, that to reform the erring and remove the causes of evil is much more efficient, as well as just, than to punish. But the judge showed us the comparative value which he set on these two kinds of *property*. But then you must remember that the boots were taken by a stranger, while the wife was insulted by her legal owner! Here it will be said, that such degrading cases are but few. For the sake of humanity, I hope they are. But as long as woman shall be oppressed by unequal laws, so long will she be degraded by man.

We have hardly an adequate idea how all-powerful law is in forming public opinion, in giving tone and character to the mass of society. To illustrate my point, look at that infamous, detestable law, which was written in human blood, and signed and sealed with life and liberty, that eternal stain on the statute book of this country, the Fugitive Slave Law. Think you that before its passage, you could have found any in the free States—except a few politicians in the market—base enough to desire such a law ? No! no! Even those who took no interest in the slave question, would have shrunk from so barbarous a thing. But no sooner was it passed, than the ignorant mass, the rabble of the self-styled Union Safety Committee, found out that we were a law-loving, law-abiding people! Such is the magic power of Law. Hence the necessity to guard against bad ones. Hence also the reason why we call on the nation to remove the legal shackles from woman, and it will have a beneficial effect on that still greater tyrant she has to contend with, Public Opinion.

Carry out the republican principle of universal suffrage, or strike it from your banners and substitute " Freedom and Power,to one half of society, and Submission and Slavery to the other." Give woman the elective franchise. Let married women have the same right to property that their husbands have; for whatever the difference in their respective occupations, the duties of the wife are as indispensable and far more arduous than the husband's. Why then should the wife, at the death of her husband, not be his heir to the same extent that he is heir to her ? In this inequality there is involved another wrong. When the wife dies, the husband is left in the undisturbed possession of all there is, and the children are left with him; no change is made, no stranger intrudes on his home and his affliction. But when the husband dies, the widow, at best receives but a mere pittance, while strangers assume authority denied to the wife. The sanctuary of affliction must be desecrated by executors; everything must be ransacked and assessed, lest she should steal something out of her own house; and to cap the climax, the children must be placed under guardians. When the husband dies poor, to be sure, no guardian is required, and the children are left for the mother to care and toil for, as best she may. But when anything is left for their maintenance, then it must be placed in the hands of strangers for safe keeping! The bringing-up and safety of the children are left with the mother, and safe they are in her hands. But a few hundred or thousand dollars can not be intrusted with her!

But, say they, "in case of a second marriage, the children must be protected in their property." Does that reason not hold as good in the case of the husband as in that of the wife? Oh, no! When *he* marries again, he still retains his identity and power to act; but *she* becomes merged once more into a mere nonentity; and therefore the first husband must rob her to prevent the second from doing so! Make the laws regulating property between husband and wife, equal for both, and all these difficulties would be removed.

According to a late act, the wife has a right to the property she brings at marriage, or receives in any way after marriage. Here is some provision for the favored few; but for the laboring many, there is none. The mass of the people commence life with no other capital than the union of heads, hearts, and hands. To the benefit of this best of capital, the wife has no right. If they are unsuccessful in married life, who suffers more the bitter consequences of poverty than the wife? But if successful, she can not call a dollar her own. The husband may will away every dollar of the personal property, and leave her destitute and penniless, and she has no redress by law. And even where real estate is left she receives but a life-interest in a third part of it, and at her death, she can not leave it to any one belonging to her: it falls back even to the remotest of his relatives. This is law, but where is the justice of it? Well might we say that laws were made to prevent, not to promote, the ends of justice.

In case of separation, why should the children be taken from the protecting care of the mother? Who has a better right to them than she? How much do fathers generally do toward bringing them up? When he comes home from business, and the child is in good humor and handsome trim, he takes the little darling on his knee and plays with it. But when the wife, with the care of the whole household on her shoulders, with little or no help, is not able to put them in the best order, how much does he do for them? Oh, no! Fathers like to have children good natured, well-behaved, and comfortable, but how to put them in that desirable condition is out of their philosophy. Children always depend more on the tender, watchful care of the mother, than of the father. Whether from nature, habit, or both, the mother is much more capable of administering to their health and comfort than the father, and therefore she has the best right to them. And where there is property, it ought to be divided equally between them, with an additional provision from the father toward the maintenance and education of the children.

Much is said about the burdens and responsibilities of married men. Responsibilities indeed there are, if they but felt them; but as to burdens, what are they? The sole province of man seems to be centered in that one thing, attending to some business. I grant that owing to the present unjust and unequal reward for labor, many have to work too hard for a subsistence; but whatever his vocation, he has to attend as much to it before as after marriage. Look at your bachelors, and see if they do not strive as much for wealth, and attend as steadily to business, as married men. No! the husband has little or no increase of burden, and every increase of comfort after marriage; while most of the burdens, cares, pains, and penalties of married life fall on the wife. How unjust and cruel, then, to have all the laws in his favor! If any difference should be made by law between husband and wife, reason, justice, and humanity, if their voices were heard, would dictate that it should be in her favor.

No! there is no reason against woman's elevation, but there are deep-rooted, hoary-headed prejudices. The main cause of them is, a pernicious falsehood propagated against her being, namely, that she is inferior by her nature. Inferior in what? What has man ever done, that woman, under the same advantages, could not do? In morals, bad as she is, she is generally considered his superior. In the intellectual sphere, give her a fair chance before you pronounce a verdict against her. Cultivate the frontal portion of her brain as much as that of man is cultivated, and she will stand his equal at least. Even now, where her mind has been called out at all, her intellect is as bright, as capacious, and as powerful as his. Will you tell us, that women have no Newtons, Shakespeares, and Byrons? Greater natural powers than even those possessed may have been destroyed in woman for want of proper culture, a just appreciation, reward for merit as an incentive to exertion, and freedom of action, without which, mind becomes cramped and stifled, for it can not expand under bolts and bars; and yet, amid all blighting, crushing circumstances—confined within the narrowest possible limits, trampled upon by prejudice and injustice, from her education and position forced to occupy herself almost exclusively with the most trivial affairs—in spite of all these difficulties, her intellect is as good as his. The few bright meteors in man's intellectual horizon could well be matched by woman, were she allowed to occupy the same elevated position. There is no need of naming the De Staëls, the Rolands, the Somervilles, the Wollstonecrofts, the Sigourneys, the Wrights, the Martineaus, the Hemanses, the Fullers, Jagellos, and many more of modern as well as ancient times, to prove her mental powers, her patriotism, her self-sacrificing devotion to the cause of humanity, and the eloquence that gushes from her pen, or from her tongue. These things are too well known to require repetition. And do you ask for fortitude, energy, and perseverance? Then look at woman under suffering, reverse of fortune, and affliction, when the strength and power of man have sunk to the lowest ebb, when his mind is overwhelmed by the dark waters of despair. She, like the tender ivy plant. bent yet unbroken by the storms of life, not only upholds her own hopeful courage, but clings around the tempest-fallen oak, to speak hope to his faltering spirit, and shelter him from the returning blast of the storm.

DOCUMENT 9 (I: 825–26): Second National Convention, Worcester, Massachusetts, October 15-16, 1851. Resolutions

1. *Resolved*, That while we would not undervalue other methods, the Right of Suffrage for Women is, in our opinion, the corner-stone of this enterprise, since we do not seek to protect woman, but rather to place her in a position to protect herself.

2. *Resolved*, That it will be woman's fault if, the ballot once in her hand, all the barbarous, demoralizing, and unequal laws relating to marriage and property, do not speedily vanish from the statute-book; and while we acknowledge that the hope of a share in the higher professions and profitable employments of society is one of the strongest motives to intellectual culture, we know, also, that an interest in political questions is an equally powerful stimulus; and we see, beside, that we do our best to insure education to an individual when we put the ballot into his hands; it being so clearly the interest of the community that one upon whose decisions depend its welfare and safety, should both have free access to the best means of education, and be urged to make use of them.

3. *Resolved*, That we do not feel called upon to assert or establish the equality of the sexes, in an intellectual or any other point of view. It is enough for our argument that natural and political justice, and the axioms of English and American liberty, alike determine that rights and burdens—taxation and representation—should be co-extensive; hence women, as individual citizens, liable to punishment for acts which the laws call criminal, or to be taxed in their labor and property for the support of government, have a self-evident and indisputable right, identically the same right that men have, to a direct voice in the enactment of those laws and the formation of that government.

4. *Resolved*, That the democrat, or reformer, who denies suffrage to women, is a democrat only because he was not born a noble, and one of those levelers who are willing to level only down to themselves.

5. *Resolved*, That while political and natural justice accords civil equality to woman; while great thinkers of every age, from Plato to Condorcet and Mill, have supported

their claim ; while voluntary associations, religious and secular, have been organized on this basis, still, it is a favorite argument against it, that no political community or nation ever existed in which women have not been in a state of political inferiority. But, in reply, we remind our opponents that the same fact has been alleged, with equal truth, in favor of slavery ; has been urged against freedom of industry, freedom of conscience, and the freedom of the press ; none of these liberties having been thought compatible with a well-ordered state, until they had proved their possibility by springing into existence as facts. Besides, there is no difficulty in understanding why the subjection of woman has been a *uniform custom*, when we recollect that we are just emerging from the ages in which *might* has been always right.

6. *Resolved*, That, so far from denying the overwhelming social and civil influence of women, we are fully aware of its vast extent ; aware, with Demosthenes, that "measures which the statesman has meditated a whole year may be overturned in a day by a woman" ; and for this very reason we proclaim it the very highest expediency to endow her with full civil rights, since only then will she exercise this mighty influence under a just sense of her duty and responsibility ; the history of all ages bearing witness, that the only safe course for nations is to add open responsibility wherever there already exists unobserved power.

7. *Resolved*, That we deny the right of any portion of the species to decide for another portion, or of any individual to decide for another individual what is and what is not their "proper sphere" ; that the proper sphere for all human beings is the largest and highest to which they are able to attain ; what this is, can not be ascertained without complete liberty of choice ; woman, therefore, ought to choose for herself what sphere she will fill, what education she will seek, and what employment she will follow, and not be held bound to accept, in submission, the rights, the education, and the sphere which man thinks proper to allow her.

8. *Resolved*, That we hold these truths to be self-evident : That all men are created equal ; that they are endowed by their Creator with certain inalienable rights : that among these are life, liberty, and the pursuit of happiness ; that, to secure these rights, governments are instituted among men, deriving their just powers from the consent of the governed ; and we charge that man with gross dishonesty or ignorance, who shall contend that "men," in the memorable document from which we quote, does not stand for the human race ; that "life, liberty, and the pursuit of happiness," are the "inalienable rights" of *half* only of the human species ; and that, by "the governed," whose consent is affirmed to be the only source of just power, is meant that *half* of mankind only who, in relation to the other, have hitherto assumed the character of *governors*.

9. *Resolved*, That we see no weight in the argument that it is necessary to exclude women from civil life because domestic cares and political engagements are incompatible ; since we do not see the fact to be so in the case of men ; and because, if the incompatibility be real, it will take care of itself, neither men nor women needing any law to exclude them from an occupation when they have undertaken another incompatible with it. Second, we see nothing in the assertion that women, themselves, do not desire a change, since we assert that superstitious fears and·dread of losing men's regard, smother all frank expression on this point ; and further, if it be their real wish to avoid civil life, laws to keep them out of it are absurd, no legislator having ever yet thought it necessary to compel people by law to follow their own inclination.

10. *Resolved*, That it is as absurd to deny all women their civil rights because the cares of household and family take up all the time of some, as it would be to exclude the whole male sex from Congress, because some men are sailors, or soldiers in active service or merchants, whose business requires all their attention and energies.

DOCUMENT 10 (I: 117–18): Woman's Rights Meeting in a Barn, May 1850, and "John's Convention," Mount Gilead, Ohio, December 1851, described by Frances D. Gage in a letter to Matilda Joslyn Gage

DEAR MADAM:—Your postal and note requesting items of history of the almost forgotten doings of thirty years ago, is at hand.

In 1850 Ohio decided by the votes of her male population to "alter and amend her Constitution." The elected delegates assembled in Cincinnati in the spring of that year.

In view of affecting this legislation the "Woman's Rights Convention" at Salem, Columbiana Co., was called in April, 1850, and memorialized the Delegate Convention, praying that Equal Rights to all citizens of the State be guaranteed by the new Constitution. In May a county meeting was called in McConnelsville, Morgan Co., Ohio. Mrs. H. M. Little, Mrs. M. T. Corner, Mrs. H. Brewster, and myself, were all the women that I knew in that region, even favorable to a movement for the help of women. Two of these only asked for more just laws for married women. One hesitated about the right of suffrage. I alone in the beginning asked for the ballot,* and equality before the law for all adult citizens of sound minds, without regard to sex or color. The Freemasons gave their hall for our meeting, but no men were admitted. I drew up a memorial for signatures, praying that the words " white " and " male " be omitted in the new Constitution. I also drew up a paper copying the unequal laws on our statute books with regard to women. We met, Mrs. Harriet Brewster presiding. Some seventy ladies of our place fell in through the day. I read my paper, and Mrs. M. T. Corner gave a historical account of noted women of the past. It was a new thing. At the close, forty names were placed on the memorial. For years I had been talking and writing, and people were used to my " craziness." But who expected Mrs. Corner and others to take such a stand ! Of course, we were heartily abused.

This led to the calling of a county meeting at Chesterfield, Morgan County. It was advertised to be held in the M. E. Church. There were only present some eight ladies, including the four above mentioned We four " scoffers " hired a hack and rode sixteen miles over the hill, before 10 A.M., to be denied admittance to church or school-house Rev. Philo Matthews had found us shelter on the threshing-floor of a fine barn, and we found about three or four hundred of the farmers, and their wives, sons, and daughters, assembled. They were nearly all

* My notoriety as an Abolitionist made it very difficult for me to reach people at home, and, consequently, I had to work through press and social circle; women dared not speak then. But the seed was sown far and wide, now bearing fruit.

" Quakers " and Abolitionists, but then not much inclined to " woman's rights." I had enlarged my argument, and there the " ox-sled " speech was made, the last part of May, 1850, date of day not remembered.

A genuine " Quaker Preacher " said to me at the close, " Frances, thee had great Freedom. The ox-cart inspired thee." The farmers' wives brought huge boxes and pans of provisions. Men and women made speeches, and many names were added to our memorial. On the whole, we had a delightful day. It was no uncommon thing in those days for Abolitionist, or Methodist, or other meetings, to be held under the trees, or in large barns, when school-houses would not hold the people. But to shut up doors against women was a new thing.

In December of 1851 I was invited to attend a Woman's Rights Convention at the town of Mount Gilead, Morrow Co., Ohio. A newspaper call promised that celebrities would be on hand, etc. I wrote I would be there. It was two days' journey, by steamboat and rail. The call was signed " John Andrews," and John Andrews promised to meet me at the cars. I went. It was fearfully cold, and John met me. He was a beardless boy of nineteen, looking much younger. We drove at once to the " Christian Church." On the way he cheered me by saying " he was afraid nobody would come, for all the people said nobody would come for his asking." When we got to the house, there was not one human soul on hand, no fire in the old rusty stove, and the rude, unpainted board benches, all topsy-turvy. I called some boys playing near, asked their names, put them on paper, five of them, and said to them, " Go to every house in this town and tell everybody that 'Aunt Fanny' will speak here at 11 A.M., and if you get me fifty to come and hear, I will give you each ten cents." They scattered off upon the run. I ordered John to right the benches, picked up chips and kindlings, borrowed a brand of fire at the next door, had a good hot stove, and the floor swept, and was ready for my audience at the appointed time. John had done his work well, and fifty at least were on hand, and a minister to make a prayer and quote St. Paul before I said a word. I said my say, and before 1 P.M., we adjourned, appointing another session at 3, and one for 7 P.M., and three for the following day. Mrs. C. M. Severance came at 6 P.M., and we had a good meeting throughout.

John's Convention was voted a success after all. He died young, worn out by his own enthusiasm and conflicts.

DOCUMENT 11 (I: 517–30, 535–42): Syracuse National
Convention, Syracuse, New York, September 8-10,
1852

This Convention, lasting three days, was in many respects remarkable, even for that " City of Conventions." It called out immense
audiences, attracted many eminent persons from different points of
the State, and was most favorably noticed by the press; the debates
were unusually earnest and brilliant, and the proceedings orderly and
harmonious throughout. Notwithstanding an admission fee of one
shilling, the City Hall was densely packed at every session, and at
the hour of adjournment it was with difficulty that the audience
could gain the street. The preliminary * editorials of the city papers
reflected their own conservative or progressive tendencies.

In no one respect were the participants in these early Conventions
more unsparingly ridiculed, and more maliciously falsified, than in
their personal appearance; it may therefore be wise to say that in
dignity and grace of manner and style of dress, the majority of these
ladies were superior to the mass of women; while the neat and
unadorned Quaker costume was worn by some, many others were
elegantly and fashionably attired; two of them in such extreme style

---

* *The Daily Standard*, Sept. 8th, 1852, said : The Woman's Rights Convention will assemble at the City Hall this morning. Some of the most able women of the country
will be present, and the discussion can not fail to be particularly interesting.

The Daily Star, a pro-slavery paper of the most pronounced and reckless character, said :
The women are coming ! They flock in upon us from every quarter, all to hear and talk
about Woman's Rights. The blue stockings are as thick as grasshoppers in hay-time,
and mighty will be the force of "jaw-logic" and "broom-stick ethics" preached by the
females of both sexes.

as to call forth much criticism from the majority, to whom a happy medium seemed desirable.

The Convention was called to order by Paulina Wright Davis, chairman of the Central Committee, and prayer offered by the Rev Samuel J. May, pastor of the Unitarian Church in Syracuse.

Although this was the first Woman's Rights Convention at which Mr. May was ever present, he had been represented in nearly all by letter, and as early as 1845 had preached an able sermon advocating the social, civil, and political rights of woman. He had been an early convert to this doctrine, and enjoyed telling the manner of his conversion. Speaking once in Providence on the question of slavery, he was attracted by the earnest attention he received from an intelligent-looking woman. At the close of the meeting, she said to him : " I have listened to you with an interest that only a woman can feel. I doubt whether you see how much of your description of the helpless dependence of slaves applies equally to all women." She ran the parallel rapidly, quoting law and custom, maintaining her assertion so perfectly that Mr. May's eyes were opened at once, and he promised the lady to give the subject his immediate consideration.

Lucy Stone read the call * and expressed the wish that every one present, even if averse to the new demands by women, would take part in the debates, as it was the truth on this question its advocates were seeking. Among the most noticeable features of these early Conventions was the welcome given to opposing arguments.

---

* THE NATIONAL WOMAN'S RIGHTS CONVENTION.

The friends of equality, justice, and truth are earnestly invited to meet in Syracuse, N. Y., Sept. 8th, 9th, and 10th, 1852, to discuss the important question of " Woman's Rights." We propose to review not only the past and consider the present, but to mark out new and broader paths for the future.

The time has come for the discussion of woman's social, civil, and religious rights, and also for a thorough and efficient organization ; a well-digested plan of operation whereby these social rights, for which our fathers fought, bled, and died, may be secured by us. Let woman no longer supinely endure the evils she may escape, but with her own right hand carve out for herself a higher, nobler destiny than has heretofore been hers. Inasmuch as through the folly and imbecility of woman, the race is what it is, dwarfed in mind and body ; and as through her alone it can yet be redeemed, all are equally interested in the objects of this Convention.

We therefore solemnly urge those men and women who desire the elevation of humanity, to be present at the coming Convention, and aid us by their wisdom. Our platform will be free to all who are capable of discussing the subject with candor and truth. On behalf of the Central Committee,

ELIZABETH CADY STANTON,
PAULINA WRIGHT DAVIS,
WILLIAM HENRY CHANNING,
LUCY STONE,
SAMUEL J. MAY.

The Nominating Committee reported the list of officers,* with Lucretia Mott as permanent President. She asked that the vote be taken separately, as there might be objections to her appointment. The entire audience (except her husband, who gave an emphatic "No!") voted in her favor. The very fact that Mrs. Mott consented, under any circumstances, to preside over a promiscuous assemblage, was proof of the progress of liberal ideas, as four years previously she had strenuously opposed placing a woman in that position, and as a member of the Society of Friends, by presiding over a meeting to which there was an admission fee, she rendered herself liable to expulsion. The vote being taken, Mrs. Mott, who sat far back in the audience, walked forward to the platform, her sweet face and placid manners at once winning the confidence of the audience. This impression was further deepened by her opening remarks. She said she was unpracticed in parliamentary proceedings, and felt herself incompetent to fulfill the duties of the position now pressed upon her, and was quite unprepared to make a suitable speech. She asked the serious and respectful attention of the Convention to the business before them, referred to the success that had thus far attended the movement, the respect shown by the press, and the favor with which the public generally had received these new demands, and closed by inviting the cordial co-operation of all present.

In commenting upon Mrs. Mott's opening address, the press of the city declared it to have been "better expressed and far more appropriate than those heard on similar occasions in political and legislative assemblages." The choice of Mrs. Mott as President was preeminently wise; of mature years, a member of the Society of Friends, in which woman was held as an equal, with undoubted right to speak in public, and the still broader experience of the Anti-Slavery

---

* *President.*—Lucretia Mott, Philadelphia.

Vice-Presidents.—Paulina Wright Davis, Rhode Island; Caroline M. Severance, Ohio; Elizabeth Oakes Smith, New York; Clarina I. H. Nichols, Vermont; Gerrit Smith, Peterboro; Sarah L. Miller, Pennsylvania.

Secretaries.—Susan B. Anthony, Martha C. Wright, Samuel J. May, Lydia F. Fowler.

Business Committee.—Elizabeth Oakes Smith, Lucy Stone, Caroline M. Severance, Harriot K. Hunt, Jane Elizabeth Jones, James Mott, Ernestine L. Rose, Elizabeth W. Phillips, Pliny Sexton, Benjamin S. Jones.

Committee on Finance.—Rosa Smith, Joseph Savage, Caroline M. Severance.

Many earnest friends beside the officers were present and took part in the discussions; among them Amy Post, Mary and Sarah Hallowell, Catharine A. F. Stebbins, Thomas and Mary Ann McClintock, Elizabeth Smith Miller, Rev. Lydia Ann Jenkins, Rev. Antoinette L. Brown, Lydia Mott, Phebe H. Jones, Mary A. Springstead, Abby H. Price, Rev. Abraham Pryne, Eliza A. Aldrich, editor *Genius of Liberty;* Dr. Cutcheon, of McGrawville College; Matilda Joslyn Gage, Lydia P. Savage, Sarah Hallock, Griffith M. Cooper.

platform, she was well fitted to guide the proceedings and encourage the expression of opinions from those to whom public speaking was an untried experiment. "It was a singular spectacle," said the *Syracuse Standard*, "to see this gray-haired matron presiding over a Convention with an ease, dignity, and grace that might be envied by the most experienced legislator in the country."

Delegates were present from Canada and eight different States. Letters were received from Mrs. Marion Reid, of England, author of an able work upon woman; from John Neal, of Maine, the veteran temperance reformer; from William Lloyd Garrison, Rev. William Henry Channing, Rev. A. D. Mayo, Margaret H. Andrews, Sarah D. Fish, Angelina Grimké Weld, Elizabeth Cady Stanton, from G. W. Johnson, chairman of the State Committee of the Liberty party, and Horace Greeley, the world-renowned editor of the *Tribune.* Mr. Johnson's letter enclosed ten dollars and the following sentiments: 1. Woman has, equally with man, the inalienable right to education, suffrage, office, property, professions, titles, and honors—to life, liberty, and the pursuit of happiness. 2. False to our sex, as well as her own, and false to herself and to God, is the woman who approves, or who submits without resistance or protest, to the social and political wrongs imposed upon her in common with the rest of her sex throughout the world.

Mrs. Stanton's letter presented three suggestions for the consideration of the Convention, viz.: That all women owning property should refuse to pay taxes as long as unrepresented; that man and woman should be educated together, and the abuse of the religious element in woman. This letter created much discussion, accompanied as it was by a series of resolutions of the most radical character, which were finally, with one exception, adopted. Thus at that early day was the action of those women, who have since refused to pay taxes, prefigured and suggested. One of the remarkable aspects of this reform, is the fact that from the first its full significance was seen by many of the women who inaugurated it.

HORACE GREELEY'S LETTER.

NEW YORK, *Sept.* 1, 1852.

MY FRIEND:—I have once or twice been urged to attend a Convention of the advocates of woman's rights; and though compliance has never been within my power, I have a right to infer that some friends of the cause desire suggestions from me with regard to the best means of advancing it. I therefore venture to submit some thoughts on that subject. To my mind the BREAD problem lies at the base of all the desirable and practical reforms which our age meditates. Not that bread is intrinsically more important to man than Temperance, Intelligence, Morality, and Religion, but that it is essential to the just appreciation of all these. Vainly do we preach the blessings of temperance to human beings cradled in hunger, and suffering at intervals the agonies of famine; idly do we commend intellectual culture to those whose minds are daily racked with the dark problem, "How shall we procure food for the morrow?" Morality, religion, are but words to him who fishes in the gutters for the means of sustaining life, and crouches behind barrels in the street for shelter from the cutting blasts of a winter's night.

Before all questions of intellectual training or political franchises for women, not to speak of such a trifle as costume, do I place the question of enlarged opportunities for work; of a more extended and diversified field of employment. The silk culture and manufacture firmly established and thriftily prosecuted to the extent of our home demand for silk, would be worth everything to American women. Our now feeble and infantile schools of design should be encouraged with the same view. A wider and more prosperous development of our Manufacturing Industry will increase the demand for female labor, thus enhancing its average reward and elevating the social position of woman. I trust the future has, therefore, much good in store for the less muscular half of the human race.

But the reform here anticipated should be inaugurated in our own households. I know how idle is the expectation of any general and permanent enhancement of the wages of any class or condition above the level of equation of Supply and Demand; yet it seems to me that the friends of woman's rights may wisely and worthily set the example of paying juster prices for female assistance in their households than those now current. If they would but resolve never to pay a capable, efficient woman less than two-thirds the wages paid to a vigorous, effective man employed in some corresponding vocation, they would very essentially aid the movement now in progress for the general recognition and conception of Equal Rights to Woman.

Society is clearly unjust to woman in according her but four to eight dollars per month for labor equally repugnant with, and more protracted than that of men of equal intelligence and relative efficiency, whose services command from ten to twenty dollars per month. If, then, the friends of Woman's Rights could set the world an example of paying for female service, not the lowest pittance which stern Necessity may compel the defenceless to accept, but as approximately fair and liberal compensation for the work actually done, as determined by a careful comparison with the recompense of other labor, I believe they would give their cause an impulse which could not be permanently resisted.

With profound esteem, yours,   HORACE GREELEY.

MRS. PAULINA W. DAVIS, Providence, R. I.

Mr. Greeley's letter bore two remarkable aspects. First, he recognized the poverty of woman as closely connected with her degradation. One of the brightest anti-slavery orators was at that time in the habit of saying, " It is not the press, nor the pulpit, which rules the country, but the counting-room " ; proving his assertion by showing the greater power of commerce and money, than of intellect and morality. So Mr. Greeley saw the purse to be woman's first need ; that she must control money in order to help herself to freedom.

Second, ignoring woman's pauperized condition just admitted, he suggested that women engaged in this reform should pay those employed in the household larger wages than was customary, although these very women were dependent upon others for their shelter, food, and clothes ; so impossible is it for a governing class to understand the helplessness of dependents, and to fully comprehend the disabilities of a subject class.

The declaration of sentiments adopted at the Westchester Convention was read by Martha C. Wright, and commented upon as follows by

CLARINA HOWARD NICHOLS: There *is* no limit to personal responsibility. Our duties are as wide as the world, and as far-reaching as the bounds of human endeavor. Woman and man must act together; she, *his* helper. She has no sphere peculiar to herself, because she could not then be his helper. It is only since I have met the varied responsibilities of life, that I have comprehended woman's sphere; and I have come to regard it as lying within the whole circumference of humanity. If, as is claimed by the most ultra opponents of the wife's legal individuality, the *interests of the parties are identical,* then I claim as a legitimate conclusion that their spheres are also identical. For interests determine duties, and duties are the land-marks of spheres. The dependence of the sexes is mutual.

It is in behalf of our sons, the future men of the Republic, as well as of our daughters, its future mothers, that we claim the full development of our energies by education, and legal protection in the control of all the issues and profits of our lives called *property.* Woman must seek influence, independence, representation, that she may have power to aid in the elevation of the human race. When men kindly set aside woman from the National Councils, they say the moral field belongs to her; and the strongest reason why woman should seek a more elevated position, is because her moral susceptibilities are greater than those of man.

Mrs. MOTT thought differently from Mrs. Nichols; she did not believe that woman's moral feelings were more elevated than man's; but that with the same opportunities for development, with the same restrictions and penalties, there would probably be about an equal manifestation of virtue.

ELIZABETH OAKES SMITH: My friends, do we realize for what purpose we are convened ? Do we fully understand that we aim at nothing less than an entire subversion of the present order of society, a dissolution of the whole existing social compact ? Do we see that it is not an error of to-day, nor of yesterday, against which we are lifting up the voice of dissent, but that it is against the hoary-headed error of all times—error borne onward from the foot-prints of the first pair ejected from Paradise, down to our own time ? In view of all this, it does seem to me that we should each and all feel as if anointed, sanctified, set apart as to a great mission. It seems to me that we who struggle to restore the divine order to the world, should feel as if under the very eye of the Eternal Searcher of all hearts, who will reject any sacrifice other than a pure offering.

We are said to be a " few disaffected, embittered women, met for the purpose of giving vent to petty personal spleen and domestic discontent." I repel the charge; and I call upon every woman here to repel the charge. If we have personal wrongs, here is not the place for redress. If we have private griefs (and what human heart, in a large sense, is without them ?), we do not come here to recount them. The grave will lay its cold honors over the hearts of all here present, before the good we ask for our kind will be realized to the world. We shall pass onward to other spheres of existence, but I trust the seed we shall here plant will ripen to a glorious harvest. We " see the end from the beginning," and rejoice in spirit. We care not that we shall not reach the fruits of our toil, for we know in times to come it will be seen to be a glorious work.

Bitterness is the child of wrong; if any one of our number has become embittered (which, God forbid!), it is because social wrong has so penetrated to the inner life that we are crucified thereby, and taste the gall and vinegar with the Divine Master. All who take their stand against false institutions, are in some sense embittered. The conviction of wrong has wrought mightily in them. Their large hearts took in the whole sense of human woe, and bled for those who had become brutalized by its weight, and they spoke as never man spoke in his own individualism, but as the embodied race will speak, when the full time shall come Thus Huss and Wickliffe and Luther spoke, and the men of '76.

No woman has come here to talk over private griefs, and detail the small coin of personal anecdote; and yet did woman speak of the wrongs which unjust legislation; the wrongs which corrupt public opinion; the wrongs which false social aspects have fastened upon us; wrongs which she hides beneath smiles, and conceals with womanly endurance; did she give voice to all this, her smiles would seem hollow and her endurance pitiable.

I hope this Convention will be an acting Convention. Let us pledge ourselves to the support of a paper in which our views shall be fairly presented to the world. At our last Convention in Worcester, I presented a prospectus for such a paper, which I will request hereafter to be read here. We can do little or nothing without such an organ. We have no opportunity now to repel slander, and are restricted in disseminating truth, from the want of such an organ. *The Tribune*, and some other papers in the country, have treated us generously; but a paper to represent us must be sustained by ourselves. We must look to our own resources. We must work out our own salvation, and God grant it be not in fear and trembling! Woman must henceforth be the redeemer, the regenerator of the world. We plead not for ourselves alone, but for Humanity. We must place woman on a higher platform, and she will raise the race to her side. We should have a literature of our own, a printing-press and a publishing-house, and tract writers and distributors, as well as lectures and conventions; and yet I say this to a race of beggars, for women have no pecuniary resources.

Well, then, we must work, we must hold property, and claim the consequent right to representation, or refuse to be taxed. Our aim is nothing less than an overthrow of our present partial legislation, that every American citizen, whether man or woman, may have a voice in the laws by which we are governed. We do not aim at idle distinction, but while we would pull down our present worn-out and imperfect human institutions, we would help to reconstruct them upon a new and broader foundation.

LUCY STONE: It seems to me that the claims we make at these Conventions are self-evident truths. The second resolution affirms the right of human beings to their persons and earnings. Is not that self-evident ? Yet the common law which regulates the relation of husband and wife, and which is modified only in a very few instances where there are statutes to the contrary, gives the " custody " of the wife's person to her husband, so that he has a right to her even against herself. It gives him her earnings, no matter with what weariness they have been acquired, or how greatly she may need them for herself or her children. It gives him a right to her personal property, which he may will entirely from her, also the use of her real estate; and in some of the States, married women, insane persons, and idiots are ranked together as not fit to make a will. So that she is left with only one right, which she enjoys in common with the pauper, viz.: the right of maintenance. Indeed when she has taken the sacred marriage vow, her legal existence ceases.

And what is our position politically ? Why, the foreigner who can't speak his mother tongue correctly; the negro, who to our own shame, we regard as fit only for a boot-black (whose dead even we bury by themselves), and the drunkard, all are entrusted with the ballot, all placed by men politically higher than their own mothers, sisters, wives, and daughters. The woman who, seeing and feeling this, dare not maintain her rights, is the woman to hang her head and blush. We ask only for justice and equal rights—the right to vote, the right to our own earnings, equality before the law—these are the Gibraltar of our cause.

Rev. ANTOINETTE L. BROWN: Man can not represent woman. They differ in their nature and relations. The law is wholly masculine; it is created and executed by man. The framers of all legal compacts are restricted to the masculine stand-point of observation, to the thought, feelings, and biases of man. The law then could give us no representation as woman, and therefore no impartial justice even if the present lawmakers were honestly intent upon this; for we can be represented only by our peers. It is expected then under the present administration, that woman should be the legal subject of man, legally reduced to pecuniary dependence upon him; that the mother should have lower legal claims upon the children than the father, and that, in short, woman should be in all respects the legal inferior of man, though entitled to full equality.

Here is the fact and its cause. When woman is tried for crime, her jury, her judges, her advocates, are all men; and yet there may have been temptations and various palliating circumstances connected with her peculiar nature as woman, such as man can not appreciate. Common justice demands that a part of the law-makers and law executors should be of her own sex. In questions of marriage and divorce, affecting interests dearer than life, both parties in the compact are entitled to an equal voice. Then the influences which arise from the relations of the sexes, when left to be exerted in our halls of justice, would at least cause decency and propriety of conduct to be maintained there; but now. low-minded men are encouraged to jest openly in court over the most sacred and most delicate subjects. From the nature of things, the guilty woman can not now have justice done her before the professed tribunals of justice; and the innocent but wronged woman is constrained to suffer on in silence rather than ask for redress.

CLARINA HOWARD NICHOLS said: There is one peculiarity in the laws affecting woman's property rights, which as it has not to my knowledge been presented for the consideration of the public, except by myself to a limited extent in private conversation and otherwise, I wish to speak of here. It is the unconstitutionality of laws cutting off the wife's right of dower. It is a provision of our National and State Constitutions, that property rights shall not be confiscated for political or other offences against the laws. Yet in all the States, if I am rightly informed, the wife forfeits her right of dower in case of divorce for infidelity to the marriage vow. In Massachusetts and several other States, if the wife desert her husband for any cause, and he procure a divorce on the ground of her desertion, she forfeits her right of dower. But it is worthy of remark that in no case is the right of the husband to possess and control the estate which is their joint accumulation, set aside; no, not even when the wife procures a divorce for the most aggravated abuse and infidelity combined. She, the innocent party, goes out childless and portionless, by decree of law; and he, the criminal, retains the home and the children, by the favor of the same law. I claim, friends, that the laws which cut off the wife's right of dower, in any case do confiscate property rights, and hence are *unconstitutional*. The property laws compel the wife to seek divorce in order to protect her earnings for the support of her children. A rum-drinker took his wife's clothing to pay his rum bill, and the justice decided that the clothing could be held, because the wife belonged to him.

Only under the Common Law of England has woman been deprived of her natural rights. Instances are frequent where the husband's aged parents are supported by the wife's earnings, and the wife's parents left paupers.

Mrs. Nichols here offered the following resolution:

Resolved, That equally involved as they are in all the Natural Relations which lie at the base of society, the sexes are equally entitled to all the rights necessary to the discharge of the duties of those relations.

ELIZABETH OAKES SMITH presented the following resolution offered by Lucretia Mott:

Resolved, That as the imbruted slave, who is content with his own lot, and would not be free if he could, if any such there be, only gives evidence of the depth of his degradation; so the woman who is satisfied with her inferior condition, avering that she has all the rights she wants, does but exhibit the enervating effects of the wrongs to which she is subjected.

Susan B. Anthony read the resolutions.* The audience called upon Hon. Gerrit Smith for a speech. His rising was received with cheers. This was Mr. Smith's first appearance upon our platform, although in letters to different Conventions he had already expressed his sympathy. His commanding presence, his benevolent countenance, and deep rich voice, made a profound impression, and intensified the power of his glowing words. Being well known in Syracuse for his philanthropy, his presence added dignity and influence to the assembly.†

Mr. SMITH said: The women who are engaged in this movement are ridiculed for aspiring to be doctors, lawyers, clergymen, sea captains, generals, presidents. For the sake of argument admitting this to be true, what then ? Shall we block the way to any individual aspiration ? But women are totally unfit for these places. Let them try, and their failure will settle the matter to their own satisfaction. There is not the slightest danger of a human being holding any position that he is incapable of attaining. We can not lay down a rule for all women. Because all women are not born with a genius for navigation, shall we say that one who is by skill and education able to take observations, who understands the chart and compass, the dangerous shores, currents, and latitudes, shall not, if she chooses, be a sea captain ? Suppose we apply that rule to man. Because I can not stand on my head, shall we deny that right to all acrobats in our circuses ? Because I can not make a steam engine, shall all other men be denied that right ? Because all men can not stand on a platform and make a speech, shall I be denied the exercise of that right ? Each individual has a sphere, and that sphere is the largest place that he or she can fill.

These women complain that they have been robbed of great and essential rights. They do not ask favors; they demand rights, the right to do whatever they have the capacity to accomplish, the right to dictate their

---

* *The Syracuse Journal* said : " Miss Anthony has a capital voice and deserves to be made clerk of the Assembly."

† When Gerrit Smith was in Congress, elected on account of his anti-slavery principles, his power to make friends even among foes was fully illustrated. At his elegant dinners distinguished Southerners were frequent guests. Hence it was said of him that he dined with slaveholders, and would have wined with them but for his temperance principles.

own sphere of action, and to have a voice in the laws and rulers under which they live. Suppose I should go to vote, and some man should push me back and say, "You want to be Governor, don't you ?" "No," I reply, "I want to exercise my God-given right to vote." Such a taunt as this would be no more insulting than those now cast at women, when they demand rights so unjustly denied.

I make no claim that woman is fit to be a member of Congress or President; all I ask for her is what I ask for the negro, a fair field. All will admit that woman has a right to herself, to her own powers of locomotion, to her own earnings, but how few are prepared to admit her right to the ballot. But all rights are held by a precarious tenure, if this one be denied. When women are the constituents of men who make and administer the laws, they will pay due consideration to their interests and not before. The right of suffrage is the great right that guarantees all others.

Mr. Smith set forth the education, the dignity, the power of self-government, and took his seat amid great applause.

LUCY STONE said: It is the duty of woman to resist taxation as long as she is not represented. It may involve the loss of friends as it surely will the loss of property. But let them all go; friends, house, garden spot, and all. The principle at issue requires the sacrifice. Resist, let the case be tried in the courts; be your own lawyers; base your cause on the admitted self-evident truth, that taxation and representation are inseparable. One such resistance, by the agitation that will grow out of it, will do more to set this question right than all the conventions in the world. There are $15,000,000 of taxable property owned by women of Boston who have no voice either in the use or imposition of the tax.

J. B. BRIGHAM, a school teacher, said: That the natures of men and women showed that their spheres were not the same, and woman was only truly lovely and happy when in her own element. He wished woman to recognize the feminine element in her being, for if she understood this, it would guide her in everything. In the domestic animals even this difference was manifest. Women should be keepers at home, and mind domestic concerns. The true object of this Convention is, I fear, not so much to acquire any real or supposed rights, as to make the speakers and actors conspicuous. I urge those engaged in this movement to claim nothing masculine for woman.

Mrs. NICHOLS said: Mr. Brigham's allusion to the animal world is not a happy one, as no animal has been discovered which legislated away the rights of the female.

GERRIT SMITH said: He would hand his esteemed friend over to Lucretia Mott, that he might be slain like Abimelech of old, by the hand of a woman; as evidently from his estimate of the sex, that would be the most humiliating death he could suffer. I trust no gentleman on this platform will consent to play the part of the armor-bearer in his behalf, and rescue him from his impending fate.

LUCRETIA MOTT said: It was impossible for one man to have arbitrary power over another without becoming despotic. She did not expect man to see how woman is robbed. Slaveholders did not see that they were oppressors, but slaves did. Gerrit Smith alluded to one woman that he intends me to personify, whom our friend would consider far out of her sphere. Yet if he believes his Bible, he must acknowledge that Deborah, a mother in Israel, arose by divine command, and led the armies of Israel,—the wife of Heber the Kenite, who drove the nail into the head of the Canaanite General, and her praises were chanted in the songs of Israel. The preaching of women, too, is approved in the Bible. Paul gives special directions to women how to preach, and he exhorts them to qualify themselves for this function and not to pin their faith on the sleeves of the clergy. I would advise Mr. Bingham not to set up his wisdom against the plain decrees of the Almighty. As to woman's voice being too weak to be heard as a public speaker, did Mr. Brigham send a protest to England against Victoria's proroguing Parliament?

Mr. MAY moved that Mrs. Stephen Smith be placed on a Committee in his stead.

The PRESIDENT quickly replied: Woman's Rights' women do not like to be called by their husbands' names, but by their own.

Mr. MAY corrected himself and said—*Rosa Smith.*

Matilda Joslyn Gage made her first public appearance in an address to this Convention. She pressed the adoption of some settled plan for the future—brought up many notable examples of woman's intellectual ability, and urged that girls be trained to self-reliance. Although Mrs. Gage, whose residence was Onondaga County, had not before taken part in a Convention, yet from the moment she read of an organized effort for the rights of woman, she had united in it heart and soul, merely waiting a convenient opportunity to publicly identify herself with this reform; an opportunity given by the Syracuse Convention. Personally acquainted with none of the leaders except Mr. May, it was quite a test of moral courage for Mrs. Gage, then quite a young woman, in fact the youngest person who took part in that Convention, to speak upon this occasion. She consulted no one as to time or opportunity, but when her courage had reached a sufficiently high point, with palpitating heart she ascended the platform, where she was cordially given place by Mrs. Mott, whose kindness to her at this supreme moment of her life was never forgotten.

Mrs. GAGE said: This Convention has assembled to discuss the subject of Woman's Rights, and form some settled plan of action for the future. While so much is said of the inferior intellect of woman, it is by a strange absurdity conceded that very many eminent men owe their station in life to their mothers. Women are now in the situation of the mass of mankind a few years since, when science and learning were in the hands of the priests, and property was held by vassalage. The Pope and the priests claimed to be not only the teachers, but the guides of the people; the laity were not permitted to examine for themselves; education was held to be unfit for the masses, while the tenure of their landed property was such as kept them in a continual state of dependence on their feudal lords.

It was but a short time since the most common rudiments of education were deemed sufficient for any woman; could she but read tolerably and write her own name it was enough. Trammeled as women have been by might and custom, there are still many shining examples, which serve as beacon lights to show what may be attained by genius, labor, energy, and perseverance combined. "The longer I live in the world," says Göethe, "the more I am certain that the difference between the great and the insignificant, is energy, invincible determination, an honest purpose once fixed, and then victory."

Although so much has been said of woman's unfitness for public life, it can be seen, from Semiramis to Victoria, that she has a peculiar fitness for governing. In poetry, Sappho was honored with the title of the Tenth Muse. Helena Lucretia Corano, in the seventeenth century, was of such rare scientific attainments, that the most illustrious persons in passing through Venice, were more anxious to see her than all the curiosities of the city; she was made a doctor, receiving the title of Unalterable. Mary Cunity, of Silesia, in the sixteenth century, was one of the most able astronomers of her time, forming astronomical tables that acquired for her a great reputation. Anna Maria Schureman was a sculptor, engraver, musician, and painter; she especially excelled in miniature painting. Constantina Grierson, an Irish girl, of humble parentage, was celebrated for her literary acquirements, though dying at the early age of twenty-seven.

With the learning, energy, and perseverance of Lady Jane Grey, Mary and Elizabeth, all are familiar. Mrs. Cowper was spoken of by Montague as standing at the head of all that is called learned, and that every critic veiled his bonnet at her superior judgment. Joanna Baillie has been termed the woman Shakespeare. Caroline Herschell shares the fame of her brother as an astronomer. The greatest triumphs of the present age in the drama, music, and literature have been achieved by women, among whom may be mentioned, Charlotte Cushman, Jenny Lind, the Misses Carey, Mrs. Stowe, and Margaret Fuller. Mrs. Somerville's renown has long been spread over both continents as one of the first mathematicians of the present age.

Self-reliance is one of the first lessons to be taught our daughters; they should be educated with our sons, and equally with them, taught to look forward to some independent means of support, either to one of the professions or the business best fitted to exercise their talents. Being placed in a position compelling them to act, has caused many persons to discover talents in themselves they were before unaware of possessing. Great emergencies produce great leaders, by arousing hitherto dormant energies.

Let us look at the rights it is boasted women now possess. After marriage the husband and wife are considered as one person in law, which I hold to be false from the very laws applicable to married parties. Were it so, the act of one would be as binding as the act of the other, and wise legislators would not need to enact statutes defining the peculiar rights of each; were it so, a woman could not legally be a man's inferior. Such a thing would be a veritable impossibility. One-half of a person can not be made the protection or direction of the other half. Blackstone says "a woman may indeed be attorney for her husband, for that implies no separation from, but rather a representation of, her lord. And a husband may also bequeath anything to his wife by will; for it can not take effect till the coverture is determined by his death." After stating at considerable length, the reasons showing their unity, the learned commentator proceeds to cut the knot, and show they are not one, but are considered as two persons, one superior, the one inferior, and not only so, but the inferior in the eye of the law as acting from compulsion.

J. ELIZABETH JONES of Ohio: This is a time of progress; and man may sooner arrest the progress of the lightning, or the clouds, or stay the waves of the sea, than the onward march of Truth with her hand on her sword and her banner unfurled. I am not in the habit of talking much about rights; I am one of those who take them. I have occupied pulpits all over the country five days out of seven, in lecturing on science, and have found no objection.

I do not know what all the women want, but I do know what I want myself, and that is, what men are most unwilling to grant; the right to vote. That includes all other rights. I want to go into the Legislative Hall, sit on the Judicial Bench, and fill the Executive Chair. Now do you understand me? This I claim on the ground of humanity; and on the ground that taxation and representation go together. The whole question resolves itself into this; there has been no attempt to dispute this. No man will venture to deny the right of woman to vote. He may urge many objections against the expediency of her exercising it, but the right is hers.

But though women are deprived of political rights, there are other rights which no law prevents. We can take our rights as merchants and in other avocations, by investing our capital in them; but we stand back and wait till it is popular for us to become merchants, doctors, lecturers, or practitioners of the mechanic arts. I know girls who have mechanical genius sufficient to become Arkwrights and Fultons, but their mothers would not apprentice them. Which of the women of this Convention have sent their daughters as apprentices to a watchmaker? There is no law against this!!

Mrs. MOTT: The Church and public opinion are stronger than law.

LYDIA JENKINS: Is there any law to prevent women voting in this State? The Constitution says "white male citizens" may vote, but does not say that white female citizens may not.

Mrs. JONES said: I do not understand that point sufficiently well to explain, but whether the statute book is in favor or opposed, every citizen in a republic (and a woman is a citizen) has a natural right to vote which no human laws can abrogate; the right to vote is the right of self-government.

ANTOINETTE BROWN said: I know instances of colored persons voting under the same circumstances, and their votes being allowed by the legal authorities; but John A. Dix declared the proceedings of a school meeting void because two women voted at it.

BENJAMIN S. JONES said, in Ohio where there is much splitting of hairs between white and black blood, the judges decided in favor of a certain colored man's right to vote, because there was 50 per cent. of white blood in the person in question.

Mrs. DAVIS: The first draft of the Rhode Island Constitution said "all citizens," but as soon as some one suggested that the door was thus left open for women to vote, the word "male" was promptly inserted.

. * * *

Dr. Harriot K. Hunt attracted much attention from the fact of her yearly protest against taxation. In the course of her remarks she said, " Unseen spirits have been with us in this Convention; the spirits of our Shaker sisters whom untold sorrows have driven into those communal societies, the convents of our civilization."

After quite a brilliant discussion, in which Mr. Brigham made himself a target for Lucy Stone, Martha C. Wright, Eliza Aldrich, Clarina Howard Nichols, Harriot K. Hunt, and Mrs. Palmer to shoot at, Antoinette L. Brown offered the following resolution, and made a few good points on the Bible argument:

Resolved, That the Bible recognizes the rights, duties, and privileges of woman as a public teacher, as every way equal with those of man; that it enjoins upon her no subjection that is not enjoined upon him; and that it truly and practically recognizes neither male nor female in Christ Jesus.

God created the first human pair equal in rights, possessions, and authority. He bequeathed the earth to them as a joint inheritance; gave them joint dominion over the irrational creation; but none over each other. (Gen. i. 28). They sinned. God announced to them the results of sin. One of these results was the rule which man would exercise over woman. (Gen. iii. 16). This rule was no more approved, endorsed, or sanctioned by God, than was the twin-born prophecy, "thou (Satan) shalt bruise his (Christ's) heel." God could not, from His nature, command Satan to injure Christ, or any other of the seed of woman. What particle of evidence is there then for supposing that in the parallel announcement He commanded man to rule over woman? Both passages should have been translated will, instead of shall. Either auxiliary is used indifferently according to the sense, in rendering that form of the Hebrew verb into English.

Because thou hast done this, is God's preface to the announcement. The results are the effects of sin. Can woman then receive evil from this rule, and man receive good? Man should be blessed in exercising this power, if he is divinely appointed to do so; but the two who are one flesh have an identity of interests, therefore if it is a curse or evil to woman, it must be so to man also. We mock God, when we make Him approve of man's thus cursing himself and woman.

The submission enjoined upon the wife in the New Testament, is not the unrighteous rule predicted in the Old. It is a Christian submission due from man towards man, and from man towards woman: " Yea, all of you be subject one to another " (1 Pet. v. 5; Eph. v. 21; Rom. xii. 10, etc.) In 1 Cor. xvi. 16, the disciples are besought to submit themselves " to every one that helpeth with us and laboreth." The same apostle says, " help those women which labored with me in the Gospel, with Clement also, and with other of my fellow-laborers."

Man is the head of the woman. True, but only in the sense in which Christ is represented as head of His body, the Church. In a different sense He is head of all things—of wicked men and devils. If man is woman's head in this sense, he may exercise over her all the prerogatives of God Himself. This would be blasphemous. The mystical Head and Body, or Christ and His Church, symbolize oneness, union. Christ so loved the Church He gave Himself for it, made it His own body, part and parcel of Himself. So ought men to love their wives. Then the rule which grew out of sin, will cease with the sin.

It is said woman is commanded not to teach in the Church. There is no such command in the Bible. It is said (1 Cor. xiv. 34), " Let your women keep silence in the churches; for it is not permitted unto them to speak." This injunction, taken out of its connection, forbids singing also; interpreted by its context, woman is merely told not to talk unless she does teach. On the same principle, one who has the gift of tongues is told not to use it in the Church, unless there is an interpreter. The rule enforced from the beginning to the end of the chapter is, " Let all things be done unto edifying." Their women, who had not been previously instructed like the men, were very naturally guilty of asking questions which did not edify the assembly. It was better that they should wait till they got home for the desired information, rather than put an individual good before the good of the Church. Nothing else is forbidden. There is not a word here against woman's teaching. The apostle says to the whole Church, woman included, " Ye may all prophesy, one by one."

In 1 Tim. ii. 12, the writer forbids woman's teaching over man, or usurping authority over him ; that is, he prohibits dogmatizing, tutoring, teaching in a dictatorial spirit. This is prohibited both in public and private ; but a proper kind of teaching is not prohibited. Verse 14—a reference to Eve, who, though created last, sinned first, is merely such a suggestion as we would make to a daughter whose mother had been in fault. The daughters are not blamed for the mother's sin, merely warned by it ; and cautioned against self-confidence, which could make them presume to teach over man. The Bible tells us of many prophetesses approved of God. The Bible is truly democratic. Do as you would be done by, is its golden commandment, recognizing neither male nor female in Christ Jesus.

ERNESTINE L. ROSE : If the able theologian who has just spoken had been in Indiana when the Constitution was revised, she might have had a chance to give her definitions on the Bible argument to some effect. At that Convention Robert Dale Owen introduced a clause to give a married woman the right to her property. The clause had passed, but by the influence of a minister was recalled ; and by his appealing to the superstition of the members, and bringing the whole force of Bible argument to bear against the right of woman to her property, it was lost. Had Miss Brown been there, she might have beaten him with his own weapons. For my part, I see no need to appeal to any written authority, particularly when it is so obscure and indefinite as to admit of different interpretations. When the inhabitants of Boston converted their harbor into a teapot rather than submit to unjust taxes, they did not go to the Bible for their authority; for if they had, they would have been told from the same authority to " give unto Cæsar what belonged to Cæsar." Had the people, when they rose in the might of their right to throw off the British yoke, appealed to the Bible for authority, it would have answered them, " Submit to the powers that be, for they are from God." No! on Human Rights and Freedom, on a subject that is as self-evident as that two and two make four, there is no need of any written authority. But this is not what I intended to speak upon. I wish to introduce a resolution, and leave it to the action of the Convention :

Resolved, That we ask not for our rights as a gift of charity, but as an act of justice. For it is in accordance with the principles of republicanism that, as woman has to pay taxes to maintain government, she has a right to participate in the formation and administration of it. That as she is amenable to the laws of her country, she is entitled to a voice in their enactment, and to all the protective advantages they can bestow ; and as she is as liable as man to all the vicissitudes of life, she ought to enjoy the same social rights and privileges. And any difference, therefore, in political, civil, and social rights, on account of sex, is in direct violation of the principles of justice and humanity, and as such ought to be held up to the contempt and derision of every lover of human freedom.

. . . . But we call upon the law-makers and law-breakers of the nation, to defend themselves for violating the fundamental principles of the Republic, or disprove their validity. Yes! they stand arrayed before the bar, not only of injured womanhood, but before the bar of moral consistency; for this question is awakening an interest abroad, as well as at home. Whatever human rights are claimed for man, moral consistency points to the equal rights of woman ; but statesmen dare not openly face the subject, knowing well they can not confute it, and they have not moral courage enough to admit it ; and hence, all they can do is to shelter themselves under a subterfuge which, though solidified by age, ignorance, and prejudice, is transparent enough for the most benighted vision to penetrate. A strong evidence of this, is given in a reply of Mr. Roebuck, member of Parliament, at a meeting of electors in Sheffield, England. Mr. R., who advocated the extension of the franchise to the occupants of five-pound tenements, was asked whether he would favor the extension of the same to women who pay an equal amount of rent? That was a simple, straight-forward question of justice ; one worthy to be asked even in our republican legislative halls. But what was the honorable gentleman's reply? Did he meet it openly and fairly? Oh, no! but hear him, and I hope the ladies will pay particular attention, for the greater part of the reply contains the draught poor, deluded woman has been accustomed to swallow—Flattery :

" There is no man who owes more than I do to woman. My education was formed by one whose very recollections at this moment make me tremble. There is nothing which, for the honor of the sex, I would not do ; the happiness of my life is bound up with it ; mother, wife, daughter, woman, to me have been the oasis of the desert of life, and, I have to ask myself, would it conduce to the happiness of society to bring woman more distinctly than she now is brought, into the arena of politics? Honestly I confess to you I believe not. I will tell you why. All their influences, if I may so term it, are gentle influences. In the rude battle and business of life, we come home to find a nook and shelter of quiet comfort after the hard and severe, and, I may say, the sharp ire and the disputes of the House of Commons. I hie me home, knowing that I shall there find personal solicitude and anxiety. My head rests upon a bosom throbbing with emotion for me and our child; and I feel a more hearty man in the cause of my country, the next day, because of the perfect, soothing, gentle peace which a mind sullied by politics is unable to feel. Oh! I can not rob myself of that inexpressible benefit, and therefore I say, No."

Well, this is certainly a nice little romantic bit of parliamentary declamation. What a pity that he should give up all these enjoyments to give woman a vote! Poor man! his happiness must be balanced on the very verge of a precipice, when the simple act of depositing a vote by the hand of woman, would overthrow and destroy it forever. I don't doubt the honorable gentleman meant what he said, particularly the last part of it, for such are the views of the unthinking, unreflecting mass of the public, here as well as there. But like a true politician, he commenced very patriotically, for the happiness of society, and finished by describing his own individual interests. His reply is a curious mixture of truth, political sophistry, false assumption, and blind selfishness. But he was placed in a dilemma, and got himself out as he could. In advocating the franchise to five-pound tenement-holders, it did not occur to him that woman may possess the same qualification that man has, and in justice, therefore, ought to have the same rights; and when the simple question was put to him (simple questions are very troublesome to statesmen), having too much sense not to see the justness of it, and too little moral courage to admit it, he entered into quite an interesting account of what a delightful little creature woman is, provided only she is kept quietly at home, waiting for the arrival of her lord and master, ready to administer a dose of purification, "which his politically sullied mind is unable to feel." Well! I have no desire to dispute the necessity of it, nor that he owes to woman all that makes life desirable— comforts, happiness, aye, and common sense too, for it's a well-known fact that smart mothers always have smart sons, unless they take after their father. But what of that? Are the benefits woman is capable of bestowing on man, reasons why she must pay the same amount of rent and taxes, without enjoying the same rights that man does?

But the justice of the case was not considered. The honorable gentleman was only concerned about the "happiness of society." Society! what does the term mean? As a foreigner, I understand by it a collection or union of human beings—men, women, and children, under one general government, and for mutual interest. But Mr. Roebuck, being a native Briton and a member of Parliament, gave us a parliamentary definition, namely: society means the male sex only; for in his solicitude to consult "the happiness of society," he enumerated the benefits man enjoys from keeping woman from her rights, without even dreaming that woman was at all considered in it; and this is the true parliamentary definition, for statesmen never include woman in their solicitude for the happiness of society. Oh, no! she is not yet recognized as belonging to the honorable body, unless taxes are required for its benefit, or the penalties of the law have to be enforced for its security.

Thus, being either unwilling or afraid to do woman justice, he first flattered her, then, in his ignorance of her true nature, he assumed that if she has her rights equal with man, she would cease to be woman—forsake the partner of her existence, the child of her bosom, dry up her sympathies, stifle her affections, turn recreant to her own nature. Then his blind selfishness took the alarm, lest, if woman were more independent, she might not be willing to be the obedient, servile tool, implicitly to obey and minister to the passions and follies of man; "and as he could not rob himself of these inexpressible bene-fits, therefore he said, No."

The speech of Antoinette Brown, and the resolution she presented opened the question of authority as against individual judgment, and roused a prolonged and somewhat bitter discussion, to which Mrs. Stanton's letter, read in a most emphatic manner by Susan B. Anthony, added intensity. It continued at intervals for two days, calling out great diversity of sentiment. Rev. Junius Hatch, a Con-gregational minister from Massachusetts, questioned the officers of the Convention as to their belief in the paramount authority of the Bible, saying the impression had gone abroad that the Convention was in-fidel in character. The President ruled that question not before the Convention.

Thomas McClintock † said, to go back to a particular era for a standard of religion and morality, is to adopt an imperfect standard and impede the progress of truth. The best minds of to-day surely understand the vital issues of this hour better than those possibly could who have slumbered in their graves for centuries. Mrs. Nichols, whom the city press spoke of as wielding a trenchant blade, announced herself as having been a member of a Baptist church since the age of eight years, thus sufficiently proving her orthodoxy. Mrs. Rose, expressing the conviction that belief does not depend upon voluntary inclination, deemed it right to interpret the Bible as he or she thought best, but objected to any such inter-pretation going forth as the doctrine of the Convention, as, at best, it was but mere opinion and not authority.

The debate upon Miss Brown's resolution was renewed in the afternoon, during which the Rev. Junius Hatch made so coarse a speech that the President was obliged to call him to order. ‡   Paying

---

† This noble man was among the first to append his name to the declaration of rights issued at Seneca Falls, and he did not withdraw it when the press began to ridicule the proceedings of the Convention.

‡ Rev. Mr. Hatch gave his idea of female loveliness. It consisted in that shrinking delicacy which, like the modest violet, hid itself until sought; that modesty which led women to blush, to cast down their eyes when meeting men, or walking up the aisle of a church to drop the veil; to wear long skirts, instead of imitating the sun-flower, which lifted up its head, seeming to say: "Come and admire me." He repeated the remarks made near the door on some of the speakers. The President hoped he would keep in order, and not relate the vulgar conversation of his associates. He went on in a similar strain until the indignation of the audience became universal, when he was summarily stopped.

In the midst of his remarks Miss Anthony suggested that the Reverend gentleman doubtless belonged to the pin-cushion ministry, educated by women's sewing societies! which, on inquiry, proved true. It was almost always the case that the "poor but pious" young man, who had studied his profession at the expense of women, proved most narrow and bigoted in his teachings.

no heed to this reprimand he continued in a strain so derogatory to his own dignity and so insulting to the Convention, that the audience called out, " Sit down ! Sit down ! Shut up ! " forcing the Reverend gentleman to his seat. The discussion still continued between the members of the Convention ; Miss Brown sustaining her resoultion, Mrs. Rose opposing it.

Mrs. MOTT, vacating the chair, spoke in opposition to the resolution, and related her anti-slavery experience upon the Bible question; one party taking great pains to show that the Bible was opposed to slavery, while the other side quoted texts to prove it of divine origin, thus wasting their time by bandying Scripture texts, and interfering with the business of their meetings. The advocates of emancipation soon learned to adhere to their own great work—that of declaring the inherent right of man to himself and his earnings—and that self-evident truths needed no argument or outward authority. We already see the disadvantage of such discussions here. It is not to be supposed that all the advice given by the apostles to the women of their day is applicable to our more intelligent age ; nor is there any passage of Scripture making those texts binding upon us.

A GENTLEMAN said : " All Scripture is given by inspiration of God, and profitable, etc." Does not this apply to the latest period ?

LUCRETIA MOTT : If the speaker will turn to the passage he will find that the word " is," being in italics, was inserted by the translators. She accepted it as in the original, " All Scriptures *given* by inspiration of God, is profitable, etc." She was somewhat familar with the Scriptures, and at a suitable time would have no objection to discuss the question. She concluded by moving that the resolution be laid on the table, which was unanimously carried.

On the morning of the last day the President stated that the sub-ject of organizing a National Society was to be discussed, and at her suggestion Mr. May read a long and interesting letter from Angelina Grimké Weld, from which we give the salient points :

" Organization is two-fold—natural and artificial, divine and human. Natu-ral organizations are based on the principle of progression; the eternal law of change. But human or artificial organizations are built upon the principle of crystallization; they *fix* the conditions of society; they seek to daguerreotype themselves, not on the present age only, but on future generations ; hence, they fet-ter and distort the expanding mind. Organizations do not protect the sacredness of the individual; their tendency is to sink the individual in the mass, to sacri-fice his rights, and immolate him on the altar of some fancied good.

It is not to organization that I object, but to an *artificial society* that must prove a burden, a clog, an incumbrance, rather than a help. Such an organ-ization as now actually exists among the women of America I hail with heartfelt joy. We are bound together by the natural ties of spiritual affinity ; we are drawn to each other because we are attracted toward one common center—the good of humanity. We need no external bonds to bind us together, no cum-brous machinery to keep our minds and hearts in unity of purpose and effort ;

we are not the lifeless staves of a barrel which can be held together only by the iron hoops of an artificial organization.

The present aspect of organizations, whether in Church, or State, or society at large, foretokens dissolution. The wrinkles and totterings of age are on them. The power of organization has been deemed necessary only because the power of Truth has not been appreciated, and just in proportion as we reverence the individual, and trust the unaided potency of Truth, we shall find it useless. What organization in the world's history has not encumbered the unfettered action of those who created it? Indeed, has not been used as an engine of oppression.

The importance of this question can hardly be duly magnified. How few organizations have ever had the power which this is destined to wield! The prayers and sympathies of the ripest and richest minds will be ours. Vast is the influence which true-hearted women will exert in the coming age. It is a beautiful coincidence, that just as the old epochs of despotism and slavery, Priestcraft and Political intrigue are dying out, just as the spiritual part of man is rising into the ascendency, Woman's Rights are being canvassed and conceded, so that when she becomes his partner in office, higher and holier principles of action will form the basis of Governmental administration.

ANGELINA GRIMKÉ WELD.

The reading of Mrs. Weld's letter was followed by a spirited discussion, resulting in the continuance of the Central Committee, composed of representative men and women of the several States, which was the only form of National Organization until after the war.

MARY SPRINGSTEAD moved that the Convention proceed to organize a National Woman's Rights Society.

Mrs. SMITH and Mrs. DAVIS did not like to be bound by a Constitution longer than during the sessions of the Convention. Both recommended the formation of State Societies.

Dr. HARRIOT K. HUNT spoke as a physician in deeming spontaneity as a law of nature.

ERNESTINE L. ROSE declared organizations to be like Chinese bandages. In political, moral, and religious bodies they hindered the growth of men; they were incubi ; she herself had cut loose from an organization into which she had been born ;* she knew what it had cost her, and having bought that little freedom for what was dearer to her than life itself, she prized it too highly to ever put herself in the same shackles again.

LUCY STONE said, that like a burnt child that dreads the fire, they had all been in permanent organizations, and therefore dread them. She herself had had enough of thumb-screws and soul screws ever to wish to be placed under them again. The present duty is agitation.

Rev. SAMUEL J. MAY deemed a system of action and co-operation all that was needed. There is probably not one woman in a thousand, not one in ten thousand who has well considered the disabilities, literary, pecuniary, social, politi-

---

* The Jewish.

cal, under which she labors. Ample provision must be made for woman's education, as liberal and thorough as that provided for the other sex.

Mrs. C. I. H. NICHOLS favored organization as a means to collect and render operative the fragmentary elements now favoring the cause.

Rev. ABRAM PRYNE, in an able speech, favored National and State organization.

The discussion was closed by the adoption of the following resolution, introduced by Paulina Wright Davis:

Resolved, That this National Convention earnestly recommends to those who are members of it from several States, and to those persons in any or all of our States, who are interested in this great reform, that they call meetings of the States or the counties in which they live, certainly as often as once a year, to consider the principles of this reform, and devise measures for their promulgation, and thus co-operate with all throughout the nation and the world, for the elevation of woman to a proper place in the mental, moral, social, religious, and political world.

It is impossible to more than give the spirit of the Convention, though glimpses of it and its participants may be caught in the brief sketch of its proceedings. In accordance with the call, woman's social, civil, and religious rights were all discussed. Lucy Stone made a brilliant closing address, the doxology was sung to " Old Hundred," and the Convention adjourned.

IV. Temperance and Woman's Rights

By THE 1850s, TEMPERANCE, like antislavery, served as an arena for woman's rights agitation. From the 1810s through the 1830s, an eastern, essentially elite, and predominantly male temperance campaign railed against widespread drinking, which had increased since the American Revolution. With the settling of the western territories and spread of religious revivalism, a new and more popularly based movement grew and changed the tenor of the campaign. As the western abolitionists demanded immediate emancipation, the western temperance advocates preached total abstinence as a supreme value. This movement peaked in the mid-1830s and declined as the economic recession and the rise of antislavery agitation shunted the drinking issue aside. In the 1840s, the movement was revived through organizations of former drunkards and their sympathizers who pledged to keep themselves free from alcohol. Like the legislative battles to enact local option and more restrictive state regulations, these societies relegated women's role to an ancillary one. Despite (and no doubt in part because of) the legislative success in several states, temperance agitation again dampened in the 1850s. Now Stanton, Anthony, and others moved to fill the vacuum by asserting women's right and obligation to play a leading role.

As Stanton's convention report showed, woman's rights advocates regarded temperance not only as the logical extension of other kinds of agitations but also as a stepping stone for many women from charity work to engagement with the broader society. Through temperance campaigns, women gained personal self-confidence, organizational skills, and political acumen. Over the century, thousands of women would move from temperance agitation to the issues of antislavery, suffrage, populism, and socialism, looking beyond effects to the social cause of evil.

The World Temperance Convention of 1853, like the

London Convention of 1840, offered an object lesson in the limits of male reformers' convictions. Excluded from this convention, which women sarcastically labeled the "Half-world," they organized one of their own. Temperance reform faded rapidly, however, to be revived in the 1870s with a distinct feminist orientation. Other causes were more pressing. As the editors of the *History of Woman Suffrage* noted following the debacle of 1853,

Most of the liberal men and women now withdrew from all temperance organizations, leaving the movement in the hands of time-serving priests and politicians, who, being in the majority, effectually blocked the progress of the reform for the time—destroying, as they did, the enthusiasm of the women trying to press it as a moral principle, and the hope of the men, who intended to carry it as a political measure. . . . Hence [the women] turned their attention to rolling up petitions for the civil and political rights of women, to hearings before legislatures and constitutional conventions, giving their persistent efforts to the reform technically called "Woman's Rights."[1]

1. Vol. I, 512–13.

DOCUMENT 12 (I: 476–78): Mary C. Vaughan, Address, Daughters of Temperance Assembly, Albany, New York, January 28, 1852

We have met to consider what we, as women, can do and may do, to forward the temperance reform. We have met, because, as members of the human family, we share in all the sufferings which error and crime bring upon the race, and because we are learning that our part in the drama of life is something beside inactive suffering and passive endurance. We would act as well as endure; and we meet here to-day because many of us have been trying to act, and we would combine our individual experiences, and together devise plans for the future, out of which shall arise well-based hopes of good results to humanity. We are aware that this proceeding of ours, this calling together of a body of women to deliberate publicly upon plans to carry out a specified reform, will rub rather harshly upon the mould of prejudice, which has gathered thick upon the common mind.

. . . . There are plenty of women, as well as men, who can labor for reforms without neglecting business or duty. It is an error that clings most tenaciously to the public mind, that because a part of the sex are wives and mothers and have absorbing duties, that all the sex should be denied any other sphere of effort. To deprive every unmarried woman, spinster, or widow, or every childless wife, of the power of exercising her warm sympathies for the good of others, is to deprive her of the greatest happiness of which she is capable; to rob her highest faculties of their legitimate operation and reward; to belittle and narrow her mind; to dwarf her affections; to turn the harmonies of her nature to discord; and, as the human mind must be active, to compel her to employ hers with low and grovelling thoughts, which lead to contemptible actions.

There is no reform in which woman can act better or more appropriately than temperance. I know not how she can resist or turn aside from the duty of acting in this; its effects fall so crushingly upon her and those whose interests are identical with her own; she has so often seen its slow, insidious, but not the less surely fatal advances, gaining upon its victim; she has seen the intellect which was her dearest pride, debased; the affections which were her life-giving springs of action, estranged; the children once loved, abused, disgraced and impoverished; the home once an earthly paradise, rendered a fit abode for lost spirits; has felt in her own person all the misery, degradation, and woe of the drunkard's wife; has shrunk from revilings and cowered beneath blows; has labored and toiled to have her poor earnings transferred to the rum-seller's ill-gotten hoard; while her children, ragged, fireless, poor, starving, gathered shivering about her. and with hollow eyes, from which all smiles had fled, begged vainly for the bread she had not to bestow. Oh! the misery, the utter, hopeless misery of the drunkard's wife!

. . . . We account it no reason why we should desist, when conscience, an awakened sense of duty, and aroused heart-sympathies, would lead us to show ourselves something different than an impersonation of the vague ideal which has been named, Woman, and with which woman has long striven to identify herself. A creature all softness and sensibility, who must necessarily enjoy and suffer in the extreme, while sharing with man the pleasures and the ills of life; bearing happiness meekly, and sorrow with fortitude; gentle, mild, submissive, forbearing under all circumstances; a softened reflex of the opinions and ideas of the masculines who, by relationship, hold mastery over her; without individualism, a mere adjunct of man, the chief object of whose creation was to adorn and beautify his existence, or to minister to some form of his selfishness. This is nearly the masculine idea of womanhood, and poor womanhood strives to personify it. But not all women. This is an age of iconoclasms; and daring hands are raised to sweep from its pedestal, and dash to fragments, this false image of woman. We care not how soon, if the true woman but take its place. This is also, and most emphatically, an age of progress. One old idea, one mouldering form of prejudice after another, is rapidly swept away. Thought, written and spoken, acts upon the mass of mind in this day of railroads and telegraphs, with a thousandfold more celerity than in the days of pillions and slow coaches. Scarce have the lips that uttered great thoughts ceased to move, or the pen which wrote them dropped from the weary hand, ere they vibrate through the inmost recesses of a thousand hearts, and awaken deep and true responses in a thousand living, truthful souls. Thence they grow, expand, fructify, and the result is Progress.

DOCUMENT 13 (I: 501–3): Lucy Stone, Letter to *The Una*, May 1853

LUCY STONE, in a letter to *The Una*, says: Last week, at New York, we had a foretaste of what woman is to expect when she attempts to exercise her equal rights as a human being. In conformity with a resolution adopted by the Mass Convention recently held in Boston, a call was issued, inviting "the *friends of temperance*" to meet in New York, May 11th, and prepare for a "World's Convention." Under that call, the Woman's State Society of New York, an active and efficient body, sent delegates; but though regularly elected, their credentials were rejected with scorn. The chairman of the committee reported that those who called the meeting never intended to include women. Think of it, a *World's* Convention, in which woman is voted not of the world!!

Rev. Dr. Hewitt affirmed it a burning shame for women to be there; and though it was entirely out of order, he discussed the question of "Woman's Rights," taking the ground that women should be nowhere but at home. Rev. E. M. Jackson, gave it as his opinion, that "the women came there expressly to disturb." The Rev. Mr. Fowler, of Utica, showed the same contempt for woman that he did last year, at the N. Y. State Temperance Society, at Syracuse. Rev. Mr. Chambers was particularly bitter.

It would have been well for those women who accept the foolish flattery of men, to have been present to see the real estimate in which woman is held by these men who surely represent a large class. The President of the meeting, Mayor Barstow, of your city, indignantly refused to put the motion made—that Susan B. Anthony should be on a committee, declaring "that he would resign rather than do it." He said it "was not fit that a woman should be in such places." After we left, if the papers reported him correctly, he used language which proved that he was not fit to be where decent people are. It was next to impossible for us or our friends to get a hearing. The "previous question" was called, or we were voted out of order, or half a dozen of the opposing party talked at once to keep us silent. Rev. T. W. Higginson declined serving on a committee from which women were excluded, and when it became apparent that only half of the world could be represented, he entered his protest, and invited those who were in favor of a *Whole* World's Temperance Convention to meet that afternoon at Dr. Trall's. A large minority withdrew, including several ministers, and arranged for a Convention that shall know "neither male nor female," to be held in New York sometime during The World's Fair.

A large and enthusiastic meeting was held at the Broadway Tabernacle, to protest against the above proceedings, and although twelve and a half cents were charged at the door, every seat was occupied, and much of the "standing room" also.

The same gentlemen! who excluded us, held a meeting subsequently in Metropolitan Hall. There your Major Barstow said: "God has placed woman in the moral world where he has the sun in the physical, to regulate, enlighten, and cheer." C. C. Burleigh, alluding to this remark, in our meeting at the Tabernacle, said: "Thus he calls his Convention, in which Mars, Jupiter, Saturn, Mercury, and Neptune are appointed a committee of arrangements, and says the Sun shall be excluded."

At this meeting, *ladies* were especially invited to vote, as though they had a heart in it, and were urged also to give their money to aid these very men by whom every soul of us had been insulted. I am sorry to say some gave. But taught such lessons, by such masters, woman will one day be wiser. Yours, for humanity, without distinction of sex,

LUCY STONE.

DOCUMENT 14 (I: 493–97): Elizabeth Cady Stanton, Address, First Annual Meeting of the Woman's State Temperance Society, Rochester, New York, June 1, 1853

A little more than one year ago, in this same hall, we formed the first Woman's State Temperance Society. We believed that the time had come for woman to speak on this question, and to insist on her right to be heard in the councils of Church and State. It was proposed at that time that we, instead of forming a society, should go *en masse* into the Men's State Temperance Society. We were assured that in becoming members by paying the sum of $1, we should thereby secure the right to speak and vote in their meetings.

We who had watched the jealousy with which man had ever eyed the slow aggressions of woman, warned you against the insidious proposition made by agents from that Society. We told you they would no doubt gladly receive the dollar, but that you would never be allowed to speak or vote in their meetings. Many of you thought us suspicious and unjust toward the temperance men of the Empire State. The fact that Abby Kelly had been permitted to speak in one of their public meetings, was brought up as an argument by some agent of that Society to prove our fears unfounded. We suggested that she spoke by favor and not

right, and our right there as equals to speak and vote, we well knew
would never be acknowledged.   A long debate saved you from that false
step, and our predictions have been fully realized in the treatment our
delegates received at the annual meeting held at Syracuse last July, and
at the recent Brick Church meeting in New York.

In forming our Society, the mass of us being radical and liberal, we
left our platform free; we are no respecters of persons, all are alike
welcome here without regard to sect, sex, color, or caste.   There have
been, however, many objections made to one feature in our Constitution, and that is, that although we admit men as members with
equal right to speak in our meetings, we claim the offices for women
alone.   We felt, in starting, the necessity of throwing all the responsibility on woman, which we knew she never would take, if there were any
men at hand to think, act, and plan for her.   The result has shown the wisdom of what seemed so objectionable to many.   It was, however, a temporary expedient, and as that seeming violation of man's rights prevents
some true friends of the cause from becoming members of our Society,
and as the officers are now well skilled in the practical business of getting up meetings, raising funds, etc., and have fairly learned how to
stand and walk alone, it may perhaps be safe to raise man to an entire
equality with ourselves, hoping, however, that he will modestly permit
the women to continue the work they have so successfully begun.   I
would suggest, therefore, that after the business of the past year be
disposed of, this objectionable feature of our Constitution be brought
under consideration.

Our experience thus far as a Society has been most encouraging.   We
number over two thousand members.   We have four agents who have
traveled in various parts of the State, and I need not say what is well
known to all present, that their labors thus far have given entire satisfaction to the Society and the public.   I was surprised and rejoiced to
find that women, without the least preparation or experience, who had
never raised their voices in public one year ago, should with so much
self-reliance, dignity, and force, enter at once such a field of labor, and
so ably perform the work.   In the metropolis of our country, in the
capital of our State, before our Legislature, and in the country school-
house, they have been alike earnest and faithful to the truth.   In behalf
of our Society, I thank you for your unwearied labors during the past
year.   In the name of humanity, I bid you go on and devote yourselves
humbly to the cause you have espoused.   The noble of your sex everywhere rejoice in your success, and feel in themselves a new impulse to
struggle upward and onward; and the deep, though silent gratitude
that ascends to Heaven from the wretched outcast, the wives, the mothers, and the daughters of brutal drunkards, is well known to all who
have listened to their tales of woe, their bitter experience, the dark, sad
passages of their tragic lives.

I hope this, our first year, is prophetic of a happy future of strong,
united, and energetic action among the women of our State.   If we are
sincere and earnest in our love of this cause, in our devotion to truth, in
our desire for the happiness of the race, we shall ever lose sight of self; each

soul will, in a measure, forget its own individual interests in proclaiming great principles of justice and right.   It is only a true, a deep, and abiding love of truth, that can swallow up all petty jealousies, envies, discords, and dissensions, and make us truly magnanimous and self-sacrificing. We have every reason to think, from reports we hear on all sides, that our Society has given this cause a new impulse, and if the condition of our treasury is a test, we have abundant reason to believe that in the hearts of the people we are approved, and that by their purses we shall be sustained.

It has been objected to our Society that we do not confine ourselves to the subject of temperance, but talk too much about woman's rights, divorce, and the Church.   It could be easily shown how the considera- tion of this great question carries us legitimately into the discussion of these various subjects.   One class of minds would deal with effects alone; another would inquire into causes; the work of the former is easily per- ceived and quickly done; that of the latter requires deep thought, great patience, much time, and a wise self-denial.   Our physicians of the pres- ent day are a good type of the mass of our reformers.   They take out cancers, cut off tonsils, drive the poison which nature has wisely thrown to the surface, back again, quiet unsteady nerves with valerian, and by means of ether infuse an artificial courage into a patient that he may bravely endure some painful operation.   It requires but little thought to feel that the wise physician who shall trace out the true causes of suffer- ing; who shall teach us the great, immutable laws of life and health; who shall show us how and where in our every-day life, we are violating these laws, and the true point to begin the reform, is doing a much higher, broader, and deeper work than he who shall bend all his ener- gies to the temporary relief of suffering.   Those temperance men or women whose whole work consists in denouncing rum-sellers, appealing to legislatures, eulogizing Neal Dow, and shouting Maine Law, are super- ficial reformers, mere surface-workers.   True, this outside work is well, and must be done; let those who see no other do this, but let them lay no hindrances in the way of that class of mind, who, seeing in our pres- ent false social relations the causes of the moral deformities of the race, would fain declare the immutable laws that govern mind as well as mat- ter, and point out the true causes of the evils we see about us, whether lurking under the shadow of the altar, the sacredness of the marriage institution, or the assumed superiority of man.

1. We have been obliged to preach woman's rights, because many, in- stead of listening to what we had to say on temperance, have questioned the right of a woman to speak on any subject.   In courts of justice and legislative assemblies, if the right of the speaker to be there is ques- tioned, all business waits until that point is settled.   Now, it is not set- tled in the mass of minds that woman has any rights on this footstool, and much less a right to stand on an even pedestal with man, look him in the face as an equal, and rebuke the sins of her day and generation. Let it be clearly understood, then, that we are a woman's rights Society; that we believe it is woman's duty to speak whenever she feels the im- pression to do so; that it is her right to be present in all the councils of

Church and State. The fact that our agents are women, settles the question of our character on this point.

Again, in discussing the question of temperance, all lecturers, from the beginning, have made mention of the drunkards' wives and children, of widows' groans and orphans' tears; shall these classes of sufferers be introduced but as themes for rhetorical flourish, as pathetic touches of the speaker's eloquence; shall we passively shed tears over their condition, or by giving them their rights, bravely open to them the doors of escape from a wretched and degraded life ? Is it not legitimate in this to discuss the social degradation, the legal disabilities of the drunkard's wife ? If in showing her wrongs, we prove the right of all womankind to the elective franchise; to a fair representation in the government; to the right in criminal cases to be tried by peers of her own choosing, shall it be said that we transcend the bounds of our subject ? If in pointing out her social degradation, we show you how the present laws outrage the sacredness of the marriage institution; if in proving to you that justice and mercy demand a legal separation from drunkards, we grasp the higher idea that a unity of soul alone constitutes and sanctifies true marriage, and that any law or public sentiment that forces two immortal, high-born souls to live together as husband and wife, unless held there by love, is false to God and humanity; who shall say that the discussion of this question does not lead us legitimately into the consideration of the important subject of divorce?

But why attack the Church ? We do not attack the Church; we defend ourselves merely against its attacks. It is true that the Church and reformers have always been in an antagonistic position from the time of Luther down to our own day, and will continue to be until the devotional and practical types of Christianity shall be united in one harmonious whole. To those who see the philosophy of this position, there seems to be no cause for fearful forebodings or helpless regret. By the light of reason and truth, in good time, all these seeming differences will pass away. I have no special fault to find with that part of humanity that gathers into our churches; to me, human nature seems to manifest itself in very much the same way in the Church and out of it. Go through any community you please—into the nursery, kitchen, the parlor, the places of merchandise, the market-place, and exchange, and who can tell the church member from the outsider ? I see no reason why we should expect more of them than other men. Why, say you, they lay claim to greater holiness; to more rigid creeds; to a belief in a sterner God; to a closer observance of forms. The Bible, with them, is the rule of life, the foundation of faith, and why should we not look to them for patterns of purity, goodness, and truth above all other men ? I deny the assumption. Reformers on all sides claim for themselves a higher position than the Church. Our God is a God of justice, mercy, and truth. Their God sanctions violence, oppression, and wine-bibbing, and winks at gross moral delinquencies. Our Bible commands us to love our enemies; to resist not evil; to break every yoke and let the oppressed go free; and makes a noble life of more importance than a stern faith. Their Bible permits war, slavery, capital punishment, and makes salvation depend on faith and ordinances. In their creed it is a sin to dance, to pick up sticks on the Sabbath day, to go to the theater, or large parties during Lent, to read a notice of any reform meeting from the altar, or permit a woman to speak in the church. In our creed it is a sin to hold a slave; to hang a man on the gallows; to make war on defenseless nations, or to sell rum to a weak brother, and rob the widow and the orphan of a protector and a home. Thus may we write out some of our differences, but from the similarity in the conduct of the human family, it is fair to infer that our differences are more intellectual than spiritual, and the great truths we hear so clearly uttered on all sides, have been incorporated as vital principles into the inner life of but few indeed.

We must not expect the Church to leap *en masse* to a higher position. She sends forth her missionaries of truth one by one. All of our reformers have, in a measure, been developed in the Church, and all our reforms have started there. The advocates and opposers of the reforms of our day, have grown up side by side, partaking of the same ordinances and officiating at the same altars; but one, by applying more fully his Christian principles to life, and pursuing an admitted truth to its legitimate results, has unwittingly found himself in antagonism with his brother.

Belief is not voluntary, and change is the natural result of growth and development. We would fain have all church members sons and daughters of temperance; but if the Church, in her wisdom, has made her platform so broad that wine-bibbers and rum-sellers may repose in ease thereon, we who are always preaching liberality ought to be the last to complain.

DOCUMENT 15 (I: 507): Antoinette Brown, Statement on World Temperance Convention, September 1853

HORACE GREELEY says, in the *Tribune*, September 7, 1853: "This convention has completed three of its four business sessions, and the results may be summed up as follows:
" *First Day*—Crowding a woman off the platform.
" *Second Day*—Gagging her.
" *Third Day*—Voting that she shall stay gagged. Having thus disposed of the main question, we presume the incidentals will be finished this morning."

Antoinette Brown was asked why she went to that Convention, knowing, as she must, that she would be rejected.

"I went there," she said, "to assert a principle—a principle relevant to the circumstances of that convention, and one which would promote *all* good causes and retard *all* bad ones. I went there, as an item of the world, to contend that the sons and daughters of the race, without distinction of sex, sect, class or color, should be recognized as belonging to the world, and I planted my feet upon the simple *rights of a delegate.* I asked no favor as a woman, or in behalf of woman; no favor as a woman advocating temperance; no recognition of the cause of woman above the cause of humanity; the indorsement of no 'ism' and of no measure; but I claimed, in the name of the world, the rights of a delegate in a world's convention.

"Is it asked, Why did you make that issue at that time? I answer, I have made it at all times and in all places, whenever and wherever Providence has given me the opportunity, and in whatever way it could be made to appear most prominent. Last spring, when woman claimed the supremacy—the right to hold all the offices in the Woman's State Temperance Society—I contended, from this platform, for the equality of man; the equal rights of all the members of this society. I have claimed everywhere the equality of humanity in Church and in State; God helping me, I here pledge myself anew to Him, and to you all, to be true everywhere to the central principle—the soul of the Divine commandment, 'Thou shalt love thy neighbor as thyself.' The temperance cause was not injured by our course at that Convention. We went there with thoughtful hearts. Said Wendell Phillips: 'Take courage, and remember that whether you are received or rejected, you are going to make the most effectual speech for temperance, for woman, and humanity that you have ever made in your life.' 'God bless you,' were the fervent words of Mr. Channing, in a moment when there was most need of Divine assistance; and when I stood on the platform for an hour and a half, waiting to be heard, I could read in the faces of men such as these, and in the faces, too, of our opposers, the calm assurance, 'You are making the most effectual speech for temperance, for woman, and humanity, that you have ever made in your life.' I believed it then; I believe it now."

V. END OF AN ERA

FROM THE MID-1850S, the convention phase of woman's rights drew to a close. Its success in proclaiming the individual rights of women might be measured in an ostensibly private event: the "Marriage of Lucy Stone Under Protest." While Thomas Wentworth Higginson performed the ceremony uniting Stone and Henry B. Blackwell, husband and wife issued a personal manifesto:[1]

PROTEST.

While acknowledging our mutual affection by publicly assuming the relationship of husband and wife, yet in justice to ourselves and a great principle, we deem it a duty to declare that this act on our part implies no sanction of, nor promise of voluntary obedience to such of the present laws of marriage, as refuse to recognize the wife as an independent, rational being, while they confer upon the husband an injurious and unnatural superiority, investing him with legal powers which no honorable man would exercise, and which no man should possess. We protest especially against the laws which give to the husband:

1. The custody of the wife's person.

2. The exclusive control and guardianship of their children.

3. The sole ownership of her personal, and use of her real estate, unless previously settled upon her, or placed in the hands of trustees, as in the case of minors, lunatics, and idiots.

4. The absolute right to the product of her industry.

5. Also against laws which give to the widower so much larger and more permanent an interest in the property of his deceased wife, than they give to the widow in that of the deceased husband.

6. Finally, against the whole system by which "the legal existence of the wife is suspended during marriage," so that in most States, she neither has a legal part in the choice of her residence, nor can she make a will, nor sue or be sued in her own name, nor inherit property.

1. Vol. I, 260–61.

> We believe that personal independence and equal human rights can never be forfeited, except for crime; that marriage should be an equal and permanent partnership, and so recognized by law; that until it is so recognized, married partners should provide against the radical injustice of present laws, by every means in their power.
>
> We believe that where domestic difficulties arise, no appeal should be made to legal tribunals under existing laws, but that all difficulties should be submitted to the equitable adjustment of arbitrators mutually chosen.
>
> Thus reverencing law, we enter our protest against rules and customs which are unworthy of the name, since they violate justice, the essence of law.
>
>   (Signed),   HENRY B. BLACKWELL,
> *Worcester Spy*, 1855.   LUCY STONE.

The social implications of this declaration were manifest in the efforts to change state property laws. Women and their allies directed an attack upon the *Commentaries on the Laws of England*, the eighteenth-century work of Sir William Blackstone that had served as a basic treatise on jurisprudence in the American Republic. The legal definition of the married couple as "one person, and that person the husband" had been frequently violated by state measures concerning equity, but woman's rights activists pointed to *femme couvert* as the legal principle circumscribing their social status. As early as 1836 New York State had, for unique reasons, secured some advanced rights for women in other respects, most important the inheritance of property. Similar bills passed in Rhode Island in 1844, Vermont in 1847, and a scattering of states in the next several years. In 1848 New York enacted the most comprehensive bill hitherto, seen retrospectively as the death blow to Blackstone's dictum in the United States.

Nevertheless a sharp battle ensued for women to gain control over their own earnings, the right to guardianship of their children in the event of divorce, and the ultimate goal of suffrage. At Susan B. Anthony's initiative in 1853, sixty female "captains" were appointed to gather signatures on petitions for these demands. Over the winter, some six thousand signatures were collected. Next, Anthony planned a woman's rights convention during a legislative session in Albany, where Stanton delivered a major statement assailing the representatives. She said, in part:

> You may say that the mass of the women of this state do not make the demand. . . . You are mistaken, the mass speak through us. A very large majority of the women of this State support themselves and their children, and many their husbands too. Go into any village you please, of three or four thousand inhabitants, and you will find as many as fifty men or more, whose only business is to discuss religion and politics, as they watch the trains come and go at the depot, or the passage of a canal boat through a lock; to laugh at the vagaries of some drunken brother, or the capers of a monkey dancing to the music of his master's organ. All these are supported by their mothers, wives, or sisters. . . . If to this long list you add the laboring women who are loudly demanding remuneration for their unending toil; those women who teach in our seminaries, academies, and public schools for a miserable pittance; the widows who are taxed without mercy; the unfortunate ones in our work-houses, poor-houses and prisons; who are they that we do not now represent? But a small class of the fashionable butterflies, who, through the short summer days, seek the sunshine and the flowers; but the cool breezes of autumn and the hoary frosts of winter will soon chase all these away; then they, too, will need and ask protection, and through other lips demand in their turn justice and equity at your hands.[2]

A bill was finally passed in 1860, "securing to married women their own inheritance absolutely, to use, will, and dispose of as they see fit; to do business in their name, make contracts, sue and be sued." Not even the partial repeal of these provisions by the New York legislature in 1862 could undo the essential labors: the precedent, once set, was eventually established throughout the country.

The legislative campaign had other benefits. Stanton and Anthony were drawn together and grew individually from the work of the 1850s. When Stanton convinced Anthony of the ballot's centrality to woman's rights, Anthony began her efforts to push Stanton toward fuller utilization of the latter's

2. Vol. I, 604–5.

talents. And while Anthony gained agitational experience from the petition drives, Stanton deepened her theoretical knowledge greatly from the necessity of preparing her address to the New York legislature.

But the clarification of differences within the movement continued apace. By its very nature, the issue of marriage was more complex and divisive than those of women's other civil rights. Whereas the moral belief in the virtue of temperance could easily be reinforced by practical concerns for the drunkard's wife, the belief in the divine nature of marriage was challenged by those who sought its redefinition in legal, rational terms. The divergent conclusions were illustrated by the conservatism of Antoinette Brown Blackwell and the radicalism of Ernestine Rose. The importance of the issue at the 1860 Woman's Rights Convention was underlined by the determination of Wendell Phillips to close debate and bar it from the record, and the resolve of Stanton to keep the subject open. The issue was not merely abstract, as leading figures acted on their own conclusions. Stone's marriage under protest was a gesture of equality between partners but certainly not subversive of the institution itself. Susan B. Anthony, on the other hand, was to take a more daring position by aiding the escape of a mother and child from a husband who had previously committed the woman to an insane asylum. To Anthony and Stanton, such fugitive women were akin to fugitive slaves. To allies like Phillips, Anthony's actions were a tactical zealotry which might threaten the entire reform movement. The issues were pushed aside during the political emergency of the Civil War and Reconstruction, but they were to reemerge to divide activists again afterward.

By 1860, the struggles of woman's rights had established the principle of woman as an individual. Susan B. Anthony, Ernestine Rose, and Elizabeth Jones could roll off with pride the names of women who had attained new heights of accomplishment in literature and the professions. But pressed to their conclusion, the rights of woman as an individual challenged the legal sanctity of the family, threatened to reform it drastically or destroy it. In part because "personal" issues of marriage and morality could not be resolved, suffrage returned to the spotlight after the property rights agitation had faded. Only suffrage could allow women to make the necessary decisions for themselves, whatever those decisions might be. Not even the Civil War could dim the clarity of this vision.

DOCUMENT 16 (I: 632–33): Lucy Stone, Address to Seventh National Woman's Rights Convention, New York City, November 25-26, 1856

LUCY STONE, on taking the chair, said : I am sure that all present will agree with me that this is a day of congratulation. It is our Seventh Annual National Woman's Rights Convention. Our first effort was made in a small room in Boston, where a few women were gathered, who had learned woman's rights by woman's wrongs. There had been only one meeting in Ohio, and two in New York. The laws were yet against us, custom was against us, prejudice was against us, and more than all, women were against us. We were strong only "in the might of our right"—and, now, when this seventh year has brought us together again, we can say as did a laborer in the Republican party, though all is not gained, "we are without a wound in our faith, without a wound in our hope, and stronger than when we began." Never before has any reformatory movement gained so much in so short a time. When we began, the statute books were covered with laws against women, which an eminent jurist (Judge Walker) said would be a disgrace to the statute books of any heathen nation.

Now almost every Northern State has more or less modified its laws. The Legislature of Maine, after having granted nearly all other property rights to wives, found a bill before it asking that a wife should be entitled to what she earns, but a certain member grew fearful that wives would bring in bills for their daily service, and, by an eloquent appeal to pockets, the measure was lost for the time, but that which has secured other rights will secure this. In Massachusetts, by the old laws, a wife owned nothing but the fee simple in her real estate. And even for that, she could not make a will without the written endorsement of her husband, permitting her to do so. Two years ago the law was so changed that she now holds the absolute right to her entire property, earnings included. Vermont, New Hampshire, and Rhode Island have also very much amended their statutes. New York, the proud Empire State, has, by the direct effort of this movement, secured to wives every property right except earnings. During two years a bill has been before the Legislature, which provides that if a husband be a drunkard, a profligate, or has abandoned his wife, she may have a right to her own earnings. It has not passed. Two hundred years hence that bill will be quoted as a proof of the barbarism of the times ; now it is a proof of progress.

Ohio, Illinois, and Indiana have also very materially modified their laws. And Wisconsin—God bless these young States—has granted almost all that has been asked except the right of suffrage. And even this, Senator Sholes, in an able minority report on the subject, said, "is only a question of time, and as sure to triumph as God is just." It proposed that the Convention which meets in two years to amend the Constitution of the State should consider the subject. In Michigan, too, it has been moved that women should have a right to their own babies, which none of you, ladies, have here in New York. The motion caused much discussion in the Legislature, and it would probably have been carried had not a disciple of Brigham Young's, a Mormon

157

member, defeated the bill. In Nebraska everything is bright for our cause. Mrs. Bloomer is there, and she has circulated petitions, claiming for women the right to vote. A bill to that effect passed the House of Representatives, and was lost in the Senate, only because of the too early closing of the session. That act of justice to woman would be gained in Nebraska first, and scores of women would go there that they might be made citizens, and be no longer subjects.

In addition to these great legal changes, achieved so directly by this reform, we find also that women have entered upon many new and more remunerative industrial pursuits; thus being enabled to save themselves from the bitterness of dependent positions, or from lives of infamy. Our demand that Harvard and Yale Colleges should admit women, though not yielded, only waits for a little more time. And while they wait, numerous petty "female colleges" have sprung into being, indicative of the justice of our claim that a college education should be granted to women. Not one of these female colleges (which are all second or third rate, and their whole course of study only about equal to what completes the sophomore year in our best colleges) meets the demand of the age, and so will eventually perish. Oberlin and Antioch Colleges in Ohio, and Lima College in New York, admit women on terms nearly equal with men.

In England, too, the claims of women are making progress. The most influential papers in London have urged the propriety of women physicians. Also a petition was sent to Parliament last year, signed by the Brownings, the Howitts, Harriet Martineau, Mrs. Gaskell, and Mrs. Jameson, asking for just such rights as we claim here. It was presented by Lord Brougham, and was respectfully received by Parliament. The ballot has not yet been yielded; but it can not be far off when, as in the last Presidential contest, women were urged to attend political meetings, and a woman's name was made one of the rallying cries of the party of progress. The enthusiasm which everywhere greeted the name of Jessie† was so far a recognition of woman's right to participate in politics. Encouraged by the success of these seven years of effort, let us continue with unfailing fidelity to labor for the practical recognition of the great truth, that all human rights inhere in each human being. We welcome to this platform men and women irrespective of creed, country, or color; those who dissent from us as freely as those who agree with us.

DOCUMENT 17 (I: 689–99): Susan B. Anthony,
Ernestine L. Rose, and Elizabeth Jones, Addresses to the
Tenth National Woman's Rights Convention, New York
City, May 10-11, 1860

Susan B. Anthony was then introduced, and read the following
report:

For our encouragement in laboring for the elevation of woman, it is well ever
and anon to review the advancing steps. Each year we hail with pleasure new
accessions to our faith. Strong words of cheer have come to us on every
breeze. Brave men and true, from the higher walks of literature and art, from
the bar, the bench, the pulpit, and legislative halls, are ready now to help
woman wherever she claims to stand. The Press, too, has changed its tone.
Instead of ridicule, we now have grave debate. And still more substantial
praises of gold and silver have come to us. A gift of $5,000 from unknown
hands; a rich legacy from the coffers of a Boston merchant prince—the late
Charles F. Hovey; and, but a few days ago, $400,000 from Mr. Vassar, of
Poughkeepsie, to found a college for girls, equal in all respects to Yale and
Harvard.

We had in New York a legislative act passed at the last session, securing to
married women their rights to their earnings and their children. Other States
have taken onward steps. And, from what is being done on all sides, we have
reason to believe that, as the Northern States shall one by one remodel their
Constitutions, the right of suffrage will be granted to women. Six years hence
New York proposes to revise her Constitution. These should be years of effort
with all those who believe that it is the right and the duty of every citizen of a
State to have a voice in the laws that govern them.

Woman is being so educated that she will feel herself capable of assuming
grave responsibilities as lawgiver and administrator. She is crowding into

higher avocations and new branches of industry. She already occupies the highest places in literature and art. The more liberal lyceums are open to her, and she is herself the subject of the most popular lectures now before the public. The young women of our academies and high schools are asserting their right to the discipline of declamation and discussion, and the departments of science and mathematics. Pewholders, of the most orthodox sects, are taking their right to a voice in the government of the church, and in the face of priests, crying "let your women keep silence in the churches," yes, at the very horns of the altar, calmly, deliberately, and persistently casting their votes in the choice of church officers and pastors.* Mass-meetings to sympathize with the "strikers" of Massachusetts are being called in this metropolis by women. Women are ordained ministers, and licensed physicians. Elizabeth Blackwell has founded a hospital in this city, where she proposes a thorough medical education, both theoretical and practical, for young women. And this Institute in which we are now assembled, with its school of design, its library and reading-room, where the arts and sciences are freely taught to women, and this hall, so cheerfully granted to our Convention, shows the magnanimity of its founder, Peter Cooper. All these are the results of our twenty years of agitation. And it matters not to us, though the men and the women who echo back our thought do fail to recognize the source of power, and while they rejoice in each onward step achieved in the face of ridicule and persecution, ostracise those who have done the work. Who of our literary women has yet ventured one word of praise or recognition of the heroic enunciators of the great idea of woman's equality—of Mary Woolstonecraft, Frances Wright, Ernestine L. Rose, Lucretia Mott, Elizabeth Cady Stanton? It matters not to those who live for the race, and not for self alone, who has the praise, so that justice be done to woman in Church, in State, and at the fireside—an equal everywhere with man—they will not complain, though even *The New York Observer* itself does claim to have done for them the work.

During the past six years this State has been thoroughly canvassed, and every county that has been visited by our lecturers and tracts has rolled up

---

* In the Scotch Presbyterian Church at Johnstown, N. Y., there was great excitement at one time on the question of temperance, the pastor being a very active friend to that movement. The opposition were determined to get rid of him, and called a church meeting for that purpose. To the surprise of the leading men of the congregation, the women came in force, armed with ballots, to defeat their proposed measures. When the time came to vote, according to arrangement, my mother headed the line marching up to the altar, where stood the deacon, hat in hand, to receive the ballots. As soon as he saw the women coming, he retreated behind the railing in the altar, closing the little door after him, which the women deliberately opened, and soon filled the space, completely surrounding *the inspector of election*, and, whichever way he turned, the ballots were thrown into the hat; and, when all had voted, my mother put her hand into the hat and stirred them up with the men's votes, so that it would be impossible to separate them. The pastor, representing the interests of temperance, had a large majority for his retention. But the men declared the election void because of the illegal voting, and, barricading the women out, with closed doors, voted their own measures the next day. Rev. Jeremiah Wood presided on the occasion, and whilst the women were contending for their rights under the very shadow of the altar, he recited various Scriptural texts on woman's sphere, to which these rebellious ones paid not the slightest attention. One dignified Scotch matron, looking him steadily in the face, indignant at the behavior of the men, said with sternness and emphasis: "I protest against such high-handed proceedings." The result of this outbreak, was a decree by the Judicature of the Church, "that the women of the congregation should have the right to vote in all business matters," which they have most judiciously done ever since.   E. C. S.

petitions by the hundreds and thousands, asking for woman's right to vote and hold office—her right to her person, her wages, her children, and her home. Again and again have we held Conventions at the capital, and addressed our Legislature, demanding the exercise of all our rights as citizens of the Empire State. During the past year, we have had six women * lecturing in New York for several months each. Conventions have been held in forty counties, one or more lectures delivered in one hundred and fifty towns and villages, our petitions circulated, and our tracts and documents sold and gratuitously distributed throughout the entire length and breadth of the State.

A State Convention was held at Albany early in February. Large numbers of the members of the Legislature listened respectfully and attentively to the discussions of its several sessions, and expressed themselves converts to the claims for woman. The bills for woman's right to her property, her earnings, and the guardianship of her children passed both branches of the Legislature with scarce a dissenting voice, and received the prompt signature of the Governor.

Our Legislature passed yet another bill that brings great relief to a large class of women. It was called the Boarding-House Bill. It provides that the keepers of private boarding-houses shall have the right of lien on the property of boarders, precisely the same as do hotel-keepers. We closed our work by a joint hearing before the Committees of the Judiciary at the Capitol on the 19th of March. Elizabeth Cady Stanton addressed them. The Assembly Chamber was densely packed, and she was listened to with marked attention and respect. The Judiciary Committees of neither House reported on our petition for the right of suffrage, though the Chairman, with a large minority of the House Committee and a majority of the Senate Committee, favored the claim. The Hon. A. J. Colvin, of the Senate Committee, in a letter to me, says:

"The subject was presented at so late a day as to preclude action. While a majority of the Senate Committee I think were favorable, a majority of the House Committee, so far as I could learn, were opposed. So many progressive measures had passed both Houses that I felt apprehensive we might perhaps be running too great a risk by urging this question of justice and reform at this session. I did not therefore press it. Should I remain in the Senate, I may take occasion at an early day in the next session to bring up the subject and present my views at length. The more reflection I give, the more my mind becomes convinced that in a Republican Government, we have no right to deny to woman the privileges she claims. Besides, the moral element which those privileges would bring into existence would, in my judgment, have a powerful influence in perpetuating our form of government. It may be deemed best, at the next session, to urge an early Constitutional Convention. In case one should be called, your friends should be prepared to meet the emergency. Is the public mind sufficiently enlightened to accept a constitution recognizing the right of women to vote and hold office? You should consider this."

The entire expense of the New York State work during the past year is

* Frances D. Gage, Hannah Tracy Cutler, J. Elizabeth Jones, Antoinette Brown Blackwell, Lucy N. Colman, and Susan B. Anthony.

nearly four thousand dollars. The present year we propose to expend our funds and efforts mostly in Ohio, to obtain, if possible, for the women of that State, the liberal laws we have secured for ourselves. Ohio, too, is soon to revise her Constitution, and we trust she will not be far behind New York in recognizing the full equality of woman. We who have grasped the idea of woman's destiny, her power and influence, the trinity of her existence as woman, wife, and mother, can most earnestly work for her elevation to that high position that it is the will of God she should ever fill. Though we have not yet realized the fullness of our hopes, let us rest in the belief that in all these years of struggle, no earnest thought, or word, or prayer has been breathed in vain. The influence has gone forth, the great ocean has been moved, and those who watch, e'en now may see the mighty waves of truth slowly swelling on the shores of time.

> "One accent of the Holy Ghost,
> A heedless word hath never lost."

ERNESTINE L. ROSE being introduced, said: Frances Wright was the first woman in this country who spoke on the equality of the sexes. She had indeed a hard task before her. The elements were entirely unprepared. She had to break up the time-hardened soil of conservatism, and her reward was sure—the same reward that is always bestowed upon those who are in the vanguard of any great movement. She was subjected to public odium, slander, and persecution. But these were not the only things that she received. Oh, she had her reward !—that reward of which no enemies could deprive her, which no slanders could make less precious—the eternal reward of knowing that she had done her duty; the reward springing from the consciousness of right, of endeavoring to benefit unborn generations. How delightful to see the molding of the minds around you, the infusing of your thoughts and aspirations into others, until one by one they stand by your side, without knowing how they came there ! That reward she had. It has been her glory, it is the glory of her memory; and the time will come when society will have outgrown its old prejudices, and stepped with one foot, at least, upon the elevated platform on which she took her position. But owing to the fact that the elements were unprepared, she naturally could not succeed to any great extent.

After her, in 1837, the subject of woman's rights was again taken hold of—aye, taken hold of by woman; and the soil having been already somewhat prepared, she began to sow the seeds for the future growth, the fruits of which we now begin to enjoy. Petitions were circulated and sent to our Legislature, and who can tell the hardships that then met those who undertook that great work ! I went from house to house with a petition for signatures simply asking our Legislature to allow married women to hold real estate in their own name. What did I meet with ? Why, the very name exposed one to ridicule, if not to worse treatment. The women said: "We have rights enough; we want no more"; and the men, as a matter of course, echoed it, and said: "You have rights enough; nay, you have too many already." (Laughter). But by perseverance in sending petitions to the Legislature, and, at the same time, enlightening the public mind on the subject, we at last accomplished our purpose. We had to adopt the method which physicians sometimes use, when they are called to a patient who is so hopelessly sick that he is unconscious of his pain and suffering. We had to describe to women their own position, to explain to them the burdens that rested so heavily upon them, and through these means, as a wholesome irritant, we roused public opinion on the subject, and through public opinion, we acted upon the Legislature, and in 1848–'49, they gave us the great boon for which we asked, by enacting that a woman who possessed property previous to marriage, or obtained it after marriage, should be allowed to hold it in her own name. Thus far, thus good; but it was only a beginning, and we went on. In 1848 we had the first Woman's Rights Convention, and then some of our papers thought it only a very small affair, called together by a few "strong-minded women," and would pass away like a nine-days' wonder. They little knew woman! They little knew that if woman takes anything earnestly in her hands, she will not lay it aside unaccomplished. (Applause). We have continued our Conventions ever since. A few years ago, when we sent a petition to our Legislature, we obtained, with but very little effort, upward of thirteen thousand signatures. What a contrast between this number and the five signatures attached to the first petition, in 1837! Since then, we might have had hundreds of thousands of signatures, but it is no longer necessary. Public opinion is too well known to require a long array of names.

We have been often asked, "What is the use of Conventions? Why talk? Why not go to work?" Just as if the thought did not precede the act! Those who act without previously thinking, are not good for much. Thought is first required, then the expression of it, and that leads to action; and action based upon thought never needs to be reversed; it is lasting and profitable, and produces the desired effect. I know that there are many who take advantage of this movement, and then say: "You are doing nothing; only talking." Yes, doing nothing! We have only broken up the ground and sowed the seed; they are reaping the benefit, and yet they tell us we have done nothing! Mrs. Swisshelm, who has proclaimed herself to be "no woman's rights woman," has accepted a position as Inspector of logs and lumber. (Laughter). Well, I have no objection to her having that avocation, if she have a taste and capacity for it—far from it. But she has accepted still more, and I doubt not with a great deal more zest and satisfaction—the five hundred dollars salary; and I hope she will enjoy it. Then, having accepted both the office and the salary, she folds her arms, and says: "I am none of your strong-minded women; I don't go for woman's rights." Well, she is still welcome to it. I have not the slightest objection that those who proclaim themselves not strong-minded, should still reap the benefit of a strong mind (applause and laughter); it is for them we work. So there are some ladies who think a great deal can be done in the Legislature without petitions, without conventions, without lectures, without public claim, in fact, without anything, but a little lobbying. Well, if they have a taste for it, they are welcome to engage in it; I have not the slightest objection. Yes, I have. I, as a woman, being conscious of the evil that is done by these lobby loafers in our Legislature and in the halls of Congress, object to it. (Loud cheers). I will wait five years longer to have a right given to me legitimately, from a sense of justice, rather than buy it in an underhand way by lobbying. Whatever my sentiments may be, good bad, or indifferent, I express them, and they are known. Nevertheless, if any desire it, let them do that work. But what has induced them, what has enabled them to do that work ? The Woman's Rights movement, although they are afraid or ashamed even of the name "woman's rights."

You have been told, and much more might be said on the subject, that already the Woman's Rights platform has upon it lawyers, ministers, and statesmen—men who are among the highest in the nation. I need not mention Wm. Lloyd Garrison, or Wendell Phillips; but there are others, those even who are afraid of the name of reformer, who have stood upon our platform. Brady ! Who would ever have expected it ? Chapin! Beecher ! Think of it for a moment ! A minister advocating the rights of woman, even her right at the ballot-box ! What has done it ? Our agitation has purified the atmosphere, and enabled them to see the injustice that is done to woman.

Mrs. ELIZABETH JONES, of Ohio, was the next speaker. She said: I wish to preface my remarks with this resolution:

Resolved, That woman's sphere can not be bounded. Its prescribed orbit is the largest place that in her highest development she can fill. The laws of mind are as immutable as are those of the planetary world, and the true woman must ever revolve around the great moral sun of light and truth.

As a general proposition, we say that capacity determines the true sphere of action, and indicates the kind of labor to be performed. I often hear women discussing this subject, much more in earnest than in jest, though they profess to be simply amusing themselves. One says: "If I were a man, I should be a mechanic"; another says: "I should be a merchant." One says: "I am sure I should be rich"; another, in the excess of her humor, thinks she should be distinguished. Why do women talk thus ? Because one feels that she has mechanical genius; the power to construct, to perfect. Another understands the secrets of trade, and would like to incur the heavy responsibilities it involves. A third is conscious that she was born a financier; while a fourth has an intuitive perception of the elements of success.

Many women are beginning to judge for themselves the proper sphere of action, and are not only jesting about what they should do under other circumstances, but are already entering upon such paths as their taste and capacity indicate. Some will doubtless make mistakes, which experience will rectify, and others will perhaps persist in striving to do that which it will be very evident they have no ability to perform. This is the case with men who have had freedom in every sphere. Look at the American pulpit, for instance. Go through the country, and listen to those who claim to be the messengers of God, and if you do not say that many are destitute of capacity to fill the sphere they have chosen, we shall regard it as an act of obedience on your part to the command which says: "Judge not, lest ye be judged." (Laughter). Let adaptation be the rule for pulpit occupancy, and while it would eject some who are now no honor to the station, and no benefit to the people, it would open the place to many an Anna and Miriam and Deborah to fulfill the mission which God has.clearly indicated by the talents He has bestowed.

The world says now, man is God's minister, and woman is not fit to call sinners to repentance; but let it say: "Those who have faith in the principles of eternal right, and have power to give it utterance; those who have the clearest perceptions of moral truth; those who understand the wants of the people, are the proper persons, whether they be men or women, to dispense to the needy multitude the bread of life." This would elevate the standard of pulpit qualifications, and bring into the field a far greater amount of talent to choose from, and thus would the intellectual and spiritual needs of the people be more fully answered. What is true of this profession will apply with equal force to others. Should I be told that the American bar needs no more talent, I would reply that it needs decency, and a well-founded self-respect. When you enter a court-room, and listen to a cross-examination of a delicate nature, one where woman is concerned, and she would rather die a hundred deaths, if she could, than to have the case dragged before the public, you will see it treated in the coarsest way, as if her holiest affections and her most sacred functions were fitting themes for brutish men to jeer at. And even in the most ordinary cases, gentlemen who would spurn the imputation of incivility in social life, will so browbeat and badger a witness, that the most disgusting bear-baiting would become by comparison a refined amusement. If the young aspirants for legal honors should meet among the advocates and judges sensible, dignified, and highly cultivated women, they would, if I am not much mistaken, get the benefit of certain lessons, upon manners and morals, that it is essential for all young men to learn. (Applause). It appears to me that by association of men and women in this profession, the bar might be purged of this indecorum, and possess the humanity, the wisdom, and the dignity that should ever characterize a Court of Justice.

You need not tell me that the profession would be overstocked, if women should enter it, for, like men, they must stand on their merits. Let there be no proscription on account of sex. Let talent be brought fairly into competition, and although many a young man, as well as young woman, would sit down forever briefless, having neither the capacity nor the acquirements to bring or retain clients, yet their loss would be for the public good, and for the honor and respectability of the profession. Let the talents of women be fully developed, and no man will lose any place that he is qualified to fill in consequence, and no woman will obtain that place who has not peculiar fitness. All these matters will find their own level, ultimately. I can point you to localities now where the people prefer women for teachers. A Union School in Northern Ohio, which is made up of ten departments, employs women for teachers, and a woman as superintendent of the whole. The people reason this way: We prefer women, because they bring us the best talent. Not that they have better talents than men, but with the latter, teaching is generally a stepping-stone to a profession. Woman accepts it as her highest post, and brings her best energies. With man, it is often a subordinate interest, and his best talents will be exercised upon what he regards as something higher and better. As in this, so in other things. The time will come when talent or capacity will govern the choice and not sex. It is so now in Art, to a great extent. I think there is not much known of sex there. The world does not care who wrote "Aurora Leigh." It does not recognize it as the production of a woman, but as the work of genius. Let the artists say what they please, the world does not care who chisels Zenobia, so that Zenobia be well chiseled. It does not care whether Landseer or Rosa Bonheur paints animals, so that animals are well painted. No one says this or that is well done for a woman, but he says, this is the work of an artist, that has no merit; not because a woman did it, not because a man did it, but because the author was destitute of capacity to embody the idea.

Again, read the little village newspapers, got out by little editors, and you will find, in many cases, an utter want of ability to fill the place that has been chosen. I hope young women will not make such mistakes as these young men have done, who might have been supposed to know something, if they had only kept still. (Laughter). If these papers, to which I have referred, were all in the hands of women, and so destitute of editorial pith and point as they now are, I should counsel against any further efforts for the elevation of the sex, believing the case to be hopeless. (Applause). If I mistake not, women have a peculiar fitness for trade. Mrs. Dall says, in her second lecture, that on the Island of Nantucket, women have engaged in commerce very successfully. They did it in the war, and afterward, when destitution drove the men to the whale fisheries, and again when they went to California. They have had much experience; and Eliza Barney tells of seventy women who engaged in trade, and retired with a competence, and besides brought up and educated large families of children. She says, also, that failures were very uncommon when women managed the business, and some of the largest and safest fortunes in Boston were founded by women. Whenever, therefore, one shows any ability for trade, that is her license for engaging in it—a license granted under the higher law, and therefore valid. I went into a bonnet store the other day, and saw a man-milliner holding up a bonnet on his soft white hand to a lady customer, and expatiating upon the beauties of the article with an earnestness, if not the eloquence, of an orator. She tried it on, and he went into ecstacies. (Laughter). It was so becoming! It was so charming! He complimented her, and he complimented the bonnet, and had she not been a strong-minded woman, I do not know how much of the flattery she would have taken for truth. I thought that man was out of his sphere; and not only that, but he had crowded some woman out of her appropriate place, out of the realm of taste and fashion. (Applause). When I passed out on the street, the harsh, discordant tone of a fish-woman fell upon my ear. I saw that she bore a heavy tub upon her head, evidently seeking by this branch of merchandise to procure a living for herself and family. So few were the avenues open to her, as she thought, and so much had men monopolized the places she could fill, that she was compelled to carry fish on her head, until she could raise money enough to procure a better conveyance.

Again, I see young men selling artificial flowers, and laces and embroidery, crinolines and balmorals, and I think to myself they had better be out digging coal or making brick. When I go back home to the West, I could take a car-load with me, and set them to work, and I would greatly benefit their condition, while the places they vacate here might be filled by the girls who are now starving in your garrets. (Applause). At a shoe-store, instead of finding a sprightly miss, to select and fit the ladies gaiters, you often see a strong, healthy man, kneeling before the customer with a gallantry that would be admirable in a drawing-room, and worth infinitely more than the price of the article he is selling; and he fusses over the gaiters and over the lady's foot, until you wonder if she is not tempted to propel him into a more appropriate sphere. (Laughter). Whatever possessed men to imagine that God designed them to fit ladies' gaiters, is more than I can imagine. (Applause). I am unable to realize how they obtained the revelation that for a woman to thus officiate would take her out of her appropriate sphere. Shall I be held to my principles here, and told that these men succeed in business, and success being the test of sphere, therefore they are in their place? It remains to be proved that they have succeeded. A man may jump Jim Crow from morning till night, or make a fool of himself in any other way, and succeed admirably in pleasing auditors and gathering pennies; but when you take into consideration his high and heavenly origin, and the noble purposes for which he was made, you can hardly call it a success. Neither should I think a woman was in suitable business, even if it were ever so lucrative and well done, unless that business developed her talents; made her stronger, more self-reliant, and better fitted her for life and its duties. These stores would be a good discipline for young girls, but not for men.

This whole question lies in a small compass. Our reform would leave woman just where God placed her—a moral, accountable being, endowed with talents whose scope and character indicate the work she is to do; and who is responsible primarily to her Creator for the use she makes of those talents. He says to every man and to every woman, Go work in my vineyard! That vineyard I understand to be the world, embracing all the varied responsibilities of life. Whether man shall pursue science, literature, or art, whether he shall engage in agriculture, manufactures, or mechanics, is for *him* to determine, and whether woman shall engage in any of these things is for *her* to determine. Nothing but an internal consciousness of power to perform certain work, and that it will be for her own good, can aid her in her choice. If a woman can write vigorous verse, then let her write verse. If she can build ships, then let her be a ship-builder. I know no reason why. If she can keep house, and that takes as much brains as any other occupation, let her be a housekeeper. They tell us that "eternal vigilance is the price of liberty"; eternal vigilance is the price of a well-ordered home, and every woman before me knows it. (Applause). I know that the conservative, in his fear, says, Surely you would not have woman till the soil, sail the seas, run up the rigging of a ship like a monkey (I use the language of one of your most distinguished men), go to war, engage in political brawls ? No ! I would not have her do anything. She must be her own judge. In relation to tilling the soil, the last census of the United Kingdom reports 128,418 women employed in agriculture. Examples are by no means rare where a woman carries on a farm which her deceased husband has left, and I have seen much skill evinced in the management. "In Media, Pa., two girls named Miller carry on a farm of 300 acres, raising hay and grain, hiring labor, but working mostly themselves." I have been on a farm in your own State where I saw, not Tennyson's six mighty daughters of the plow, but I saw three* who plowed, and not only that, but they plowed well. Doubtless, some of our fastidious young ladies would be greatly shocked at such an exhibition, and I must acknowledge that it was to me a novel sight; but the more I considered it, the more I thought that I would rather see a young woman holding the plow, than to see her leading such an aimless, silly life as many a young lady leads. I would rather see a young woman holding the plow, than to see her decked out in her finery, and sitting idle in the parlor, waiting for an offer of marriage. (Applause). I hope women will not copy the vices of men. I hope they will not go to war; I wish men would not. I hope they will not be contentious politicians; I am sorry that men are. I hope they will not regard their freedom as a license to do wrong; I am ashamed to acknowledge that men do. But we need not fear. We may safely trust the judgment of those who tell us that politics and morals, and every department into which woman may enter, will be elevated and re-fined by her influence.

So far as navigation is concerned, I think many women would not be attracted to that life. There might be now and then a Betsy Miller, who could walk the quarter-deck in a gale, and that certainly would indicate constitutional ability to become a sailor. I do not suppose so much violence would be done to her nature by navigating the seas, as by helping a drunken husband to navigate the streets habitually. (Applause). In relation to running up the rigging like a monkey, or in regard to any other monkey performance, I do not believe that women will ever enter into competition with men in these things, because the latter have shown such remarkable aptitude for that business. (Laughter and applause). But after all that may be said on this subject, we fail to reach one class in the community who have spare time, spare energies, abundance of power for work. I mean young ladies of wealth and rank. The world shows a degree of toleration now toward any young woman who from necessity has engaged in any industrial avocation to which women have not heretofore applied themselves. But there is no such toleration for the rich. Many of these are now striving to kill time with fancy-work and fiction, with flirtation and flaunting. Some are destitute of aspiration for anything better. These could be moved only by some convulsion in the social system, like the earthquake, or like the volcano that opens the ground at our feet and shows us our danger. But there are others whose convictions lead them to desire something better; who feel that they are living to no purpose; who know that their own powers, good as any God ever created, are lying in inglorious repose. Some of the advocates

---

* Mrs. Roberts and her daughters in Niagara County.

of our cause have said that for these there is no profession but marriage. If they are not literary, artistic, or philanthropic, what can they do? They are held by a cable, made up of home influence, of fashion, and of perverted Scripture, which binds them down to an insipid existence. Hence, they suppress all desire for a fuller, larger life; they smile graciously upon their fetters; they profess to be the happiest of all happy women, and thus they glide along through the thoroughfares of society with a lying tongue and an aching heart.

I wish these had enough vitality of soul and enough energy of character to rise superior to the circumstances around them, and make some approach to their own ideal. I know this is asking them to martyrize themselves. But could they see the beauty and the glory that will invest the future woman, when she shall have her proper place among the children of the Father; when she shall infuse her love, her moral perceptions, her sense of justice, into the ethics and governments of the earth; when she shall be united to man in a Divine harmony, and her children shall go forth to bless all coming generations, they would regard martyrdom but dust in the balance compared with such blessing. And when the world shall see the moral grandeur, the sublime position of a race redeemed by the sanctifying influences of this Divine harmony, it will weave for them a brighter chaplet than it has ever woven for any of its martyrs who have suffered at the stake. (Loud applause).

DOCUMENT 18 (I: 716–35): Debates on Marriage and Divorce, Tenth National Woman's Rights Convention, New York City, May 10-11, 1860

Elizabeth Cady Stanton then presented a series of resolutions,* in support of which she addressed the Convention as follows:

Mrs. PRESIDENT:—In our common law, in our whole system of jurisprudence, we find man's highest idea of right. The object of law is to secure justice. But

---

* 1. *Resolved*, That, in the language (slightly varied) of John Milton, "Those who marry intend as little to conspire their own ruin, as those who swear allegiance, and as a whole people is to an ill government, so is one man or woman to an ill marriage. If a whole people, against any authority, covenant, or statute, may, by the sovereign edict of charity, save not only their lives, but honest liberties, from unworthy bondage, as well may a married party, against any private covenant, which he or she never entered, to his or her mischief, be redeemed from unsupportable disturbances, to honest peace and just contentment."

2. *Resolved*, That all men are created equal, and all women, in their natural rights, are the equals of men, and endowed by their Creator with the same inalienable right to the pursuit of happiness.

3. *Resolved*, That any constitution, compact, or covenant between human beings, that failed to produce or promote human happiness, could not, in the nature of things, be of any force or authority; and it would be not only a right, but a duty, to abolish it.

4. *Resolved*, That though marriage be in itself divinely founded, and is fortified as an institution by innumerable analogies in the whole kingdom of universal nature, still, a true marriage is only known by its results; and, like the fountain, if pure, will reveal only pure manifestations. Nor need it ever be said, "What God hath joined together, let no man put asunder," for man could not put it asunder; nor can he any more unite what God and nature have not joined together. ·

5. *Resolved*, That of all insulting mockeries of heavenly truth and holy law, none can be greater than that physical impotency is cause sufficient for divorce, while no amount of mental or moral or spiritual imbecility is ever to be pleaded in support of such a demand.

6. *Resolved*, That such a law was worthy those dark periods when marriage was held by the greatest doctors and priests of the Church to be a work of the flesh only, and

170

inasmuch as fallible man is the maker and administrator of law, we must look for many and gross blunders in the application of its general principles to individual cases.

The science of theology, of civil, political, moral, and social life, all teach the common idea, that man ever has been, and ever must be, sacrificed to the highest good of society; the one to the many—the poor to the rich—the weak to the powerful—and all to the institutions of his own creation. Look, what thunderbolts of power man has forged in the ages for his own destruction!—at the organizations to enslave himself! And through those times of darkness, those generations of superstition, behold all along the relics of his power and skill, that stand like mile-stones, here and there, to show how far back man was great and glorious! Who can stand in those vast cathedrals of the old world, as the deep-toned organ reverberates from arch to arch, and not feel the grandeur of humanity? These are the workmanship of him, beneath whose stately dome the architect himself now bows in fear and doubt, knows not himself, and knows not God—a mere slave to symbols—and with holy water signs the Cross, whilst He who died thereon declared man God.

I repudiate the popular idea of man's degradation and total depravity. I place man above all governments, all institutions—ecclesiastical and civil—all constitutions and laws. (Applause). It is a mistaken idea, that the same law that oppresses the individual can promote the highest good of society. The best interests of a community never can require the sacrifice of one innocent being—of one sacred right. In the settlement, then, of any question, we must simply consider the highest good of the individual. It is the inalienable right of all to be happy. It is the highest duty of all to seek those conditions in life, those surroundings, which may develop what is noblest and best, remembering that the lessons of these passing hours are not for time alone, but for the ages of eternity. They tell us, in that future home—the heavenly paradise—that the human family shall be sifted out, and the good and pure shall dwell together

---

almost, if not altogether, a defilement; denied wholly to the clergy, and a second time, forbidden to all.

7. *Resolved*, That an unfortunate or ill-assorted marriage is ever a calamity, but not ever, perhaps never, a crime—and when society or government, by its laws or customs, compels its continuance, always to the grief of one of the parties, and the actual loss and damage of both, it usurps an authority never delegated to man, nor exercised by God himself.

8. *Resolved*, That observation and experience daily show how incompetent are men, as individuals, or as governments, to select partners in business, teachers for their children, ministers of their religion, or makers, adjudicators, or administrators of their laws; and as the same weakness and blindness must attend in the selection of matrimonial partners, the dictates of humanity and common sense alike show that the latter and most important contract should no more be perpetual than either or all of the former.

9. *Resolved*, That children born in these unhappy and unhallowed connections are, in the most solemn sense, of unlawful birth—the fruit of lust, but not of love—and so not of God, divinely descended, but from beneath, whence proceed all manner of evil and uncleanliness.

10. *Resolved*, That next to the calamity of such a birth to the child, is the misfortune of being trained in the atmosphere of a household where love is not the law, but where discord and bitterness abound; stamping their demoniac features on the moral nature, with all their odious peculiarities—thus continuing the race in a weakness and depravity that must be a sure precursor of its ruin, as a just penalty of long-violated law.

in peace.   If that be the heavenly order, is it not our duty to render earth as near like heaven as we may ?

For years, there has been before the Legislature of this State a variety of bills, asking for divorce in cases of drunkenness, insanity, desertion, cruel and brutal treatment, endangering life.   My attention was called to this question very early in life, by the sufferings of a friend of my girlhood, a victim of one of those unfortunate unions, called marriage.   What my great love for that young girl, and my holy intuitions, then decided to be right, has not been changed by years of experience, observation, and reason.   I have pondered well these things in my heart, and ever felt the deepest interest in all that has been written and said upon the subject, and the most profound respect and loving sympathy for those heroic women, who, in the face of law and public sentiment, have dared to sunder the unholy ties of a joyless, loveless union.

If marriage is a human institution, about which man may legislate, it seems but just that he should treat this branch of his legislation with the same common-sense that he applies to all others.   If it is a mere legal contract, then should it be subject to the restraints and privileges of all other contracts.   A contract, to be valid in law, must be formed between parties of mature age, with an honest intention in said parties to do what they agree.   The least concealment, fraud, or deception, if proved, annuls the contract.   A boy can not contract for an acre of land, or a horse, until he is twenty-one, but he may contract for a wife at fourteen.   If a man sell a horse, and the purchaser find in him great incompatibility of temper—a disposition to stand still when the owner is in haste to go—the sale is null and void, and the man and his horse part company.   But in marriage, no matter how much fraud and deception are practiced, nor how cruelly one or both parties have been misled ; no matter how young, inexperienced,or thoughtless the parties, nor how unequal their condition and position in life, the contract can not be annulled.   Think of a husband telling a young and trusting girl, but one short month his wife,that he married her for her money; that those letters so precious to her, that she had read and re-read, and kissed and cherished, were written by another ; that their splendid home, of which, on their wedding-day, her father gave him the deed, is already in the hands of his creditors ; that she must give up the elegance and luxury that now surround her, unless she can draw fresh supplies of money to meet their wants !   When she told the story of her wrongs to me—the abuse to which she was subject, and the dread in which she lived—I impulsively urged her to fly from such a monster and villain, as she would before the hot breath of a ferocious beast of the wilderness. (Applause). And she did fly ; and it was well with her. Many times since, as I have felt her throbbing heart against my own, she has said, "Oh, but for your love and sympathy, your encouragement, I should never have escaped from that bondage.   Before I could, of myself, have found courage to break those chains my heart would have broken in the effort."

Marriage, as it now exists, must seem to all of you a mere human institution. Look through the universe of matter and mind—all God's arrangements are perfect, harmonious, and complete !   There is no discord, friction, or failure in His eternal plans.   Immutability, perfection, beauty, are stamped on all His laws.   Love is the vital essence that pervades and permeates, from the center to the circumference, the graduating circles of all thought and action. Love is the talisman of human weal and woe—the open sesame to every human soul.

Where two beings are drawn together, by the natural laws of likeness and affinity, union and happiness are the result. Such marriages might be Divine. But how is it now? You all know our marriage is, in many cases, a mere outward tie, impelled by custom, policy, interest, necessity; founded not even in friendship, to say nothing of love; with every possible inequality of condition and development. In these heterogeneous unions, we find youth and old age, beauty and deformity, refinement and vulgarity, virtue and vice, the educated and the ignorant, angels of grace and goodness, with devils of malice and malignity: and the sum of all this is human wretchedness and despair; cold fathers, sad mothers, and hapless children, who shiver at the hearthstone, where the fires of love have all gone out. The wide world, and the stranger's unsympathizing gaze, are not more to be dreaded for young hearts than homes like these. Now, who shall say that it is right to take two beings, so unlike, and anchor them right side by side, fast bound—to stay all time, until God shall summon one away?

Do wise, Christian legislators need any arguments to convince them that the sacredness of the family relation should be protected at all hazards? The family, that great conservator of national virtue and strength, how can you hope to build it up in the midst of violence, debauchery, and excess? Can there be anything sacred at that family altar, where the chief-priest who ministers makes sacrifice of human beings, of the weak and the innocent? where the incense offered up is not to the God of justice and mercy, but to those heathen divinities, who best may represent the lost man in all his grossness and deformity? Call that sacred, where woman, the mother of the race—of a Jesus of Nazareth—unconscious of the true dignity of her nature, of her high and holy destiny, consents to live in legalized prostitution !—her whole soul revolting at such gross association !—her flesh shivering at the cold contamination of that embrace, held there by no tie but the iron chain of the law, and a false and most unnatural public sentiment? Call that sacred, where innocent children, trembling with fear, fly to the corners and dark places of the house, to hide themselves from the wrath of drunken, brutal fathers, but, forgetting their past sufferings, rush out again at their mother's frantic screams, "Help, oh help"? Behold the agonies of those young hearts, as they see the only being on earth they love, dragged about the room by the hair of the head, kicked and pounded, and left half dead and bleeding on the floor ! Call that sacred, where fathers like these have the power and legal right to hand down their natures to other beings, to curse other generations with such moral deformity and death?

Men and brethren, look into your asylums for the blind, the deaf and dumb, the idiot, the imbecile, the deformed, the insane; go out into the by-lanes and dens of this vast metropolis, and contemplate that reeking mass of depravity; pause before the terrible revelations made by statistics, of the rapid increase of all this moral and physical impotency, and learn how fearful a thing it is to violate the immutable laws of the beneficent Ruler of the universe; and there behold the terrible retributions of your violence on woman ! Learn how false and cruel are those institutions, which, with a coarse materialism, set aside those holy instincts of the woman to bear no children but those of love ! In the best condition of marriage, as we now have it, to woman comes all the penalties and sacrifices. A man, in the full tide of business or pleasure, can marry and not change his life one iota; he can be husband, father, and everything beside; but in marriage, woman gives up all. Home is her sphere, her realm. Well, be it so. If here you will make us all-supreme, take to yourselves the universe beside; explore the North Pole; and, in your airy car, all space; in your Northern homes and cloud-capt towers, go feast on walrus flesh and air, and lay you down to sleep your six months' night away, and leave us to make these laws that govern the inner sanctuary of our own homes, and faithful satellites we will ever be to the dinner-pot, the cradle, and the old arm-chair. (Applause).

Fathers, do you say, let your daughters pay a life-long penalty for one unfortunate step ? How could they, on the threshold of life, full of joy and hope, believing all things to be as they seemed on the surface, judge of the dark windings of the human soul ? How could they foresee that the young man, to-day so noble, so generous, would in a few short years be transformed into a cowardly, mean tyrant, or a foul-mouthed, bloated drunkard ? What father could rest at his home by night, knowing that his lovely daughter was at the mercy of a strong man drunk with wine and passion, and that, do what he might, he was backed up by law and public sentiment ? The best interests of the individual, the family, the State, the nation, cry out against these legalized marriages of force and endurance. There can be no heaven without love, and nothing is sacred in the family and home, but just so far as it is built up and anchored in love. Our newspapers teem with startling accounts of husbands and wives having shot or poisoned each other, or committed suicide, choosing death rather than the indissoluble tie; and, still worse, the living death of faithless wives and daughters, from the first families in this State, dragged from the privacy of home into the public prints and courts, with all the painful details of sad, false lives. What say you to facts like these ? Now, do you believe, men and women, that all these wretched matches are made in heaven ? that all these sad, miserable people are bound together by God ? I know Horace Greeley has been most eloquent, for weeks past, on the holy sacrament of ill-assorted marriages; but let us hope that all wisdom does not live, and will not die with Horace Greeley. I think, if he had been married to *The New York Herald*, instead of the Republican party, he would have found out some Scriptural arguments against life-long unions, where great incompatibility of temper existed between the parties. (Laughter and applause).

Our law-makers have dug a pit, and the innocent have fallen into it; and now will you coolly cover them over with statute laws, *Tribunes*, and Weeds,* and tell them to stay there and pay the life-long penalty of having fallen in ? Nero was thought the chief of tyrants, because he made laws and hung them up so high that his subjects could not read them, and then punished them for every act of disobedience. What better are

---

* Thurlow Weed, editor of *The Albany Evening Journal*, opposed the passage of the Divorce Bill before the New York Legislature in 1860.

our Republican legislators ? The mass of the women of this nation know nothing about the laws, yet all their specially barbarous legislation is for woman. Where have they made any provision for her to learn the laws ? Where is the Law School for our daughters ? where the law office, the bar, or the bench, now urging them to take part in the jurisprudence of the nation ?

But, say you, does not separation cover all these difficulties ? No one objects to separation when the parties are so disposed. But, to separation there are two very serious objections. First, so long as you insist on marriage as a divine institution, as an indissoluble tie, so long as you maintain your present laws against divorce, you make separation, even, so odious, that the most noble, virtuous, and sensitive men and women choose a life of concealed misery, rather than a partial, disgraceful release. Secondly, those who, in their impetuosity and despair, do, in spite of public sentiment, separate, find themselves in their new position beset with many temptations to lead a false, unreal life. This isolation bears especially hard on woman. Marriage is not all of life to man. His resources for amusement and occupation are boundless. He has the whole world for his home. His business, his politics, his club, his friendships with either sex, can help to fill up the void made by an unfortunate union or separation. But to woman, marriage is all and everything; her sole object in life—that for which she is educated— the subject of all her sleeping and her waking dreams. Now, if a noble, generous girl of eighteen marries, and is unfortunate, because the cruelty of her husband compels separation, in her dreary isolation, would you drive her to a nunnery; and shall she be a nun indeed ? Her solitude is nothing less, as, in the present undeveloped condition of woman, it is only through our fathers, brothers, husbands, sons, that we feel the pulsations of the great outer world.

One unhappy, discordant man or woman in a neighborhood, may mar the happiness of all the rest. You can not shut up discord, any more than you can small-pox. There can be no morality where there is a settled discontent. A very wise father once remarked, that in the government of his children, he forbade as few things as possible; a wise legislation would do the same. It is folly to make laws on subjects beyond human prerogative, knowing that in the very nature of things they must be set aside. To make laws that man can not and will not obey, serves to bring all law into contempt. It is very important in a republic, that the people should respect the laws, for if we throw them to the winds, what becomes of civil government ? What do our present divorce laws amount to ? Those who wish to evade them have only to go into another State to accomplish what they desire. If any of our citizens can not secure their inalienable rights in New York State, they may in Connecticut and Indiana. Why is it that all agreements, covenants, partnerships, are left wholly at the discretion of the parties, except the contract, which of all others is considered most holy and important, both for the individual and the race ? This question of divorce, they tell us, is hedged about with difficulties; that it can not be approached with the ordinary rules of logic and common-sense. It is too holy, too sacred to

be discussed, and few seem disposed to touch it. From man's standpoint, this may be all true, as to him they say belong reason, and the
power of ratiocination. Fortunately, I belong to that class endowed with
mere intuitions, a kind of moral instinct, by which we feel out right and
wrong. In presenting to you, therefore, my views of divorce, you will of
course give them the weight only of the woman's intuitions. But inasmuch as that is all God saw fit to give us, it is evident we need nothing
more. Hence, what we do perceive of truth must be as reliable as what
man grinds out by the longer process of reason, authority, and speculation.

Horace Greeley, in his recent discussion with Robert Dale Owen, said,
this whole question has been tried, in all its varieties and conditions, from
indissoluble monogamic marriage down to free love; that the ground has
been all gone over and explored. Let me assure him that but just one-
half of the ground has been surveyed, and that half but by one of the
parties, and that party certainly not the most interested in the matter.
Moreover, there is one kind of marriage that has not been tried, and that
is, a contract made by equal parties to live an equal life, with equal restraints and privileges on either side. Thus far, we have had the man
marriage, and nothing more. From the beginning, man has had the sole
and whole regulation of the matter. He has spoken in Scripture, he has
spoken in law. As an individual, he has decided the time and cause for
putting away a wife, and as a judge and legislator, he still holds the entire control. In all history, sacred and profane, the woman is regarded
and spoken of simply as the toy of man—made for his special use—to meet
his most gross and sensuous desires. She is taken or put away, given or
received, bought or sold, just as the interest of the parties might dictate.
But the woman has been no more recognized in all these transactions,
through all the different periods and conditions of the race, than if she
had had no part nor lot in the whole matter. The right of woman to put
away a husband, be he ever so impure, is never hinted at in sacred history. Even Jesus himself failed to recognize the sacred rights of the holy
mother of the race. We can not take our gauge of womanhood from the
past, but from the solemn convictions of our own souls, in the higher development of the race. No parchments, however venerable with the
mould of ages, no human institutions, can bound the immortal wants of
the royal sons and daughters of the great I Am,—rightful heirs of the
joys of time, and joint heirs of the glories of eternity.

If in marriage either party claims the right to stand supreme, to woman, the
mother of the race, belongs the scepter and the crown. Her life is one long
sacrifice for man. You tell us that among all womankind there is no Moses,
Christ, or Paul,—no Michael Angelo, Beethoven, or Shakspeare,—no Columbus,
or Galileo,—no Locke or Bacon. Behold those mighty minds attuned to music
and the arts, so great, so grand, so comprehensive,—these are our great works of
which we boast! Into you, O sons of earth, go all of us that is immortal. In
you center our very life-thoughts, our hopes, our intensest love. For you we
gladly pour out our heart's blood and die, knowing that from our suffering comes
forth a new and more glorious resurrection of thought and life. (Loud applause).

Rev. Antoinette Brown Blackwell followed, and prefaced her remarks by saying: " Ours has always been a free platform. We have believed in the fullest freedom of thought and in the free expression of individual opinion. I propose to speak upon the subject discussed by our friend, Mrs. Stanton. It is often said that there are two sides to every question; but there are three sides, many sides, to every question. Let Mrs. Stanton take hers; let Horace Greeley take his; I only ask the privilege of stating mine. (Applause). I have embodied my thought, hastily, in a series of resolutions,* and my remarks following them will be very brief."

Resolved, That marriage is the voluntary alliance of two persons of opposite sexes into one family, and that such an alliance, with its possible incidents of children, its common interests, etc., must be, from the nature of things, as permanent as the life of the parties.

Resolved, That if human law attempts to regulate marriage at all, it should aim to regulate it according to the fundamental principles of marriage ; and that as the institution is inherently as continuous as the life of the parties, so all laws should look to its control and preservation as such.

Resolved, That as a parent can never annul his obligations towards even a profligate child, because of the inseparable relationship of the parties, so the married partner can not annul his obligations towards the other, while both live, no matter how profligate that other's conduct may be, because of their still closer and alike permanent relationship ; and, therefore, that all divorce is naturally and morally impossible, even though we should succeed in annulling all legalities.

Resolved, That gross fraud and want of good faith in one of the parties contracting this alliance, such as would invalidate any other voluntary relation, are the only causes which can invalidate this, and this, too, solely upon the ground that the relation never virtually existed, and that there are, therefore, no resulting moral obligations.

Resolved, however, That both men and women have a first and inviolable right to themselves, physically, mentally, and morally, and that it can never be the duty of either to surrender his personal freedom in any direction to his own hurt.

Resolved, That the great duty of every human being is to secure his own highest moral development, and that he can not owe to society, or to an individual, any obligation which shall be degrading to himself.

Resolved, That self-devotion to the good of another, and especially to the good of the sinful and guilty, like all disinterestedness, must redound to the highest good of its author, and that the husband or wife who thus seeks the best interests of the other, is obedient to the highest law of benevolence.

Resolved, That this is a very different thing from the culpable weakness which allows itself to be immolated by the selfishness of another, to the hurt of both ; and that the miserable practice, now so common among wives, of allowing themselves, their children and family interests, to be sacrificed to a degraded husband and father, is most reprehensible.

Resolved, That human law is imperatively obligated to give either party ample protection to himself, to their offspring, and to all other family interests, against wrong, injustice, and usurpation on the part of the other, and that, if it be necessary to this, it should grant a legal separation ; and yet, that even such separation can not invalidate any real marriage obligation.

Resolved, That every married person is imperatively obligated to do his utmost thus to protect himself and all family interests against injustice and wrong, let it arise from what source it may.

Resolved, That every woman is morally obligated to maintain her equality in human rights in all her relations in life, and that if she consents to her own subjugation, either

Mrs. Blackwell continued:

I believe that the highest laws of life are those which we find written within our being; that the first moral laws which we are to obey are the laws which God's own finger has traced upon our own souls. Therefore, our first duty is to ourselves, and we may never, under any circumstances, yield this to any other. I say we are first responsible to ourselves, and to the God who has laid the obligation upon us, to make ourselves the grandest we may. Marriage grows out of the relations of parties. The law of our development comes wholly from within; but the relation of marriage supposes two persons as being united to each other, and from this relation originates the law. Mrs. Stanton calls marriage a "tie." No, marriage is a *relation*; and, once formed, that relation continues as long as the parties continue with the natures which they now essentially have. Let, then, the two parties deliberately, voluntarily consent to enter into this relation. It is one which, from its very nature, must be permanent. Can the mother ever destroy the relation which exists between herself and her child? Can the father annul the relation which exists between himself and his child? Then, can the father and mother annul the relation which exists between themselves, the parents of the child? It can not be. The interests of marriage are such that they can not be destroyed, and the only question must be, " Has there been a marriage in this case or not?" If there has, then the social law, the obligations growing out of the relation, must be life-long.

But I assert that every woman, in the present state of society, is bound to maintain her own independence and her own integrity of character; to assert herself, earnestly and firmly, as the equal of man, who is only her peer. This is her first right, her first duty; and if she lives in a country where the law supposes that she is to be subjected to her husband, and she consents to this subjection, I do insist that she consents to degradation; that this is sin, and it is impossible to make it other than sin. True, in this State, and in nearly all the States, the idea of marriage is that of subjection, in all respects, of the wife to the husband—personal subjection, subjection in the rights over their children and over their property; but this is a false relation. Marriage is a union of equals—equal interests being involved, equal duties at stake; and if any woman has been married to a man who chooses to take advantage of the laws as they now stand, who chooses to subject her, ignobly, to his will, against her own, to take from her the earnings which belong to the family, and to take from her the children which belong to the family, I hold that that woman, if she can not, by her influence, change this state of things, is solemnly obligated to go to some State where she can be legally divorced; and then she would be as solemnly bound to return again, and, standing for herself and her children, regard herself, in the sight of God, as being bound still to the father of those children, to work for his best interests, while she still maintains her own sov-

---

in the family, Church or State, she is as guilty as the slave is in consenting to be a slave.

Resolved, That a perfect union can not be expected to exist until we first have perfect units, and that every marriage of finite beings must be gradually perfected through the growth and assimilation of the parties.

Resolved, That the permanence and indissolubility of marriage tend more directly than anything else toward this result.

ereignty. Of course, she must be governed by the circumstances of the case. She may be obliged, for the protection of the family, to live on one continent while her husband is on the other : but she is never to forget that in the sight of God and her own soul, she is his wife, and that she owes to him the wife's loyalty; that to work for his redemption is her highest social obligation, and that to teach her children to do the same is her first motherly duty. Legal divorce may be necessary for personal and family protection; if so, let every woman obtain it. This, God helping me, is what I would certainly do, for under no circumstances will I ever give my consent to be subjected to the will of another, in any relation, for God has bidden me not to do it. But the idea of most women is, that they must be timid, weak, helpless, and full of ignoble submission. Only last week, a lady who has just been divorced from her husband said to me—"I used to be required to go into the field and do the hardest laborer's work, when I was not able to do it; and my husband would declare, that if I would not thus labor, I should not be allowed to eat, and I was obliged to submit." I say the fault was as much with the woman as with the man; she should never have submitted.

Our trouble is not with marriage as a relation between two; it is all individual. We have few men or women fit to be married. They neither fully respect themselves and their own rights and duties, nor yet those of another. They have no idea how noble, how godlike is the relation which ought to exist between the husband and wife.

Tell me, is marriage to be merely a contract — something entered into for a time, and then broken again—or is the true marriage permanent? One resolution read by Mrs. Stanton said that, as men are incompetent to select partners in business, teachers for their children, ministers of their religion, or makers, adjudicators, or administrators of their laws, and as the same weakness and blindness must attend in the selection of matrimonial partners, the latter and most important contract should no more be perpetual than either or all of the former. I do not believe that, rightly understood, she quite holds to that position herself. Marriage must be either permanent, or capable of being any time dissolved. Which ground shall we take? I insist that, from the nature of things, marriage must be as permanent and indissoluble as the relation of parent and child. If so, let us legislate toward the right. Though evils must sometimes result, we are still to seek the highest law of the relation.

Self-devotion is always sublimely beautiful, but the law has no right to require either a woman to be sacrificed to any man, or a man to be sacrificed to any woman, or either to the good of society; but if either chooses to devote himself to the good of the other, no matter how low that other may have fallen, no matter how degraded he may be, let the willing partner strive to lift him up, not by going down and sitting side by side with him—that is wrong—but by steadily trying to win him back to the right; keeping his own sovereignty, but trying to redeem the fallen one as long as life shall endure. I do not wish to go to the other state of being, and state what shall be our duty there, but I do say, that where there is sin and suffering in this universe of ours, we may none of us sit still until we have overcome that sin and suffering. Then if my husband was wretched and degraded in this life, I believe God would give me strength to work for him while life lasted. I would do that for the lowest drunkard in the street, and certainly I would do as much for my husband. I

believe that the greatest boon of existence is the privilege of working for those
who are oppressed and fallen; and those who have oppressed their own natures
are those who need the most help. My great hope is, that I may be able to lift
them upwards. The great responsibility that has been laid upon me is the
responsibility never to sit down and sing to myself psalms of happiness and
content while anybody suffers. (Applause). Then, if I find a wretched man in
the gutter, and feel that, as a human sister, I must go and lift him up, and that
I can never enjoy peace or rest until I have thus redeemed him and brought
him out of his sins, shall I, if the man whom I solemnly swore to love, to associate with in all the interests of home and its holiest relations — shall I, if he
falls into sin, turn him off, and go on enjoying life, while he is sunk in wretchedness and sin? I will not do it. To me there is a higher idea of life. If, as
an intelligent human being, I promised to co-work with him in all the higher
interests of life, and if he proves false, I will not turn from him, but I
must seek first to regenerate him, the nearest and dearest to me, as I would
work, secondly, to save my children, who are next, and then my brothers, my
sisters, and the whole human family. (Applause).

Mrs. Stanton asks, "Would you send a young girl into a nunnery,
when she has made a mistake?" Does Mrs. Stanton not know that nun-
neries belong to a past age, that people who had nothing to do might go
there and try to expiate their own sins? I would teach the young girl a
higher way. I do not say to her, "If you have foolishly united yourself
to another" (not "if you have been tied by the law"; for, remember, it
was not the law that tied her; she said, "I will do it," and the law said,
"So let it be!")—"sunder the bond"; but I say to her, that her duty is
to reflect, "Now that I see my mistake, I will commence being true to
myself; I will become a true unit, strong and noble in myself; and if I
can never make our union a true one, I will work toward that good result,
I will live for this great work—for truth and all its interests." Let me
tell you, if she is not great enough to do this, she is not great enough
to enter into any union!

Look at those who believe in thus easily dissolving the marriage obligation! In very many cases they can not be truly married, or truly
happy in this relation, because there is something incompatible with it
in their own natures. It is not always so; but when one feels that it is a
relation easily to be dissolved, of course, incompatibility at once seems
to arise in the other, and every difficulty that occurs, instead of being
overlooked, as it ought to be, in a spirit of forgiveness, is magnified, and
the evil naturally increased. We purchase a house, the deed is put into
our hands, and we take possession. We feel at once that it is really very
convenient. It suits us, and we are surprised that we like it so much
better than we supposed. The secret is, that it is our house, and until
we are ready to part with it, we make ourselves content with it as it is.
We go to live in some country town. At first we do not like it; it is
not like the home we came from; but soon we begin to be reconciled, and
feel that, as Dr. Holmes said of Boston, our town is the hub of the universe. So, when we are content to allow our relations to remain as they
are, we adapt ourselves to them, and they adapt themselves to us, and
we constantly, unconsciously (because God made us so) work toward the

perfecting of all the interests arising from those relations. But the moment we wish to sell a house, or remove from a town, how many defects we discover! The place has not the same appearance to us at all; we wish we could get out of it; we feel all the time more and more dissatisfied. So, let any married person take the idea that he may dissolve this relation, and enter into a new one, and how many faults he may discover that otherwise never would have been noticed! The marriage will become intolerable. The theory will work that result; it is in the nature of things, and that to me is everything.

Of course, I would not have man or woman sacrificed—by no means. First of all, let every human being maintain his own position as a self-protecting human being. At all hazards, let him never sin, or consent to be sacrificed to the hurt of himself or of another; and when he has taken this stand, let him act in harmony with it. Would I say to any woman, " You are bound, because you are legally married to one who is debased to the level of the brute, to be the mother of his children?" I say to her, "No! while the law of God continues, you are bound never to make one whom you do not honor and respect, as well as love, the father of any child of yours. It is your first and highest duty to be true to yourself, true to posterity, and true to society." (Applause). Thus, let each decide for himself and for herself what is right. But, I repeat, either marriage is in its very nature a relation which, once formed, never can be dissolved, and either the essential obligations growing out of it exist forever, or the relation may at any time be dissolved, and at any time those obligations be annulled. And what are those obligations? Two persons, if I understand marriage, covenant to work together, to uphold each other in all excellence, and to mutually blend their lives and interests into a common harmony. I believe that God has so made man and woman, that it is not good for them to be alone, that they each need a co-worker. There is no work on God's footstool which man can do alone and do well, and there is no work which woman can do alone and do well. (Applause). We need that the two should stand side by side everywhere. All over the world, we need this co-operation of the two classes—not because they are alike, but because they are unlike—in trying to make the whole world better. Then we need something more than these class workers. Two persons need to stand side by side, to stay up each other's hands, to take an interest in each other's welfare, to build up a family, to cluster about it all the beauties and excellencies of home life; in short, to be to each other what only one man and one woman can be to each other in all God's earth.

No grown-up human being ought to rush blindly into this most intimate, most important, most enduring of human relations; and will you let a young man, at the age of fourteen, contract marriage, or a young maiden either? If the law undertakes to regulate the matter at all, let it regulate it upon principles of common-sense. But this is a matter which must be very much regulated by public opinion, by our teachers. What do you, the guides of our youth, say? You say to the young girl, "You ought to expect to be married before you are twenty, or about that time; you should intend to be; and from the time you are fifteen, it should be made your one life purpose; and in all human probability, you may expect to spend the next ten or twenty years in the nursery, and at forty or fifty, you will be an old woman, your life will be well-nigh worn out." I stand here to say that this is all false. Let the young girl be instructed that, above her personal interests, her home, and social life, she is to have a great life purpose, as broad as the rights and interests of humanity. I say, let every young girl feel this, as much as every young man does. We have no right, we, who expect to live forever, to play about here as if we were mere flies, enjoying ourselves in the sunshine. We ought to have an earnest purpose outside of home, outside of our family relations. Then let the young girl fit herself for this. Let her be taught that she ought not to be married in her teens. Let her wait, as a young man does, if he is sensible, until she is twenty-five or thirty. (Applause). She will then know how to choose properly, and probably she will not be deceived in her estimate of character; she will have had a certain life-discipline, which will enable her to control her household matters with wise judgment, so that, while she is looking after her family, she may still keep her great life purpose, for which she was educated, and to which she has given her best energies, steadily in view. She need not absorb herself in her home, and God never intended that she should; and then, if she has lived according to the laws of physiology, and according to the laws of common-sense, she ought to be, at the age of fifty years, just where man is, just where our great men are, in the very prime of life ! When her young children have gone out of her home, then let her enter in earnest upon the great work of life outside of home and its relations. (Applause).

It is a shame for our women to have no steady purpose or pursuit, and to make the mere fact of womanhood a valid plea for indolence; it is a greater shame that they should be instructed thus to throw all the responsibility of working for the general good upon the other sex. God has not intended it. But as long as you make women helpless, inefficient beings, who never expect to earn a farthing in their lives, who never expect to do anything outside of the family, but to be cared for and protected by others throughout life, you can not have true marriages; and if you try to break up the old ones, you will do it against the woman and in favor of the man. Last week I went back to a town where I used to live, and was told that a woman, whose husband was notoriously the most miserable man in the town, had in despair taken her own life. I asked what had become of the husband, and the answer was, "Married again." And yet everybody there knows that he is the vilest and most contemptible man in the whole neighborhood. Any man, no matter how wretched he may be, will find plenty of women to accept him, while they are rendered so helpless and weak by their whole education that they must be supported or starve. The advantage, if this theory of marriage is adopted, will not be on the side of woman, but altogether on the side of man. The cure for the evils that now exist is not in dissolving marriage, but it is in giving to the married woman her own natural independence and self-sovereignty, by which she can maintain herself.

Yes, our women and our men are both degenerate; they are weak and ignoble. "Dear me!" said a pretty, indolent young lady, "I had a great deal rather my husband would take care of me, than to be obliged to do it for myself." "Of course you would," said a blunt old lady who was present; "and your brother would a great deal rather marry an heiress, and lie upon a sofa eating lollypops, bought with her money, than to do anything manly or noble. The only difference is, that as heiresses are not very plenty, he may probably have to marry a poor girl, and then society will insist that he shall exert himself to earn a living for the family; but you, poor thing, will only have to open your mouth, all your life long, like a clam, and eat." (Applause and laughter). So long as society is constituted in such a way that woman is expected to do nothing if she have a father, brother, or husband able to support her, there is no salvation for her, in or out of marriage. When you tie up your arm, it will become weak and feeble; and when you tie up woman, she will become weak and helpless. Give her, then, some earnest purpose in life, hold up to her the true ideal of marriage, and it is enough—I am content! (Loud applause).

ERNESTINE L. ROSE said:—Mrs. President—The question of a Divorce law seems to me one of the greatest importance to all parties, but I presume that the very advocacy of divorce will be called "Free Love." For my part (and I wish distinctly to define my position), I do not know what others understand by that term; to me, in its truest significance, love must be free, or it ceases to be love. In its low and degrading sense, it is not love at all, and I have as little to do with its name as its reality.

The Rev. Mrs. Blackwell gave us quite a sermon on what woman ought to be, what she ought to do, and what marriage ought to be; an excellent sermon in its proper place, but not when the important question of a Divorce law is under consideration. She treats woman as some ethereal being. It is very well to be ethereal to some extent, but I tell you, my friends, it is quite requisite to be a little material, also. At all events, we are so, and, being so, it proves a law of our nature. (Applause).

It were indeed well if woman could be what she ought to be, man what he ought to be, and marriage what it ought to be; and it is to be hoped that through the Woman's Rights movement—the equalizing of the laws, making them more just, and making woman more independent—we will hasten the coming of the millennium, when marriage shall indeed be a bond of union and affection. But, alas! it is not yet; and I fear that sermons, however well meant, will not produce that desirable end; and as long as the evil is here, we must look it in the face without shrinking, grapple with it manfully, and the more complicated it is, the more courageously must it be analyzed, combated, and destroyed. (Applause).

Mrs. Blackwell told us that, marriage being based on the perfect equality of husband and wife, it can not be destroyed. But is it so? Where? Where and when have the sexes yet been equal in physical or mental education, in position, or in law? When and where have they yet been recognized by society, or by themselves, as equals? "Equal in rights," says Mrs. B. But are they equal in rights? If they were, we would need no conventions to claim our rights. "She can assert her equality." Yes, she can assert it, but does that assertion constitute a true marriage? And when the husband holds the iron heel of legal oppres io ι on the subjugated neck of the wife until every spark of womahood is crushed out, will it heal the wounded heart, the lacerated spirit, the destroyed hope, to assert her equality? And shall she still continue the wife? Is that a marriage which must not be dissolved? (Applause).

According to Mr. Greeley's definition, viz., that there is no marriage unless the ceremony is performed by a minister and in a church, the tens of thousands married according to the laws of this and most of the other States, by a lawyer or justice of the peace, a mayor or an alderman, are not married at all. According to the definition of our reverend sister, no one has ever yet been married, as woman has never yet been perfectly equal with man. I say to both, take your position, and abide by the consequences. If the few only, or no one, is really married, why do you object to a law that shall acknowledge the fact? You certainly ought not to force people to live together who are not married. (Applause).

Mr. Greeley tells us, that, marriage being a Divine institution, nothing but death should ever separate the parties; but when he was asked, "Would you have a being who, innocent and inexperienced, in the youth and ardor of affection, in the fond hope that the sentiment was reciprocated, united herself to one she loved and cherished, and then found (no matter from what cause) that his profession was false, his heart hollow, his acts cruel, that she was degraded by his vice, despised for his crimes, cursed by his very presence, and treated with every conceivable ignominy—would you have her drag out a miserable existence as his wife?" "No, no," says he; "in that case, they ought to separate." Separate? But what becomes of the union divinely instituted, which death only should part? (Applause).

The papers have of late been filled with the heart-sickening accounts of wife-poisoning. Whence come these terrible crimes? From the want of a Divorce law. Could the Hardings be legally separated, they would not be driven to the commission of murder to be free from each other; and which is preferable, a Divorce law, to dissolve an unholy union, which all parties agree is no true marriage, or a murder of one, and an execution (legal murder) of the other party? But had the unfortunate woman, just before the poisoned cup was presented to her lips, pleaded for a divorce, Mrs. Blackwell would have read her a sermon equal to St. Paul's "Wives, be obedient to your husbands," only she would have added, "You must assert your equality," but "you must keep with your husband and work for his redemption, as I would do for my husband"; and Mr. Greeley would say, "As you chose to marry him, it is your own fault; you must abide the consequences, for it is a 'divine institution, a union for life, which nothing but death can end.'" (Applause). *The Tribune* had recently a long sermon, almost equal to the one we had this morning from our reverend sister, on "Fast Women." The evils it spoke of were terrible indeed, but, like all other sermons, it was one-sided. Not one single word was said about fast men, except that the "poor victim had to spend so much money." The writer forgot that it is the demand which calls the supply into existence. But what was the primary cause of that tragic end? Echo answers, "what?" Ask the lifeless form of the murdered woman, and she may disclose the terrible secret, and show you that, could she have been legally divorced, she might not have been driven to the watery grave of a "fast woman." (Applause).

But what is marriage? A human institution, called out by the needs of social, affectional human nature, for human purposes, its objects are, first, the happiness of the parties immediately concerned, and, secondly, the welfare of society. Define it as you please, these are only its objects; and therefore if, from well-ascertained facts, it is demonstrated that the real objects are frustrated, that instead of union and happiness, there are only discord and misery to themselves, and vice and crime to society, I ask, in the name of individual, happiness and social morality and well-being, why such a marriage should be binding for life?—why one human being should be chained for life to the dead body of another? "But they may separate and still remain married." What a perversion of the very term! Is that the union which "death only should part"? It may be according to the definition of the Rev. Mrs. Blackwell's theology and Mr. Greeley's dictionary, but it certainly is not according to common-sense or the dictates of morality. No, no! "It is not well for man to be alone," before nor after marriage. (Applause).

I therefore ask for a Divorce law. Divorce is now granted for some crimes ; I ask it for others also. It is granted for a State's prison offense. I ask that personal cruelty to a wife, whom he swore to "love, cherish, and protect," may be made a heinous crime—a perjury and a State's prison offense, for which divorce shall be granted. Willful desertion for one year should be a sufficient cause for divore, for the willful deserter forfeits the sacred title of husband or wife. Habitual intemperance, or any other vice which makes the husband or wife intolerable and abhorrent to the other, ought to be sufficient cause for divorce. I ask for a law of Divorce, so as to secure the real objects and blessings of married life, to prevent the crimes and immoralities now practiced, to prevent "Free Love," in its most hideous form, such as is now carried on but too often under the very name of marriage, where hypocrisy is added to the crime of legalized prostitution. "Free Love," in its degraded sense, asks for no Divorce law. It acknowledges no marriage, and therefore requires no divorce. I believe in true marriages, and therefore I ask for a law to free men and women from false ones. (Applause).

But it is said that if divorce were easily granted, "men and women would marry to-day and unmarry to-morrow." Those who say that, only prove that they have no confidence in themselves, and therefore can have no confidence in others. But the assertion is false; it is a libel on human nature. It is the indissoluble chain that corrodes the flesh. Remove the indissolubility, and there would be less separation than now, for it would place the parties on their good behavior, the same as during courtship. Human nature is not quite so changeable; give it more freedom, and it will be less so. We are a good deal the creatures of habit, but we will not be forced. We live (I speak from experience) in uncomfortable houses for years, rather than move, though we have the privilege to do so every year ; but force any one to live for life in one house, and he would run away from it, though it were a palace.

But Mr. Greeley asks, "How could the mother look the child in the face, if she married a second time?" With infinitely better grace and better conscience than to live as some do now, and show their children the degrading example, how utterly father and mother despise and hate each other, and still live together as husband and wife. She could say to her child, "As, unfortunately, your father proved himself unworthy, your mother could not be so unworthy as to continue to live with him. As he failed to be a true father to you, I have endeavored to supply his place with one, who, though not entitled to the name, will, I hope, prove himself one in the performance of a father's duties." (Applause).

Finally, educate woman, to enable her to promote her independence, and she will not be obliged to marry for a home and a subsistence. Give the wife an equal right with the husband in the property acquired after marriage, and it will be a bond of union between them. Diamond cement, applied on both sides of a fractured vase, re-unites the parts, and prevents them from falling asunder. A gold band is more efficacious than an iron law. Until now, the gold has all been on one side, and the iron law on the other. Remove it; place the golden band of justice and mutual interest around both husband and wife, and it will hide the little fractures which may have occurred, even from their own perception, and allow them effectually to re-unite. A union of interest helps to preserve a union of hearts. (Loud applause).

WENDELL PHILLIPS then said: I object to entering these resolutions upon the journal of this Convention. (Applause). I would move to lay them on the table; but my conviction that they are out of order is so emphatic, that I wish to go further than that, and move that they do not appear on the journals of this Convention. If the resolutions were merely the expressions of individual sentiments, then they ought not to appear in the form of resolutions, but as speeches, because a resolution has a certain emphasis and authority. It is assumed to give the voice of an assembly, and is not taken as an individual expression, which a speech is.

Of course, every person must be interested in the question of marriage, and the branch that grows out of it, the question of divorce; and no one could deny, who has listened for an hour, that we have been favored with an exceedingly able discussion of those questions. But here we have nothing to do with them, any more than with the question of intemperance, or Kansas, in my opinion. This Convention is no Marriage Convention—if it were, the subject would be in order; but this Convention, if I understand it, assembles to discuss the laws that rest unequally upon women, not those that rest equally upon men and women. It is the laws that make distinctions between the sexes. Now, whether a man and a woman are married for a year or a life is a question which affects the man just as much as the woman. At the end of a month, the man is without a wife exactly as much as the woman is without a husband. The question whether, having entered into a contract, you shall be bound to an unworthy partner, affects the man as much as the woman. Certainly, there are cases where men are bound to women carcasses as well as where women are bound to men carcasses. (Laughter and applause). We have nothing to do with a question which affects both sexes equally. Therefore, it seems to me we have nothing to do with the theory of marriage, which is the basis, as Mrs. Rose has very clearly shown, of divorce. One question grows out of the other; and therefore the question of the permanence of marriage, and the laws relating to marriage, in the essential meaning of that word, are not for our consideration. Of course I know, as everybody else does, that the results of marriage, in the present condition of society, are often more disastrous to woman than to men. Intemperance, for instance, burdens a wife worse than a husband, owing to the present state of society. It is not the fault of the statute-book, and no change in the duration of marriage would alter that inequality.

The reason why I object so emphatically to the introduction of the question here is because it is a question which admits of so many theories, physiological and religious, and what is technically called "free-love," that it is large enough for a movement of its own. Our question is only unnecessarily burdened with it. It can not be kept within the convenient limits of this enterprise; for this Woman's Rights Convention is not Man's Convention, and I hold that I, as a man, have an exactly equal interest in the essential question of marriage as woman has. I move, then, that these series of resolutions do not appear at all upon the journal of the Convention. If the speeches are reported, of course the resolutions will go with them. Most journals will report them as adopted. But I say to those who use this platform to make speeches on this question, that they do far worse than take more than their fair share of the time; they open a gulf into which our distinctive movement will be plunged, and its success postponed two years for every one that it need necessarily be.

Of course, in these remarks, I intend no reflection upon those whose views differ from mine in regard to introducing this subject before the Convention; but we had an experience two years ago on this point, and it seems to me that we might have learned by that lesson. No question —Anti-Slavery, Temperance, Woman's Rights—can move forward efficiently, unless it keeps its platform separate and unmixed with extraneous issues, unmixed with discussions which carry us into endless realms of debate. We have now, under our present civilization, to deal with the simple question which we propose—how to make that statute-book look upon woman exactly as it does upon man. Under the law of Divorce, one stands exactly like the other. All we have asked in regard to the law of property has been, that the statute-book of New York shall make the wife exactly like the husband; we do not go another step, and state what that right shall be. We do not ask law-makers whether there shall be rights of dower and courtesy—rights to equal shares—rights to this or that interest in property. That is not our business. All we say is, "Gentlemen law-makers, we represent woman; make what laws you please about marriage and property, but let woman stand under them exactly as man does; let sex deprive her of no right, let sex confer no special right; and that is all we claim." (Applause). Society has done that as to marriage and divorce, and we have nothing more to ask of it on this question, as a Woman's Rights body.

ABBY HOPPER GIBBONS, of New York City, seconded the motion of Mr. Phillips, and said that she wished the whole subject of marriage and divorce might be swept from that platform, as it was manifestly not the place for it.

Mr. GARRISON said he fully concurred in opinion with his friend, Mr. Phillips, that they had not come together to settle definitely the question of marriage, as such, on that platform; still, he should be sorry to have the motion adopted, as against the resolutions of Mrs. Stanton, because they were a part of her speech, and her speech was an elucidation of her resolutions, which were offered on her own responsibility, not on behalf of the Business Committee, and which did not, therefore, make the Convention responsible for them. It seemed to him that, in the liberty usually taken on that platform, both by way of argument and illustration, to show the various methods by which woman was unjustly, yet legally, subjected to the absolute control of man, she ought to be permitted to present her own sentiments. It was not the specific object of an Anti-Slavery Convention—for example—to discuss the conduct of Rev. Nehemiah Adams, or the position of Stephen A. Douglas, or the course of *The York Herald;* yet they did, incidentally, discuss all these, and many other matters closely related to the great struggle for the freedom of the slave. So this question of marriage came in as at least incidental to the main question of the equal rights of woman.

Mrs. BLACKWELL: I should like to say a few words in explanation. I do not understand whether our friend Wendell Phillips objects to both series of resolutions on the subject of divorce, or merely to mine.

Mr. PHILLIPS: To both.

Mrs. BLACKWELL: I wish simply to say, that I did not come to the Convention proposing to speak on this subject, but on another ; but finding that these resolutions were to be introduced, and believing the subject legitimate, I said, "I will take my own position." So I prepared the resolutions, as they enabled me at the moment better to express my thought than I could do by merely extemporizing.

Now does this question grow legitimately out of the great question of woman's equality? The world says, marriage is not an alliance between equals in human rights. My whole argument was based on the position that it is. If this question is not legitimate, what is? Then do we not ask for laws which are not equal between man and woman? What have we been doing here in New York State? I spent three months asking the State to allow the drunkard's wife her own earnings. Do I believe that the wife ought to take her own earnings, as her own earnings? No; I do not believe it. I believe that in a true marriage, the husband and wife earn for the family, and that the property is the family's — belongs jointly to the husband and wife. But if the law says that the property is the husband's, if it says that he may take the wages of his wife, just as the master does those of the slave, and she has no right to them, we must seek a temporary redress. We must take the first step, by compelling legislators, who will not look at great principles, to protect the wife of the drunkard, by giving her her own earnings to expend upon herself and her children, and not allow them to be wasted by the husband. I say that it is legitimate for us to ask for a law which we believe is merely a temporary expedient, not based upon the great principle of human and marriage equality. Just so with this question of marriage. It must come upon this platform, for at present it is a relation which legally and socially bears unequally upon woman. We must have temporary redress for the wife. The whole subject must be incidentally opened for discussion. The only question is one of present fitness. Was it best, under all the circumstances, to introduce it now? I have not taken the responsibility of answering in the affirmative. But it must come here and be settled, sooner or later, because its interests are everywhere, and all human relations center in this one marriage relation. (Applause).

SUSAN B. ANTHONY: I hope Mr. Phillips will withdraw his motion that these resolutions shall not appear on the records of the Convention. I am very sure that it would be contrary to all parliamentary usage to say, that when the speeches which enforced and advocated the resolutions are reported and published in the proceedings, the resolutions shall not be placed there. And as to the point that this question does not belong to this platform,—from that I totally dissent. Marriage has ever been a one-sided matter, resting most unequally upon the sexes. By it, man gains all—woman loses all; tyrant law and lust reign supreme with him—meek submission and ready obedience alone befit her. Woman has never been consulted; her wish has never been taken into consideration as regards the terms of the marriage compact. By law, public sentiment and religion, from the time of Moses down to the present day, woman has never been thought of other than as a piece of property, to be disposed of at the will and pleasure of man. And this very hour, by our statute-books, by our (so called) enlightened Christian civilization, she has no voice whatever in saying what shall be the basis of the relation. She must accept marriage as man proffers it, or not at all.

And then again, on Mr. Phillips' own ground, the discussion is perfectly in order, since nearly all the wrongs of which we complain grow out of the inequality, the injustice of the marriage laws, that rob the wife of the right to herself and her children—that make her the slave of the man she marries.

I hope, therefore, the resolutions will be allowed to go out to the public, that there may be a fair report of the ideas which have actually been presented here, that they may not be left to the mercy of the secular press. I trust the Convention will not vote to forbid the publication of those resolutions with the proceedings.

REV. WM. HOISINGTON, the blind preacher: Publish all that you have said and done here, and let the public know it.

The question was then put on the motion of Mr. Phillips, and it was lost.

PART TWO: THE CIVIL WAR TO 1885

I. WOMAN'S NATIONAL LOYAL LEAGUE

THE CIVIL WAR INSPIRED a fervent patriotic response from Union women, who did men's work in many places and played a vital auxiliary role elsewhere. The task of woman's rights advocates was to give this energy a goal beyond military victory. Their agitation raised the level of women's self-consciousness and participation in the political process.

The official woman's rights movement declared a temporary moratorium. Only Susan B. Anthony felt the continuation of activities in wartime to be essential. In 1862-63, two events stirred the women leaders into action. The New York legislature repealed the substance of the Married Women's Property Acts of 1860, and Charles Sumner led a Congressional struggle to extend the Emancipation Proclamation to all American territories. In response, Stanton and Anthony called a conference of the "Loyal Women of the Nation."

The Woman's National Loyal League was designed to give women an ideological perspective on the war and on their own activities, so that women would "labor for a principle" rather than merely pour out their energies into an unfocused volunteerism. The war was to be fought for freedom, not only for the one-sixth in racial bondage but the half in sexual oppression. "True loyalty" was the demand that the fight be carried to a conclusion.

WNLL called for congressional support for the Thirteenth Amendment. Following in the tradition of abolitionist and woman's rights agitation, a "mammoth" petition campaign was begun with a goal of collecting one million signatures. Some four hundred thousand were actually secured before the passage of the amendment in 1865.

WNLL activity expanded women's political work within the Union states and strengthened the support for Radical Republicanism. In the long run, these two effects would prove paradoxical. The success of WNLL's organizational

initiatives dampened much of the antebellum prejudice
within the woman's rights movement against organizations of
any kind and paved the way for more structured association.
At the same time, the very nature of WNLL's work, even
with the underlying emphasis on women's emancipation,
increased the woman's movement's reliance on its antislavery
allies.

DOCUMENT 19 (II: 1–3): Woman's Patriotism in the War, written by Matilda Joslyn Gage

OUR first volume closed with the period when the American people stood waiting with apprehension the signal of the coming conflict between the Northern and Southern States. On April 12, 1861, the first gun was fired on Sumter, and on the 14th it was surrendered. On the 15th, the President called out 75,000 militia, and summoned Congress to meet July 4th, when 400,000 men and $400,000,000 were voted to carry on the war.

These startling events roused the entire people, and turned the current of their thoughts in new directions. While the nation's life hung in the balance, and the dread artillery of war drowned alike the voices of commerce, politics, religion and reform, all hearts were filled with anxious forebodings, all hands were busy in solemn preparations for the awful tragedies to come.

At this eventful hour the patriotism of woman shone forth as fervently and spontaneously as did that of man; and her self-sacrifice and devotion were displayed in as many varied fields of action. While he buckled on his knapsack and marched forth to conquer the enemy, she planned the campaigns which brought the nation victory; fought in the ranks when she could do so without detection; inspired the sanitary commission; gathered needed supplies for the grand army; provided nurses for the hospitals; comforted the sick; smoothed the pillows of the dying; inscribed the last messages of love to those far away; and marked the resting-places where the brave men fell. The labor women accomplished, the hardships they endured, the time and strength they sacrificed in the war that summoned three million men to arms, can never be fully appreciated.

Think of the busy hands from the Atlantic to the Pacific, making garments, canning fruits and vegetables, packing boxes, preparing lint and bandages* for soldiers at the front; think of the mothers, wives and daughters on the far-off prairies, gathering in the harvests, that their fathers, husbands, brothers, and sons might fight the battles of freedom ; of those month after month walking the wards of the hospital; and those on the battle-field at the midnight hour, ministering to the wounded and dying, with none but the cold stars to keep them company.

Think of the multitude of delicate, refined women, unused to care and toil, thrown suddenly on their own resources, to struggle evermore with poverty and solitude; their hopes and ambitions all freighted in the brave young men that marched forth from their native hills, with flying flags and marshal music, to return no more forever. The untiring labors, the trembling apprehensions, the wrecked hopes, the dreary solitude of the fatherless, the widowed, the childless in that great national upheaval, have never been measured or recorded ; their brave deeds never told in story or in song, no monuments built to their memories, no immortal wreaths to mark their last resting-places.

How much easier it is to march forth with gay companions and marshal music; with the excitement of the battle, the camp, the ever-shifting scenes of war, sustained by the hope of victory ; the promise of reward ; the ambition for distinction ; the fire of patriotism kindling every thought, and stimulating every nerve and muscle to action ! How much easier is all this, than to wait and watch alone with nothing to stimulate hope or ambition.

The evils of bad government fall ever most heavily on the mothers of the race, who, however wise and far-seeing, have no voice in its administration, no power to protect themselves and their children against a male dynasty of violence and force.

While the mass of women never philosophize on the principles that underlie national existence, there were those in our late war who understood the political significance of the struggle: the " irrepressible conflict" between freedom and slavery ; between national and State rights. They saw that to provide lint, bandages, and supplies for the army, while the war was not conducted on a wise policy, was labor in vain ; and while many organizations, active, vigilant, self-sacrificing, were multiplied to look after the material

---

* Before one man was slain the lint and bandages were so piled. up in Washington, that the hospital surgeons in self-defence cried out, enough !

wants of the army, these few formed themselves into a National Loyal League to teach sound principles of government, and to press on the nation's conscience, that " freedom to the slaves was the only way to victory."   Accustomed as most women had been to works of charity, to the relief of outward suffering, it was difficult to rouse their enthusiasm for an idea, to persuade them to labor for a principle. They clamored for practical work, something for their hands to do ; for fairs, sewing societies to raise money for soldier's families, for tableaux, readings, theatricals, anything but conventions to discuss principles and to circulate petitions for emancipation.   They could not see that the best service they could render the army was to suppress the rebellion, and that the most effective way to accomplish that was to transform the slaves into soldiers.   This Woman's Loyal League voiced the solemn lessons of the war : liberty to all ; national protection for every citizen under our flag; universal suffrage, and universal amnesty.

As no national recognition has been accorded the grand women who did faithful service in the late war ; no national honors nor profitable offices bestowed on them, the noble deeds of a few representative women should be recorded.   The military services of Anna Ella Carroll in planning the campaign on the Tennessee ; the labors of Clara Barton on the battle-field ; of Dorothea Dix in the hospital ; of Dr. Elizabeth Blackwell in the Sanitary ; of Josephine S. Griffing in the Freedman's Bureau ; and the political triumphs of Anna Dickinson in the Presidential campaign, reflecting as they do all honor on their sex in general, should ever be proudly remembered by their countrywomen.

DOCUMENT 20 (II: 53): Call to the Woman's National Loyal League Meeting of May 14, 1863

The call for a meeting of the Loyal Women of the Nation :

In this crisis of our country's destiny, it is the duty of every citizen to consider the peculiar blessings of a republican form of government, and decide what sacrifices of wealth and life are demanded for its defence and preservation. The policy of the war, our whole future life, depends on a clearly-defined idea of the end proposed, and the immense advantages to be secured to ourselves and all mankind, by its accomplishment. No mere party or sectional cry, no technicalities of Constitution or military law, no mottoes of craft or policy are big enough to touch the great heart of a nation in the midst of revolution. A grand idea, such as freedom or justice, is needful to kindle and sustain the fires of a high enthusiasm.

At this hour, the best word and work of every man and woman are imperatively demanded. To man, by common consent, is assigned the forum, camp, and field. What is woman's legitimate work, and how she may best accomplish it, is worthy our earnest counsel one with another. We have heard many complaints of the lack of enthusiasm among Northern women ; but, when a mother lays her son on the altar of her country, she asks an object equal to the sacrifice. In nursing the sick and wounded, knitting socks, scraping lint, and making jellies, the bravest and best may weary if the thoughts mount not in faith to something beyond and above it all. Work is worship only when a noble purpose fills the soul. Woman is equally interested and responsible with man in the final settlement of this problem of self-government ; therefore let none stand idle spectators now. When every hour is big with destiny, and each delay but complicates our difficulties, it is high time for the daughters of the revolution, in solemn council, to unseal the last will and testament of the Fathers—lay hold of their birthright of freedom, and keep it a sacred trust for all coming generations.

To this end we ask the Loyal Women of the Nation to meet in the church of the Puritans (Dr. Cheever's), New York, on Thursday, the 14th of May next.

Let the women of every State be largely represented both in person and by letter.

On behalf of the Woman's Central Committee,

ELIZABETH CADY STANTON.
SUSAN B. ANTHONY.

DOCUMENT 21 (II: 57–66): Resolutions and Debate,
Woman's National Loyal League Meeting, New York
City, May 14, 1863

Susan B. Anthony presented a series of resolutions,* and said:

There is great fear expressed on all sides lest this war shall be made a
war for the negro. I am willing that it shall be. It is a war to found an
empire on the negro in slavery, and shame on us if we do not make it a
war to establish the negro in freedom—against whom the whole nation,
North and South, East and West, in one mighty conspiracy, has combined from the beginning.

Instead of suppressing the real cause of the war, it should have been
proclaimed, not only by the people, but by the President, Congress, Cabinet, and every military commander. Instead of President Lincoln's
waiting two long years before calling to the side of the Government the
four millions of allies whom we have had within the territory of rebel-
dom, it should have been the first decree he sent forth. Every hour's delay,
every life sacrificed up to the proclamation that called the slave to freedom and to arms, was nothing less than downright murder by the Government. For by all the laws of common-sense—to say nothing of laws
military or national—if the President, as Commander-in-Chief of the
Army and Navy, could have devised any possible means whereby he
might hope to suppress the rebellion, without the sacrifice of the life of one
loyal citizen, without the sacrifice of one dollar of the loyal North, it was
clearly his duty to have done so. Every interest of the insurgents, every
dollar of their property, every institution, however peculiar, every life in
every rebel State, even, if necessary, should have been sacrificed, before one
dollar or one man should have been drawn from the free States. How
much more, then, was it the President's duty to confer freedom on the
four million slaves, transform them into a peaceful army for the Union,
cripple the rebellion, and establish justice, the only sure foundation of

---

* *Resolved,* 2. That we heartily approve that part of the President's Proclamation which
decrees freedom to the slaves of rebel masters, and we earnestly urge him to devise measures for emancipating all slaves throughout the country.
  Resolved, 3. That the national pledge to the freedmen must be redeemed, and the integrity of the Government in making it vindicated, at whatever cost.
  Resolved, 4. That while we welcome to legal freedom the recent slaves, we solemnly remonstrate against all State or National legislation which may exclude them from any lo-
cality, or debar them from any rights or privileges as free and equal citizens of a common
Republic.
  Resolved, 5. There never can be a true peace in this Republic until the civil and political
rights of all citizens of African descent and all women are practically established.
  Resolved, 7. That the women of the Revolution were not wanting in heroism and self-
sacrifice, and we, their daughters, are ready in this war to pledge our time, our means, our
talents, and our lives, if need be, to secure the final and complete consecration of America
to freedom.

peace! I therefore hail the day when the Government shall recognize that it is a war for freedom. We talk about returning to the old Union—"the Union as it was," and "the Constitution as it is"—about "restoring our country to peace and prosperity—to the blessed conditions that existed before the war!" I ask you what sort of peace, what sort of prosperity, have we had? Since the first slave-ship sailed up the James River with its human cargo, and there, on the soil of the *Old* Dominion, sold it to the highest bidder, we have had nothing but war. When that pirate captain landed on the shores of Africa, and there kidnapped the first stalwart negro, and fastened the first manacle, the struggle between that captain and that negro was the commencement of the terrible war in the midst of which we are to-day. Between the slave and the master there has been war, and war only. This is only a new form of it. No, no; we ask for no return to the *old* conditions. We ask for something better. We want a Union that is a Union in fact, a Union in spirit, not a sham. (Applause).

By the Constitution as it is, the North has stood pledged to protect slavery in the States where it existed. We have been bound, in case of insurrections, to go to the aid, not of those struggling for liberty, but of the oppressors. It was politicians who made this pledge at the beginning, and who have renewed it from year to year to this day. These same men have had control of the churches, the Sabbath-schools, and all religious influences; and the women have been a party in complicity with slavery. They have made the large majority in all the different religious organizations throughout the country, and have without protest, fellowshiped the slave-holder as a Christian; accepted pro-slavery preaching from their pulpits; suffered the words "slavery a crime" to be expurgated from all the lessons taught their children, in defiance of the Golden Rule, "Do unto others as you would that others should do unto you." They have had no right to vote in their churches. and, like slaves, have meekly accepted whatever morals and religion the selfish interest of politics and trade dictated.

Woman must now assume her God-given responsibilities, and make herself what she is clearly designed to be, the educator of the race. Let her no longer be the mere reflector, the echo of the worldly pride and ambition of man. (Applause). Had the women of the North studied to know and to teach their sons the law of justice to the black man, regardless of the frown or the smile of pro-slavery priest and politician, they would not now be called upon to offer the loved of their households to the bloody Moloch of war. And now, women of the North, I ask you to rise up with earnest, honest purpose, and go forward in the way of right, fearlessly, as independent human beings, responsible to God alone for the discharge of every duty, for the faithful use of every gift, the good Father has given you. Forget conventionalisms; forget what the world will say, whether you are in your place or out of your place; think your best thoughts, speak your best words, do your best works, looking to your own conscience for approval.

Mrs. Hoyt, of Wisconsin : Thus far this meeting has been conducted in such a way as would lead one to suppose that it was an anti-slavery convention. There are ladies here who have come hundreds of miles to attend a business meeting of the Loyal Women of the North; and good as anti-slavery conventions are, and anti-slavery speeches are, in their way, I think that here we should attend to our own business.

Mrs. CHALKSTONE, of California: My speech shall be as brief as possible and I ask for an excuse for my broken language. Our field is very small, and God has given us character and abilities to follow it out. We do not need to stand at the ballot-boxes and cast our votes, neither to stand and plead as lawyers; but in our homes we have a great office. I consider women a great deal superior to men. (Laughter and applause). Men are physically strong, but women are morally better. I speak of pure women, good women. It is woman who keeps the world in the balance.

I am from Germany, where my brothers all fought against the Government and tried to make us free, but were unsuccessful. My only son, seventeen years old, is in our great and noble army of the Union. He has fought in many of the battles here, and I only came from California to see him once more. I have not seen him yet; though I was down in the camp, I could not get any pass. But I am willing to lay down all this sacrifice for the cause of liberty. We foreigners know the preciousness of that great, noble gift a great deal better than you, because you never were in slavery, but we are born in it. Germany pines for freedom. In Germany we sacrificed our wealth and ornaments for it, and the women in this country ought to do the same. We can not fight in the battles, but we can do this, and it is all we can do. The speaker, before me, remarked that Abraham Lincoln was two years before he emancipated slaves. She thought it wrong. It took eighteen hundred years in Europe to emancipate the Jews, and they are not emancipated now. Among great and intelligent peoples like Germany and France, until 1814 no Jew had the right to go on the pavement; they had to go in the middle of the street, where the horses walked! It took more than two years to emancipate the people of the North from the idea that the negro was not a human being, and that he had the right to be a free man. A great many will find fault in the resolution that the negro shall be free and equal, because our equal not every human being can be; but free every human being has a right to be. He can only be equal in his rights. (Applause).

Mrs. ROSE called for the reading of the resolutions, which after a spirited discussion, all except the fifth, were unanimously adopted.

Mrs. HOYT, of Wisconsin, said: *Mrs. President*—I object to the passage of the fifth resolution, not because I object to the sentiment expressed; but I do not think it is the time to bring before this meeting, assembled for the purpose of devising the best ways and means by which women may properly assist the Government in its struggle against treason, anything which could in the least prejudice the interest in this cause which is so dear to us all. We all know that Woman's Rights as an *ism* has not been received with entire favor by the women of the country, and I know that there are thousands of earnest, loyal, and able women who will not go into any movement of this kind, if this idea is made prominent. (Applause). I came here from Wisconsin hoping to meet the earnest women of the country. I hoped that nothing that would in any way damage the cause so dear to us all would be brought forward by any of the members. I object to this, because our object should be to maintain, as women properly may, the integrity of our Government; to vindicate its authority; to re-establish it upon a far more enduring basis. We can do this if we do not involve ourselves in any purely political matter, or any *ism* obnoxious to the people. The one idea should be the maintenance of the authority of the Government as it is, and the integrity of the Republican idea. For this, women may properly work, and I hope this resolution will not pass.

SARAH H. HALLECK, of Milton, N. Y.: I would make the suggestion that those who approve of this resolution can afford to give way, and allow that part of it which is objectionable to be stricken out. The negroes have suffered more than the women, and the women, perhaps, can afford to give them the preference. Let it stand as regards them, and blot out the word "woman." It may possibly be woman's place to suffer. At any rate, let her suffer, if, by that means, *man*kind may suffer less.

A VOICE: You are too self-sacrificing.

ERNESTINE L. ROSE: I always sympathize with those who seem to be in the minority. I know it requires a great deal of moral courage to object to anything that appears to have been favorably received. I know very well from long experience how it feels to stand in a minority of one; and I am glad that my friend on the other side (Mrs. Halleck) has already added one to make a minority of two, though that is by far too small to be comfortable. I, for one, object to the proposition to throw woman out of the race for freedom. (Applause). And do you know why? Because she needs freedom for the freedom of man. (Applause). Our ancestors made a great mistake in not recognizing woman in the rights of man. It has been justly stated that the negro at present suffers more than woman, but it can do him no injury to place woman in the same category with him. I, for one, object to having that term stricken out, for it can have no possible bearing against anything that we want to promote: we desire to promote human rights and human freedom. It can do no injury, but must do good, for it is a painful fact that woman under the law has been in the same category with the slave. Of late years she has had some small privileges conceded to her. Now, mind, I say *conceded;* for publicly it has not yet been recognized by the laws of the land that she has a right to an equality with man. In that resolution it simply states a fact, that in a republic based upon freedom, woman, as well as the negro, should be recognized as an equal with the whole human race. (Applause).

ANGELINE G. WELD: *Mrs. President*—I rejoice exceedingly that that resolution should combine us with the negro. I feel that we have been with him; that the iron has entered into our souls. True, we have not felt the slave-holder's lash; true, we have not had our hands manacled, but our *hearts* have been crushed. Was there a single institution in this country that would throw open its doors to the acknowledgment of woman's equality with man in the race for science and the languages, until Oberlin, Antioch, Lima, and a very few others opened their doors, twenty years ago? Have I not heard women say—I said thus to my own brother, as I used to receive from him instruction and reading: "Oh, brother, that I could go to college with you! that I could have the instruction you do! but I am crushed! I hear nothing, I know nothing, except in the fashionable circle." A teacher said to a young lady, who had been studying for several years, on the day she finished her course of instruction, "I thought you would be very glad that you were so soon to go home, so soon to leave your studies." She looked up, and said, "What was I made for? When I go home I shall live in a circle of fashion and folly. I was not made for embroidery and dancing; I was made a woman; but I can not be a true woman, a full-grown woman, in America."

Now, my friends, I do not want to find fault with the past. I believe that men did for women the best that they knew how to do. They did not know their own rights; they did not recognize the rights of any man who had a black face. We can not wonder that, in their tenderness for woman, they wanted to shelter and protect her, and they made those laws from true, human, generous feelings. Woman was then too undeveloped to demand anything else. But woman is full-grown to-day, whether man knows it or not, equal to her rights, and equal to the responsibilities of the hour. I want to be identified with the negro; until he gets his rights, we never shall have ours. (Applause).

SUSAN B. ANTHONY: This resolution brings in no question, no *ism*. It merely makes the assertion that in a true democracy, in a genuine republic, every citizen who lives under the government must have the right of representation. You remember the maxim, "Governments derive their just powers from the consent of the governed." This is the fundamental principle of democracy; and before our Government can be a true democracy—before our republic can be placed upon lasting and enduring foundations — the civil and political rights of every citizen must be practically established. This is the assertion of the resolution. It is a philosophical statement. It is not because women suffer, it is not because slaves suffer, it is not because of any individual rights or wrongs—it is the simple assertion of the great fundamental truth of democracy that was proclaimed by our Revolutionary fathers. I hope the discussion will no longer be continued as to the comparative rights or wrongs of one class or another. The question before us is: Is it possible that peace and union shall be established in this country; is it possible for this Government to be a true democracy, a genuine republic, while one-sixth or one-half of the people are disfranchised?

MRS. HOYT: I do not object to the philosophy of these resolutions. I believe in the advancement of the human race, and certainly not in a retrograde movement of the Woman's Rights question; but at the same time I do insist that nothing that has become obnoxious to a portion of the people of the country shall be dragged into this meeting. (Applause). The women of the North were invited here to meet in convention, not to hold a Temperance meeting, not to hold an Anti-Slavery meeting, not to hold a Woman's Rights Convention, but to consult as to the best practical way for the advancement of the loyal cause. To my certain knowledge there are ladies in this house who have come hundreds of miles, who will withdraw from this convention, who will go home disappointed, and be thrown back on their own resources, and form other plans of orgánization ; whereas they would much prefer to co-operate with the National Convention if this matter were not introduced. This movement must be sacred to the one object of assisting our Government. I would add one more remark, that though the women of the Revolution did help our Government in that early struggle, they did not find it necessary to set forth in any theoretical or clamorous way their right to equal suffrage or equal political position, though doubtless they believed, as much as any of us, in the advancement of woman.

A LADY: I want to ask the lady who just spoke if the women of the Revolution found it necessary to form Loyal Leagues? We are not bound to do just as the women of the Revolution did. (Applause and laughter).

LUCY N. COLEMAN, of Rochester, N. Y.: I wish to say, in the first place, something a little remote from the point, which I have in my mind just now. A peculiar sensitiveness seems to have come over some of the ladies here in reference to the anti-slavery spirit of the resolutions. It seems to me impossible that a company of women could stand upon this platform without catching something of the anti-slavery spirit, and without expressing, to some extent, their sympathy with the advancement of human rights. It is the Anti-Slavery women and the Woman's Rights women who called this meeting, and who have most effectually aided in this movement. Their hearts bleed to the very core that our nation is to-day suffering to its depths, and they came together to devise means whereby they could help the country in its great calamity. I respect the woman who opposed this resolution, for daring to say so much. She says that it is an Anti-Slavery Convention that is in session. So it is, and something more. (Applause). She says it is a Woman's Rights Convention. So it is, and even more than that; it is a World's Convention. (Applause). Another woman (I rejoice to hear that lisping, foreign tongue) says that our sphere is so narrow that we should be careful to keep within it. All honor to her, that she dared to say even that. I recognize for myself no narrow sphere. (Applause). Where you may work, my brother, I may work. I would willingly stand upon the battle-field, and would be glad to receive the balls in my person, if in that way I could do more for my country's good than in any other. I recognize no right of any man or of any woman to say that I sho.ld not stand there. Our sphere is *not* narrow—it is broad.

In reference to this resolution, Mrs. Halleck thinks it might be well to leave out woman. No, no. Do you remember, friends, long, long ago here in New York, an Anti-Slavery convention broke up in high dudgeon, because a woman was put upon a committee? But that Anti-Slavery Society, notwithstanding those persons who felt so sensitive withdrew from it, has lived thirty years, and to-day it has the honor of being credited as the cause of this war. Perhaps if the principle which was then at stake—that a woman had a right to be on a committee—had been waived, from the very fact that the principle of right was overruled, that Society would have failed. I would not yield one iota, one particle, to this clamor for compromise. Be it understood that it is a Woman's Rights matter; for the Woman's Rights women have the same right to dictate to a Loyal League that the Anti-Woman's Rights women have, and the side that is strongest will carry the resolution, of course. But do not withdraw it. Do not say, " We will take it away because it is objectionable."

I want the people to understand that this Loyal League—because it is a Loyal League—must of necessity bring in Anti-Slavery and Woman's Rights. (Applause). Is it possible that any of you believe that there is such a being in this country to-day as a loyal man or woman who is not anti-slavery to the backbone? (Applause). Neither is there a loyal man or woman whose intellect is clear enough to take in a broad, large idea, who is not to the very core a Woman's Rights man or woman. (Applause).

MRS. HOYT: As I have said before, I am not opposed to Anti-Slavery. I stand here an Abolitionist from the earliest childhood, and a stronger anti-slavery woman lives not on the soil of America. (Applause). I voted Yea on the anti-slavery resolution, and I would vote it ten times over. But, at the same time, in the West, which I represent, there is a very strong objection to Woman's Rights; in fact, this Woman's Rights matter is odious to some of us from the *manner* in which it has been conducted; not that we object to the philosophy—we believe in the philosophy—but object to this matter being tacked on to a purely loyal convention. . . . . I will make one more statement which bears upon the point which I have been trying to make. I have never before spoken except in private meetings, and therefore must ask the indulgence of the audience. The women of Madison, Wisconsin, feeling the necessity and importance of doing something more than women were doing to assist the Government in this struggle, organized a Ladies' Union League, which has been in operation some time, and is very efficient.

A VOICE:—What are they doing? Please state.

MRS. HOYT: In Madison we had a very large and flourishing "Soldiers' Aid Society." We were the headquarters for that part of the State. A great many ladies worked in our Aid Society, and assisted us, who utterly refused to join with the Loyal League, because, they said, it would damage the Aid Society. We recognized that fact, and kept it purely distinct as a Ladies' Loyal League, for the promotion of the loyal sentiment of the North, and to reach the soldiers in the field by the most direct and practical means which were in our power. We have a great many very flourishing Ladies' Loyal Leagues throughout the West, and we have kept them sacred from Anti-Slavery, Woman's Rights, Temperance, and everything else, good though they may be. In our League we have three objects in view. The first is, retrenchment in household expenses, to the end that the material resources of the Government may be, so far as possible, applied to the entire and thorough vindication of its authority. Second, to strengthen the loyal sentiment of the people at home, and instil a deeper love of the national flag. The third and most important object is, to write to the soldiers in the field, thus reaching nearly every private in the army, to encourage and stimulate him in the way that ladies know how to do. I state again, it is not an Anti-Slavery objection. I will vote for every Anti-Slavery movement in this Convention. I object to the Woman's Rights resolutions, and nothing else.

ERNESTINE L. ROSE: It is exceedingly amusing to hear persons talk about throwing out Woman's Rights, when, if it had not been for Woman's Rights, that lady would not have had the courage to stand here and say what she did. (Applause). Pray, what means "loyal"? Loyal means to be true to one's highest conviction. Justice, like charity, begins at home. It is because we are loyal to truth, loyal to justice, loyal to right, loyal to humanity, that woman is included in that resolution. Now, what does this discussion mean? The lady acknowledges that it is not against Woman's Rights itself; she is *for* Woman's Rights. We are here to endeavor to help the cause of human rights and human freedom. We ought not to be afraid. You may depend upon it, if there are any of those who are called copperheads—but I don't like to call names, for even a copperhead is better than no head at all—(laughter)— if there are any copperheads here, I am perfectly sure they will object to this whole Convention; and if we want to consult them, let us adjourn *sine die*. If we are loyal to our highest convictions, we need not care how far it may lead. For truth, like water, will find its own level. No, friends, in the name of consistency let us not wrangle here simply because we associate the name of woman with human justice and human rights. Although I always like to see opposition on any subject, for it elicits truth much better than any speech, still I think it will be exceedingly inconsistent if, because some women out in the West are opposed to the Woman's Rights movement—though at the same time they take advantage of it—that therefore we shall throw it out of this resolution.

Mrs. SPENCE, of New York: I didn't come to this meeting to participate—only to listen. I don't claim to be a Northerner or a Southerner; but I claim to be a human being, and to belong to the human family (Applause). I belong to no sect or creed of politics or religion; I stand as an individual, defending the rights of every one as far as I can see them. It seems to me we have met here to come to some unity of action. If we attempt to bring in religious, political, or moral questions, we all must of necessity differ. We came here hoping to be inspired by each other to lay some plan by which we can unite in practical action. I have not heard such a proposition made; but I anticipate that it will be. (Hear, hear). Then if we are to unite on some proposition which is to be presented, it seems to me that our resolutions should be practical and directed to the main business. Let the object of the meeting be unity of action and expression in behalf of what we feel to be the highest right, our highest idea of liberty.

THE PRESIDENT (Lucy Stone): Every good cause can afford to be just. The lady from Wisconsin, who differs from some of us here, says she is an Anti-Slavery woman. We ought to believe her. She accepts the principles of the Woman's Rights movement, but she does not like the way in which it has been carried on. We ought to believe her. It is not, then, that she objects to the idea of the equality of women and negroes, but because she does not wish to have anything "tacked on" to the Loyal League, that to the mass of people does not seem to belong there. She seems to me to stand precisely in the position of those good people just at the close of the war of the Revolution. The people then, as now, had their hearts aching with the memory of their buried dead. They had had years of war from which they had garnered out sorrows as well as hopes; and when they came to establish a Union, they found that one black, unmitigated curse of slavery rooted in the soil. Some men said, "We can have no true Union where there is not justice to the negro. The black man is a human being, like us, with the same equal rights." They had given to the world the Declaration of Independence, grand and brave and beautiful. They said, "How can we form a true Union?" Some people representing the class that Mrs. Hoyt represents, answered, "Let us have a Union. We are weak; we have been beset for seven long years; do not let us meddle with the negro question. What we are for is a Union; let us have a Union at all hazards." There were earnest men, men of talent, who could speak well and earnestly, and they persuaded the others to silence. So they said nothing about slavery, and let the wretched monster live.

To-day, over all our land, the unburied bones of our fathers and sons and brothers tell the sad mistake that those men made when long ago they left this one great wrong in the land. They could not accomplish good by passing over a wrong. If the right of one single human being is to be disregarded by us, we fail in our loyalty to the country. All over this land women have no political existence. Laws pass over our heads that we can not unmake. Our property is taken from us without our consent. The babes we bear in anguish and carry in our arms are not ours. The few rights that we have, have been wrung from the Legislature by the Woman's Rights movement. We come to-day to say to those who are administering our Government and fighting our battles, "While you are going through this valley of humiliation, do not forget that you must be true alike to the women and the negroes." We can never be truly "loyal" if we leave them out. Leave them out, and we take the same backward step that our fathers took when they left out slavery. If justice to the negro and to woman is right, it can not hurt our loyalty to the country and the Union. If it is not right, let it go out of the way; but if it is right, there is no occasion that we should reject it, or ignore it. We make the statement that the Government derives its just powers from the consent of the governed, and that all human beings have equal rights. This is not an *ism*—it is simply an assertion that we shall be true to the highest truth.

A MAN IN THE AUDIENCE: The question was asked, as I entered this house, "Is it right for women to meet here and intermeddle in our public affairs?" It is the greatest possible absurdity for women to stand on that platform and talk of loyalty to a Government in which nine-tenths of the politicians of the land say they have no right to interfere, and still oppose Woman's Rights. The very act of standing there is an endorsement of Woman's Rights.

A VOICE: I believe this is a woman's meeting. Men have no right to speak here.

THE GENTLEMAN CONTINUED: It is on woman more than on man that the real evils of this war settle. It is not the soldier on the battle-field that suffers most; it is the wife, the mother, the daughter. (Applause. Cries of " Question, question ").

A VOICE: You are not a woman, sit down.

SUSAN B. ANTHONY: Some of us who sit upon this platform have many a time been clamored down, and told that we had no right to speak, and that we were out of our place in public meetings; far be it from us, when women assemble, and a man has a thought in his soul, burning for utterance, to retaliate upon him. (Laughter and applause).

The resolution was then put to vote.

A VOICE : Allow me to inquire if men have a right to vote on this question ?

THE PRESIDENT : I suppose men who are used to business know that they should *not* vote here. We give them the privilege of speaking.

The resolution was carried by a large majority.

SUSAN B. ANTHONY: The resolution recommending the practical work, has not yet been prepared. We have a grand platform on which to stand, and I hope we shall be able to present a plan of work equally grand. But, Mrs. President, if we should fail in doing this, we shall not fail to enunciate the principles of democracy and republicanism which underlie the structure of a free government. When the heads and hearts of the women of the North are fully imbued with the true idea, their hands will find a way to secure its accomplishment.

There is evidently very great earnestness on the part of all present to settle upon some practical work. I therefore ask that the women from every State of the Union, who are delegates here from Loyal Leagues and Aid Societies, shall retire, at the close of this meeting, to the lecture-room of this church, and there we will endeavor to fix upon the best possible plan we can gather from the counsels of the many. I hope this enthusiasm may be directed to good and legitimate ends, and not allowed to evaporate into thin air. I hope we shall aid greatly in the establishment of this Government on the everlasting foundation of justice to all.

DOCUMENT 22 (II: 78–80): Prayer of One Hundred
Thousand, presented by Charles Sumner, U. S. Senate,
February 9, 1864

The entire year was spent in rolling up the mammoth petition.
Many hands were busy sending out letters and petitions, counting and
assorting the names returned.   Each State was rolled up separately in
yellow paper, and tied with the regulation red tape, with the number of men and women who had signed, endorsed on the outside.
Nearly four hundred thousand were thus sent, and may now be
found in the archives at Washington.   The passage of the Thirteenth
Amendment made the continuance of the work unnecessary.   The
first installment of 100,000 was presented by Charles Sumner, in an
appropriate speech, Feb. 9th, 1864.

THE PRAYER OF ONE HUNDRED THOUSAND.

*Speech of Hon. Chas. Sumner on the Presentation of the First Installment
of the Emancipation Petition of the Woman's National League.*

In the Senate of the United States, Tuesday, February 9, 1864.

Mr. SUMNER.—Mr. President: I offer a petition which is now lying on
the desk before me.   It is too bulky for me to take up.   I need not add
that it is too bulky for any of the pages of this body to carry.

This petition marks a stage of public opinion in the history of slavery,
and also in the suppression of the rebellion.   As it is short I will read it:

"To the Senate and House of Representatives of the United
    States:

"The undersigned, women of the United States above the age of
eighteen years, earnestly pray that your honorable body will pass at the
earliest practicable day an act emancipating all persons of African descent held to involuntary service or labor in the United States."

There is also a duplicate of this petition signed by "men above the
age of eighteen years."

It will be perceived that the petition is in rolls. Each roll represents
a State.* For instance, here is New York with a list of seventeen thousand seven hundred and six names; Illinois with fifteen thousand three
hundred and eighty; and Massachusetts with eleven thousand six hundred and forty-one. These several petitions are consolidated into one
petition, being another illustration of the motto on our coin—*E pluribus
unum.*

This petition is signed by one hundred thousand men and women, who
unite in this unparalleled number to support its prayer. They are from
all parts of the country and from every condition of life. They are from
the sea-board, fanned by the free airs of the ocean, and from the Mississippi and the prairies of the West, fanned by the free airs which fer-
tilize that extensive region. They are from the families of the educated
and uneducated, rich and poor, of every profession, business, and calling in life, representing every sentiment, thought, hope, passion, activity,
intelligence which inspires, strengthens, and adorns our social system.

---

* The following is the abstract :

State.	Men.	Women.	Total.
New York	6,519	11,187	17,706
Illinois	6,382	8,998	15,380
Massachusetts	4,248	7,392	11,641
Pennsylvania	2,259	6,366	8,625
Ohio	3,676	4,654	8,330
Michigan	1,741	4,441	6,182
Iowa	2,025	4,014	6,039
Maine	1,225	4,362	5,587
Wisconsin	1,639	2,391	4,030
Indiana	1,075	2,591	3,666
New Hampshire	393	2,261	2,654
New Jersey	824	1,709	2,533
Rhode Island	827	1,451	2,278
Vermont	375	1,183	1,558
Connecticut	393	1,162	1,555
Minnesota	396	1,094	1,490
West Virginia	82	100	182
Maryland	115	50	165
Kansas	84	74	158
Delaware	67	70	137
Nebraska	13	20	33
Kentucky	21		21
Louisiana (New Orleans)		14	14
Citizens of the U. S. living in New Brunswick	19	17	36
	34,399	65,601	100,000

Here they are, a mighty army, one hundred thousand strong, without arms or banners; the advance-guard of a yet larger army.

But though memorable for their numbers, these petitioners are more memorable still for the prayer in which they unite. They ask nothing less than universal emancipation; and this they ask directly at the hands of Congress. No reason is assigned. The prayer speaks for itself. It is simple, positive. So far as it proceeds from the women of the country, it is naturally a petition, and not an argument. But I need not remind the Senate that there is no reason so strong as the reason of the heart. Do not all great thoughts come from the heart?

It is not for me, on presenting this petition, to assign reasons which the army of petitioners has forborne to assign. But I may not improperly add that, naturally and obviously, they all feel in their hearts, what reason and knowledge confirm: not only that slavery *as a unit*, one and indivisible, is the guilty origin of the rebellion, but that its influence everywhere, even outside the rebel States, has been hostile to the Union, always impairing loyalty, and sometimes openly menacing the national government. It requires no difficult logic to conclude that such a monster, wherever it shows its head, is a *national enemy*, to be pursued and destroyed as such, or at least a nuisance to the national cause to be abated as such. The petitioners know well that Congress is the depository of those supreme powers by which the rebellion, alike in its root and in its distant offshoots, may be surely crushed, and by which unity and peace may be permanently secured. They know well that the action of Congress may be with the co-operation of the slave-masters, or even without the co-operation, under the overruling law of military necessity, or the commanding precept of the Constitution " to guarantee to every State a Republican form of government." Above all, they know well that to save the country from peril, especially to save the national life, there is no power, in the ample arsenal of self-defense, which Congress may not grasp; for to Congress, under the Constitution, belongs the prerogative of the Roman Dictator to see that the Republic receives no detriment. Therefore to Congress these petitioners now appeal. I ask the reference of the petition to the Select Committee on Slavery and Freedmen.

It was referred, after earnest discussion, as Mr. Sumner proposed.

II. Reconstruction Alliances

THE WOMAN'S RIGHTS MOVEMENT reappeared at the end of the Civil War, its leaders determined to propel Reconstruction toward the realization of equal political rights for all citizens. The impress of the war experience lay clearly outlined upon the logic and methods of this effort in the second half of the 1860s. Woman suffrage advocates looked to their friends and potential allies in positions of national power and sought to wheedle and cajole politicians into a favorable bloc, confident that as Abolitionists' efforts had forced national policy shifts, so the women's long-standing protest would be converted at last into an important political issue.

Reformers' meetings were inspired by the sense of historic opportunity but remained nevertheless remarkably far-reaching in philosophical as well as strategic and tactical questions. In a sense, these meetings were a final, brief renaissance of the convention phase of the 1840s and 1850s, with outstanding veterans like Ernestine Rose, Lucretia Mott, and Abby Kelley Foster making their last series of public appearances. Once more, too, the echoes of the European revolutions of 1848 were heard, most notably in the oratory of Franziska Anneke, leading German-American woman suffrage leader. Joined by Frederick Douglass, the most prominent black political figure in the United States, by rising temperance movement stars such as Mary A. Livermore, and by representatives of working women, these meetings presented a veritable congress of radical reform, past and future.

Moral outrage, so brilliantly expressed against the unwillingness of major party politicians to take the question of woman suffrage seriously, had a real public importance for gathering a reform constituency. But perhaps the key role of oratory was to rally the convinced rather than widen significantly the circle of supporters. Woman's rights advocates exposed the limits of Radical Reconstruction and of the Republican party's dedication to equal rights. They could sketch out the requirements of a higher political morality but were lacking in strength to bring this morality into practice.

Defeat fed the flames of disagreement. The inner tragedy of the woman suffrage movement in these years was the bitter discord engendered among old friends and natural allies. No simple resolutions would be found because the whole strategy of postwar reform seemed at stake. Indeed, some of the sharpest debates among reformers were developed outward precisely from the suffrage question. Could formal Black equality be raised above all other, and at the possible expense of other questions? Should alliances be sought among those self-avowed radicals on other questions like Land and Irish freedom, even if the potential allies revealed a racist taint? Who was most fit to join the electorate if a choice had to be made—the educated and refined women or the mass of largely illiterate Black freedmen? Could the necessary transformation of American society proceed step by step through measured coalitions, or did the situation require a new party standing above the morass of Republican-Democratic corruption? The irony of the suffrage supporters' ardent debates of those questions was that the political mechanisms for national decision-making lay elsewhere, beyond the reach of these reformers. The Republican party's rightward turn and the futility of third-party efforts forced suffrage forces to rely on their own efforts. And the consequent awareness of powerlessness turned strategic decisions into moral claims, widening the distance between opponents. At times old comradeships, as between Frederick Douglass and Elizabeth Cady Stanton, were renewed even amidst the harshest arguments. But in the end, friendly sentiments and sweet memories were insufficient. The split between proponents of different strategies marked not only a new era for suffrage but the eclipse of a grand old phase of universal reformism. The unrecalcitrant radicals' final effort to create a "People's Party" in 1872 merely revealed their weakness and hurtled them back to Ulysses Grant and the Republican party they had so proudly left behind.

DOCUMENT 23 (II: 90–97): Congressional Action, 1866

LIBERTY victorious over slavery on the battle-field had now more powerful enemies to encounter at Washington. The slave set free; the master conquered; the South desolate; the two races standing face to face, sharing alike the sad results of war, turned with appealing looks to the General Government, as if to say, "How stand we now?" "What next?" Questions, our statesmen, beset with dangers, fears for the nation's life, of party divisions, of personal defeat, were wholly unprepared to answer. The reconstruction of the South involved the reconsideration of the fundamental principles of our Government, and the natural rights of man. The nation's heart was thrilled with prolonged debates in Congress and State Legislatures, in the pulpits and public journals, and at every fireside on these vital questions, which took final shape in three historic amendments.

The first point, his emancipation, settled, the political status of the negro was next in order; and to this end various propositions were submitted to Congress. But to demand his enfranchisement on the broad principle of natural rights, was hedged about with difficulties, as the logical result of such action must be the enfranchisement of all ostracised classes; not only the white women of the entire country, but the slave women of the South. Though our Senators and Representatives had an honest aversion to any proscriptive legislation against loyal women, in view of their varied and self-sacrificing work during the war, yet the only way they could open the constitutional door just wide enough to let the black *man* pass in, was to introduce the word "male" into the national Constitution. After the generous devotion of such women as Anna Carroll and Anna Dickinson in sustaining the policy of the Republicans, both in peace and war, they felt it would come with an ill-grace from that party, to place new barriers in woman's path to freedom. But how could the amendment be written without the word "male"? was the question.

Robert Dale Owen, being at Washington and behind the scenes at the time, sent copies of the various bills to the officers of the Loyal League in New York, and related to them some of the amusing discussions. One of the Committee proposed "persons" instead of "males." "That will never do," said another, "it would enfranchise all the Southern wenches." "Suffrage for black men will be all the strain the Republican party can stand," said another. Charles Sumner said, years afterward, that he wrote over nineteen pages of foolscap to get rid of the word "male" and yet keep "negro suffrage" as a party measure intact; but it could not be done.

Miss Anthony and Mrs. Stanton, ever on the watch-tower for legislation affecting women, were the first to see the full significance of the word "male" in the 14th Amendment, and at once sounded the alarm, and sent out petitions* for a constitutional amendment

---

* FORM OF PETITION. — *To the Senate and House of Representatives :* —The undersigned women of the United States, respectfully ask an amendment of the Constitution that shall prohibit the several States from disfranchising any of their citizens on the ground of sex.

In making our demand for Suffrage, we would call your attention to the fact that we represent fifteen million people—one-half the entire population of the country—intelligent, virtuous, native-born American citizens ; and yet stand outside the pale of political recognition. The Constitution classes us as " free people," and counts us *whole* persons in the basis of representation ; and yet are we governed without our consent, compelled to pay taxes without appeal, and punished for violations of law without choice of judge or juror. The experience of all ages, the Declarations of the Fathers, the Statute Laws of our own day, and the fearful revolution through which we have just passed, all prove the uncertain tenure of life, liberty, and property so long as the ballot—the only weapon of self-protection—is not in the hand of every citizen.

Therefore, as you are now amending the Constitution, and, in harmony with advancing civilization, placing new safeguards round the individual rights of four millions of emancipated slaves, we ask that you extend the right of Suffrage to Woman—the only remaining class of disfranchised citizens—and thus fulfill your constitutional obligation "to guarantee to every State in the Union a Republican form of Government." As all partial application of Republican principles must ever breed a complicated legislation as well as a discontented people, we would pray your Honorable Body, in order to simplify the machinery of Government and ensure domestic tranquillity, that you legislate hereafter for persons, citizens, tax-payers, and not for class or caste. For justice and equality your petitioners will ever pray.

to "prohibit the States from disfranchising any of their citizens on the ground of sex."*

Miss Anthony, who had spent the year in Kansas, started for New York the moment she saw the propositions before Congress to put the word "male" into the National Constitution, and made haste to rouse the women in the East to the fact that the time had come to begin vigorous work again for woman's enfranchisement.†

Mr. Tilton (December 27, 1865) proposed the formation of a National Equal Rights Society, demanding suffrage for black men and women alike, of which Wendell Phillips should be President, and the *National Anti-Slavery Standard* its organ. Mr. Beecher promised to give a lecture (January 30th) for the benefit of this universal suffrage

---

* JOINT RESOLUTIONS BEFORE CONGRESS AFFECTING WOMEN.

*To the Editor of the Standard—Sir :—*Mr. Broomall, of Pennsylvania ; Mr. Schenck, of Ohio ; Mr. Jenckes, of Rhode Island ; Mr. Stevens, of Pennsylvania, have each a resolution before Congress to amend the Constitution.

Article 1st, Section 2d, reads thus : " Representatives and direct taxes shall be apportioned among the several States which may be included within this Union according to their respective number."

Mr. Broomall proposes to amend by saying " male electors," Mr. Schenck " male citizens," Mr. Jenckes " male citizens," Mr. Stevens " legal voters." There is no objection to the amendment proposed by Mr. Stevens, as in process of time women may be made " legal voters " in the several States, and would then meet that requirement of the Constitution. But those urged by the other gentlemen, neither time, effort, nor State Constitutions could enable us to meet, unless, by a liberal interpretation of the amendment, a coat of mail to be worn at the polls might be judged all-sufficient. Mr. Jenckes and Mr. Schenck, in their bills, have the grace not to say a word about taxes, remembering perhaps that " taxation without representation is tyranny." But Mr. Broomall, though unwilling to share with us the honors of Government, would fain secure us a place in its burdens ; for while he apportions representatives to " male electors " only, he admits " *all the inhabitants* " into the rights, privileges, and immunities of taxation. Magnanimous M. C. !

I would call the attention of the women of the nation to the fact that under the Federal Constitution, as it now exists, there is not one word that limits the right of suffrage to any privileged class. This attempt to turn the wheels of civilization backward, on the part of Republicans claiming to be *the* Liberal party, should rouse every woman in the nation to a prompt exercise of the only right she has in the Government, the right of petition. To this end a committee in New York have sent out thousands of petitions, which should be circulated in every district and sent to its Representative at Washington as soon as possible.   ELIZABETH CADY STANTON.

NEW YORK, *January* 2, 1866.

† Leaving Rochester October 11th, she called on Martha Wright, Auburn ; Phebe Jones and Lydia Mott, Albany ; Mrs. Rose, Gibbons, Davis, Stanton, New York ; Lucy Stone and Antoinette Brown Blackwell, New Jersey ; Stephen and Abby Foster, Worcester ; Mrs. Severance, Dall, Nowell, Dr. Harriot K. Hunt, Dr. Zakzyewska, Mr. Phillips and Garrison, in Boston, urging them to join in sending protests to Washington against the pending legislation. Mr. Phillips at once consented to vote $500 from the " Jackson Fund " to commence the work. Miss Anthony and Mrs. Stanton spent all their " Christmas holidays " in writing letters and addressing appeals and petitions to every part of the country, and before the close of the session of 1865–66 ten thousand signatures were poured into Congress.

movement.   The *New York Independent* (Theodore Tilton, editor) gave the following timely and just rebuke of the proposed retrogressive legislation:

A LAW AGAINST WOMEN.

The spider-crab walks backward. Borrowing this creature's mossy legs, two or three gentlemen in Washington are seeking to fix these upon the Federal Constitution, to make that instrument walk backward in like style. For instance, the Constitution has never laid any legal disabilities upon woman. Whatever denials of rights it formerly made to our slaves, it denied nothing to our wives and daughters. The legal rights of an American woman—for instance, her right to her own property, as against a squandering husband; or her right to her own children, as against a malicious father—have grown, year by year, into a more generous and just statement in American laws. This beautiful result is owing in great measure to the persistent efforts of many noble women who, for years past, both publicly and privately, both by pen and speech, have appealed to legislative committees, and to the whole community, for an enlargement of the legal and civil status of their fellow-country women. Signal, honorable, and beneficent have been the works and words of Lucretia Mott, Lydia Maria Child, Paulina W. Davis, Abby Kelly Foster, Frances D. Gage, Lucy Stone, Caroline H. Dall, Antoinette Brown Blackwell, Susan B. Anthony, Elizabeth Cady Stanton, and many others. Not in all the land lives a poor woman, or a widow, who does not owe some portion of her present safety under the law to the brave exertions of these faithful laborers in a good cause.

Now, all forward-looking minds know that, sooner or later, the chief public question in this country will be woman's claim to the ballot. The Federal Constitution, as it now stands, leaves this question an open one for the several States to settle as they choose. Two bills, however, now lie before Congress proposing to array the fundamental law of the land against the multitude of American women by ordaining a denial of the political rights of a whole sex. To this injustice we object totally ! Such an amendment is a snap judgment before discussion; it is an obstacle to future progress; it is a gratuitous bruise inflicted upon the most tender and humane sentiment that has ever entered into American politics. If the present Congress is not called to legislate *for* the rights of women, let it not legislate *against* them.

But Americans now live who shall not go down into the grave till they have left behind them a Republican Government; and no republic is Republican which denies to half its citizens those rights which the Declaration of Independence, and which a true Christian Democracy make equal to all. Meanwhile, let us break the legs of the spider-crab !

While the 13th Amendment was pending, Senator Sumner wrote many letters to the officers of the Loyal League, saying, " Send on the petitions ; they give me opportunity for speech." " You are doing a noble work." " I am grateful to your Association for what you have done to arouse the country to insist on the extinction of slavery." And our petitions were sent again and again, 300,000 strong, and months after the measure was carried, they still rolled in from every quarter where the tracts and appeals had been scattered. But when the proposition for the 14th Amendment was pending, and the same women petitioned for their own civil and political rights, they received no letters of encouragement from Republicans nor Abolitionists; and now came some of the severest trials the women demanding the right of suffrage were ever called on to endure. Though loyal to the Government and the rights of the colored race, they found themselves in antagonism with all with whom they had heretofore sympathized. Though Unionists, Republicans, and Abolitionists, they could not without protest see themselves robbed of their birth-right as citizens of the republic by the proposed amendment. Republicans presented their petitions in a way to destroy their significance, as petitions for "universal suffrage," which to the public meant "manhood suffrage." Abolitionists refused to sign them, saying, "This is the negro's hour."*

---

* "THIS IS THE NEGRO'S HOUR."

To the Editor of the Standard—Sir :—By an amendment of the Constitution, ratified by three-fourths of the loyal States, the black man is declared free. The largest and most influential political party is demanding suffrage for him throughout the Union, which right in many of the States is already conceded. Although this may remain a question for politicians to wrangle over for five or ten years, the black man is still, in a political point of view, far above the educated women of the country. The representative women of the nation have done their uttermost for the last thirty years to secure freedom for the negro, and so long as he was lowest in the scale of being we were willing to press *his* claims; but now, as the celestial gate to civil rights is slowly moving on its hinges, it becomes a serious question whether we had better stand aside and see "Sambo" walk into the kingdom first. As self-preservation is the first law of nature, would it not be wiser to keep our lamps trimmed and burning, and when the constitutional door is open, avail ourselves of the strong arm and blue uniform of the black soldier to walk in by his side, and thus make the gap so wide that no privileged class could ever again close it against the humblest citizen of the republic?

"This is the negro's hour." Are we sure that he, once entrenched in all his inalienable rights, may not be an added power to hold us at bay? Have not "black male citizens" been heard to say they doubted the wisdom of extending the right of suffrage to women? Why should the African prove more just and generous than his Saxon compeers? If the two millions of Southern black women are not to be secured in their rights of person, property, wages, and children, their emancipation is but another form of slavery. In fact, it is better to be the slave of an educated white man, than of a degraded, ignorant black one. We who know what absolute power the statute laws of most of the States give man, in all his civil, political, and social relations, demand that in changing the status of the four millions of Africans, the women as well as the men shall be secured in all the rights, privileges, and immunities of citizens.

It is all very well for the privileged order to look down complacently and tell us, "This is the negro's hour; do not clog his way; do not embarrass the Republican party with any new issue; be generous and magnanimous; the negro once safe, the woman comes next." Now, if our prayer involved a new set of measures, or a new train of thought, it would be cruel to tax "white male citizens" with even two simple questions at a time; but the disfranchised all make the same demand, and the same logic and jus-

Colored men themselves opposed us, saying, do not block our chance by lumbering the Republican party with Woman Suffrage.

The Democrats readily saw how completely the Republicans were stultifying themselves and violating every principle urged in the debates on the 13th Amendment, and volunteered to help the women fight their battle. The Republicans had declared again and again that suffrage was a natural right that belonged to every citizen that paid taxes and helped to support the State. They had declared that the ballot was the only weapon by which one class could protect itself against the aggressions of another. Charles Sumner had rounded out one of his eloquent periods, by saying, " The ballot is the Columbiad of our political life, and every citizen who holds it is a full-armed monitor."

The Democrats had listened to all the glowing debates on these great principles of freedom until the argument was as familiar as a, b, c, and continually pressed the Republicans with their own weapons. Then those loyal women were taunted with having gone over to the Democrats and the Disunionists. But neither taunts nor persuasions moved them from their purpose to prevent, if possible, the introduction of the word " male " into the Federal Constitution, where it never had been before. They could not see the progress—in purging the Constitution of all invidious distinctions on the ground of color—while creating such distinctions for the first time in regard to sex.

In the face of all opposition they scattered their petitions broadcast, and in one session of Congress they rolled in upwards of ten thousand. The Democrats treated the petitioners with respect, and called attention in every way to the question.* But even such Re-

---

tice that secures suffrage to one class gives it to all. The struggle of the last thirty years has not been merely on the black man as such, but on the broader ground of his humanity. Our Fathers, at the end of the first revolution, in their desire for a speedy readjustment of all their difficulties, and in order to present to Great Britain, their common enemy, an united front, accepted the compromise urged on them by South Carolina, and a century of wrong, ending in another revolution, has been the result of their action. This is our opportunity to retrieve the errors of the past and mould anew the elements of Democracy. The nation is ready for a long step in the right direction ; party lines are obliterated, and all men are thinking for themselves. If our rulers have the justice to give the black man suffrage, woman should avail herself of that new-born virtue to secure her rights ; if not, she should begin with renewed earnestness to educate the people into the idea of universal suffrage.   ELIZABETH CADY STANTON.
NEW YORK, *December* 26, 1865.

* From the *New York Evening Express.*

SCENES IN THE HOUSE OF REPRESENTATIVES.—*Negroes are to Vote—Why not Coolies in California—Indians everywhere, and First of all, Fifteen Millions of our Countrywomen.*

The following occurred in the House, 'Tuesday, upon Thaddeus Stevens' resolution,

publicans as Charles Sumner presented them, if at all, under protest. A petition from Massachusetts, with the name of Lydia Maria
Child at the head, was presented by the great Senator under protest

from the Reconstruction Committee, to deprive the South of representation, unless the
South lets the negroes vote there. . . . .

Mr. CHANDLER, of New York, having the floor for an hour, said : Before proceeding with
my remarks, I will yield the floor for ten minutes to my colleague [Mr. Brooks].

Mr. BROOKS : Mr. Speaker, I do not rise, of course, to debate this resolution, in the
few minutes allowed me by my colleague, nor, in my judgment, does the resolution
need any discussion unless it may be for the mere purpose of agitation. I do not suppose that there is an honorable gentleman upon the floor of this House who believes for
a moment that any movement of this character is likely to become the fundamental law
of the land, and these propositions are, therefore, introduced only for the purpose of
agitation. If the honorable gentleman from Pennsylvania [Mr. Stevens] had been quite
confident of adopting this amendment, he would at the start have named what are States
of this Union. The opinion of the honorable gentleman himself, that there are no States
in this Union but those that are now represented upon this floor, I know full well, but
he knows as well that the President of the United States recognizes thirty-six States of
this Union, and that it is necessary to obtain the consent of three-fourths of those thirty-
six States, which number it is not possible to obtain. He knows very well that if his
amendment should be adopted by the Legislatures of States enough, in his judgment, to
carry it, before it could pass the tribunal of the Executive Chamber it would be obliged
to receive the assent of twenty-seven States in order to become an amendment to the
Constitution. The whole resolution, therefore, is for the purpose of mere agitation. It
is an appeal from this House to the outside constituencies that we know by the name of
buncombe. Here it was born, and here, after its agitation in the States, it will die.
Hence, I asked the gentleman from Pennsylvania this morning to be consistent in his
proposition. In one thing he is consistent, and that is in admitting the whole of the
Asiatic immigration, which, by the connection of our steamers with China and Japan
and the East Indies, is about to pour forth in mighty masses upon the Pacific coast to
the overwhelming even of the white population there.

Mr. STEVENS : I wish to correct the gentleman. I said it excluded Chinese.

Mr. BROOKS : How exclude them, when Chinese are to be included in the basis of
representation ?

Mr. STEVENS : I say it excludes them.

Mr. BROOKS : How exclude them ?

Mr. STEVENS : They are not included in the basis of representation.

Mr. BROOKS : Yes, if the States exclude them from the elective franchise ; and the
States of California and Oregon and Nevada are to be deprived of representation according to their population upon the floor of this House by this amendment. I asked him,
also, if the Indian was not a man and a brother, and I obtained no satisfactory answer
from the honorable gentleman. I speak now, in order to make his resolution consistent,
for no one hundred thousand coolies or wild savages, but I raise my voice here in behalf
of fifteen million of our countrywomen, the fairest, brightest portion of creation, and I
ask why they are not permitted to vote for Representatives under this resolution ? Why,
in organizing a system of liberality and justice, not recognize in the case of free women
as well as free negroes the right of representation ?

Mr. STEVENS : The gentleman will allow me to say that this bill does not exclude
women. It does not say who shall vote.

Mr. BROOKS : I comprehend all that ; but the whole object of this amendment is to
obtain votes for the negroes. That is its purport, tendency, and meaning ; and it pun-
ishes those who will not give a vote to the negroes in the Southern States of our Union.
That is the object of the resolution, and the ground upon which it is presented to this
House and to the country. This is a new era ; this is an age of progress. Indians are not
only Indians, but men and brothers ; and why not, in a resolution like this, include the fair
sex too, and give them the right to representation ? Will it be said that this sex does

as " most inopportune!"   As if there could be a more fitting time
for action than when the bills were pending.

During the morning hour of February 21st, Senator Henderson,
of Missouri, presented a petition from New York.

---

not claim a right to representation? Many members here have petitions from these
fifteen millions of women, or a large portion of them, for representation, and for the
right to vote on equal terms with the stronger sex, who they say are now depriving
them of it. To show that such is their wish and desire, I will send to the Clerk's desk
to be read certain documents, to which I ask the attention of the honorable gentleman
from Pennsylvania [Mr. Stevens], for in one of them he will find he is somewhat interested.

The Clerk read as follows:

STANDARD OFFICE, 48 Beekman Street, New York, *Jan.* 20, 1866.

Dear Sir:—I send you the inclosed copy of petition and signatures sent to Thaddeus
Stevens last week. I then urged Mr. Stevens, if their committee of fifteen could not
report favorably on our petitions, they would, at least, not interpose any new barrier
against woman's right to the ballot.

Mrs. Stanton has sent you a petition—I trust you will present that at your earliest con-
venience. The Democrats are now in minority. May they drive the Republicans to do
good works—not merely to hold the rebel States in check until negro men shall be
guaranteed their right to a voice in their governments, but to hold the party to a logical
consistency that shall give every responsible citizen in every State equal right to the
ballot. Will you, sir, please send me whatever is said or done with our petitions? Will
you also give me the names of members whom you think would present petitions for us?

Hon. JAMES BROOKS.   Respectfully yours,   SUSAN B. ANTHONY.

A PETITION FOR UNIVERSAL SUFFRAGE.

To the Senate and House of Representatives:—[The petition here presented has been
already in *The Express*. The following are the signatures to the petition sent to Mr.
Stevens]: Elizabeth Cady Stanton, New York; Susan B. Anthony, Rochester, N. Y.;
Antoinette Brown Blackwell, New York; Lucy Stone, Newark, N. J.; Ernestine L. Rose,
New York; Joanna S. Morse, 48 Livingston St., Brooklyn; Elizabeth R. Tilton, 48 Liv-
ingston St., Brooklyn; Ellen Hoxie Squier, 34 St. Felix St., Brooklyn; Mary Fowler
Gilbert, 294 West 19th St., New York; Mary E. Gilbert, 294 West 19th St., New York;
Mattie Griffith, New York.

The SPEAKER: The ten minutes of the gentleman from New York [Mr. Brooks] have
expired.

Mr. BROOKS: I will only say that at the proper time I will move to amend—or if I do
not I would suggest to some gentleman on the other side to move it—this proposed
amendment by inserting the words "or sex" after the word "color," so that it will read:

Provided, That whenever the elective franchise shall be denied or abridged in any State
on account of race or color or sex, all persons of such race or color or sex shall be excluded from the basis of representation.

Mr. STEVENS: Is the gentleman from N. Y. [Mr. Brooks] in favor of that amendment?

Mr. BROOKS: I am if negroes are permitted to vote.

Mr. STEVENS: That does not answer my question. Is the gentleman in favor of the
amendment he has indicated?

Mr. BROOKS: I suggested that I would move it at a convenient time.

Mr. STEVENS: Is the gentleman in favor of his own amendment?

Mr. BROOKS: I am in favor of my own color in preference to any other color, and I
prefer the white women of my country to the negro. [Applause on the floor and in the
galleries promptly checked by the Speaker]. The Speaker said he saw a number of persons clapping in the galleries. He would endeavor, to the best of his ability, whether
supported by the House or not, to preserve order. Applause was just as much out of
order as manifestations of disapproval, and hisses not more than clapping of hands. Instead of general applause on the floor, gentlemen on the floor should set a good example.

DOCUMENT 24 (II: 152–54, 168–71, 174–75): Woman's Rights Convention, New York City, May 10, 1866, including Address to Congress adopted by the Convention

The first Woman's Rights Convention* after the war was held in the Church of the Puritans, New York, May 10th, 1866.

As the same persons were identified with the Anti-slavery and

---

* CALL FOR THE ELEVENTH NATIONAL WOMAN'S RIGHTS CONVENTION.—The Convention will be held in the City of New York, at the Church of the Puritans, Union Square, on Thursday, the 10th of May, 1866, at 10 o'clock. Addresses will be delivered by ERNESTINE L. ROSE, FRANCES D. GAGE, WENDELL PHILLIPS, THEODORE TILTON, ELIZABETH CADY STANTON, and (probably) LUCRETIA MOTT and ANNA E. DICKINSON.

Those who tell us the republican idea is a failure, do not see the deep gulf between our broad theory and partial legislation ; do not see that our Government for the last century has been but the repetition of the old experiments of class and caste. Hence, the failure is not in the principle, but in the lack of virtue on our part to apply it. The question now is, have we the wisdom and conscience, from the present upheavings of our political system, to reconstruct a government on the one enduring basis that has never yet been tried—" EQUAL RIGHTS TO ALL."

From the proposed class legislation in Congress, it is evident we have not yet learned wisdom from the experience of the past ; for, while our representatives at Washington are discussing the right of suffrage for the black man, as the only protection to life, liberty and happiness, they deny that " necessity of citizenship " to woman, by proposing to introduce the word " male " into the Federal Constitution. In securing suffrage but to another shade of *manhood*, while we disfranchise fifteen million tax-payers, we come not one line nearer the republican idea. Can a ballot in the hand of woman, and dignity on her brow, more unsex her than do a scepter and a crown ? Shall an American Congress pay less honor to the daughter of a President than a British Parliament to the daughter of a King ? Should not our petitions command as respectful a hearing in a republican Senate as a speech of Victoria in the House of Lords ? Do we not claim that here all men and women are nobles — all heirs apparent to the throne ? The fact that this backward legislation has roused so little thought or protest from the women of the country, but proves what some of our ablest thinkers have already declared, that the greatest barrier to a government of equality was the aristocracy of its women. For, while woman holds an ideal position above man and the work of life, poorly imitating the pomp, heraldry, and distinction of an effete European civilization, we as a nation can never realize the divine idea of equality.

To build a true republic, the church and the home must undergo the same upheavings

223

Woman's Rights Societies, and as by the "Proclamation of Emancipation" the colored man was now a freeman, and a citizen; and as bills were pending in Congress to secure him in the right of suffrage, the same right women were demanding, it was proposed to merge the societies into one, under the name of "The American Equal Rights Association," that the same conventions, appeals, and petitions, might include both classes of disfranchised citizens. The proposition was approved by the majority of those present, and the new organization completed at an adjourned session. Though Mr. Garrison, with many other abolitionists, feeling that the Anti-slavery work was finished, had retired, and thus partly disorganized that Society, yet, in its executive session, Wendell Phillips, President, refused to entertain the proposition, on the ground that such action required an amendment to the constitution, which could not be made without three months previous notice. Nevertheless there was a marked division of opinion among the anti-slavery friends present.

At an early hour Dr. Cheever's church was well filled with an audience chiefly of ladies, who received the officers and speakers* of the Convention with hearty applause. Elizabeth Cady Stanton, President of the "National Woman's Rights Committee," called the Convention to order, and said:

We have assembled to-day to discuss the right and duty of women to claim and use the ballot. Now in the reconstruction is the opportunity, perhaps for the century, to base our government on the broad principle of equal rights to all. The representative women of the nation feel that they have an interest and duty equal with man in the struggles and triumphs of this hour.

----

we now see in the State;—for, while our egotism, selfishness, luxury and ease are baptized in the name of Him whose life was a sacrifice,—while at the family altar we are taught to worship wealth, power and position, rather than humanity, it is vain to talk of a republican government:—The fair fruits of liberty, equality and fraternity must be blighted in the bud, till cherished in the heart of woman. At this hour the nation needs the highest thought and inspiration of a true womanhood infused into every vein and artery of its life; and woman needs a broader, deeper education, such as a pure religion and lofty patriotism alone can give. From the baptism of this second revolution should she not rise up with new strength and dignity, clothed in all those "rights, privileges and immunities" that shall best enable her to fulfill her highest duties to Humanity, her Country, her Family and Herself?

On behalf of the National Woman's Rights Central Committee,

ELIZABETH CADY STANTON, President.

SUSAN B. ANTHONY, Secretary.

New York (48 Beekman street), March 31, 1866.

* Ernestine L. Rose, Wendell Phillips, John T. Sargeant, O. B. Frothingham, Frances D. Gage, Elizabeth Cady Stanton, Susan B. Anthony, Theodore Tilton, Lucretia Mott, Martha C. Wright, Stephen S. and Abbey Kelley Foster, Margaret Winchester and Parker Pillsbury.

It may not be known to all of you that, during the past year, thousands of petitions, asking the ballot for woman, have been circulated through the Northern States and sent to Congress. Onr thanks are due to the Hon. James Brooks for his kindness in franking our petitions, and his skill in calling to them the attention of the nation. As we have lost this champion in the House, I trust his more fortunate successor will not *dodge* his responsibilities to his countrywomen who are taxed but not represented. This should be a year of great activity among the women of this State. As New York is to have a constitutional convention in '67, it behooves us now to make an earnest demand, by appeals and petitions, to have the word " male " as well as " white " stricken from our Constitution.

SUSAN B. ANTHONY, presented several resolutions for consideration.

5. *Resolved*, That disfranchisement *in a republic* is as great an anomaly, if not cruelty, as slavery itself. It is, therefore, the solemn duty of Congress, in "*guaranteeing a republican form of government to every State of this Union,*" to see that there be no abridgment of suffrage among persons responsible to law, on account of color or sex.

6. *Resolved*, That the Joint Resolutions and report of the " Committee of Fifteen," now before Congress, to introduce the word "*male*" into the Federal Constitution, are a desecration of the last will and testament of the Fathers, a violation of the spirit of republicanism, and cruel injustice to the women of the nation.

7. *Resolved*, That while we return our thanks to those members of Congress who, recognizing the sacred right of petition, gave our prayer for the ballot a respectful consideration, we also remind those who, with scornful silence laid them on the table, or with flippant sentimentality pretended to exalt us to the clouds, above man, the ballot and the work of life, that we consider no position more dignified and womanly than on an even platform with man worthy to lay the corner-stone of a republic in equality and justice.

8. *Resolved*, That we recommend to the women of the several States to petition their Legislatures to take the necessary steps to so amend their constitutions as to secure the right of suffrage to every citizen, without distinction of race, color or sex ; and especially in those States that are soon to hold their constitutional conventions.

* * *

ADDRESS TO CONGRESS.

Adopted by the Eleventh National Woman's Rights Convention, held in New York City, Thursday, May 10, 1866.

To the Senate and House of Representatives :

We have already appeared many times during the present session before your honorable body, in petitions, asking the enfranchisement of woman ; and now, from this National Convention we again make our appeal, and urge you to lay no hand on that "pyramid of rights," the Constitution of the Fathers," unless to add glory to its height and strength to its foundation.

We will not rehearse the oft-repeated arguments on the natural rights of every citizen, pressed as they have been on the nation's conscience for the last thirty years in securing freedom for the black man, and so grandly echoed on the floor of Congress during the past winter. We can not add one line or precept to the inexhaustible speech recently made by Charles Sumner in the Senate, to prove that "no just government can be formed without the consent of the governed ;" to prove the dignity, the education, the power, the necessity, the salvation of the ballot in the hand of every man and woman ; to prove that a just government and a true church rest alike on the sacred rights of the individual.

As you are familiar with that speech of the session on "EQUAL RIGHTS TO ALL," so convincing in facts, so clear in philosophy, and so elaborate in quotations from the great minds of the past, without reproducing the chain of argument, permit us to call your attention to a few of its unanswerable assertions on the ballot :

I plead now for the ballot, as the great guarantee ; and *the only sufficient guarantee*—being in itself peacemaker, reconciler, schoolmaster and protector—to which we are bound by every necessity and every reason ; and I speak also for the good of the States lately in rebellion, as well as for the glory and safety of the Republic, that it may be an example to mankind.

Ay, sir, the ballot is the Columbiad of our political life, and every citizen who has it is a full-armed Monitor.

The ballot is *schoolmaster*. Reading and writing are of inestimable value, but the ballot teaches what these can not teach.

Plutarch records that the wise men of Athens charmed the people by saying that *Equality causes no war*, and "both the rich and the poor repeated it."

The ballot is like charity, which never faileth, and without which man is only as sounding brass or a tinkling cymbal. The ballot is the one thing needful, without which rights of testimony and all other rights will be no better than cobwebs, which the master will break through with impunity. To him who has the ballot all other things shall be given—protection, opportunity, education, a homestead. The ballot is like the Horn of Abundance, out of which overflow rights of every kind, with corn, cotton, rice, and all the fruits of the earth. Or, better still, it is like the hand of the body, without which man, who is now only a little lower than the angels, must have continued only a little above the brutes. They are fearfully and wonderfully made ; but as is the hand in the work of civilization, so is the ballot in the work of government. "Give me the ballot, and I can move the world."

Do you wish to see harmony truly prevail, so that industry, society, government, civilization, may all prosper, and the Republic may wear a crown of true greatness ? Then do not neglect the ballot.

Lamartine said, "Universal Suffrage is the first truth and only basis of every national republic."

In regard to "Taxation without representation," Mr. Sumner quotes from Lord Coke:

The Supreme Power cannot take from any man any part of his property *without consent in person, or by representation.*

Taxes are not to be laid on the people, but by their consent in person, or by representation.

I can see no reason to doubt but that the imposition of taxes, whether on trade, or on land, or houses, or ships, or real or personal, fixed or floating, property in the colonies, is absolutely irreconcilable with the rights of the colonies, as British subjects, *and as men.* I say men, for in a state of nature no man can take any property from me without my consent. *If he does, he deprives me of my liberty and makes me a slave.* The very act of taxing, exercised over those who are not represented, appears to me to deprive them of one of their most essential rights as freemen, and if continued seems to be in effect an entire disfranchisement of every civil right. For what one civil right is worth a rush, after a man's property is subject to be taken from him at pleasure without his consent ?

In demanding suffrage for the black man you recognize the fact that as a freedman he is no longer a " part of the family," and that, therefore, his master is no longer his representative ; hence, as he will now be liable to taxation, he must also have representation. Woman, on the contrary, has never been such a " part of the family " as to escape taxation. Although there has been no formal proclamation giving her an individual existence, she has always had the right to property and wages, the right to make contracts and do business in her own name. And even married women, by recent legislation, have been secured in these civil rights. Woman now holds a vast amount of the property in the country, and pays her full proportion of taxes, revenue included. On what principle, then, do you deny her representation ? By what process of reasoning Charles Sumner was able to stand up in the Senate, a few days after these sublime utterances, and rebuke 15,000,000 disfranchised tax-payers for the exercise of their right of petition merely, is past understanding. If he felt that this was not the time for woman to even mention her right to representation, why did he not take breath in some of his splendid periods, and propose to release the poor shirtmakers, milliners and dressmakers, and all women of property, from the tyranny of taxation ?

We propose no new theories. We simply ask that you secure to ALL the practical application of the immutable principles of our government, without distinction of race, color or sex. And we urge our demand *now*, because you have the opportunity and the power to take this onward step in legislation. The nations of the earth stand watching and waiting to see if our Revolutionary idea, "all men are created equal," can be realized in government. Crush not, we pray you, the million hopes that hang on our success. Peril not another bloody war. Men and parties must pass away, but justice is eternal. And they only who work in harmony with its laws are immortal. All who have carefully noted the proceedings of this Congress, and contrasted your speeches with those made under the old *régime* of slavery, must have seen the added power and eloquence that greater freedom gives. But still you propose no action on your grand ideas. Your Joint Resolutions, your Reconstruction Reports, do not reflect your highest thought. The constitution, in basing representation on " respective numbers," covers a broader ground than any you have yet proposed. Is not the only amendment needed to Article 1st, Section 3d, to strike out the exceptions which follow "respective numbers ?" And is it not your duty, by securing a republican form of government to every State, to see that these "respective numbers" are made up of enfranchised citizens ? Thus bringing your legislation up to the Constitution—not the Constitution down to your party possibilities ! ! The only tenable ground of representation is UNIVERSAL SUFFRAGE, as it is only through Universal Suffrage that the principle of "Equal Rights to All" can be realized. All prohibitions based on race, color, sex, property, or education, are violations of the republican idea; and the various qualifications now proposed are but so many plausible pretexts to debar new classes from the ballot-box. The limitations of property and intelligence, though unfair, can be met ; as with freedom must come the repeal of statute-laws that deny schools and wages to the negro. So time makes him a voter. But color and sex ! Neither time nor statutes can make black white, or woman man ! You assume to be the representatives of 15,000,000 women—American citizens —who already possess every *attainable* qualification for the ballot. Women read and write, hold many offices under government, pay taxes, and the penalties of crime, and yet are allowed to exercise but the one right of petition.

For twenty years we have labored to bring the statute laws of the several States into harmony with the broad principles of the Constitution, and have been so far successful that in many, little remains to be done but to secure the right of suffrage. Hence, our prompt protest against the propositions before Congress to introduce the word "male" into the Federal Constitution, which, if successful, would block all State action in giving the ballot to woman. As the only way disfranchised citizens can appear before you, we availed ourselves of the sacred right of petition. And, as our representatives, it was your duty to give those petitions a respectful reading and a serious consideration. How well a Republican Senate performed that duty, is already inscribed on the page of history. Some tell us it is not judicious to press the claims of women *now ;* that this is not the time. Time ? When you propose legislation so fatal to the best interests of woman and the nation, shall we be silent till the deed is done ? No ! As we love republican ideas, we must resist tyranny   As we honor the position of American Senator, we must appeal from the politician to the man.

With man, woman shared the dangers of the Mayflower on a stormy sea, the dreary landing on Plymouth Rock, the rigors of a New England winter, and the privations of a seven years' war. With him she bravely threw off the British yoke, felt every pulsation of his heart for freedom, and inspired the glowing eloquence that maintained it through the century. With you, we have just passed through the agony and death, the resurrection and triumph, of another revolution, doing all in our power to mitigate its horrors and gild its glories. And now, think you we have no souls to fire, no brains to weigh your arguments ; that, after education such as this, we can stand silent witnesses while you sell our birth-right of liberty, to save from a timely death an effete political organization ? No, as we respect womanhood, we must protest against this desecration of the magna charta of American liberties : and with an importunity not to be repelled, our demand must ever be: " No compromise of human rights "—" No admission in the Constitution of inequality of rights, or disfranchisement on account of color or sex."

In the oft-repeated experiments of class and caste, who can number the nations that have risen but to fall ? Do not imagine you come one line nearer the demand of justice by enfranchising but another shade of *man*hood; for, in denying representation to woman you still cling to the same principle on which all the governments of the past have been wrecked. The right way, the safe way, is so clear, the path of duty is so straight and simple, that we who are equally interested with yourselves in the result, conjure you to act not for the passing hour, not with reference to transient benefits, but to do now the one grand deed that shall mark the progress of the century—proclaim EQUAL RIGHTS TO ALL. We press our demand for the ballot at this time in no narrow, captious or selfish spirit; from no contempt of the black man's claims, nor antagonism with you, who in the progress of civilization are now the privileged order; but from the purest patriotism, for the highest good of every citizen, for the safety of the Republic, and as a spotless example to the nations of the earth.

*   *   *

Anthony proposed a list of names as officers* of the Association.
Mrs. Stanton thanked the Convention for the honor proposed, to
make her President, but said she should prefer to see Lucretia Mott
in that office; that thus that office might ever be held sacred in the
memory that it had first been filled by one so loved and honored by
all. "I shall be happy as Vice-President to relieve my dear friend
of the arduous duties of her office, if she will but give us the blessing of her name as President." Mrs. Stanton then moved that Mrs.
Mott be the President, which was seconded by many voices, and
carried by a unanimous vote.

Mrs. Mott, escorted to the Chair by Stephen S. Foster, remarked
that her age and feebleness unfitted her for any public duties, but
she rejoiced in the inauguration of a movement broad enough to
cover class, color, and sex, and would be happy to give her name and
influence, if thus she might encourage the young and strong to carry
on the good work. On motion of Theodore Tilton, Mrs. Stanton
was made first Vice-President. The rest of the names were approved.

Mrs. STANTON said, It had been the desire of her heart to see the Anti-
Slavery and Woman's Rights organizations merged into an Equal Rights
Association, as the two questions were now one. With emancipation, all
that the black man asks is the right of suffrage. With the special legislation of the last twenty years, all that woman asks is the right of suffrage. Hence it seems an unnecessary expenditure of force and substance for the same men and women to meet in convention on Tuesday
to discuss the right of one class to the ballot, and on Thursday to discuss the right of another class to the same. Has not the time come, Mrs.
President, to bury the black man and the woman in the citizen, and our
two organizations in the broader work of reconstruction? They who have
been trained in the school of anti-slavery; they who, for the last thirty
years, have discussed the whole question of human rights, which involves
every other question of trade, commerce, finance, political economy, jurisprudence, morals and religion, are the true statesmen for the new republic—the best enunciators of our future policy of justice and equality.
Any work short of this is narrow and partial and fails to meet the requirements of the hour. What is so plain to me, may, I trust, be so to
all before the lapse of many months, that all who have worked together
thus far, may still stand side by side in this crisis of our nation's history.

JAMES MOTT said, he rejoiced that the women had seen fit to re-organ-

---

* President, Elizabeth Cady Stanton; Vice-Presidents, Frederick Douglass, Frances D.
Gage, Robert Purvis, Theodore Tilton, Josephine S. Griffing, Martha C. Wright, Rebecca
W. Mott; Corresponding Secretaries, Susan B. Anthony, Mattie Griffith, Caroline M. Sev-
erance; Recording Secretary, Henry B. Blackwell; Treasurer, Ludlow Patton; Execu-
tive Committee, Elizabeth Cady Stanton, Lucy Stone, Edwin A. Studwell, Margaret E.
Winchester, Aaron M. Powell, Susan B. Anthony, Parker Pillsbury, Elizabeth Gay, Mary
F. Gilbert, Stephen S. Foster, Lydia Mott, Antoinette B. Blackwell, Wendell Phillips
Garrison.

ize their movement into one for equal rights to all, that he felt the time had come to broaden our work. He felt the highest good of the nation demanded the recognition of woman as a citizen. We could have no true government until all the people gave their consent to the laws that govern them.

STEPHEN S. FOSTER said, Many seemed to think that the one question for this hour was negro suffrage. The question for every man and woman, he thought, was the true basis of the reconstruction of our government, not the rights of woman, or the negro, but the rights of all men and women. Suffrage for woman was even a more vital question than for the negro; for in giving the ballot to the black·man, we bring no new element into the national life—simply another class of men. And for one, he could not ask woman to go up and down the length and breadth of the land demanding the political recognition of any class of disfranchised citizens, while her own rights are ignored. Thank God, the human family are so linked together, that no one man can ever enjoy life, liberty, or happiness, so long as the humblest being is crippled in a single right. I have demanded the freedom of the slave the last thirty years, because he was a human being, and I now demand suffrage for the negro because he is a human being, and for the same reason I demand the ballot for woman. Therefore, our demand for this hour is equal suffrage to all disfranchised classes, for the one and the same reason—they are all human beings.

MARTHA C. WRIGHT said: Some one had remarked that we wished to merge ourselves into an Equal Rights Association to get rid of the odious name of Woman's Rights. This she repudiated as unworthy and untrue. Every good cause had been odious some time, even the name Christian has had its odium in all nations. We desire the change, because we feel that at this hour our highest claims are as citizens, and not as women. I for one have always gloried in the name of Woman's Rights, and pitied those of my sex who ignobly declared they had all the rights they wanted. We take the new name for the broader work because we see it is no longer woman's province to be merely a humble petitioner for redress of grievances, but that she must now enter into the fullness of her mission, that of helping to make the laws, and administer justice.

DOCUMENT 25 (II: 235–37): Henry Blackwell, Letter
from the Kansas Campaign, April 21, 1867

JUNCTION CITY, KANSAS, *April* 21, 1867.
DEAR FRIENDS, E. C. STANTON AND SUSAN B. ANTHONY:

You will be glad to know that Lucy and I are going over the length and
breadth of this State speaking every day, and sometimes twice, journeying
from twenty-five to forty miles daily, sometimes in a carriage and sometimes
in an open wagon, with or without springs. We climb hills and dash down
ravines, ford creeks, and ferry over rivers, rattle across limestone ledges,
struggle through muddy bottoms, fight the high winds on the high rolling
upland prairies, and address the most astonishing (and astonished) audiences
in the most extraordinary places. To-night it may be a log school house, to-
morrow a stone church; next day a store with planks for seats, and in one
place, if it had not rained, we should have held forth in an unfinished court
house, with only four stone walls but no roof whatever.

The people are a queer mixture of roughness and intelligence, recklessness, and conservatism. One swears at women who want to wear the breeches; another wonders whether we ever heard of a fellow named Paul; a third is not going to put women on an equality with niggers. One woman told Lucy that no decent woman would be running over the country talking nigger and woman. Her brother told Lucy that "he had had a woman who was under the sod, but that if she had ever said she wanted to vote he would have pounded her to death!"

The fact is, however, that we have on our side all the shrewdest politicians and all the best class of men and women in this State. Our meetings are doing much towards organizing and concentrating public sentiment in our favor, and the papers are beginning to show front in our favor. We fought and won a pitched battle at Topeka in the convention, and have possession of the machine. By the time we get through with the proposed series of meetings, it will be about the 20th of May, if Lucy's voice and strength hold out. The scenery of this State is lovely. In summer it must be very fine indeed, especially in this Western section the valleys are beautiful, and the bluffs quite bold and romantic.

I think we shall probably succeed in Kansas next fall if the State is thoroughly canvassed, not else. We are fortunate in having Col. Sam N. Wood as an organizer and worker. We owe everything to Wood, and he is really a thoroughly noble, good fellow, and a hero. He is a short, rather thick set, somewhat awkward, and "slouchy" man, extremely careless in his dress, blunt and abrupt in his manner, with a queer inexpressive face, little blue eyes which can look dull or flash fire or twinkle with the wickedest fun. He is so witty, sarcastic, and cutting, that he is a terrible foe, and will put the laugh even on his best friends. The son of a Quaker mother, he held the baby while his wife acted as one of the officers, and his mother another, in a Woman's Rights Convention seventeen years ago. Wood has helped off more runaway slaves than any man in Kansas. He has always been *true* both to the negro and the woman. But the negroes dislike and distrust him because he has never allowed the word white to be struck out, unless the word male should be struck out also. He takes exactly Mrs. Stanton's ground, that the colored men and women shall enter the kingdom *together*, if at all. So, while he advocates both, he fully realizes the wider scope and far greater grandeur of the battle for *woman*. Lucy and I like Wood very much. We have seen a good deal of him, first at Topeka, again at Cottonwood Falls, his home, and on the journey thence to Council Grove and to this place. Our arrangements for conveyances failed, and Wood with characteristic energy and at great personal inconvenience brought us through himself. It is worth a journey to Kansas to know him for he is an original and a genius. If he should die next month I should consider the election lost. But if he live, and we all in the East drop other work and spend September and October in Kansas, we shall succeed. I am glad to say that our friend D. R. Anthony is out for both propositions in the *Leavenworth Bulletin*. But his sympathies are so especially with the negro question that we must have Susan out here to strengthen his hands. We must have Mrs. Stanton, Susan, Mrs. Gage, and Anna Dickinson, this fall. Also Ben Wade and Carl Schurz, if possible. We must also try to get 10,000 each of Mrs. Stanton's address, of Lucy Stone's address, and of Mrs. Mills article on the Enfranchisement of Women, printed for us by the Hovey Fund.

Kansas is to be *the battle ground* for 1867. *It must not be allowed to fail.* The politicians here, except Wood and Robinson, are generally " on the fence." But they dare not oppose us openly. And the Democratic leaders are quite disposed to take us up. If the Republicans come out against us the Democrats will take us up. Do not let anything prevent your being here September 1 *for the campaign*, which will end in November. There will be a big fight and a great excitement. After the fight is over Mrs. Stanton will never have *use* for *notes* or *written* speeches any more.

Yours truly,   HENRY B. BLACKWELL.

DOCUMENT 26 (II: 193–94): Sojourner Truth, Address to the First Annual Meeting of the American Equal Rights Association, New York City, May 9, 1867

My friends, I am rejoiced that you are glad, but I don't know how you will feel when I get through. I come from another field—the country of the slave. They have got their liberty—so much good luck to have slavery partly destroyed; not entirely. I want it root and branch destroyed. Then we will all be free indeed. I feel that if I have to answer for the deeds done in my body just as much as a man, I have a right to have just as much as a man. There is a great stir about colored men getting their rights, but not a word about the colored women; and if colored men get their rights, and not colored women theirs, you see the colored men will be masters over the women, and it will be just as bad as it was before. So I am for keeping the thing going while things are stirring; because if we wait till it is still, it will take a great while to get it going again. White women are a great deal smarter, and know more than colored women, while colored women do not know scarcely anything. They go out washing, which is about as high as a colored woman gets, and their men go about idle, strutting up and down; and when the women come home, they ask for their money and take it all, and then scold because there is no food. I want you to consider on that, chil'n. I call you chil'n; you are somebody's chil'n, and I am old enough to be mother of all that is here. I want women to have their rights. In the courts women have no right, no voice; nobody speaks for them. I wish woman to have her voice there among the pettifoggers. If it is not a fit place for women, it is unfit for men to be there.

I am above eighty years old; it is about time for me to be going. I have been forty years a slave and forty years free, and would be here forty years more to have equal rights for all. I suppose I am kept here because something remains for me to do; I suppose I am yet to help to break the chain. I have done a great deal of work; as much as a man, but did not get so much pay. I used to work in the field and bind grain, keeping up with the cradler; but men doing no more, got twice as much pay; so with the German women. They work in the field and do as much work, but do not get the pay. We do as much, we eat as much, we want as much. I suppose I am about the only colored woman that goes about to speak for the rights of the colored women. I want to keep the thing stirring, now that the ice is cracked. What we want is a little money. You men know that you get as much again as women when you write, or for what you do. When we get our rights we shall not have to come to you for money, for then we shall have money enough in our own pockets; and may be you will ask us for money. But help us now until we get it. It is a good consolation to know that when we have got this battle once fought we shall not be coming to you any more. You have been having our rights so long, that you think, like a slave-holder, that you own us. I know that it is hard for one who has held the reins for so long to give up; it cuts like a knife. It will feel all the better when it closes up again. I have been in Washington about three years, seeing about these colored people. Now colored men have the right to vote. There ought to be equal rights now more than ever, since colored people have got their freedom. I am going to talk several times while I am here; so now I will do a little singing. I have not heard any singing since I came here.

Accordingly, suiting the action to the word, Sojourner sang, "We are going home." "There, children," said she, "in heaven we shall rest from all our labors; first do all we have to do here. There I am determined to go, not to stop short of that beautiful place, and I do not mean to stop till I get there, and meet you there, too."

DOCUMENT 27 (II: 213–20): Resolutions and Debate, First Annual Meeting of the American Equal Rights Association, New York City, May 10, 1867

SECOND DAY.

FRIDAY MORNING, *May* 10, 1867.

The meeting was called to order by the President, and the Secretary read some additional resolutions.*

---

* *Resolved,* That the ballot alike to women and men means bread, education, self-protection, self-reliance, and self-respect; to the wife it means the control of her own person, property, and earnings; to the mother it means the equal guardianship of her children; to the daughter it means diversified employment and a fair day's wages for a fair day's work; to all it means free access to skilled labor, to colleges and professions, and to every avenue of advantage and preferment.

Resolved, That Henry Ward Beecher, Elizabeth Cady Stanton, and Frederick Douglass, be invited to represent the Equal Rights Association in the Constitutional Convention to be held in this State in the month of June next.

Resolved, That while we are grateful to Wendell Phillips, Theodore Tilton, and Horace Greeley, for the respectful mention of woman's right to the ballot in the journals through which they speak, we ask them now, when we are reconstructing both our State and Na-

237

CHARLES L. REMOND objected to the last of the resolution, and desired that the word "colored" might be stricken out. It might be that colored men would obtain their rights before women; but if so, he was confident they would heartily acquiesce in admitting women also to the right of suffrage.

The PRESIDENT (Mrs. Mott) said that woman had a right to be a little jealous of the addition of so large a number of men to the voting class, for the colored men would naturally throw all their strength upon the side of those opposed to woman's enfranchisement.

GEORGE T. DOWNING wished to know whether he had rightly understood that Mrs. Stanton and Mrs. Mott were opposed to the enfranchisement of the colored man, unless the ballot should also be accorded to woman at the same time.

Mrs. STANTON said: All history proves that despotisms, whether of one man or millions, can not stand, and there is no use of wasting centuries of men and means in trying that experiment again. Hence I have no faith or interest in any reconstruction on that old basis. To say that politicians always do one thing at a time is no reason why philosophers should not enunciate the broad principles that underlie that one thing and a dozen others. We do not take the right step for this hour in demanding suffrage for any class; as a matter of principle I claim it for all. But in a narrow view of the question as a matter of feeling between classes, when Mr. Downing puts the question to me, are you willing to have the colored man enfranchised before the woman, I say, no; I would not trust him with all my rights; degraded, oppressed himself, he would be more despotic with the governing power than even our Saxon rulers are. I desire that we go into the kingdom together, for individual and national safety demand that not another man be enfranchised without the woman by his side.

STEPHEN S. FOSTER, basing the demand for the ballot upon the natural right of the citizen, felt bound to aid in conferring it upon any citizen deprived of it irrespective of its being granted or denied to others. Even, therefore, if the enfranchisement of the colored man would probably retard the enfranchisement of woman, we had no right for that reason to deprive him of his right. The right of each should be accorded at the earliest possible moment, neither being denied for any supposed benefit to the other.

---

tional Governments, to demand that the right of suffrage be secured to all citizens—to women as well as black men, for, until this is done, the government stands on the unsafe basis of class legislation.

Resolved, That on this our first anniversary we congratulate each other and the country on the unexampled progress of our cause, as seen: 1. In the action of Congress extending the right of suffrage to the colored men of the States lately in rebellion, and in the very long and able discussion of woman's equal right to the ballot in the United States Senate, and the vote upon it. 2. In the action of the Legislatures of Kansas and Wisconsin, submitting to the people a proposition to extend the ballot to woman. 3. In the agitation upon the same measure in the Legislatures of several other States. 4. In the friendly tone of so large a portion of the press, both political and religious; and finally, in the general awaking to the importance of human elevation and enfranchisement, abroad as well as at home; particularly in Great Britain, Russia, and Brazil; and encouraged by past successes and the present prospect, we pledge ourselves to renewed and untiring exertions, until equal suffrage and citizenship are acknowledged throughout our entire country, irrespective of sex or color.

CHARLES L. REMOND said that if he were to lose sight of expediency, he must side with Mrs. Stanton, although to do so was extremely trying; for he could not conceive of a more unhappy position than that occupied by millions of American men bearing the name of freedmen while the rights and privileges of *free* men are still denied them.

Mrs. STANTON said: That is equaled only by the condition of the women by their side. There is a depth of degradation known to the slave women that man can never feel. To give the ballot to the black man is no security to the woman. Saxon men have the ballot, yet look at their women, crowded into a few half-paid employments. Look at the starving, degraded class in our 10,000 dens of infamy and vice if you would know how wisely and generously man legislates for woman.

Rev. SAMUEL J. MAY, in reply to Mr. Remond's objection to the resolution, said that the word "colored" was necessary to convey the meaning, since there is no demand now made for the enfranchisement of men, as a class. His amendment would take all the color out of the resolution. No man in this country had made such sacrifices for the cause of liberty as Wendell Phillips; and if just at this moment, when the great question for which he has struggled thirty years seemed about to be settled, he was unwilling that anything should be added to it which might in any way prejudice the success about to crown his efforts, it was not to be wondered at. He was himself of the opinion, on the contrary, that by asking for the rights of all, we should be much more likely to obtain the rights of the colored man, than by making that a special question. He would rejoice at the enfranchisement of colored men, and believed that Mrs. Stanton would, though that were all we could get at the time. Yet, if we rest there, and allow the reconstruction to be completed, leaving out the better half of humanity, we must expect further trouble; and it might be a more awful and sanguinary civil war than that which we have just experienced.

GEORGE T. DOWNING desired that the Convention should express its opinion upon the point he had raised; and, therefore, offered the following resolution:

Resolved, That while we regret that the right sentiment, which would secure to women the ballot, is not as general as we would have it, nevertheless we wish it distinctly understood that we rejoice at the increasing sentiment which favors the enfranchisement of the colored man.

Mr. DOWNING understood Mrs. Stanton to refuse to rejoice at a *part* of the good results to be accomplished, if she could not achieve the whole, and he wished to ask if she was unwilling the colored man should have the vote until the women could have it also? He said we had no right to refuse an act of justice upon the assumption that it would be followed by an act of injustice.

Mrs. STANTON replied she demanded the ballot for all. She asked for reconstruction on the basis of self-government; but if we are to have further class legislation, she thought the wisest order of enfranchisement was to take the educated classes first. If women are still to be represented by men, then I say let only the highest type of manhood stand at the helm of State. But if all men are to vote, black and white, lettered and unlettered, washed and unwashed, the safety of the nation as well as the interests of woman demand that we outweigh this incoming tide of ignorance, poverty, and vice, with the virtue, wealth, and education of the women of the country. With the black man you have no new force in government—it is manhood still; but with the enfranchisement of woman, you have a new and essential element of life and power. Would Horace Greeley, Wendell Phillips, Gerrit Smith, or Theodore Tilton be willing to stand aside and trust their individual interests, and the whole welfare of the nation, to the lowest strata of manhood? If not, why ask educated women, who love their country, who desire to mould its institutions on the highest idea of justice and equality, who feel that their enfranchisement is of vital importance to this end, why ask them to stand aside while 2,000,000 ignorant men are ushered into the halls of legislation?

EDWARD M. DAVIS asked what had been done with Mr. Burleigh's amendment.

The CHAIR—No action was taken upon it, as no one seconded it.

ABBY KELLY FOSTER said: I am in New York for medical treatment, not for speech-making; yet I must say a few words in relation to a remark recently made on this platform—that "The negro should not enter the kingdom of politics before woman, because he would be an additional weight against her enfranchisement." Were the negro and woman in the same civil, social, and religious status to-day, I should respond aye, with all my heart, to this sentiment. What are the facts? You say the negro has the civil rights bill, also the military reconstruction bill granting him suffrage. It has been well said, "he has the title deed to liberty, but is not yet in the possession of liberty." He is treated as a slave to-day in the several districts of the South. Without wages, without family rights, whipped and beaten by thousands, given up to the most horrible outrages, without that protection which his value as property formerly gave him. Again, he is liable without farther guarantees, to be plunged into peonage, serfdom or even into chattel slavery. Have we any true sense of justice, are we not dead to the sentiment of humanity if we shall wish to postpone his security against present woes and future enslavement till woman shall obtain political rights?

Rev. HENRY WARD BEECHER said: It seems that my modesty in not lending my name has been a matter of some grief. I will try hereafter to be less modest. When I get my growth I hope to overcome that. I certainly should not have been present to-day, except that a friend said to me that some who were expected had not come. When a cause is well launched and is prospering, I never feel specially called to help it. When a cause that I believe to be just is in the minority, and is struggling for a hearing, then I should always be glad to be counted among those who were laboring for it in the days when it lacked friends. I come to bear testimony, not as if I had not already done it, but again, as confirmed by all that I have read, whether of things written in England or spoken in America, in the belief that this movement is not the mere progeny of a fitful and feverish *ism* — that it is not a mere frothing eddy whose spirit is but the chafing of the water upon the rock—but that it is a part of that great tide which follows the drawing of heaven itself. I believe it to be so. I trust that it will not be invidious if I say, therefore, I hope the friends of this cause will not fall out by the way. If the division of opinion amounts merely to this, that you have two blades, and therefore can cut, I have no objection to it; but if there is such a division of opinion in respect to mere details, how important those details are, among friends that are one at the bottom where principles are, that there is to be a falling out there, I shall exceedingly regret it; I shall regret that our strength is weakened, when we need it to be augmented most, or concentrated.

All my lifetime the great trouble has been that in merely speculative things theologians have been such furious logicians, have picked up their premises, and rushed with them with race-horse speed to such remote conclusions, that in the region of ideas our logical minds have become accustomed to draw results as remote as the very eternities from any premises given. My difficulty on the other hand, has been that in practical matters, owing to the existence of this great mephitic swamp of slavery, men have been utterly unwilling to draw conclusions at all; and that the most familiar principles of political economy or politics have been enunciated, and then always docked off short. Men would not allow them to go to their natural results, in the class of questions in society. We have had raised up before us the necessity of maintaining the Union by denying conclusions. The most dear and sacred and animating principles of religion have been restrained, because they would have such a bearing upon slavery, and men felt bound to hold their peace. Our most profound and broadly acknowledged principles of liberty have been enunciated and passed over, without carrying them out and applying them to society, because it would interrupt the peace of the nation. That time is passed away; and as the result of it has come in a joy and a perfect appetite on the part of the public.

I have been a careful observer for more than thirty-five years, for I came into public life, I believe, about the same time with the lady who has just sat down (Mrs. Foster), although I am not so much worn by my labors as she seems to have been. For thirty-five years I have observed in society its impetus checked, and a kind of lethargy and deadness in practical ethics, arising from fear of this prejudicial effect upon public economy. I have noticed that in the last five years there has been a revolution as perfect as if it had been God's resurrection in the graveyard. The dead men are living, and the live men are thrice alive. I can scarcely express my sense of the leap the public mind and the public moral sense have taken within this time. The barrier is out of the way. That which made the American mind untrue logically to itself is smitten down by the hand of God; and there is just at this time an immense tendency in the public mind to carry out all principles to their legitimate conclusions, go where they will. There never was a time when men were so practical, and so ready to learn. I am not a farmer, but I know that the spring comes but once in the year. When the furrow is open is the time to put in your seed, if you would gather a harvest in its season. Now, when the red-hot plowshare of war has opened a furrow in this nation, is the time to put in the seed. If any man says to me, "Why will you agitate the woman's question, when it is the hour for the black man?" I answer, it is the hour for every man, black or white. (Applause.) The bees go out in the morning to gather the honey from the morning-glories. They take it when they are open, for by ten o'clock they are shut, and they never open again until the next crop comes. When the public mind is open, if you have anything to say, say it. If you have any

radical principles to urge, any organizing wisdom to make known, don't
wait until quiet times come.   Don't wait until the public mind shuts up altogether.

War has opened the way for impulse to extend itself.   But progress goes
by periods, by jumps and spurts.   We are in the favored hour; and if you
have great principles to make known, this is the time to advance those
principles.   If you can organize them into institutions, this is the time to
organize them.   I therefore say, whatever truth is to be known for the next
fifty years in this nation let it be spoken now—let it be enforced now.   The
truth that I have to urge is not that women have the right of suffrage—not
that Chinamen or Irishmen have the right of suffrage—not that native born
Yankees have the right of suffrage—but that suffrage is the inherent right
of mankind.   I say that man has the right of suffrage as I say that man has
the right to himself.   For although it may not be true under the Russian
government, where the government does not rest on the people, and although
under our own government a man has not a right to himself, except in accordance with the spirit and action of our own institutions, yet our institutions make the government depend on the people, and make the people depend on the government; and no man is a full citizen, or fully competent to
take care of himself, or to defend himself, who has not all those rights that
belong to his fellows.   I therefore advocate no sectional rights, no class
rights, no sex rights, but the most universal form of right for all that live
and breathe on the continent.   I do not put back the black man's emancipation; nor do I put back for a single day or for an hour his admission.   I
ask not that he should wait.   I demand that this work shall be done, not
upon the ground that it is politically expedient now to enfranchise black
men; but I propose that you take expediency out of the way, and that you
put a principle that is more enduring than expediency in the place of it—
manhood and womanhood suffrage for all.   That is the question.   You may
just as well meet it now as at any other time.   You never will have so favorable an occasion, so sympathetic a heart, never a public reason so willing
to be convinced as to-day.   If anything is to be done for the black man, or
the black woman, or for the disfranchised classes among the whites, let it be
done, in the name of God, while his Providence says, "Come; come all, and
come welcome."

But I take wisdom from some with whom I have not always trained.   If
you would get ten steps, has been the practical philosophy of some who are
not here to-day, demand twenty, and then you will get ten.   Now, even if I
were to confine—as I by no means do—my expectation to gaining the vote
for the black man, I think we should be much more likely to gain that by
demanding the vote for everybody.   I remember that when I was a boy Dr.
Spurzheim came to this country to advocate phrenology, but everybody held
up both hands—"Phrenology!   You must be running mad to have the idea
that phrenology can be true!"   It was not long after that, mesmerism came
along; and then the people said, "Mesmerism!   We can go phrenology;
there is some sense in that; but as for mesmerism—!"   Very soon spiritualism made its appearance, and then the same people began to say, "Spiritualism!   Why it is nothing but mesmerism; we can believe in that; but as for
spiritualism—!"   (Laughter.)   The way to get a man to take a position is to

take one in advance of it, and then he will drop into the one you want him to take. So that if, being crafty, I desire to catch men with guile, and desire them to adopt suffrage for colored men, as good a trap as I know of is to claim it for women also. Bait your trap with the white woman, and I think you will catch the black man. (Laughter.) I would not, certainly, have it understood that we are standing here to advocate this universal application of the principle merely to secure the enfranchisement of the colored citizen. We do it in good faith. I believe it is just as easy to carry the enfranchisement of all as the enfranchisement of any class, and easier to carry it than carry the enfranchisement of class after class—class after class. (Applause.)

I make this demand because I have the deepest sense of what is before us. We have entered upon an era such as never before has come to any nation. We are at a point in the history of the world where we need a prophet, and have none to describe to us those events rising in the horizon thick and fast. Sometimes it seems to me that that Latter Day glory which the prophets dimly saw, and which saints have ever since, with faintness of heart, longed for and prayed for with wavering faith, is just before us. I see the fountains of the great deep broken up. I think we are to have a nation born in a day among us, greater in power of thought, greater in power of conscience, greater therefore in self-government, greater still in the power of material development. Such thrift, such skill, such enterprise, such power of self-sustentation I think is about to be developed, to say nothing of the advance already made before the nations, as will surprise even the most sanguine and far-sighted. Nevertheless, while so much is promised, there are all the attendant evils. It is a serious thing to bring unwashed, uncombed, untutored men, scarcely redeemed from savagery, to the ballot-box. It is a dangerous thing to bring the foreigner, whose whole secular education was under the throne of the tyrant, and put his hand upon the helm of affairs in this free nation. It is a dangerous thing to bring men without property, or the expectation of it, into the legislative halls to legislate upon property. It is a dangerous thing to bring woman, unaccustomed to and undrilled in the art of government, suddenly into the field to vote. These are dangerous things; I admit it. But I think God says to us, " By that danger I put every man of you under the solemn responsibility of preparing these persons effectually for their citizenship." Are you a rich man, afraid of your money? By that fear you are called to educate the men who you are afraid will vote against you. We are in a time of danger. I say to the top of society, just as sure as you despise the bottom, you shall be left like the oak tree that rebelled against its own roots—better that it be struck with lightning. Take a man from the top of society or the bottom, and if you will but give himself to himself, give him his reason, his moral nature, and his affections; take him with all his passions and his appetites, and develop him, and you will find he has the same instinct for self-government that you have. God made a man just as much to govern himself as a pyramid to stand on its own bottom. Self-government is a boon intended for all. This is shown in the very organization of the human mind, with its counterbalances and checks. . . . . We are underpinning and undergirding society. Let us put under it no political expediency, but the great principle of manhood and womanhood, not merely cheating ourselves by a partial measure, but carry-

ing the nation forward to its great and illustrious future, in which it will enjoy more safety, more dignity, more sublime proportions, and a health that
will know no death. (Applause.)

HENRY C. WRIGHT said that circumstances had made Wendell Phillips
and others, leaders in the Anti-Slavery movement, as they had made Mrs.
Stanton and others leaders in this; and while they all desired the enfranchisement of both classes, it was no more than right that each should devote his energies to his own movement. There need not be, and should not
be any antagonism between the two.

Miss ANTHONY said—The question is not, is this or that person right, but
what are the principles under discussion. As I understand the difference
between Abolitionists, some think this is harvest time for the black man,
and seed-sowing time for woman. Others, with whom I agree, think we
have been sowing the seed of individual rights, the foundation idea of a republic for the last century, and that this is the harvest time for all citizens
who pay taxes, obey the laws and are loyal to the government. (Applause.)

Mr. REMOND said : In an hour like this I repudiate the idea of expediency. All I ask for myself I claim for my wife and sister. Let our action
be based upon the rock of everlasting principle. No class of citizens in this
country can be deprived of the ballot without injuring every other class. I
see how equality of suffrage in the State of New York is necessary to maintain emancipation in South Carolina. Do not moral principles, like water,
seek a common level? Slavery in the Southern States crushed the right of
free speech in Massachusetts and made slaves of Saxon men and women,
just as the $250 qualification in the Constitution of this State degrades and
enslaves black men all over the Union.

Mr. PILLSBURY protested against the use of the few last moments of this
meeting in these discussions. We should be now only "a committee of ways
and means," and future work should be the business in hand. Mr. Downing
presented an unnecessary issue. Government will never ask us which should
enter into citizenship first, the woman or the colored man, or whether we
prefer one to the other. Indeed government has given the colored man the
ballot already. We are demanding suffrage equally, not unequally. Mrs.
Stanton's private opinion, be it what it may, has nothing to do with the general question. The white voters are mostly opposed to woman's suffrage.
So will the colored men be, probably; at least so she believes, as Mrs. Mott
also suggested very strongly, and a million or more of them added to the
present opposition and indifference, are not a slight consideration. Mrs.
Stanton does not believe in loving her neighbor *better* than herself. Justice
to one class does not mean injustice to another. Woman has as good a
right to the ballot as the black man—no better. Were I a colored man, and
had reason to believe that should woman obtain her rights she would use
them to the prejudice of mine, how could I labor very zealously in her behalf? It should be enough for Mr. Downing and all who stand with him
that Mrs. Stanton does not demand one thing for herself as to rights, or time
of obtaining them, which she does not cheerfully, earnestly demand for all
others, regardless of color or sex.

DOCUMENT 28 (II: 309–12): American Equal Rights Association Anniversary, New York City, May 14, 1868

The American Equal Rights Association held its annual meeting in Cooper Institute, New York, May 14, 1868. Its officers*, with but few changes, were the same as before.

The HUTCHINSON FAMILY, the branch of John, was present, and with their sister, Abby Hutchinson Patten, opened the meeting with their song, "We Come to Greet You." Lucy Stone read a letter from John Stuart Mill, expressing sympathy with the movement. Letters were also read from Rev. Robert Collyer of Chicago, Maria Giddings, the daughter of Hon. Joshua R. Giddings, of Ohio, Frances Dana Gage, and several others. Miss Anthony invited all delegates of Equal Rights Societies to seats on the platform; she also moved that Mrs. Rose, Mrs. Stanton, Mr. Burleigh and Mr. Foster be a committee to prepare resolutions.

HENRY B. BLACKWELL reported the success of the campaign of the women of this Society in Kansas, where Rev. Olympia Brown, Lucy Stone, Mrs. Stanton and Susan B. Anthony had canvassed. Their eloquence and determination gave great promise of success; but in an inopportune moment, Horace Greeley and others saw fit in the Constitutional Convention to report unfavorably on the proposition to extend suffrage to the women of the Empire State, and that influenced the sentiment of the younger Western States, and their enterprise was crushed. Even the Republicans in Kansas, after witnessing this example, set their faces against the extension of suffrage to women. The negroes got but a few more votes than did the women.

LUCY STONE gave a resume of the progress of the cause in this country and in England. Col. Higginson and Mrs. Rose made excellent remarks. "Keep the ball rolling" was gracefully rendered by Mrs. Abby Hutchinson Patton,

---

* *President*—Lucretia Mott.

Vice-Presidents—Elizabeth Cady Stanton, N.Y.; Frederick Douglass, N.Y.; Henry Ward Beecher, N.Y.; Martha C. Wright, N.Y.; Elizabeth B. Chace, R. I.; C. Prince, Ct.; Frances D. Gage, N.Y.; Robert Purvis, Penn.; Parker Pillsbury, N.H.; Antoinette Brown Blackwell, N. J.; Josephine S. Griffing, D. C.; Thomas Garrett, Del.; Stephen H. Camp, Ohio; Euphemia Cochrane, Mich.; Mary A. Livermore, Ill.; Mrs. Isaac H. Sturgeon, Mo.; Amelia Bloomer, Iowa; Helen Ekin Starrett, Kansas; Virginia Penny, Kentucky; Olympia Brown, Mass.

Corresponding Secretary—Mary E. Gage.

Recording Secretaries—Henry B. Blackwell, Hattie Purvis.

Treasurer—John J. Merritt.

Executive Committee—Lucy Stone, Edward S. Bunker, Elizabeth R. Tilton, Ernestine L. Rose, Robert J. Johnston, Edwin A. Studwell, Anna Cromwell Field, Susan B. Anthony, Theodore Tilton, Margaret E. Winchester, Abby Hutchinson Patton.

the whole audience joining in the chorus. Mrs. Stone presented two forms of petition to Congress; one to extend suffrage to women in the District of Columbia and the Territories, the other for the submission of a proposition for a 16th Amendment to prohibit the States from disfranchising citizens on account of sex. Frederick Douglass made an acceptable speech in favor of the petitions. The President announced that Mrs. Patten headed the subscription list to aid the association in its work for the coming year with $50. Miss Anthony presented the various tracts published by the Society, and *The Revolution*, urging the friends of the cause to aid in the circulation of the paper, as it was the only one owned and edited by women, wholly devoted to the cause of Equal Rights. Rev. Dr. Blanchard, of Brooklyn, opened the evening session with prayer; a resolution was proposed and adopted, on the death of James Mott, husband of Lucretia Mott, President of the first Woman's Rights Convention at Seneca Falls.

Rev. OLYMPIA BROWN: It is said that Nature is against us. In the Massachusetts Legislature, Mr. Dana, Chairman of the Committee before whom we had a hearing, said: "Nature is against it. It will take the romance out of life to grant what you desire"! If the romance of life is a falsehood and a fiction, we want to get back to truth, nature and God. We all love liberty and desire to possess it. No one worthy the name of man or woman is willing to surrender liberty and become subservient to another. Woman may be shut out of politics by law, but her influence will be felt there. Some of our leading reformers work for other objects first; the enfranchisement of the negro, the eight hour law, the temperance cause; and leave the woman suffrage question in the background; but woman will be enfranchised in spite of them. It is no use to tell us to wait until something else is done. *Now* is the accepted time for the enfranchisement of woman. The abolition of slavery was thought to be premature, but that mistake is now clearly seen. Now is the time for every disfranchised class to make known its wants. The Republican party is no better than the Democratic. It sacrificed principle and nominated a man for President to *save the party*, whom they were afraid the Democrats would nominate if they did not! The Republican party controlled Kansas, and yet repudiated woman's rights in the canvass of last year. We want a party (and would like the Republican party) who will adopt a platform of Universal Suffrage for every color and every sex. "The Republican party must be saved," is the cry; but its great danger is in not being true to principle. We will push on, keeping in view the rights of our common nature until woman is the peer of man in every sphere of life.

ELIZABETH A. KINGSLEY, of Philadelphia, CHARLES BURLEIGH, Rev. HENRY BLANCHARD and Mrs. ROSE made brief addresses.

FREDERICK DOUGLASS deprecated the seeming assertion of Rev. O. B. Frothingham, that one good cause was in opposition to another. I champion the right of the negro to vote. It is with us a matter of life and death, and therefore can not be postponed. I have always championed woman's right to vote; but it will be seen that the present claim for the negro is one of the most *urgent* necessity. The assertion of the right of women to vote meets nothing but ridicule; there is no deep seated malignity in the hearts of the people against her; but name the right of the negro to vote, all hell is turned loose and the Ku-klux and Regulators hunt and slay the unoffending black man. The government of this country loves women. They are the sisters, mothers, wives and daughters of our rulers; but the negro is loathed. Women should not censure Mr. Phillips, Mr. Greeley, or Mr. Tilton, all have spoken eloquently for woman's rights. We are all talking for woman's rights, and we should be just to all our friends and enemies. There is a difference between the Republican and Democratic parties.

OLYMPIA BROWN: What is it?

FREDERICK DOUGLASS: The Democratic party has, during the whole war, been in sympathy with the rebellion, while the Republican party has supported the Government.

OLYMPIA BROWN: How is it now?

FREDERICK DOUGLASS: The Democratic party opposes impeachment, and desires a white man's government.

OLYMPIA BROWN: What is the difference in *principle* between the position of the Democratic party opposing the enfranchisement of 2,000,000 negro men, and the Republican party opposing the emancipation of 17,000,000 white women?

FREDERICK DOUGLASS: The Democratic party opposes suffrage to both; but the Republican party is in favor of enfranchising the negro, and is largely in favor of enfranchising woman. Where is the Democrat who favors woman suffrage? (A voice in the audience, "Train!") Yes, he hates the negro, and that is what stimulates him to substitute the cry of emancipation for women. The negro needs suffrage to protect his life and property, and to ensure him respect and education. He needs it for the safety of reconstruction and the salvation of the Union; for his own elevation from the position of a drudge to that of an influential member of society. If you want women to forget and forsake frivolity, and the negro to take pride in becoming a useful and respectable member of society, give them both the ballot.

OLYMPIA BROWN: Why did Republican Kansas vote down negro suffrage?

FREDERICK DOUGLASS: Because of your ally, George Francis Train!

OLYMPIA BROWN: How about Minnesota without Train? The Republican party is a party and cares for nothing but party! It has repudiated both negro suffrage and woman suffrage.

FREDERICK DOUGLASS: Minnesota lacked only 1,200 votes of carrying ·negro suffrage. All the Democrats voted against it, while only a small portion of the Republicans did so. And this was substantially the same in Ohio and Connecticut. The Republican party is about to bring ten States into the Union; and Thaddeus Stevens has reported a bill to admit seven, all on the fundamental basis of constitutions guaranteeing negro suffrage forever.

OLYMPIA BROWN again insisted that the party was false, and that now was the time for every true patriot to demand that no new State should be admitted except on the basis of suffrage to women as well as negroes.

LUCY STONE controverted Mr. Douglass' statement that women were not persecuted for endeavoring to obtain their rights, and depicted in glowing colors the wrongs of women and the inadequacy of the laws to redress them.   Mrs. Stone also charged the Republican party as false to principle unless it protected women as well as colored men in the exercise of their right to vote.

The Tribune said the resolutions adopted declare that suffrage is an inalienable right without qualification of sex or race; that our State and National Governments are anti-Republican in form, and anti-Democratic in fact; that the only way to decide whether women want to vote is to give them an opportunity of doing so ; that the Republicans are bound to extend the application of manhood suffrage to women; that Reconstruction will fail to secure peace, unless it gives women the right to vote; they invite the National Conventions of both parties to put a woman suffrage plank in their platforms; petition Congress to extend suffrage to the women of the District of Columbia, and to propose a Constitutional Amendment prohibiting political distinctions on account of sex; assert that the laws depriving married women of the equal custody of their children and of the control of their property, are a disgrace to civilization; and thank the men of Kansas who voted for Woman Suffrage.

DOCUMENT 29 (II: 348–55): Elizabeth Cady Stanton, Address to the National Woman Suffrage Convention, Washington, D.C., January 19, 1869

Mrs. Stanton's speech the first evening of the convention gave a fair statement of the hostile feelings of women toward the amendments; we give the main part of it. Of all the other speeches, which were extemporaneous, only meagre and unsatisfactory reports can be found.

Mrs. STANTON said:—A great idea of progress is near its consummation, when statesmen in the councils of the nation propose to frame it into statutes and constitutions; when Reverend Fathers recognize it by a new interpretation of their creeds and canons; when the Bar and Bench at its command set aside the legislation of centuries, and girls of twenty put their heels on the Cokes and Blackstones of the past.

Those who represent what is called "the Woman's Rights Movement," have argued their right to political equality from every standpoint of justice, religion, and logic, for the last twenty years. They have quoted the Constitution, the Declaration of Independence, the Bible, the opinions of great men and women in all ages; they have plead the theory of our government; suffrage a natural, inalienable right; shown from the lessons of history, that one class can not legislate for another; that disfranchised classes must ever be neglected and degraded; and that all privileges are but mockery to the citizen, until he has a voice in the making and administering of law. Such arguments have been made over and over in conventions and before the legislatures of the several States. Judges, lawyers, priests, and politicians have said again and again, that our logic was unanswerable, and although much nonsense has emanated from the male tongue and pen on this subject, no man has yet made a fair, argument on the other side. Knowing that we hold the Gibraltar rock of reason on this question, they resort to ridicule and petty objections. Compelled to follow our assailants, wherever they go, and fight them with their own weapons; when cornered with wit and sarcasm, some cry out, you have no logic on your platform, forgetting that we have no use for logic until they give us logicians at whom to hurl it, and if, for the pure love of it, we now and then rehearse the logic that is like a, b, c, to all of us, others cry out—the same old speeches we have heard these twenty years. It would be safe to say a hundred years, for they are the same our fathers used when battling old King George and the British Parliament for their right to representation, and a voice in the laws by which they were governed. There are no new arguments to be made on human rights, our work to-day is to apply to ourselves those so familiar to all; to teach man that woman is not an anomalous being, outside all laws and constitutions, but one whose rights are to be established by the same process of reason as that by which he demands his own.

When our Fathers made out their famous bill of impeachment against England, they specified eighteen grievances. When the women of this country surveyed the situation in their first convention, they found they had precisely that number, and quite similar in character; and reading over the old revolutionary arguments of Jefferson, Patrick Henry, Otis, and Adams, they found they applied remarkably well to their case. The same arguments made in this country for extending suffrage from time to time, to white men, native born citizens, without property and education, and to foreigners; the same used by John Bright in England, to extend it to a million new voters, and the same used by the great Republican party to enfranchise a million black men in the South, all these arguments we have to-day to offer for woman, and one, in addition, stronger than all besides, the difference in man and woman. Because man and woman are the complement of one another, we need woman's thought in national affairs to make a safe and stable government.

The Republican party to-day congratulates itself on having carried the Fifteenth Amendment of the Constitution, thus securing "manhood suffrage" and establishing an aristocracy of sex on this continent. As several bills to secure Woman's Suffrage in the District and the Territories have been already presented in both houses of Congress, and as by Mr. Julian's bill, the question of so amending the Constitution as to extend suffrage to all the women of the country has been presented to the nation for consideration, it is not only the right but the duty of every thoughtful woman to express her opinion on a Sixteenth Amenment. While I hail the late discussions in Congress and the various bills presented as so many signs of progress, I am especially gratified with those of Messrs. Julian and Pomeroy, which forbid any State to deny the right of suffrage to any of its citizens on account of sex or color.

This fundamental principle of our government—the equality of all the citizens of the republic—should be incorporated in the Federal Constitution, there to remain forever. To leave this question to the States and partial acts of Congress, is to defer indefinitely its settlement, for what is done by this Congress may be repealed by the next; and politics in the several States differ so widely, that no harmonious action on any question can ever be secured, except as a strict party measure. Hence, we appeal to the party now in power, everywhere, to end this protracted debate on suffrage, and declare it the inalienable right of every citizen who is amenable to the laws of the land, who pays taxes and the penalty of crime. We have a splendid theory of a genuine republic, why not realize it and make our government homogeneous, from Maine to California. The Republican party has the power to do this, and now is its only opportunity. Woman's Suffrage, in 1872, may be as good a card for the Republicans as Gen. Grant was in the last election. It is said that the Republican party made him President, not because they thought him the most desirable man in the nation for that office, but they were afraid the Democrats would take him if they did not. We would suggest, there may be the same danger of Democrats taking up Woman Suffrage if they do not. God, in his providence, may have purified that party in the furnace of affliction. They have had the opportunity, safe from the turmoil of political life and the temptations of office, to study and apply the divine principles of justice and equality to life; for minorities are always in a position to carry principles to their logical results, while majorities are governed only by votes. You see my faith in Democrats is based on sound philosophy. In the next Congress, the Democratic party will gain thirty-four new members, hence the Republicans have had their last chance to do justice to woman. It will be no enviable record for the Fortieth Congress that in the darkest days of the republic it placed our free institutions in the care and keeping of every type of manhood, ignoring womanhood, all the elevating and purifying influences of the most virtuous and humane half of the American people. . . . .

I urge a speedy adoption of a Sixteenth Amendment for the following reasons:

1. A government, based on the principle of caste and class, can not stand. The aristocratic idea, in any form, is opposed to the genius of our free institutions, to our own declaration of rights, and to the civilization of the age. All artificial distinctions, whether of family, blood, wealth, color, or sex, are equally oppressive to the subject classes, and equally destructive to national life and prosperity. Governments based on every form of aristocracy,

on every degree and variety of inequality, have been tried in despotisms, monarchies, and republics, and all alike have perished. In the panorama of the past behold the mighty nations that have risen, one by one, but to fall. Behold their temples, thrones, and pyramids, their gorgeous palaces and stately monuments now crumbled all to dust. Behold every monarch in Europe at this very hour trembling on his throne. Behold the republics on this Western continent convulsed, distracted, divided, the hosts scattered, the leaders fallen, the scouts lost in the wilderness, the once inspired prophets blind and dumb, while on all sides the cry is echoed, "Republicanism is a failure," though that great principle of a government "by the people, of the people, for the people," has never been tried. Thus far, all nations have been built on caste and failed. Why, in this hour of reconstruction, with the experience of generations before us, make another experiment in the same direction? If serfdom, peasantry, and slavery have shattered kingdoms, deluged continents with blood, scattered republics like dust before the wind, and rent our own Union asunder, what kind of a government, think you, American statesmen, you can build, with the mothers of the race crouching at your feet, while iron-heeled peasants, serfs, and slaves, exalted by your hands, tread our inalienable rights into the dust? While all men, everywhere, are rejoicing in new-found liberties, shall woman alone be denied the rights, privileges, and immunities of citizenship? While in England men are coming up from the coal mines of Cornwall, from the factories of Birmingham and Manchester, demanding the suffrage; while in frigid Russia the 22,000,000 newly-emancipated serfs are already claiming a voice in the government; while here, in our own land, slaves, but just rejoicing in the proclamation of emancipation, ignorant alike of its power and significance, have the ballot unasked, unsought, already laid at their feet— think you the daughters of Adams, Jefferson, and Patrick Henry, in whose veins flows the blood of two Revolutions, will forever linger round the campfires of an old barbarism, with no longings to join this grand army of freedom in its onward march to roll back the golden gates of a higher and better civilization? Of all kinds of aristocracy, that of sex is the most odious and unnatural; invading, as it does, our homes, desecrating our family altars, dividing those whom God has joined together, exalting the son above the mother who bore him, and subjugating, everywhere, moral power to brute force. Such a government would not be worth the blood and treasure so freely poured out in its long struggles for freedom. . . . .

2. I urge a Sixteenth Amendment, because "manhood suffrage" or a man's government, is civil, religious, and social disorganization. The male element is a destructive force, stern, selfish, aggrandizing, loving war, violence, conquest, acquisition, breeding in the material and moral world alike discord, disorder, disease, and death. See what a record of blood and cruelty the pages of history reveal! Through what slavery, slaughter, and sacrifice, through what inquisitions and imprisonments, pains and persecutions, black codes and gloomy creeds, the soul of humanity has struggled for the centuries, while mercy has veiled her face and all hearts have been dead alike to love and hope! The male element has held high carnival thus far, it has fairly run riot from the beginning, overpowering the feminine element everywhere, crushing out all the diviner qualities in human nature,

until we know but little of true manhood and womanhood, of the latter comparatively nothing, for it has scarce been recognized as a power until within the last century. Society is but the reflection of man himself, untempered by woman's thought, the hard iron rule we feel alike in the church, the state, and the home. No one need wonder at the disorganization, at the fragmentary condition of everything, when we remember that man, who represents but half a complete being, with but half an idea on every subject, has undertaken the absolute control of all sublunary matters.

People object to the demands of those whom they choose to call the strong-minded, because they say, "the right of suffrage will make the women masculine." That is just the difficulty in which we are involved to-day. Though disfranchised we have few women in the best sense, we have simply so many reflections, varieties, and dilutions of the masculine gender. The strong, natural characteristics of womanhood are repressed and ignored in dependence, for so long as man feeds woman she will try to please the giver and adapt herself to his condition. To keep a foothold in society woman must be as near like man as possible, reflect his ideas, opinions, virtues, motives, prejudices, and vices. She must respect his statutes, though they strip her of every inalienable right, and conflict with that higher law written by the finger of God on her own soul. She must believe his theology, though it pave the highways of hell with the skulls of new-born infants, and make God a monster of vengeance and hypocrisy. She must look at everything from its dollar and cent point of view, or she is a mere romancer. She must accept things as they are and make the best of them. To mourn over the miseries of others, the poverty of the poor, their hardships in jails, prisons, asylums, the horrors of war, cruelty, and brutality in every form, all this would be mere sentimentalizing. To protest against the intrigue, bribery, and corruption of public life, to desire that her sons might follow some business that did not involve lying, cheating, and a hard, grinding selfishness, would be arrant nonsense. In this way man has been moulding woman to his ideas by direct and positive influences, while she, if not a negation, has used indirect means to control him, and in most cases developed the very characteristics both in him and herself that needed repression. And now man himself stands appalled at the results of his own excesses, and mourns in bitterness that falsehood, selfishness and violence are the law of life. The need of this hour is not territory, gold mines, railroads, or specie payments, but a new evangel of womanhood, to exalt purity, virtue, morality, true religion, to lift man up into the higher realms of thought and action.

We ask woman's enfranchisement, as the first step toward the recognition of that essential element in government that can only secure the health, strength, and prosperity of the nation. Whatever is done to lift woman to her true position will help to usher in a new day of peace and perfection for the race. In speaking of the masculine element, I do not wish to be understood to say that all men are hard, selfish, and brutal, for many of the most beautiful spirits the world has known have been clothed with manhood ; but I refer to those characteristics, though often marked in woman, that distinguish what is called the stronger sex. For example, the love of acquisition and conquest, the very pioneers of civilization, when expended on the earth, the sea, the elements, the riches and forces of Nature, are powers of destruction when used to subjugate one man to another or to sacrifice nations to ambition.   Here that great conservator of woman's love, if permitted to assert itself, as it naturally would in free-dom against oppression, violence, and war, would hold all these destruct-ive forces in check, for woman knows the cost of life better than man does, and not with her consent would one drop of blood ever be shed, one life sacrificed in vain.   With violence and disturbance in the natural world, we see a constant effort to maintain an equilibrium of forces.   Nature, like a loving mother, is ever trying to keep land and sea, mountain and valley, each in its place, to hush the angry winds and waves, balance the extremes of heat and cold, of rain and drought, that peace, harmony, and beauty may reign supreme.   There is a striking analogy between matter and mind, and the present disorganization of society warns us, that in the dethronement of woman we have let loose the elements of violence and ruin that she only has the power to curb.   If the civilization of the age calls for an extension of the suffrage, surely a government of the most virtuous, educated men and women would better represent the whole, and protect the interests of all than could the representation of either sex alone.   But govern-ment gains no new element of strength in admitting all men to the ballot-box, for we have too much of the man-power there already.   We see this in every department of legislation, and it is a common remark, that unless some new virtue is infused into our public life the nation is doomed to destruction.   Will the foreign element, the dregs of China, Germany, England, Ireland, and Africa supply this needed force, or the nobler types of American womanhood who have taught our presidents, senators, and congressmen the rudiments of all they know?

3. I urge a Sixteenth Amendment because, when " manhood suffrage " is established from Maine to California, woman has reached the lowest depths of political degradation.   So long as there is a disfranchised class in this coun-try, and that class its women, a man's government is worse than a white man's government with suffrage limited by property and educational qualifications, because in proportion as you multiply the rulers, the condition of the politi-cally ostracised is more hopeless and degraded.   John Stuart Mill, in his work on " Liberty," shows that the condition of one disfranchised man in a nation is worse than when the whole nation is under one man, because in the latter case, if the one man is despotic, the nation can easily throw him off, but what can one man do with a nation of tyrants over him?   If American women find it hard to bear the oppressions of their own Saxon fathers, the best orders of manhood, what may they not be called to endure when all the lower orders of foreigners now crowding our shores legislate for them and their daughters.   Think of Patrick and Sambo and Hans and Yung Tung, who do not know the difference between a monarchy and a republic, who can not read the Declaration of Independence or Webster's spelling-book, making laws for Lucretia Mott, Ernestine L. Rose, and Anna E. Dickinson. Think of jurors and jailors drawn from these ranks to watch and try young girls for the crime of infanticide, to decide the moral code by which the mothers of this Republic shall be governed?   This manhood suffrage is an appalling question, and it would be well for thinking women, who seem to

consider it so magnanimous to hold their own claims in abeyance until all men are crowned with citizenship, to remember that the most ignorant men are ever the most hostile to the equality of women, as they have known them only in slavery and degradation.

Go to our courts of justice, our jails and prisons; go into the world of work; into the trades and professions; into the temples of science and learning, and see what is meted out everywhere to women—to those who have no advocates in our courts, no representatives in the councils of the nation. Shall we prolong and perpetuate such injustice, and by increasing this power risk worse oppressions for ourselves and daughters? It is an open, deliberate insult to American womanhood to be cast down under the iron-heeled peasantry of the Old World and the slaves of the New, as we shall be in the practical working of the Fifteenth Amendment, and the only atonement the Republican party can make is now to complete its work, by enfranchising the women of the nation. I have not forgotten their action four years ago, when Article XIV., Sec. 2, was amended* by invidiously introducing the word "male" into the Federal Constitution, where it had never been before, thus counting out of the basis of representation all men not permitted to vote, thereby making it the interest of every State to enfranchise its male citizens, and virtually declaring it no crime to disfranchise its women. As political sagacity moved our rulers thus to guard the interests of the negro for party purposes, common justice might have compelled them to show like respect for their own mothers, by counting woman too out of the basis of representation, that she might no longer swell the numbers to legislate adversely to her interests. And this desecration of the last will and testament of the fathers, this retrogressive legislation for woman, was in the face of the earnest protests of thousands of the best educated, most refined and cultivated women of the North.

Now, when the attention of the whole world is turned to this question of suffrage, and women themselves are throwing off the lethargy of ages, and in England, France, Germany, Switzerland, and Russia are holding their conventions, and their rulers are everywhere giving them a respectful hearing, shall American statesmen, claiming to be liberal, so amend their constitutions as to make their wives and mothers the political inferiors of unlettered and unwashed ditch-diggers, boot-blacks, butchers, and barbers, fresh from the slave plantations of the South, and the effete civilizations of the Old World? While poets and philosophers, statesmen and men of science are all alike pointing to woman as the new hope for the redemption of the race, shall the freest Government on the earth be the first to establish an aristocracy based on sex alone? to exalt ignorance above education, vice above virtue, brutality and barbarism above refinement and religion? Not since God first called light out of darkness and order out of chaos, was there ever made so base a proposition as "manhood suffrage" in this American Republic, after all the discussions we have had on human

---

* The amendment as proposed by the Hon. Thaddeus Stevens, of Pennsylvania, extended the right of suffrage to "all citizens," which included both white and black women. At the bare thought of such an impending calamity, the more timid Republicans were filled with alarm, and the word "male" promptly inserted.

rights in the last century. On all the blackest pages of history there is no record of an act like this, in any nation, where native born citizens, having the same religion, speaking the same language, equal to their rulers in wealth, family, and education, have been politically ostracised by their own countrymen, outlawed with savages, and subjected to the government of outside barbarians. Remember the Fifteenth Amendment takes in a larger population than the 2,000,000 black men on the Southern plantation. It takes in all the foreigners daily landing in our eastern cities, the Chinese crowding our western shores, the inhabitants of Alaska, and all those western isles that will soon be ours. American statesmen may flatter themselves that by superior intelligence and political sagacity the higher orders of men will always govern, but when the ignorant foreign vote already holds the balance of power in all the large cities by sheer force of numbers, it is simply a question of impulse or passion, bribery or fraud, how our elections will be carried. When the highest offices in the gift of the people are bought and sold in Wall Street, it is a mere chance who will be our rulers. Whither is a nation tending when brains count for less than bullion, and clowns make laws for queens? It is a startling assertion, but nevertheless true, that in none of the nations of modern Europe are the higher classes of women politically so degraded as are the women of this Republic to-day. In the Old World, where the government is the aristocracy, where it is considered a mark of nobility to share its offices and powers, women of rank have certain hereditary rights which raise them above a majority of the men, certain honors and privileges not granted to serfs and peasants. There women are queens, hold subordinate offices, and vote on many questions. In our Southern States even, before the war, women were not degraded below the working population. They were not humiliated in seeing their coachmen, gardeners, and waiters go to the polls to legislate for them; but here, in this boasted Northern civilization, women of wealth and education, who pay taxes and obey the laws, who in morals and intellect are the peers of their proudest rulers, are thrust outside the pale of political consideration with minors, paupers, lunatics, traitors, idiots, with those guilty of bribery, larceny, and infamous crimes.

Would those gentlemen who are on all sides telling the women of the nation not to press their claims until the negro is safe beyond peradventure, be willing themselves to stand aside and trust all their interests to hands like these? The educated women of this nation feel as much interest in republican institutions, the preservation of the country, the good of the race, their own elevation and success, as any man possibly can, and we have the same distrust in man's power to legislate for us, that he has in woman's power to legislate wisely for herself.

4. I would press a Sixteenth Amendment, because the history of American statesmanship does not inspire me with confidence in man's capacity to govern the nation alone, with justice and mercy. I have come to this conclusion, not only from my own observation, but from what our rulers say of themselves. Honorable Senators have risen in their places again and again, and told the people of the wastefulness and corruption of the present administration. Others have set forth, with equal clearness, the ignorance of our rulers on the question of finance. . . . .

DOCUMENT 30 (II: 381–98): Debates at the American
Equal Rights Association Meeting, New York City,
May 12–14, 1869

STEPHEN FOSTER laid down the principle that when any persons on account
of strong objections against them in the minds of some, prevented harmony
in a society and efficiency in its operations, those persons should retire from
prominent positions in that society. He said he had taken that course
when, as agent of the Anti-Slavery Society, he became obnoxious on account
of his position on some questions. He objected, to certain nominations
made by the committee for various reasons. The first was that the persons
nominated had publicly repudiated the principles of the society. One of
these was the presiding officer.

Mrs. STANTON :—I would like you to say in what respect.

Mr. FOSTER :—I will with pleasure ; for, ladies and gentlemen, I admire
our talented President with all my heart, and love the woman. (Great
laughter.) But I believe she has publicly repudiated the principles of the
society.

Mrs. STANTON :—I would like Mr. Foster to state in what way.

Mr. FOSTER :—What are these principles ? The equality of men—universal
suffrage. These ladies stand at the head of a paper which has adopted as its
motto Educated Suffrage. I put myself on this platform as an enemy of educated suffrage, as an enemy of white suffrage, as an enemy of man suffrage,
as an enemy of every kind of suffrage except universal suffrage. *The Revolution* lately had an article headed " That Infamous Fifteenth Amendment."
It is true it was not written by our President, yet it comes from a person
whom she has over and over again publicly indorsed. I am not willing to
take George Francis Train on this platform with his ridicule of the negro
and opposition to his enfranchisement.

Mrs. MARY A. LIVERMORE :—Is it quite generous to bring George Francis
Train on this platform when he has retired from *The Revolution* entirely ?

Mr. FOSTER :—If *The Revolution*, which has so often indorsed George Francis Train, will repudiate him because of his course in respect to the negro's
rights, I have nothing further to say. But it does not repudiate him. He
goes out ; it does not cast him out.

Miss ANTHONY :—Of course it does not.

Mr. FOSTER—My friend says yes to what I have said. I thought it was so. I only wanted to tell you why the Massachusetts society can not coalesce with the party here, and why we want these women to retire and leave us to nominate officers who can receive the respect of both parties. The Massachusetts Abolitionists can not co-operate with this society as it is now organized. If you choose to put officers here that ridicule the negro, and pronounce the Amendment infamous, why I must retire ; I can not work with you. You can not have my support, and you must not use my name. I can not shoulder the responsibility of electing officers who publicly repudiate the principles of the society.

HENRY B. BLACKWELL said : In regard to the criticisms on our officers, I will agree that many unwise things have been written in *The Revolution* by a gentleman who furnished part of the means by which that paper has been carried on. But that gentleman has withdrawn, and you, who know the real opinions of Miss Anthony and Mrs. Stanton on the question of negro suffrage, do not believe that they mean to create antagonism between the negro and the woman question. If they did disbelieve in negro suffrage, it would be no reason for excluding them. We should no more exclude a person from our platform for disbelieving negro suffrage than a person should be excluded from the anti-slavery platform for disbelieving woman suffrage. But I know that Miss Anthony and Mrs. Stanton believe in the right of the negro to vote. We are united on that point. There is no question of principle between us.

The vote on the report of the Committee on Organization was now taken, and adopted by a large majority.

Mr. DOUGLASS :—I came here more as a listener than to speak, and I have listened with a great deal of pleasure to the eloquent address of the Rev. Mr. Frothingham and the splendid address of the President. There is no name greater than that of Elizabeth Cady Stanton in the matter of woman's rights and equal rights, but my sentiments are tinged a little against *The Revolution*. There was in the address to which I allude the employment of certain names, such as " Sambo," and the gardener, and the bootblack, and the daughters of Jefferson and Washington, and all the rest that I can not coincide with. I have asked what difference there is between the daughters of Jefferson and Washington and other daughters. (Laughter.) I must say that I do not see how any one can pretend that there is the same urgency in giving the ballot to woman as to the negro. With us, the matter is a question of life and death, at least, in fifteen States of the Union. When women, because they are women, are hunted down through the cities of New York and New Orleans ; when they are dragged from their houses and hung upon lamp-posts ; when their children are torn from their arms, and their brains dashed out upon the pavement ; when they are objects of insult and outrage at every turn ; when they are in danger of having their homes burnt down over their heads ; when their children are not allowed to enter schools ; then they will have an urgency to obtain the ballot equal to our own. (Great applause.)

A VOICE :—Is that not all true about black women ?

Mr. DOUGLASS :—Yes, yes, yes ; it is true of the black woman, but not because she is a woman, but because she is black. (Applause.) Julia Ward

Howe at the conclusion of her great speech delivered at the convention in Boston last year, said : " I am willing that the negro shall get the ballot before me." (Applause.) Woman ! why, she has 10,000 modes of grappling with her difficulties. I believe that all the virtue of the world can take care of all the evil. I believe that all the intelligence can take care of all the ignorance. (Applause.) I am in favor of woman's suffrage in order that we shall have all the virtue and vice confronted. Let me tell you that when there were few houses in which the black man could have put his head, this woolly head of mine found a refuge in the house of Mrs. Elizabeth Cady Stanton, and if I had been blacker than sixteen midnights, without a single star, it would have been the same. (Applause.)

Miss ANTHONY :—The old anti-slavery school say women must stand back and wait until the negroes shall be recognized. But we say, if you will not give the whole loaf of suffrage to the entire people, give it to the most intelligent first. (Applause.) If intelligence, justice, and morality are to have precedence in the Government, let the question of woman be brought up first and that of the negro last. (Applause.) While I was canvassing the State with petitions and had them filled with names for our cause to the Legislature, a man dared to say to me that the freedom of women was all a theory and not a practical thing. (Applause.) When Mr. Douglass mentioned the black man first and the woman last, if he had noticed he would have seen that it was the men that clapped and not the women. There is not the woman born who desires to eat the bread of dependence, no matter whether it be from the hand of father, husband, or brother ; for any one who does so eat her bread places herself in the power of the person from whom she takes it. (Applause.) Mr. Douglass talks about the wrongs of the negro ; but with all the outrages that he to-day suffers, he would not exchange his sex and take the place of Elizabeth Cady Stanton. (Laughter and applause.)

Mr. DOUGLASS :—I want to know if granting you the right of suffrage will change the nature of our sexes ? (Great laughter.)

Miss ANTHONY :—It will change the pecuniary position of woman ; it will place her where she can earn her own bread. (Loud applause.) She will not then be driven to such employments only as man chooses for her.

Mrs. NORTON said that Mr. Douglass's remarks left her to defend the Government from the inferred inability to grapple with the two questions at once. It legislates upon many questions at one and the same time, and it has the power to decide the woman question and the negro question at one and the same time. (Applause.)

Mrs. LUCY STONE :—Mrs. Stanton will, of course, advocate the precedence for her sex, and Mr. Douglass will strive for the first position for his, and both are perhaps right. If it be true that the government derives its authority from the consent of the governed, we are safe in trusting that principle to the uttermost. If one has a right to say that you can not read and therefore can not vote, then it may be said that you are a woman and therefore can not vote. We are lost if we turn away from the middle principle and argue for one class. I was once a teacher among fugitive slaves. There was one old man, and every tooth was gone, his hair was white, and his face was full of wrinkles, yet, day after day and hour after hour, he came up to the school-house and tried with patience to learn to read, and by-and-by, when he had spelled out the first few verses of the first chapter of the Gospel of St. John, he said to me, " Now, I want to learn to write." I tried to make him satisfied with what he had acquired, but the old man said, " Mrs. Stone, somewhere in the wide world I have a son ; I have not heard from him in twenty years; if I should hear from him, I want to write to him, so take hold of my hand and teach me." I did, but before he had proceeded in many lessons, the angels came and gathered him up and bore him to his Father. Let no man speak of an educated suffrage. The gentleman who addressed you claimed that the negroes had the first right to the suffrage, and drew a picture which only his great word-power can do. He again in Massachusetts, when it had cast a majority in favor of Grant and negro suffrage, stood upon the platform and said that woman had better wait for the negro; that is, that both could not be carried, and that the negro had better be the one. But I freely forgave him because he felt as he spoke. But woman suffrage is more imperative than his own ; and I want to remind the audience that when he says what the Ku-Kluxes did all over the South, the Ku-Kluxes here in the North in the shape of men, take away the children from the mother, and separate them as completely as if done on the block of the auctioneer. Over in New Jersey they have a law which says that *any* father — he might be the most brutal man that ever existed—*any* father, it says, whether he be under age or not, may by his last will and testament dispose of the custody of his child, born or to be born, and that such disposition shall be good against all persons, and that the mother may not recover her child; and that law modified in form exists over every State in the Union except in Kansas. Woman has an ocean of wrongs too deep for any plummet, and the negro, too, has an ocean of wrongs that can not be fathomed. There are two great oceans; in the one is the black man, and in the other is the woman. But I thank God for that XV. Amendment, and hope that it will be adopted in every State. I will be thankful in my soul if *any* body can get out of the terrible pit. But I believe that the safety of the government would be more promoted by the admission of woman as an element of restoration and harmony than the negro. I believe that the influence of woman will save the country before every other power. (Applause.) I see the signs of the times pointing to this consummation, and I believe that in some parts of the country women will vote for the President of these United States in 1872. (Applause.)

At the opening of the evening session Henry B. Blackwell presented a series of resolutions.* Antoinette Brown Blackwell spoke, and was followed by Olive Logan.

---

* *Resolved*, That the extension of suffrage to woman is essential to the public safety and to the establishment and permanence of free instutions ; that the admission of woman to political recognition in our national reconstruction is as imperative as the admission of any particular class of men.

Resolved, That as woman, in private life, in the partnership of marriage, is now the conservator of private morals, so woman in public life, in the partnership of a republican State, based upon Universal suffrage, will become the conservator of public morals.

Resolved, That the petitions of more than 200,000 women to Congress and to their State Legislature during the past winter, are expressions of popular sympathy and approval,

Miss LOGAN said:—I stand here to-night full of faith, inborn faith, in the rights of woman to advance boldly in all ennobling paths. . . . . In my former sphere of life, the equality of woman was fully recognized so far as the kind of labor and the amount of reward for her labor are concerned. As an actress, there was no position in which I was not fully welcomed if I possessed the ability and industry to reach it. If I could become a Ristori, my earnings would be as great as hers, and if I was a man and could become a Kean, a Macready, or a Booth, the same reward would be obtained. If I reach no higher rank than what is called a " walking lady," I am sure of the same pay as a man who occupies the position of a "walking gentleman." In that sphere of life, be it remembered, I was reared from childhood; to that place I was so accustomed that I had no idea it was a privilege denied my sex to enter into almost every other field of endeavor.

In literature also I found myself on an equality with man. If I wrote a good article, I got as good pay; and heaven knows the pay to man or woman was small enough. (Applause). In that field, for a long time, I did not feel an interest in the subject of women's rights, and stood afar off, looking at the work of those revolutionary creatures, Mrs. Stanton and Miss Anthony. The idea of identifying myself with them was as far removed from my thoughts as becoming a female gymnast and whirling upon a trapeze. But once I wrote a lecture, and one night I delivered it. Adhering to my practice of speaking about that which was most familiar, my lecture was about the stage. I lectured, simply because I thought the pay would be better in that department; the idea that I was running counter to anybody's prejudice, never entered my head. And I was so far removed that I never read a page of *The Revolution* in my life, and, what is more, I did not want to; and when Miss Anthony passed down Broadway and saw the bills announcing my lecture she knew nothing about me, and what is more, she did not want to. (Laughter). She made a confession to me afterwards. She said to herself, " Here is a lady going to lecture about the stage," looking

---

everywhere throughout the land, and ought to silence the cavil of our opponents that " women do not want to vote."

Resolved, That while we heartily approve of the Fifteenth Amendment, extending suffrage to men, without distinction of race, we nevertheless feel profound regret that Congress has not submitted a parallel amendment for the enfranchisement of women.

Resolved, That any party professing to be democratic in spirit or republican in principle, which opposes or ignores the political rights of woman, is false to its professions, short-sighted in its policy, and unworthy of the confidence of the friends of impartial liberty.

Resolved, That we hail the report of the Joint Special Committee, just rendered to the Massachusetts Legislature, in favor of woman suffrage, as a fresh evidence of the growth of public sentiment and we earnestly hope that Massachusetts, by promptly submitting the question to a vote of her people, will maintain her historic pre-eminence in the cause of human liberty.

Resolved, That the thanks of the Convention are due to the Hon. George W Julian in the House of Representatives, and to the Hon. Henry Wilson and the Hon. S. C. Pomeroy in the Senate of the United States, for their recent active efforts to secure suffrage for woman.

Resolved, That we recommend the men and women of every Ward, Town, County, and State, to form local Associations for creating and organizing public sentiment in favor of Suffrage for Woman, and to take every possible practical means to effect her enfranchisement.

through her blessed spectacles, as I can see her (laughter)—and I can hear her muttering "a woman's rights woman." (Laughter). That is not so very long ago, a little over a year. Since this great question of woman's rights was thrust upon me, I am asked to define my position; wherever I have traveled in the fifteen months I have had to do so. A lady of society asked me, "Are you in favor of woman's rights?" I had either to answer yes or no, and "Yes," I said. (Applause). . . . .

I met, in my travels, in a New England town, an educated woman, who found herself obliged to earn her livelihood, after living a life of luxury and ease. Her husband, who had provided her with every material comfort, had gone to the grave. All his property was taken to pay his debts, and she found herself penniless. What was that woman to do? She looks abroad among the usual employments of women, and her only resource seems to be that little bit of steel around which cluster so many associations—the needle—and by the needle, with the best work and the best wages, the most she can get is two dollars a day. With this, poor as it is, she will be content; but she finds an army of other women looking for the same, and most of them looking in vain. These things have opened my eyes to a vista such as I never saw before. They have touched my heart as it never before was touched. They have aroused my conscience to the fact that this woman question is the question of the hour, and that I must take part in it. I take my stand boldly, proudly, with such earnest, thoughtful women as Susan B. Anthony, Mrs. Stanton, and Anna Dickinson, to work together with them for the enfranchisement of woman, for her elevation personally and socially, and above all for her right and opportunity to work at such employments as she can follow, with the right to such pay as men get. (Applause). There are thousands of women who have no vital interest in this question. They are happy wives and daughters, and may they ever be so; but they can not tell how soon their husbands and brothers may be lost to them, and they will find themselves destitute and penniless with no resources in themselves against misfortune. Then it will be for such that we labor. Our purpose is to help those who need help, widows and orphan girls. There is no need to do battle in this matter. In all kindness and gentleness we urge our claims. There is no need to declare war upon man, for the best of men in this country are with us heart and soul. These are with us in greater numbers even than our own sex. (A Voice—"That is true." Great applause). Do not say that we seek to break up family peace and fireside joy; far from it. (Applause). We interfere not with the wife or daughter who is happy in the strong protection thrown around her by a father or husband, but it is cowardice for such to throw obstacles in the way of those who need help. More than this, for the sake of the helpless woman, to whose unhappiness in the loss of beloved ones is added the agony of hard and griping want. For the sake of the poor girl who has no power to cope with the hard actualities of a desolate life, while her trembling feet tread the crumbling edge of the dark abyss of infamy. For the sake of this we are pleading and entertaining this great question, withhold your answer till at least you have learned to say, "God speed."

The next speaker was Miss Phoebe Couzins, a young law student from St. Louis, who spoke in a most agreeable and forcible manner.

Miss COUZINS said :—Mrs. PRESIDENT AND LADIES : I deem it the duty of every earnest woman to express herself in regard to the XVth Amendment to our Federal Constitution. I feel deeply the humiliation and insult that is offered to the women of the United States in this Amendment, and have always publicly protested against its passage. During a recent tour through the Eastern States I became still more (if that were possible) firmly fixed in my convictions. Its advocates are unwilling to have it publicly discussed, showing that they know there is an element of weakness in it which will not bear a thorough investigation.

While feeling entirely willing that the black man shall have all the rights to which he is justly entitled, I consider the claims of the black woman of paramount importance. I have had opportunities of seeing and knowing the condition of both sexes, and will bear my testimony, that the black women are, and always have been, in a far worse condition than the men. As a class, they are better, and more intelligent than the men, yet they have been subjected to greater brutalities, while compelled to perform exactly the same labor as men toiling by their side in the fields, just as hard burdens imposed upon them, just as severe punishments decreed to them, with the added cares of maternity and household work, with their children taken from them and sold into bondage ; suffering a thousandfold more than any man could suffer. Then, too, the laws for women in the Southern States, both married and single, degrade them still further. The black men, as a class, are very tyrannical in their families ; they have learned the lesson of brute force but too well, and as the marriage law allows the husband entire control over his wife's earnings and her children, she is in worse bondage than before ; because in many cases the task of providing for helpless children and an idle, lazy, husband, is imposed on the patient wife and mother ; and, with this sudden elevation to citizenship, which the mass of stupid, ignorant negroes look upon as entitling them to great honor, I regard the future state of the negro woman, without the ballot in her hand, as deplorable. And what is said of the ignorant black man can as truthfully be said of the ignorant white man ; they all regard woman as an inferior being. She is their helpless, household slave. He is her ruler, her law-giver, her conscience, her judge and jury, and the prisoner at the bar has no appeal. This XVth Amendment thrusts all women still further down in the scale of degradation, and I consider it neither praiseworthy nor magnanimous for women to assert that they are willing to hold their claims in abeyance, until all shades and types of men have the franchise. It is admitting a false principle, which all women, who are loyal to truth and justice, should immediately reject. For over twenty-five years, the advocates of woman suffrage have been trying to bring this vital question before the country. They have accomplished herculean tasks and still it is up-hill work. Shall they, after battling so long with ignorance, prejudice and unreasoning customs, stand quietly back and obsequiously say they are willing that the floodgates shall be opened and a still greater mass of ignorance, vice and degradation let in to overpower their little army, and set this question back for a century ? Their solemn duty to future generations forbids such a compromise.

The advocates of the XVth Amendment tell us we ought to accept the half loaf when we can not get the whole. I do not see that woman gets any part of the loaf, not even a crumb that falls from the rich man's table. It may appear very magnanimous for men, who have never known the degradation of being thrust down in the scale of humanity by reason of their sex, to urge these yielding measures upon women, they can not and do not know our feelings on the subject, and I regard it as neither just nor generous to eternally compel women to yield on all questions (no matter how humiliating), simply because they are women.

The Anti-Slavery party declares that with the adoption of the XVth Amendment their work is done. Have they, then, been battling for over thirty years for a fraction of a principle? If so, then the XVth Amendment is a fitting capstone to their labors. Were the earnest women who fought and endured so heroically with them, but tools in the hands of the leaders, to place "manhood suffrage" on the highest pinnacle of the temple dedicated to Truth and Justice? And are they now to bow down, and worship in abject submission this fractional part of a principle, that has hitherto proclaimed itself, as knowing neither bond nor free, male nor female, but one perfect humanity?

The XV. Amendment virtually says that every intelligent, virtuous woman is the inferior of every ignorant man, no matter how low he may be sunk in the scale of morality, and every instinct of my being rises to refute such doctrine, and God speaking within me says, No! eternally No!

Rev. GILBERT HAVEN, editor of *Zion's Herald*, was introduced, and said —Ladies and Gentlemen: As I believe that is the way to address you, or shall I merge you into one and call you fellow citizens——

MISS ANTHONY—Let me tell you how to say it. It is perfectly right for a gentleman to say "ladies and gentlemen," but a lady should say, "gentlemen and ladies." (Great applause.) You mention your friend's name before you do your own. (Applause.) I always feel like rebuking any woman who says, "ladies and gentlemen." It is a lack of good manners. (Laughter and great applause.)

MR. HAVEN—I thank the lady for the rule she has laid down. Now, Mr. Beecher has said that a minister is composed of the worst part of man and woman, and there are wealthy men who say that the pulpit should be closed against the introduction of politics, but I am glad this sentiment is not a rule; I rejoice that the country has emancipated the ministry so that a minister can speak on politics. I go further than saying that it is the mere right of the women to achieve suffrage. I say that it is an obligation imposed upon the American people to grant the demands of this large and influential class of the commonwealth. The legislation of the country concerns the woman as much as the man. Is not the wife as much interested in the preservation of property as her husband? Another reason is, that the purity of politics depends upon the admission of woman to the franchise, for without her influence morality in politics can not be secured. (Applause.)

HENRY B. BLACKWELL presented the following resolution:

Resolved, That in seeking to remove the legal disabilities which now oppress woman as wife and mother, the friends of woman suffrage are not seeking to undermine or destroy the sanctity of the marriage relation, but to ennoble marriage, making the obligations and responsibilities of the contract mutual and equal for husband and wife.

MARY A. LIVERMORE said that that was introduced by her permission, but the original resolution was stronger, and she having slept over it, thought that it should be introduced instead of that one, and offered the following:

Resolved, That while we recognize the disabilities which the legal marriage imposes upon woman as wife and mother, and while we pledge ourselves to seek their removal by putting her on equal terms with man, we abhorrently repudiate Free Loveism as horrible and mischievous to society, and disown any sympathy with it.

Mrs. LIVERMORE said that the West wanted some such resolution as that in consequence of the innuendoes that had come to their ears with regard to their striving after the ballot.

Mrs. HANAFORD spoke against such inferences not only for the ministers of her own denomination, but the Christian men and women of New England everywhere. She had heard people say that when women indorsed woman suffrage they indorsed Free Loveism, and God knows they despise it. Let me carry back to my New England home the word that you as well as your honored President, whom we love, whose labor we appreciate, and whose name has also been dragged into this inference, scout all such suggestions as contrary to the law of God and humanity.

LUCY STONE: I feel it is a mortal shame to give any foundation for the implication that we favor Free Loveism. I am ashamed that the question should be asked here. There should be nothing said about it at all. Do not let us, for the sake of our own self-respect, allow it to be hinted that we helped forge a shadow of a chain which comes in the name of Free Love. I am unwilling that it should be suggested that this great, sacred cause of ours means anything but what we have said it does. If any one says to me, " Oh, I know what you mean, you mean Free Love by this agitation," let the lie stick in his throat. You may talk about Free Love, if you please, but we are to have the right to vote. To-day we are fined, imprisoned, and hanged, without a jury trial by our peers. You shall not cheat us by getting us off to talk about something else. When we get the suffrage, then you may taunt us with anything you please, and we will then talk about it as long as you please.

ERNESTINE L. ROSE: We are informed by the people from the West that they are wiser than we are, and that those in the East are also wiser than we are. If they are wiser than we, I think it strange that this question of Free Love should have been brought upon this platform at all. I object to Mrs. Livermore's resolution, not on account of its principles, but on account of its pleading guilty. When a man comes to me and tries to convince me that he is not a thief, then I take care of my coppers. If we pass this resolution that we are not Free Lovers, people will say it is true that you are, for you try to hide it. Lucretia Mott's name has been mentioned as a friend of Free Love, but I hurl back the lie into the faces of all the ministers in the East and into the faces of the newspapers of the West, and defy them to point to one shadow of a reason why they should connect her name with that vice. We have been thirty years in this city before the public, and it is an insult to all the women who have labored in this cause; it is an insult to the thousands and tens of thousands of men and women that have listened to us in our Conventions, to say at this late hour that we are not Free Lovers.

SUSAN B. ANTHONY repudiated the resolution on the same ground as Mrs.

Rose, and said this howl came from those men who knew that when women got their rights they would be able to live honestly; no longer be compelled to sell themselves for bread, either in or out of marriage.

Mrs. Dr. L. S. BATCHELDER, a delegate appointed by the Boston Working Women's Association, said that she represented ten thousand working women of New England, and they had instructed her as their representative to introduce a resolution looking to the amelioration of the condition of the working women.

Senator WILSON spoke as follows: This is a rather new place for me to stand, and yet I am very glad to say that I have no new views in regard to this question. I learned fifteen or twenty years ago something about this reform in its earliest days, when the excellent people, who have labored so long with so much earnestness and fidelity, first launched it before the country. I never knew the time in the last fifteen or twenty years that I was not ready to give my wife the right to vote if she wanted it. I believe in the Declaration of Independence in its full scope and meaning; believing it was born of Christianity; that it came from the teachings of the New Testament; and I am willing to trust the New Testament and the Declaration of Independence anywhere on God's earth, and to adopt their doctrine in the fullest and broadest manner. I do not know that all the good in the world will be accomplished when the women of the United States have the right to vote. But it is sure to come. Truth is truth, and will stand.

Mrs. ERNESTINE L. ROSE referred to the assertion of the Rev. Mr. Haven, that the seeds of the Woman's Rights reform were sown in Massachusetts, and proceeded to disprove it. Thirty-two years ago she went round in New York city with petitions to the Legislature to obtain for married women the right to hold property in their own names. She only got five names the first year, but she and others persevered for eleven years, and finally succeeded. Who, asked Mrs. Rose, was the first to call a National Convention of women—New York or Massachusetts? [Applause.] I like to have justice done and honor given where it is due.

Mrs. SARAH F. NORTON, of the New York Working Woman's Association, referring to the former attempt to exclude the discussion of the relations of capital and labor, argued that the question was an appropriate one in any Woman's Rights Convention, and proposed that some member of the New York Working Women's Association be heard on that point.

Mrs. ELEANOR KIRK accordingly described the beginning, progress, and operations of the Association. She also replied to the recent criticism of the *World* upon the semi-literary, semi-Woman's Rights nature of the meetings of their associations, and contended that they had a perfect right to debate and read essays, and do anything else that other women might do.

Mrs. MARY F. DAVIS spoke in behalf of the rights of her own sex, but expressed her willingness to see the negro guaranteed in his rights, and would wait if only one question could be disposed of. But she thought they would not have to wait long, for the Hon. Mr. Wilson had assured them that their side is to be strongly and successfully advocated. Every step in the great cause of human rights helps the next one forward. In 1848 Mrs. Stanton called the first Convention at Seneca Falls.

Miss ANTHONY: And Lucretia Mott.

Mrs. DAVIS: Yes, and Lucretia Mott; and I love to speak of them in association. Mrs. Rose has alluded to the primary steps she took, and there were Susan B. Anthony, Lucy Stone, Antoinette Brown Blackwell, and Paulina Wright Davis, and a great galaxy who paved the way; and we stand here to proclaim the immortal principle of woman's freedom. [Great applause.] The lady then referred to the great work that lay before them in lifting out of misery and wretchedness the numbers of women in this city and elsewhere, who were experiencing all the fullness of human degradation. Even when they had finished their present work, a large field was still before them in the elevation of their sex. [Applause.]

Mrs. PAULINA W. DAVIS said she would not be altogether satisfied to have the XVth Amendment passed without the XVIth, for woman would have a race of tyrants raised above her in the South, and the black women of that country would also receive worse treatment than if the Amendment was not passed. Take any class that have been slaves, and you will find that they are the worst when free, and become the hardest masters. The colored women of the South say they do not want to get married to the negro, as their husbands can take their children away from them, and also appropriate their earnings. The black women are more intelligent than the men, because they have learned something from their mistresses. She then related incidents showing how black men whip and abuse their wives in the South. One of her sister's servants whipped his wife every Sunday regularly. [Laughter.] She thought that sort of men should not have the making of the laws for the government of the women throughout the land. [Applause.]

Mr. DOUGLASS said that all disinterested spectators would concede that this Equal Rights meeting had been pre-eminently a Woman's Rights meeting. [Applause.] They had just heard an argument with which he could not agree—that the suffrage to the black men should be postponed to that of the women. I do not believe the story that the slaves who are enfranchised become the worst of tyrants. [A voice, "Neither do I." Applause.] I know how this theory came about. When a slave was made a driver, he made himself more officious than the white driver, so that his master might not suspect that he was favoring those under him. But we do not intend to have any master over us. [Applause.]

THE PRESIDENT, Mrs. Stanton, argued that not another man should be enfranchised until enough women are admitted to the polls to outweigh those already there. [Applause.] She did not believe in allowing ignorant negroes and foreigners to make laws for her to obey. [Applause.]

Mrs. HARPER (colored) asked Mr. Blackwell to read the fifth resolution of the series he submitted, and contended that that covered the whole ground of the resolutions of Mr. Douglass. When it was a question of race, she let the lesser question of sex go. But the white women all go for sex, letting race occupy a minor position. She liked the idea of working women, but she would like to know if it was broad enough to take colored women?

Miss ANTHONY and several others: Yes, yes.

Mrs. HARPER said that when she was at Boston there were sixty women who left work because one colored woman went to gain a livelihood in their midst. [Applause.] If the nation could only handle one question, she would not have the black women put a single straw in the way, if only the men of the race could obtain what they wanted. [Great applause.]

Mr. C. C. BURLEIGH attempted to speak, but was received with some disapprobation by the audience, and confusion ensued.

Miss ANTHONY protested against the XVth Amendment because it wasn't Equal Rights. It put two million more men in position of tyrants over two million women who had until now been the equals of the men at their side.

Mr. BURLEIGH again essayed to speak. The confusion was so great that he could not be heard.

Mrs. STONE appealed for order, and her first appearance caused the most respectful silence, as did the words of every one of the ladies who addressed the audience. Mr. Burleigh again ventured, but with no better result, and Miss Anthony made another appeal to the audience to hear him. He tried again to get a word in, but was once more unsuccessful.

Mrs. LIVERMORE, after protesting against the disorderly behavior of the audience, said a few words in advocacy of the resolutions of Mr. Douglass, when a motion was made to lay them upon the table, and Mr. Blackwell moved the "previous question."

Miss ANTHONY hoped that this, the first attempt at gagging discussion, ould not be countenanced. (Applause.) She made a strong protest against this treatment of Mr. Burleigh. Sufficient silence was obtained for that gentleman to say that he had finished; but he was determined that they should hear the last word. (Hisses and laughter.) He now took his seat. The motion to lay the resolutions upon the table for discussion in the evening was then carried, and the Association adjourned till the evening, to meet in the large hall of the Cooper Institute. A letter from Jules Favre, the celebrated French advocate and *litterateur,* was read, after which addresses were delivered by Madam Anneke, of Milwaukee (in German), and by Madame de Hericourt, of Chicago (in French). Both of these ladies are of revolutionary tendencies, and left their native countries because they had rendered themselves obnoxious by a too free expression of their political opinions.

Madam ANNEKE said — *Mrs. President:* Nearly two decades have passed since, in answer to a call from our co-workers, I stood before a large assembly, over which Mrs. Mott presided, to utter, in the name of suffering and struggling womanhood, the cry of my old Fatherland for freedom and justice. At that time my voice was overwhelmed by the sound of sneers, scoffs, and hisses—the eloquence of tyranny, by which every outcry of the human heart is stifled. Then, through the support of our friends Mrs. Rose and Wendell Phillips, who are ever ready in the cause of human rights, I was allowed, in my native tongue, to echo faintly the cry for justice and freedom. What a change has been wrought since then ! To-day they greet us with deferential respect. Such giant steps are made by public opinion ! What they then derided, and sought, through physical power and rough ignorance, to render wholly impossible, to-day they greet with the voice of welcome and jubilee. Such an expression of sentiment is to us the most certain and joyful token of a gigantic revolution in public opinion—still more gratifying is it, that the history of the last few years proves that under the force of an universal necessity, reason and freedom are being consistently developed. Such is the iron step of time, that it brings forward every event to meet its rare fulfillment. Under your protection I am once more permitted, in this dawning of a new epoch which is visible to all eyes that will see, and audible to all ears that will hear, to express my hopes, my longing, my striving, and my confidence. And now, permit me to do so in the language of my childhood's play, as well as that of the earnest and free philosophy of German thinkers and workers. Not that I believe it is left to me to interest the children of my old Fatherland, here present, in the new era of truth and freedom, as if these glorious principles were not of yore implanted in their hearts—as if they could not take them up in a strange idiom—but because I am urged from my deepest soul to speak out loud and free, as I have ever felt myself constrained to do. and as I can not do in the language of my beloved adopted land. The consciousness and the holy conviction of our inalienable human rights, which I have won in the struggle of my own strangely varied life, and in the wrestling for independence which has carried me through the terrors of bloody revolution, and brought me to this effulgent shore where *Sanita Libertas* is free to all who seek it—this sacred strand, of which our German poet says: *Dich halte ich !* (I have gained thee and will not leave thee.) So I turn to you, my dear compatriots, in the language of our Fatherland—to you who are accustomed to German ways of thinking — to you who have grown up in the light which flows from thinking brains—to you whose hearts warmly cherish human rights and human worth—who are not afraid of truth when it speaks of such deep, clear, and universally important subjects as human rights and human duties. He who fears truth will find hiding places, but he who combats for it is worthy of it. The method of its adversaries is to address themselves to thoughtless passion, and thus arouse mockery and abuse against those who search for scientific knowledge to appeal to easily moved feelings and kindle sentiments of hatred and contempt. They can do this only while truth is in the minority—only until right shall become might.

You will learn to judge of woman's strength when you see that she persists strenuously in this purpose, and secures, by her energy, the rights which shall invest her with power. That which you can no longer suppress in woman—that which is free above all things—that which is pre-eminently important to mankind. and must have free play in every mind, is the natural thirst for scientific knowledge—that fountain of all peacefully progressing amelioration in human history. This longing, this effort of reason seeking knowledge of itself, of ideas, conclusions, and all higher things, has, as far as historical remembrance goes back, never been so violently suppressed in any human being as in woman. But, so far from its having been extinguished in her, it has, under the influence of this enlightened century, become a gigantic flame which shines most brightly under the protection of the star-spangled banner. There does not exist a man-made doctrine, fabricated expressly for us, and which we must learn by heart, that shall henceforth be our law. Nor shall the authority of old traditions be a standard for us—be this authority called Veda, Talmud, Koran, or Bible. No. Reason, which we recognize as our highest and only law-giver, commands us to be free. We have recognized our duty—we have heard the rustling of the golden wings of our guardian angel—we are inspired for the work!

We are no longer in the beginning of history—that age which was a constant struggle with nature, misery, ignorance, helplessness, and every kind of bondage. The moral idea of the State struggles for that fulfillment in which all individuals shall be brought into a union which shall augment a million-fold both its individual and collective force. Therefore, don't exclude us—don't exclude woman—don't exclude the whole half of the human family. Receive us—begin the work in which a new era shall dawn. In all great events we find that woman has a guiding hand—let us stay near you now, when humanity is concerned. Man has the spirit of truth, but woman alone has passion for it. All creations need love—let us, therefore, celebrate a union from which shall spring the morning of freedom for humanity. Give us our rights in the State. Honor us as your equals, and allow us to use the rights which belong to us, and which reason commands us to use. Whether it be prudent to enfranchise woman, is not the question—only whether it be right. What is positively right, must be prudent, must be wise, and must, finally, be useful. Give the lie to the monarchically disposed statesman, who says the republic of the United States is only an experiment, which earlier or later will prove a failure. Give the lie to such hopes, I say, by carrying out the whole elevated idea of the republic—by calling the entire, excluded half of mankind and every being endowed with reason, to the ballot-box, which is the people's holy palladium.

MADAME DE HERICOURT said: I wish to ask if rights have their source in ability, in functions, in qualities? No, certainly; for we see that all men, however they may differ in endowments, have equal rights. What, then, is the basis of rights? Humanity. Consequently, even if it be true that woman is inferior to man in intelligence and social ability, it is not desirable that she shut herself within what is called woman's sphere. In a philosophical light, the objections brought against her have no bearing on this question. Woman must have equal rights with man, because she is, like him, a human being; and only in establishing, through anatomical or biological proof, that she does not belong to the human race, can her rights be withheld. When such demonstration is made, my claims shall cease. In the meantime, let me say that woman—whether useful or useless—belonging to humanity, must have the rights of humanity.

But is it true that the equality of man and woman would not be useful to society? We might answer this question in the affirmative were the sexes alike, but for the very reason that they differ in many respects, is the presence of woman by the side of man, if we desire order and justice, everywhere necessary. Is it graceful, I ask, to walk on one leg? Men, since the beginning of history, have had the bad taste to prefer a lame society to one that is healthy and beautiful. We women have really too much taste to yield longer to such deformity. In law, in institutions, in every social and political matter, there are two sides. Up to the present day, man has usurped what belongs to woman. That is the reason why we have injustice, corruption, international hatred, cruelty, war, shameful laws—man assuming, in regard to woman, the sinful relation of slaveholder. Such relation must and will change, because we women have decided that it shall not exist. With you, gentlemen, we will vote, legislate, govern—not only because it is our right, but because it is time to substitute order, peace, equity, and virtue, for the disorder, war, cruelty, injustice, and corruption which you, acting alone, have established. You doubt our fitness to take part in government because we are fickle, extravagant, etc., etc., as you say. I answer, there is an inconsiderable minority which deserve such epithets; but even if all women deserved them, who is in fault? You not only prefer the weak-minded, extravagant women to the strong-minded and reasonable ones, but as soon as a woman attempts to leave her sphere, you, cowardlike, throw yourselves before her, and secure to your own profit all remunerative occupations. I could, perhaps, forgive your selfishness and injustice, but I can not forgive your want of logic nor your hypocrisy. You condemn woman to starvation, to ignorance, to extravagance, in order to please yourselves, and then reproach her for this ignorance and extravagance, while you heap blame and ridicule on those who are educated, wise, and frugal. You are, indeed, very absurd or very silly. Your judgment is so weak that you reproach woman with the faults of a slave, when it is you who have made and who keep her a slave, and who know, moreover, that no true and virtuous soul can accept slavery. You reproach woman with being an active agent in corruption and ruin, without perceiving that it is you who have condemned her to this awful work, in which only your bad passions sustain her. Whatever you may do, you can not escape her influence. If she is free, virtuous, and worthy, she will give you free, virtuous, and worthy sons, and maintain in you republican virtues. If she remain a slave, she will debase you and your sons; and your country will come under the rule of tyranny. Insane men can not understand that where there is one slave there are always two—he who wears the chain and he who rivets it. Unreasonable, shortsighted men can not understand that to enfranchise woman is to elevate man; to give him a companion who shall encourage his good and noble aspirations, instead of one who would debase and draw him down into an abyss of selfishness and dishonesty. Gentlemen, will you be just, will you preserve the republic, will you stop the moral ruin of your country; will you be worthy, virtuous, and courageous for the welfare of your nation, and, in spite of all obstacles, enfranchise your mothers, wives, daughters, and sisters? Take care that you be not too late! Such injustice and folly would be at the cost of your liberty, in which event you could claim no mercy, for tyrants deserve to be the victims of tyrants.

After her brief address, Madame de Hericourt submitted to the Conven
tion a series of resolutions for the organization of Women's Leagues.*

ERNESTINE L. ROSE said—*Mrs. Chairman, Ladies and Gentlemen :* What
we need is to arouse both men and women to the great necessity of justice and of right. The world moves. We need not seek further than
this Convention assembled here to-night to show that it moves. We
have assembled here delegates from the East and the West, from the
North and the South, from all over the United States, from England,
from France, and from Germany—all have come to give us greeting and
well-wishes, both in writing and in speech. I only wish that this whole
audience might have been able to understand and appreciate the eloquent speeches which have been delivered here to-night. They have
been uttered in support of the claim—the just demand—of woman for
the right to vote. Why is it, my friends, that Congress has enacted laws
to give the negro of the South the right to vote? Why do they not at the
same time protect the negro woman ? If Congress really means to protect
the negro race, they should have acknowledged woman just as much as
man; not only in the South, but here in the North, the only way to protect her is by the ballot. We have often heard from this platform, and
I myself have often said, that with individual man we do not find fault.
We do not war with man; we war with bad principles. And let me ask
whether we have not the right to war with these principles which stamp
the degradation of inferiority upon women.

This Society calls itself the Equal Rights Association. That I understand to be an association which has no distinction of sex, class,
or color. Congress does not seem to understand the meaning of
the term universal. I understand the word universal to include ALL.
Congress understood that Universal Suffrage meant the white man
only. Since the war we have changed the name for Impartial Suffrage. When some of our editors, such as Mr. Greeley and others,
were asked what they meant by impartial suffrage, they said, "Why,
man, of course; the man and the brother." Congress has enacted

---

* 1st. That we form a League of all women claiming their rights, both in America and
Europe.

2d. The aim of this League, which shall be called the "Universal League for Woman's
Rights and Universal Peace," is to extinguish prejudice between nations, to create a common interest through the influence of woman, in order to substitute the reign of humanity for the divisions and hatred and causes of war, and to give aid to the women of all
nations in securing their rights.

3d. That in every country Emancipation Societies shall be organized, that a National
Union may be formed which shall be in constant communication with other countries by
means of journals, pamphlets, and books.

4th. That every year a General Assembly of delegates from every country shall meet in
one of the capitals by turn. These capitals might for the present be Washington, Paris,
London, Florence, and one of the central cities of Germany.

5th. That at the stated meetings of the League there shall be an exhibition of works of
art by women.

6th. That, in traveling, women should everywhere find friendship and aid in pursuing
the end which they propose. Women, being sisters and daughters in the ranks of humanity, must feel themselves at home with their sisters of all nations. Among us there
can be no foreigners, since we are not citizens.

resolutions for the suffrage of men and brothers. They don't speak of the women and sisters. [Applause.] They have begun to change their tactics, and call it manhood suffrage. I propose to call it Woman Suffrage; then we shall know what we mean. We might commence by calling the Chinaman a man and a brother, or the Hottentot, or the Calmuck, or the Indian, the idiot or the criminal, but where shall we stop? They will bring all these in before us, and then they will bring in the babies—the *male* babies. [Laughter.] I am a foreigner. I had great difficulty in acquiring the English language, and I never shall acquire it. But I am afraid that in the meaning of language Congress is a great deal worse off than I have ever been. I go for the change of name; I will not be construed into a man and a brother. I ask the same rights for women that are extended to men—the right to life, liberty, and the pursuit of happiness; and every pursuit in life must be as free and open to me as any man in the land. [Applause.] But they will never be thrown open to me or to any of you, until we have the power of the ballot in our own hands. That little paper is a great talisman. We have often been told that the golden key can unlock all the doors. That little piece of paper can unlock doors where golden keys fail. Wherever men are—whether in the workshop, in the store, in the laboratory, or in the legislative halls—I want to see women. Wherever man is, there she is needed; wherever man has work to do—work for the benefit of humanity—there should men and women unite and co-operate together. It is not well for man to be alone or work alone; and he can not work for woman as well as woman can work for herself. I suggest that the name of this society be changed from Equal Rights Association to Woman's Suffrage Association.

LUCY STONE said she must oppose this till the colored man gained the right to vote. If they changed the name of the association for such a reason as it was evident it was proposed, they would lose the confidence of the public. I hope you will not do it.

A GENTLEMAN: Mrs. President, I hope you will do it. I move that the name of the association be changed to the " Universal Franchise Association."

MRS. STANTON: The question is already settled by our constitution, which requires a month's notice previous to the annual meeting before any change of name can be made. We will now have a song. [Laughter.]

MR. BLACKWELL said that he had just returned from the South, and that he had learned to think that the test oath required of white men who had been rebels must be abolished before the vote be given to the negro. He was willing that the negro should have the suffrage, but not under such conditions that he should rule the South. [At the allusion of Mr. Blackwell to abolishing the test oath, the audience hissed loudly.]

MRS. STANTON said—Gentlemen and Ladies : I take this as quite an insult to me. It is as if you were invited to dine with me and you turned up your nose at everything that was set on the table.

MRS. LIVERMORE said: It certainly requires a great amount of nerve to talk before you, for you have such a frankness in expressing yourselves that I am afraid of you. [Laughter and applause.] If you do not like the dish, you turn up your nose at it and say, "Take it away, take it away." [Laughter.] I was brought up in the West, and it is a good place to get rid of any superfluous modesty, but I am afraid of you. [Applause.] It seems that you are more willing to be pleased than to hear what we have to say. [Applause.] Throughout the day the men who have attended our Convention have been turbulent. [Applause.] I say it frankly, that the behavior of the majority of men has not been respectful. [Applause.] She then gave a pathetic narration of the sorrow she had seen among the depraved and destitute of our great cities, and said the work of the coming year would be to get up a monster petition of a million of names asking the Legislature for suffrage. [Applause.]

After a song from the Hutchinson Family, who had come from Chicago to entertain the audiences of the Association, the meeting adjourned.

DOCUMENT 31 (II: 516–20): National Woman Suffrage
Association, May Anniversary of 1872, New York City,
May 9-10, 1872

The National Woman Suffrage Association held its May Anniversary of 1872 in New York, at Steinway Hall.   As can be seen
by the call,* the intention was to form a political party, but the
delegates, after some discussion, decided that nominees without
electors were incongruous.   As usual a large number of States were
represented by delegates, California sending Laura de Force Gordon,
and Oregon, Abigail Scott Duniway.   This convention was chiefly
remarkable as being the first at which the presidency changed hands
—Miss Anthony, instead of Mrs. Stanton, being elected to fill the
position of chief officer.

---

* PEOPLE'S CONVENTION.—The undersigned citizens of the United States, responding
to the invitation of the National Woman Suffrage Association, propose to hold a Convention at Steinway Hall, in the city of New York, the 9th and 10th of May.

We believe the time has come for the formation of a new political party whose principles shall meet the issues of the hour, and represent equal rights for all.

As the women of the country are to take part for the first time in political action, we propose that the initiative steps in the convention shall be taken by them, that their opinions

A delegation, consisting of Mrs. Hooker, Mrs. De Force Gordon, and Miss Anthony, was sent by the National Woman Suffrage Association to the Presidential Conventions held by the Liberal Republicans at Cincinnati, the Democrats at Baltimore, and the Republicans at Philadelphia. The fruit of all the earnest labor of this delegation was a splinter in the Republican platform. This, however, was something to be grateful for, as it was the first mention of woman in the platform of either of the great political parties during our National existence. On the strength of this plank the following address was issued:

GRANT AND WILSON—APPEAL TO THE WOMEN OF AMERICA FROM THE NATIONAL WOMAN SUFFRAGE ASSOCIATION.

Women of the United States, the hour for political action has come. For the first time in the history of our country woman has been recognized in the platform of a large and dominant party. Philadelphia has spoken and woman is no longer ignored. She is now officially recognized as a part of the body politic. The fourteenth plank of its platform declares :

The Republican party mindful of its obligations to the loyal women of America expresses gratification that wider avenues of employment have been open to women, and it farther declares that her demands for additional rights should be treated with respectful consideration.

We are told that this plank does not say much, that in fact it is only a "splinter ; " and our "liberal" friends warn us not to rely upon it as a promise of the ballot to woman. What it is, we know full better than others. We recognize its meagerness; we see in it the timidity of politicians; but beyond and through it all, we farther see its promise of the

and methods may be fairly set forth, and considered by the representatives from many reform movements now ready for united action ; such as the Internationals, and other Labor Reformers—the friends of peace, temperance, and education, and by all those who believe that the time has come to carry the principles of true morality and religion into the State House, the Court, and the market place.

This convention will declare the platform of the People's Party, and consider the nomination of candidates for President and Vice-President of the United States, who shall be the best possible exponents of political and industrial reform.

The Republican party, in destroying slavery, accomplished its entire mission. In denying that "citizen" means political equality, it has been false to its own definition of Republican Government ; and in fostering land, railroad, and money monopolies, it is building up a commercial feudalism dangerous to the liberty of the people.

The Democratic party, false to its name and mission, died in the attempt to sustain slavery, and is buried beyond all hope of resurrection.

Even that portion of the Labor party which met recently at Columbus, proved its incapacity to frame a national platform to meet the demands of the hour.

We therefore invite all citizens who believe in the idea of self-government; who demand an honest administration ; the reform of political and social abuses ; the emancipation of labor, and the enfranchisement of woman, to join with us and inaugurate a political revolution which shall secure justice, liberty, and equality to every citizen of the United States.   ELIZABETH CADY STANTON, ISABELLA BEECHER HOOKER, MATILDA JOSLYN GAGE.

future. We see in it the thin edge of the entering wedge which shall break woman's slavery in pieces and make us at last a nation truly free —a nation in which the caste of sex shall fall down by the caste of color, and humanity alone shall be the criterion of all human rights. The Republican party has been the party of ideas, of progress. Under its leadership, the nation came safely through the fiery ordeal of the rebellion ; under it slavery was destroyed ; under it manhood suffrage was established. The women of the country have long looked to it in hope, and not in vain ; for to-day we are launched by it into the political arena, and the Republican party must hereafter fight our battles for us. This great party, this progressive party, having taken the initiative step, will never go back on its record. It needed this new and vital issue to keep it in life, for Cincinnati indorsed its work up to this hour ; the constitutional amendments, the payment of the bonds in gold, the civil service reform, the restoration of the States. It thanked the soldiers and sailors of the Republic, it proposed lands to actual settlers. The Republican party went up higher ; it remembered all citizens. The widows and orphans of the soldiers and sailors were not forgotten; it acknowledged its obligation to the loyal women of the Republic, and to the demands for additional rights, of all women, whatever their class, color, or birth, it promised "respectful consideration." Its second plank declared that ": complete liberty and exact equality in the enjoyment of all civil, political, and public rights should be established and maintained throughout the Union by efficient and appropriate State and Federal legislation." These two planks are the complement of each other, and are the promise of exact and equal justice to woman. They were the work of radical woman suffrage Republicans—of Wilson, Sargent, Loring, Claflin, Hoar, Fairchild, and others. They were accepted by the candidates. General Grant, in his letter, expresses his desire to see " the time when the title of 'citizen' shall carry with it all the protection and privilege to the humblest, that it does to the most exalted." His course since his elevation to the Presidency has always been favorable to increased rights for women. He has officially recognized their competency, and has given them many government positions. Senator Wilson is an old and staunch advocate of woman suffrage, and his letter in pointed terms refers to the recognition given woman by his party, and says, " to her new demands it extends the hand of grateful recognition, and it commends her demands for additional rights to the calm and careful consideration of the nation." And, too, thus early in the campaign, the strongest men of the party, among whom are Forney, of the Philadelphia *Press*, Gerrit Smith, Bowen, of the New York *Independent*, and President White, of Cornell University, speak of this recognition as introducing a new era into politics.

While the old and tried Republican party in its platform and candidates thus gives woman assurance that her claim to equal political rights is to be respected, the other party in the field gives her no promise either in its platform or the letters of its nominees. The Liberal Republican party is a new party; it has no record; it has done no work; it is wholly untried; it ignores women; and by its silence in regard to the equal rights of one-

half of the people—the most important question now in the political horizon—it proves itself unworthy of its name, unworthy of woman's confidence, and unworthy of the votes of truly liberal men.   In regard to its
candidates, Gratz Brown, once our friend, has practically denied his
record.   Horace Greeley, its chief nominee, has for years been our
most bitter opponent.   Both by tongue and pen he has heaped
abuse, ridicule, and misrepresentation upon our leading women, while
the whole power of the *Tribune* has been used to crush out our great reform.   And now that he is a candidate for election to the highest office
in the country, he still continues his bitter and hostile course toward
one half of its citizens.   He presses the iron-heel of his despotism upon
their liberties; and, in answer to our appeals, he says he "neither desires
our help nor believes us capable of giving any."

What can liberty expect from such a man?   What can woman hope
from such a party?   Women of the Republic, you can not in self-respect
give your aid to such nominees; you can not in self-respect work for such
a party.   It has repulsed you, pushed you back, said to you "go hence."

The Republican party, with Grant and Wilson as its standard-bearers,
opens its doors to you.   By its fourteenth plank it invites your aid and
co-operation.

Shall it not have it ?   Women of the South, will you not work for your
own freedom?   Women of the North, will you not strive for your own enfranchisement?

> There is a tide in the affairs of men
> Which taken at the flood leads on to fortune.
> But we must take the current when it serves our turn,
> Or lose our ventures.

For us to-day this tide has risen; for us to-day the current serves our
turn.   Let us lay aside our party preferences.   Let us one and all forget
our many grievances of the past; let us forget the many times we have
been ignored, buffeted, and spurned by politicians.   Let us throw our
whole influence of voice and pen into this campaign, and in making it a
success for the Republican party, make it a success for ourselves.

And now an especial word to the Women Suffrage organizations of the
country.   Prepare to hold mass meetings in all the large cities of your
States; be ready to co-operate with Republican committees; send into
the election districts your best women speakers, circulate addresses and
documents throughout every school district; persuade fathers, brothers,
husbands, and sons to work and vote for Grant and Wilson; offer your
own votes, as in many election districts women's votes have already been
received and counted; in every possible way throw the whole weight of
your influence on the side of the Republican party.   By persistent,
united action for one party during this Presidential canvass, the women
suffragists of the nation will make themselves felt as a power by both.

Women speakers, do not hesitate, do not vacillate; let no party or personal consideration bias you to act against the Republican party at this
momentous crisis.   Remember we owe to it a debt of gratitude that it
has made for us this opportunity, that it has thus launched our cause
into the political arena, where it must go on and on till justice and

equality to woman shall at last triumph in a true Republic; "a government of the people, for the people, and by the people."

On behalf of the National Woman Suffrage Association.

SUSAN B. ANTHONY, President,
MATILDA JOSLYN GAGE, Chair. Ex. Com.

ROCHESTER, July 19, 1872.

The Congressional Republican Committee published thousands of
this appeal, and scattered them over the country. It also telegraphed
to the President of the National Woman Suffrage Association, to go
to Washington in order to consult with the committee as to what
women could do to aid in the coming campaign. Miss Anthony's
plan was cordially accepted, and liberal appropriations placed at her
disposal by both the National and New York Republican Committees for carrying on a series of meetings.* The first of this series
was at Rochester, and was presided over by Hon. Carter Wilder,
Mayor of the city, the last in Cooper Institute, New York, at which
meeting Luther R. Marsh occupied the chair.

Mrs. Livermore and Mrs. Stanton, by special invitation of Republican State Committees, also took part in the canvass in Connecticut
and Pennsylvania.

---

* The speakers were Rev. Olympia Brown, Matilda Joslyn Gage, Susan B. Anthony,
Isabella Beecher Hooker, Elizabeth Cady Stanton, Dr. Clemence S. Lozier, Helen M.
Slocum, Lillie Devereux Blake.

III. AN INDEPENDENT STRATEGY

TURNED BACK FROM THE ROUTE of political alliances, woman suffrage advocates sought a new and independent strategy. One path was marked out by Victoria Woodhull, the principal publisher of *Woodhull & Claflin's Weekly* and an outspoken radical later mired in free-love scandals. She proposed to Congress that under the Fourteenth and Fifteenth Amendments women were already enfranchised. She received a respectful hearing, in part because the issue had already been formally introduced in Congress, first through an unsuccessful attempt to provide woman suffrage in the District of Columbia in 1866, next through proposals of a federal amendment on woman suffrage introduced by Senator S. C. Pomeroy of Kansas and Representative G. W. Julian of Indiana in 1868-69. In 1871, a committee of the House issued a favorable minority report on suffrage. But there the issue lay for decades.

A related strategy was the direct action of attempting to vote under the existing laws. In 1868, over 170 women in Vineland, New Jersey, "voted" in boxes set aside for them, after being denied the privilege of casting a true ballot. The next year some 40 women in Hyde Park, Massachusetts, including the Grimké sisters, repeated this procedure. In 1871-72, 150 women in seven states and the District of Columbia attempted to vote, a number actually succeeding. In the District of Columbia, 70 women appealed their right to the Supreme Court, arguing that the Fifteenth Amendment did not explicitly grant the Negro the right to vote and yet Negroes voted. In Rochester, Susan B. Anthony's vote was not counted, and she was prevented from carrying her appeal to the Supreme Court through a legal technicality. In the definitive case, Virginia Minor, a leading Missouri suffragist whose husband had been a counsel for the Washington, D. C., women, brought her own suit against the state of Missouri to the Supreme Court. Reviewing the evidence on the history of citizenship and voting in the nation, Chief Justice Waite ruled that suffrage was not necessarily conferred upon any citizen, and "if the courts can consider any question settled, this is one."[1]

Despite these defeats, militants could seize an occasional opportunity to renew the spirit of women's demand for full citizenship. The dramatic presentation of women's grievances at the Centennial Exposition of 1876 was a measure of the old mood. The leaders could assess the distance traveled since 1848, with many property and legal rights granted and a serious hearing allowed the women. Such consolations were, however, not greatly comforting, for the very context of Radical Reconstruction in which women had argued for the extension of suffrage was badly eroded by political reaction.

NWSA now made demands upon Congress for a special Woman Suffrage Committee and for a room in the Capitol to hold meetings; both demands were eventually granted. In 1878 the historic bill known popularly as the "Susan B. Anthony Amendment" was first introduced in Congress, derived from Sumner's phrasing of the Fifteenth Amendment and destined to be retained in identical wording for its passage forty years later. In 1882, both houses had created select committees, and major debates were held in 1886-87. Little more was accomplished for a quarter-century, but the congressional discussions gave NWSA a focus for its work and maximum publicity considering its limited strength. Stanton and Anthony continued to demand suffrage as a right to be conceded by the national government. AWSA leaders, on the contrary, put their concentration in the equally unsuccessful state referenda, appealing implicitly to the goodwill of the voters to grant suffrage. For the decades at the end of the nineteenth century, both sides could register these activities as nominal "gains" against the long wait for a breakthrough.

1. Vol. II, 742.

DOCUMENT 32 (II: 443–48): Victoria Woodhull, Memorial and Petition to the Judiciary Committee of the House of Representatives, U. S. Congress, December 19, 1870, and January 11, 1871

THE MEMORIAL OF VICTORIA C. WOODHULL.

To the Honorable the Senate and House of Representatives of the United States in Congress assembled, respectfully showeth:

That she was born in the State of Ohio, and is above the age of twenty-one years; that she has resided in the State of New York during the past three years; that she is still a resident thereof, and that she is a citizen of the United States, as declared by the XIV. Article of the Amendments to the Constitution of the United States.

That since the adoption of the XV. Article of the Amendments to the

---

* The hearing took place in the committee room, which was crowded with a goodly assemblage of men and women, Judge Bingham, of Ohio, was chairman, Gen. B. F. Butler, of Mass., was prominent in favor of the cause. Messrs. Eldridge, B. C. Cook, I. A. Peters, Ulysses Mercur, Wm. Loughridge, Michael Kerr, S. W. Kellogg, and G. W. Hitchcock formed the rest of the committee. The claimants for woman suffrage were represented by Mrs. V. C. Woodhull and Mrs. L. D. Blake, New York ; Mrs. I. B. Hooker, Rev. O. Brown, Conn.; Mrs. P. W. Davis, Miss K. Stanton, Rhode Island ; Mrs. J. Griffing, and Mrs. Lockwood, D. C.; and Miss Susan B. Anthony. The proceedings were opened by the reading of her memorial by Mrs. Woodhull. It was the first time the lady had ever appeared in public, and her voice trembled slightly with emotion which only made the reading the more effective. She claimed not a XVI. amendment ; but that under the XIV. and XV. Amendments, women have already the right to vote, and prayed Congress merely to pass a declaratory resolution to that effect.—The Washington *Republican*.

Constitution, neither the State of New York nor any other State, nor any Territory, has passed any law to abridge the right of any citizen of the United States to vote, as established by said article, neither on account of sex or otherwise. That, nevertheless, the right to vote is denied to women citizens of the United States by the operation of Election Laws in the several States and Territories, which laws were enacted prior to the adoption of the said XV. Article, and which are inconsistent with the Constitution as amended, and, therefore, are void and of no effect; but which, being still enforced by the said States and Territories, render the Constitution inoperative as regards the right of women citizens to vote:

And whereas, Article VI., Section 2, declares "That this Constitution and the laws of the United States which shall be made in pursuance thereof, and all treaties made, or which shall be made, under the authority of the United States, shall be the supreme law of the land; and all judges in every State shall be bound thereby, anything in the Constitution and laws of any State to the contrary, notwithstanding."

And whereas, no distinction between citizens is made in the Constitution of the United States on account of sex; but the XV. Article of Amendments to it provides that "No State shall make or enforce any law which shall abridge the privileges and immunities of citizens of the United States, nor deny to any person within its jurisdiction the equal protection of the laws."

And whereas, Congress has power to make laws which shall be necessary and proper for carrying into execution all powers vested by the Constitution in the Government of the United States; and to make or alter all regulations in relation to holding elections for senators or representatives, and especially to enforce, by appropiate legislation, the provisions of the said XIV. Article:

And whereas, the continuance of the enforcement of said local election laws, denying and abridging the right of citizens to vote on account of sex, is a grievance to your memorialist and to various other persons, citizens of the United States,

Therefore, your memorialist would most respectfully petition your honorable bodies to make such laws as in the wisdom of Congress shall be necessary and proper for carrying into execution the right vested by the Constitution in the citizens of the United States to vote, without regard to sex.

And your memorialist will ever pray.   VICTORIA C. WOODHULL.
New York City, Dec. 19, 1870.

ADDRESS OF VICTORIA C. WOODHULL JANUARY 11, 1871.

To the Honorable the Judiciary Committee of the House of Representatives of the Congress of the United States:

Having most respectfully memorialized Congress for the passage of such laws as in its wisdom shall seem necessary and proper to carry into effect the rights vested by the Constitution of the United States in the citizens to vote, without regard to sex, I beg leave to submit to your honorable body the following in favor of my prayer in said memorial which has been referred to your Committee.

The public law of the world is founded upon the conceded fact that sovereignty can not be forfeited or renounced. The sovereign power of this country is perpetually in the politically organized people of the United States, and can neither be relinquished nor abandoned by any portion of them. The people in this republic who confer sovereignty are its citizens: in a monarchy the people are the subjects of sovereignty. All citizens of a republic by rightful act or implication confer sovereign power. All people of a monarchy are subjects who exist under its supreme shield and enjoy its immunities. The subject of a monarch takes municipal immunities from the sovereign as a gracious favor; but the woman citizen of this country has the inalienable "sovereign" right of self-government in her own proper person. Those who look upon woman's status by the dim light of the common law, which unfolded itself under the feudal and military institutions that establish right upon physical power, can not find any analogy in the status of the woman citizen of this country, where the broad sunshine of our Constitution has enfranchised all.

As sovereignty can not be forfeited, relinquished, or abandoned, those from whom it flows—the citizens—are equal in conferring the power, and should be equal in the enjoyment of its benefits and in the exercise of its rights and privileges. One portion of citizens have no power to deprive another portion of rights and privileges such as are possessed and exercised by themselves. The male citizen has no more right to deprive the female citizen of the free, public, political, expression of opinion than the female citizen has to deprive the male citizen thereof.

The sovereign will of the people is expressed in our written Constitution, which is the supreme law of the land. The Constitution makes no distinction of sex. The Constitution defines a woman born or naturalized in the United States, and subject to the jurisdiction thereof, to be a citizen. It recognizes the right of citizens to vote. It declares that the right of citizens of the United States to vote shall not be denied or abridged by the United States or by any State on account of "race, color, or previous condition of servitude."

Women, white and black, belong to races, although to different races. A race of people comprises all the people, male and female. The right to vote can not be denied on account of race. All people included in the term race have the right to vote, unless otherwise prohibited. Women of all races are white, black, or some intermediate color. Color comprises all people, of all races and both sexes. The right to vote can not be denied on account of color. All people included in the term color have the right to vote unless otherwise prohibited.

With the right to vote sex has nothing to do. Race and color include all people of both sexes. All people of both sexes have the right to vote, unless prohibited by special limiting terms less comprehensive than race or color. No such limiting terms exist in the Constitution. Women, white and black, have from time immemorial groaned under what is properly termed in the Constitution "previous condition of servitude." Women are the equals of men before the law, and are equal in all their rights as citizens. Women are debarred from voting in some parts of the United States, although they are allowed to exercise that right elsewhere. Women were formerly permitted to vote in places where they are now debarred therefrom. The naturalization laws of the United States expressly provide for the naturalization of

women. But the right to vote has only lately been definitely declared by
the Constitution to be inalienable, under three distinct conditions—in all of
which woman is clearly embraced.

The citizen who is taxed should also have a voice in the subject matter of
taxation. "No taxation without representation" is a right which was fundamentally established at the very birth of our country's independence; and by
what ethics does any free government impose taxes on women without giving
them a voice upon the subject or a participation in the public declaration as
to how and by whom these taxes shall be applied for common public use?
Women are free to own and to control property, separate and free from
males, and they are held responsible in their own proper persons, in every
particular, as well as men, in and out of court. Women have the same inalienable right to life, liberty, and the pursuit of happiness that men have.
Why have they not this right politically, as well as men?

Women constitute a majority of the people of this country—they hold vast
portions of the nation's wealth and pay a proportionate share of the taxes.
They are intrusted with the most vital responsibilities of society; they bear,
rear, and educate men; they train and mould their characters; they inspire
the noblest impulses in men; they often hold the accumulated fortunes of a
man's life for the safety of the family and as guardians of the infants, and yet
they are debarred from uttering any opinion by public vote, as to the management by public servants of these interests; they are the secret counsel-
ors, the best advisers, the most devoted aids in the most trying periods of
men's lives, and yet men shrink from trusting them in the common questions
of ordinary politics. Men trust women in the market, in the shop, on the
highway and railroad, and in all other public places and assemblies, but
when they propose to carry a slip of paper with a name upon it to the polls,
they fear them. Nevertheless, as citizens, women have the right to vote;
they are part and parcel of that great element in which the sovereign power
of the land had birth; and it is by usurpation only that men debar them
from this right. The American nation, in its march onward and upward,
can not publicly choke the intellectual and political activity of half its citizens by narrow statutes. The will of the entire people is the true basis of
republican government, and a free expression of that will by the public vote
of all citizens, without distinctions of race, color, occupation, or sex, is the
only means by which that will can be ascertained. As the world has advanced into civilization and culture; as mind has risen in its dominion over
matter; as the principle of justice and moral right has gained sway, and
merely physical organized power has yielded thereto; as the might of right
has supplanted the right of might, so have the rights of women become
more fully recognized, and that recognition is the result of the development
of the minds of men, which through the ages she has polished, and thereby
heightened the lustre of civilization.

It was reserved for our great country to recognize by constitutional enactment that political equality of all citizens which religion, affection, and common sense should have long since accorded; it was reserved for America to
sweep away the mist of prejudice and ignorance, and that chivalric conde-
scension of a darker age, for in the language of Holy Writ, "The night is far
spent, the day is at hand, let us therefore cast off the work of darkness and

let us put on the armor of light.   Let us walk honestly as in the day." It
may be argued against the proposition that there still remains upon the
statute books of some States the word "male" to an exclusion; but as the
Constitution, in its paramount character, can only be read by the light of the
established principle, *ita lex Scripta est*, and as the subject of sex is not
mentioned, and the Constitution is not limited either in terms or by necessary implication in the general rights of citizens to vote, this right can not
be limited on account of anything in the spirit of inferior or previous enact-
ments upon a subject which is not mentioned in the supreme law.   A different construction would destroy a vested right in a portion of the citizens,
and this no legislature has a right to do without compensation, and nothing
can compensate a citizen for the loss of his or her suffrage—its value is equal
to the value of life.   Neither can it be presumed that women are to be kept from
the polls as a mere police regulation: it is to be hoped, at least, that police
regulations in their case need not be very active.   The effect of the amendments to the Constitution must be to annul the power over this subject in
the States, whether past, present, or future, which is contrary to the amendments.   The amendments would even arrest the action of the Supreme
Court in cases pending before it prior to their adoption, and operate as an
absolute prohibition to the exercise of any other jurisdiction than merely
to dismiss the suit.   3 Dall., 382: 6 Wheaton, 405; 9 ib., 868; 3d Circ. Pa.,
1832.

And if the restrictions contained in the Constitution as to color, race or
servitude, were designed to limit the State governments in reference to their
own citizens, and were intended to operate also as restrictions on the federal
power, and to prevent interference with the rights of the State and its citizens, how, then, can the State restrict citizens of the United States in the
exercise of rights not mentioned in any restrictive clause in reference to
actions on the part of those citizens having reference solely to the necessary
functions of the General Government, such as the election of representatives
and senators to Congress, whose election the Constitution expressly gives
Congress the power to regulate?   S. C., 1847: Fox vs. Ohio, 5 Howard, 410.

Your memorialist complains of the existence of State laws, and prays
Congress, by appropriate legislation, to declare them, as they are, annulled,
and to give vitality to the Constitution under its power to make and alter the
regulations of the States contravening the same.

It may be urged in opposition that the courts have power, and should declare upon this subject.   The Supreme Court has the power, and it would be
its duty so to declare the law: but the court will not do so unless a determination of such point as shall arise make it necessary to the determination of
a controversy, and hence a case must be presented in which there can be no
rational doubt.   All this would subject the aggrieved parties to much dila-
tory, expensive and needless litigation, which your memorialist prays your
honorable body to dispense with by appropriate legislation, as there can be
no purpose in special arguments "*ad inconvenienti*," enlarging or contracting the import of the language of the Constitution.

Therefore, Believing firmly in the right of citizens to freely approach those
in whose hands their destiny is placed under the Providence of God, your
memorialist has frankly, but humbly, appealed to you, and prays that the
wisdom of Congress may be moved to action in this matter for the benefit
and the increased happiness of our beloved country.

DOCUMENT 33 (II: 715–17, 732–34): Virginia L.
Minor's Petition, Circuit Court of St. Louis County,
Missouri, December 1872

St. Louis County, ss.: Virginia L. Minor and Francis Minor, her husband,
Plaintiffs, *vs.* Reese Happersett, Defendant.

The plaintiff, Virginia L. Minor (with whom is joined her husband, Francis
Minor, as required by the law of Missouri), states, that under the Constitution and law of Missouri, all persons wishing to vote at any election, must
previously have been registered in the manner pointed out by law, this being
a condition precedent to the exercise of the elective franchise.

That on the fifteenth day of October, 1872 (one of the days fixed by law for
the registration of voters), and long prior thereto, she was a native-born, free
white citizen of the United States, and of the State of Missouri, and on the
day last mentioned she was over the age of twenty-one years.

That on said day, the plaintiff was a resident of the thirteenth election district of the city and county of St. Louis, in the State of Missouri, and had

been so residing in said county and election district, for the entire period of twelve months and more, immediately preceding said fifteenth day of October, 1872, and for more than twenty years had been and is a tax-paying, law-abiding citizen of the county and State aforesaid.

That on said last mentioned day, the defendant, having been duly and legally appointed Registrar for said election district, and having accepted the said office of Registrar and entered upon the discharge of the duties thereof at the office of registration, to wit: No. 2004 Market Street, in said city and county of St. Louis, it became and was then and there his duty to register all citizens, resident in said district as aforesaid, entitled to the elective franchise, who might apply to him for that purpose.

The plaintiff further states, that wishing to exercise her privilege as a citizen of the United States, and vote for Electors for President and Vice-President of the United States, and for a Representative in Congress, and for other officers, at the General Election held in November, 1872: While said defendant was so acting as Registrar, on said 15th day of October, 1872, she appeared before him, at his office aforesaid, and then and there offered to take and subscribe the oath to support the Constitution of the United States and of the State of Missouri, as required by the registration law of said State, approved March 10, 1871, and respectfully applied to him to be registered as a lawful voter, which said defendant then and there refused to do.

The plaintiff further states, that the defendant, well knowing that she, as a citizen of the United States and of the State of Missouri, resident as aforesaid, was then and there entitled to all the privileges and immunities of citizenship, chief among which is the elective franchise, and as such, was entitled to be registered, in order to exercise said privilege: yet, unlawfully intending, contriving, and designing to deprive the plaintiff of said franchise or privilege, then and there knowingly, willfully, maliciously, and corruptly refused to place her name upon the list of registered voters, whereby she was deprived of her right to vote.

Defendant stated to plaintiff, that she was not entitled to be registered, or to vote, because she was not a "male" citizen, but a woman! That by the Constitution of Missouri, Art. II., Sec. 18, and by the aforesaid registration law of said State, approved March 10, 1871, it is provided and declared, that only "male citizens" of the United States, etc., are entitled or permitted to vote.

But the plaintiff protests against such decision, and she declares and maintains that said provisions of the Constitution and registration law of Missouri aforesaid, are in conflict with, and repugnant to the Constitution of the United States, which is paramount to State authority; and that they are especially in conflict with the following articles and clauses of said Constitution of the United States, to wit:

ART. I. Sec. 9.—Which declares that no Bill of Attainder shall be passed.

ART. I. Sec. 10.—No State shall pass any Bill of Attainder, or grant any title of nobility.

ART. IV. Sec. 2.—The citizens of each State shall be entitled to all privileges and immunities of citizens in the several States.

ART. IV. Sec. 4.—The United States shall guarantee to every State a republican form of government.

ART. VI.—This Constitution and the laws of the United States which shall be made in pursuance thereof, shall be the supreme law of the land, anything in the Constitutions or laws of any State to the contrary notwithstanding.

AMENDMENTS.

ART. V.—No person shall be . . . . deprived of life, liberty, or property without due process of law.

ART. IX.—The enumeration in the Constitution of certain rights, shall not be construed to deny or disparage others retained by the people.

ART. XIV. Sec. 1.—All persons born or naturalized in the United States, and subject to the jurisdiction thereof, are citizens of the United States and of the State wherein they reside. No State shall make or enforce any law which shall abridge the privileges or im- munities of citizens of the United States. Nor shall any State deprive any person of life, liberty, or property, without due process of law ; nor deny to any person within its juris- diction, the equal protection of the laws.

The plaintiff states, that by reason of the wrongful act of the defendant as aforesaid, she has been damaged in the sum of ten thousand dollars, for which she prays judgment.

JOHN M. KRUM,
FRANCIS MINOR,   } *Att'ys for Plffs.*
JOHN B. HENDERSON,

Demurrer. In the Circuit Court of St. Louis County: Virginia L. Minor and Francis Minor, her husband, Plaintiffs, *vs.* Reese Happersett.

The defendant, Reese Happersett, demurs to the petition of plaintiffs, and for cause of demurrer defendant states that said petition does not state facts sufficient to constitute a cause of action, for the following reasons :

1. Because said Virginia L. Minor, plaintiff, had no right to vote at the general election held in November, 1872, in said petition referred to.

2. Because said Virginia L. Minor had no right to be registered for voting by said de- fendant, at the time and in the manner in said petition alleged.

3. Because it was the duty of the defendant to refuse to place said Virginia L. Minor's name upon the list of registered voters in said petition referred to.

All of which appears by said petition.   SMITH P. GALT, *Atty for Deft.*

* * *

The first amendment to the Constitution declares that Congress shall make no law abridging freedom of speech or of the press, thus incorporating into the organic law of this country absolute freedom of thought or opinion. We presume it will not be doubted that the States are equally bound with Congress by this prohibition, not only because, as Chief-Justice Taney says, " the Constitution of the United States, and every article and clause in it, is a part of the law of every State in the Union, and is the paramount law " (Prigg *vs.* The Comm., 16 Peters R., 628), but because, in the very nature of things, freedom of speech or of thought can not be divided. It is a personal attribute, and once secured is forever secured. To vote is but one form or method of expressing this freedom of speech. Speech is a declaration of thought. A vote is the expression of the will, preference, or choice. Suf- frage is one definition of the word, while the verb is defined, to choose by suffrage, to elect, to express or signify the mind, will, or preference, either *viva voce,* or by ballot. We claim then that the right to vote, or express one's wish at the polls, is embraced in the spirit, if not the letter, of the First Amendment, and every citizen is entitled to the protection it affords. It is the merest mockery to say to this plaintiff, you may write, print, publish, or, speak your thoughts upon every occasion, except at the polls. There your lips shall be sealed. It is impossible that this can be American law!

Again, it is the opinion of some that suffrage is somehow lodged in the government, whence it is dispensed, or conferred upon the citizen, thus completely reversing the actual fact. Suffrage is never conferred by government upon the citizen. He holds it by a higher title. In this country government is the source of power, not of rights. These are vested in the individual—are personal and inalienable. Society can only acquire the authority to regulate these rights, or declare them forfeited, for cause. The time, place, and manner of their exercise are under governmental control, but their origin and source are in the individual himself.

I shall, therefore, says a writer on government, assume it as an incontrovertible position, as a first principle, that the right of private opinion, which is, in fact, no other than the right of private judgment upon any subject presented to the mind, is a sacred right, with which society can, on no pretense, authoritatively interfere, without a violation of the first principles of the law of nature. (Chipman on Government, chap. 5.)

Other liberties, says Erskine, are held under governments, but the liberty of opinion keeps governments themselves in due subjection to their duties. (Speech in defense of Thomas Paine.)

But this clause of the Missouri law further violates the XIII. Amendment, which declares that neither slavery nor involuntary servitude shall exist in the United States, except for crime, etc. This Amendment is a copy of the 6th clause of the famous Ordinance of 1787, which secured freedom for the Northwest Territory, and has now become the organic law for the entire Union. This Ordinance was drawn by the Hon. Nathan Dane, of Massachusetts.*

We say that this Missouri law violates this amendment, inasmuch as it places the plaintiff in a disfranchised condition, which is none other than a condition of servitude—of "involuntary servitude," because, although a citizen in the fullest acceptation of the term—a member of this body politic —one of the " people "—she has never consented to this law ; has never been permitted to express either consent or dissent, nor given any opportunity to express her opinion thereon, in the manner pointed out by law, while at the same time she is taxed, and her property taken to pay the very men who sat in judgment upon and condemned her !

Finally—Such is the nature of this privilege—so individual—so purely personal is its character, that its indefinite extension detracts not in the slightest degree from those who already enjoy it, and by an affirmation of the plaintiff's claim all womanhood would be elevated into that condition of self-respect that perfect freedom alone can give.

RESUME—(Minor vs. Happersett, 21 Wallace Rep., p. 164.)

1st. As a citizen of the United States, the plaintiff is entitled to any and all the "privileges and immunities" that belong to such position however defined ; and as are held, exercised, and enjoyed by other citizens of the United States.

2d. The elective franchise is a "privilege" of citizenship, in the highest sense of the word. It is the privilege preservative of all rights and privi-

---

* More recent investigation shows that this clause was originated by Mr. Jefferson in 1784. See *The Nation* for May 4, 1882, *and authorities there referred to.* See "Bancroft's " History of the United States." Vol. II., p. 115.

eges; and especially of the right of the citizen to participate in his or her government.

3d. The denial or abridgment of this privilege, if it exist at all, must be sought only in the fundamental charter of government—the Constitution of the United States. If not found there, no inferior power or jurisdiction can legally claim the right to exercise it.

4th. But the Constitution of the United States, so far from recognizing or permitting any denial or abridgment of the privileges of its citizens, expressly declares that " no State shall make or enforce any law which shall abridge the privileges or immunities of citizens of the United States."

5th. It follows that the provisions of the Missouri Constitution and registry law before recited, are in conflict with and must yield to the paramount authority of the Constitution of the United States.

A few words more and we have done. The plaintiff has sought, by this action, for the establishment of a great principle of fundamental right, applicable not only to herself, but to the class to which she belongs; for the principles here laid down (as in the Dred Scott case) extend far beyond the limits of the particular suit, and embrace the rights of millions of others, who are thus represented through her. She has a right, therefore, to be heard for her cause; and in making this plea, she seeks only to give expression to those principles upon which, as upon a rock, our Government is founded.

It is impossible that that can be a Republican government in which one half the citizens thereof are forever disfranchised. A citizen disfranchised is a citizen attainted; and this, too, in face of the fact, that you look in vain in the great charter of government, the Constitution of the United States, for any warrant or authority for such discrimination. To that instrument she appeals for protection.

DOCUMENT 34 (II: 648–49, 687–89): The United States of America *vs.* Susan B. Anthony, Circuit Court, Northern District of New York, June 17-18, 1873

UNITED STATES CIRCUIT COURT. (NORTHERN DISTRICT OF NEW YORK.)

The United States of America *vs.* Susan B. Anthony; Hon. Ward Hunt, Presiding. Appearances: For the United States: Hon: Richard Crowley, U. S. District Attorney; For the Defendant: Hon. Henry R. Selden, John Van Voorhis, Esq.

Tried at Canandaigua, Tuesday and Wednesday, June 17th and 18th, 1873, before Hon. Ward Hunt, and a jury. Jury impaneled at 2:30 P.M.

Mr. Crowley opened the case as follows :

May it please the Court and Gentlemen of the Jury:

On the 5th of November, 1872, there was held in this State, as well as in other States of the Union, a general election for different officers, and among those, for candidates to represent several districts of this State in the Congress of the United States. The defendant, Miss Susan B. Anthony, at that time resided in the city of Rochester, in the county of Monroe, Northern District of New York, and upon the 5th day of November, 1872, she voted for a representative in the Congress of the United States, to represent the 29th Congressional District of this State, and also for a representative at large for the State of New York, to represent the State in the Congress of the United States. At that time she was a woman. I suppose there will be no question about that. The question in this case, if there be a question of fact about it at all, will, in my judgment, be rather a question of law than one of fact. I suppose that there will be no question of fact, substantially, in the case when all of the evidence is out, and it will be for you to decide under the charge for his honor, the Judge, whether or not the defendant committed the offense of voting for a representative in Congress upon that occasion. We think, on the part of the Government, that there is no question about it either one way or the other, neither a question of fact, nor a question of law, and that whatever Miss Anthony's intentions may have been — whether they were good or otherwise—she did not have a right to vote upon that question, and if she did vote without having a lawful right to vote, then there is no question but what she is guilty of violating a law of the United States in that be-half enacted by the Congress of the United States.

We don't claim in this case, gentlemen, that Miss Anthony is of that class of people who go about "repeating." We don't claim that she went from place to place for the purpose of offering her vote. But we do claim that upon the 5th of November, 1872, she voted, and whether she believed that she had a right to vote or not, it being a question of law, that she is within the statute. Congress in 1870 passed the following statute: (Reads 19th Section of the Act of 1870, page 144, 16th statutes at large.) It is not necessary for me, gentlemen, at this stage of the case, to state all the facts which will be proven on the part of the Government. I shall leave that to be shown by the evidence and by the witnesses, and if any question of law shall arise his Honor will undoubtedly give you instructions as he shall deem proper. Conceded, that on the 5th day of November, 1872, Miss Susan B. Anthony was a woman.

* * *

The Court, after listening to an argument from the District Attorney, denied the motion for a new trial.

The COURT: The prisoner will stand up. Has the prisoner anything to say why sentence shall not be pronounced?

Miss ANTHONY: Yes, your honor, I have many things to say; for in your ordered verdict of guilty, you have trampled underfoot every vital principle of our government. My natural rights, my civil rights, my political rights, are all alike ignored. Robbed of the fundamental privilege of citizenship, I am degraded from the status of a citizen to that of a subject; and not only myself individually, but all of my sex, are, by your honor's verdict, doomed to political subjection under this so-called Republican government.

Judge HUNT: The Court can not listen to a rehearsal of arguments the prisoner's counsel has already consumed three hours in presenting.

Miss ANTHONY: May it please your honor, I am not arguing the question, but simply stating the reasons why sentence can not, in justice, be pronounced against me. Your denial of my citizen's right to vote is the denial of my right of consent as one of the governed, the denial of my right of representation as one of the taxed, the denial of my right to a trial by a jury of my peers as an offender against law, therefore, the denial of my sacred rights to life, liberty, property, and—

Judge HUNT: The Court can not allow the prisoner to go on.

Miss ANTHONY: But your honor will not deny me this one and only poor privilege of protest against this high-handed outrage upon my citizen's rights.   May it please the Court to remember that since the day of my arrest last November, this is the first time that either myself or any person of my disfranchised class has been allowed a word of defense before judge or jury—

Judge HUNT : The prisoner must sit down ; the Court can not allow it.

Miss ANTHONY : All my prosecutors, from the 8th Ward corner grocery politician, who entered the complaint, to the United States Marshal, Commissioner, District Attorney, District Judge, your honor on the bench, not one is my peer, but each and all are my political sovereigns ; and had your honor submitted my case to the jury, as was clearly your duty, even then I should have had just cause of protest, for not one of those men was my peer ; but, native or foreign, white or black, rich or poor, educated or ignorant, awake or asleep, sober or drunk, each and every man of them was my political superior ; hence, in no sense, my peer.   Even, under such circumstances, a commoner of England, tried before a jury of lords, would have far less cause to complain than should I, a woman, tried before a jury of men.   Even my counsel, the Hon. Henry R. Selden, who has argued my cause so ably, so earnestly, so unanswerably before your honor, is my political sovereign.   Precisely as no disfranchised person is entitled to sit upon a jury, and no woman is entitled to the franchise, so, none but a regularly admitted lawyer is allowed to practice in the courts, and no woman can gain admission to the bar—hence, jury, judge, counsel, must all be of the superior class.

Judge HUNT : The Court must insist—the prisoner has been tried according to the established forms of law.

Miss ANTHONY : Yes, your honor, but by forms of law all made by men, interpreted by men, administered by men, in favor of men, and against women ; and hence, your honor's ordered verdict of guilty, against a United States citizen for the exercise of "that citizen's right to vote," simply because that citizen was a woman and not a man.   But, yesterday, the same manmade forms of law declared it a crime punishable with $1,000 fine and six months' imprisonment, for you, or me, or any of us, to give a cup of cold water, a crust of bread, or a night's shelter to a panting fugitive as he was tracking his way to Canada.   And every man or woman in whose veins coursed a drop of human sympathy violated that wicked law, reckless of consequences, and was justified in so doing.   As then the slaves who got their freedom must take it over, or under, or through the unjust forms of law, precisely so now must women, to get their right to a voice in this Government, take it ; and I have taken mine, and mean to take it at every possible opportunity.

Judge HUNT : The Court orders the prisoner to sit down.   It will not allow another word.

Miss ANTHONY : When I was brought before your honor for trial, I hoped for a broad and liberal interpretation of the Constitution and its recent amendments, that should declare all United States citizens under its protecting ægis—that should declare equality of rights the national guarantee to all persons born or naturalized in the United States.   But failing to get this justice—failing, even, to get a trial by a jury *not* of my peers—I ask not leniency at your hands—but rather the full rigors of the law.

Judge HUNT : The Court must insist—   (Here the prisoner sat down.)

Judge HUNT: The prisoner will stand up. (Here Miss Anthony arose again.) The sentence of the Court is that you pay a fine of one hundred dollars and the costs of the prosecution.

Miss ANTHONY: May it please your honor, I shall never pay a dollar of your unjust penalty. All the stock in trade I possess is a $10,000 debt, incurred by publishing my paper—*The Revolution*—four years ago, the sole object of which was to educate all women to do precisely as I have done, rebel against your man-made, unjust, unconstitutional forms of law, that tax, fine, imprison, and hang women, while they deny them the right of representation in the Government; and I shall work on with might and main to pay every dollar of that honest debt, but not a penny shall go to this unjust claim. And I shall earnestly and persistently continue to urge all women to the practical recognition of the old revolutionary maxim, that "Resistance to tyranny is obedience to God."

Judge HUNT: Madam, the Court will not order you committed until the fine is paid.

DOCUMENT 35 (III: 28–34): United States Centennial Celebration and the Declaration of Rights, Philadelphia, Pennsylvania, July 4, 1876

Mrs. Stanton, as president of the association, wrote General Hawley, asking the opportunity to present the woman's protest and bill of rights at the close of the reading of the Declaration of Independence. Just its simple presentation and nothing more. She wrote:

We do not ask to read our declaration, only to present it to the president of the United States, that it may become an historical part of the proceedings.

Mrs. Spencer, bearer of this letter, in presenting it to General Hawley, said:

The women of the United States make a slight request on the occasion of the centennial celebration of the birth of the nation; we only ask that we may silently present our declaration of rights.

General HAWLEY replied: It seems a very slight request, but our programme is published, our speakers engaged, our arrangements for the day decided upon, and we can not make even so slight a change as that you ask.

Mrs. SPENCER replied: We are aware that your programme is published, your speakers engaged, your entire arrangements decided upon, without consulting with the women of the United States; for that very reason we desire to enter our protest. We are aware that this government has been conducted for one hundred years without consulting the women of the United States; for this reason we desire to enter our protest.

General HAWLEY replied: Undoubtedly we have not lived up to our own original Declaration of Independence in many respects. I express no opinion upon your question. It is a proper subject of discussion at the Cincinnati convention, at the St. Louis convention, in the Senate of the United States, in the State legislatures, in the courts, wherever you can obtain a hearing. But to-morrow we propose to celebrate what we have done the last hundred years; not what we have failed to do. We have much to do in the future. I understand the full significance of your very slight request. If granted, it would be the event of the day—the topic of discussion to the exclusion of all others. I am sorry to refuse so slight a demand; we cannot grant it.

General Hawley also addressed a letter to Mrs. Stanton:

DEAR MADAM: I regret to say it is impossible for us to make any change in our programme, or make any addition to it at this late hour.

Yours very respectfully,

JOS. R. HAWLEY, *President U. S. C. C.*

As General Grant was not to attend the celebration, the acting vice-president, Thomas W. Ferry, representing the government, was to officiate in his place, and he, too, was addressed by note, and courteously requested to make time for the reception of this declaration. As Mr. Ferry was a well-known sympathizer with the demands of woman for political rights, it was presumable that he would render his aid. Yet he was forgetful that in his position that day he represented, not the exposition, but the government of a hundred years, and he too refused; thus this simple request of woman for a half moment's recognition on the nation's centennial birthday was denied by all in authority.*

While the women of the nation were thus absolutely forbidden the right of public protest, lavish preparations were made for the reception and entertainment of foreign potentates and the myrmidons of monarchial institutions. Dom Pedro, emperor of Brazil, a representative of that form of government against which the United States is a perpetual defiance and protest, was welcomed with fulsome adulation, and given a seat of honor near the officers of the day; Prince Oscar of Sweden, a stripling of sixteen, on whose shoulder rests the promise of a future kingship, was seated near. Count Rochambeau of France, the Japanese commissioners, high officials from Russia and Prussia, from Austria, Spain, England, Turkey, representing the barbarism and semi-civilization of the day, found no difficulty in securing recognition and places of honor upon that platform, where representative womanhood was denied.

Though refused by their own countrymen a place and part in the centennial celebration, the women who had taken this presentation in hand were not to be conquered. They had respectfully asked for recognition; now that it had been denied, they determined to seize upon the moment when the reading of the Declaration of Independence closed, to proclaim to the world the tyranny and injustice of the nation toward one-half its people. Five officers of the National Woman Suffrage Association, with that heroic spirit which has ever animated lovers of liberty in resistance to tyranny, determined, whatever the result, to present the woman's declaration of rights at the chosen hour. They would not, they dared not sacrifice the golden opportunity

---

* On the receipt of these letters a prolonged council was held by the officers of the association at their headquarters, as to what action they should take on the Fourth of July. Mrs. Mott and Mrs. Stanton decided for themselves that after these rebuffs they would not even sit on the platform, but at the appointed time go to the church they had engaged for a meeting, and open their convention. Others more brave and determined insisted that women had an equal right to the glory of the day and the freedom of the platform, and decided to take the risk of a public insult in order to present the woman's declaration and thus make it an historic document.—[E. C. S.

to which they had so long looked forward; their work was not for themselves alone, nor for the present generation, but for all women of all time. The hopes of posterity were in their hands and they determined to place on record for the daughters of 1976, the fact that their mothers of 1876 had asserted their equality of rights, and impeached the government of that day for its injustice toward woman. Thus, in taking a grander step toward freedom than ever before, they would leave one bright remembrance for the women of the next centennial.

That historic Fourth of July dawned at last, one of the most oppressive days of that terribly heated season. Susan B. Anthony, Matilda Joslyn Gage, Sara Andrews Spencer, Lillie Devereux Blake and Phoebe W. Couzins made their way through the crowds under the broiling sun to Independence Square, carrying the Woman's Declaration of Rights. This declaration had been handsomely engrossed by one of their number, and signed by the oldest and most prominent advocates of woman's enfranchisement. Their tickets of admission proved open sesame through the military and all other barriers, and a few moments before the opening of the ceremonies, these women found themselves within the precincts from which most of their sex were excluded.

The declaration of 1776 was read by Richard Henry Lee, of Virginia, about whose family clusters so much of historic fame. The close of his reading was deemed the appropriate moment for the presentation of the woman's declaration. Not quite sure how their approach might be met—not quite certain if at this final moment they would be permitted to reach the presiding officer—those ladies arose and made their way down the aisle. The bustle of preparation for the Brazilian hymn covered their advance. The foreign guests, the military and civil officers who filled the space directly in front of the speaker's stand, courteously made way, while Miss Anthony in fitting words presented the declaration. Mr. Ferry's face paled, as bowing low, with no word, he received the declaration, which thus became part of the day's proceedings; the ladies turned, scattering printed copies, as they deliberately walked down the platform. On every side eager hands were stretched; men stood on seats and asked for them, while General Hawley, thus defied and beaten in his audacious denial to women the right to present their declaration, shouted, "Order, order!"

Passing out, these ladies made their way to a platform erected for the musicians in front of Independence Hall. Here on this old historic ground, under the shadow of Washington's statue, back of them the old bell that proclaimed " liberty to all the land, and all the inhabitants thereof," they took their places, and to a listening, applauding crowd, Miss Anthony read* the Declaration of Rights for Women by the National Woman Suffrage Association, July 4, 1876:

While the nation is buoyant with patriotism, and all hearts are attuned to praise, it is with sorrow we come to strike the one discordant note, on this one-hundredth anniversary of our country's birth. When subjects of kings, emperors, and czars, from the old world join in our national jubilee, shall the women of the republic refuse to lay their hands with benedictions on the nation's head? Surveying America's exposition, surpassing in magnificence those of London, Paris, and Vienna, shall we not rejoice at the success of the youngest rival among the nations of the earth? May not our hearts, in unison with all, swell with pride at our great achievements as a people; our free speech, free press, free schools, free church, and the rapid progress we have made in material wealth, trade, commerce and the inventive arts? And we do rejoice in the success, thus far, of our experiment of self-government. Our faith is firm and unwavering in the broad principles of human rights proclaimed in 1776, not only as abstract truths, but as the corner stones of a republic. Yet we cannot forget, even in this glad hour, that while all men of every race, and clime, and condition, have been invested with the full rights of citizenship under our hospitable flag, all women still suffer the degradation of disfranchisement.

The history of our country the past hundred years has been a series of assumptions and usurpations of power over woman, in direct opposition to the principles of just government, acknowledged by the United States as its foundation, which are :

First—The natural rights of each individual.

Second—The equality of these rights.

Third—That rights not delegated are retained by the individual.

Fourth—That no person can exercise the rights of others without delegated authority.

Fifth—That the non-use of rights does not destroy them.

And for the violation of these fundamental principles of our government, we arraign our rulers on this Fourth day of July, 1876,—and these are our articles of impeachment :

Bills of attainder have been passed by the introduction of the word " male " into all the State constitutions, denying to women the right of suffrage, and thereby mak-

---

* During the reading of the declaration to an immense concourse of people, Mrs. Gage stood beside Miss Anthony, and held an umbrella over her head, to shelter her friend from the intense heat of the noonday sun ; and thus in the same hour, on opposite sides of old Independence Hall, did the men and women express their opinions on the great principles proclaimed on the natal day of the republic. The declaration was handsomely framed and now hangs in the vice-president's room in the capitol at Washington.

ing sex a crime—an exercise of power clearly forbidden in article 1, sections 9, 10, of the United States constitution.

The writ of habeas corpus, the only protection against *lettres de cachet* and all forms of unjust imprisonment, which the constitution declares " shall not be suspended, except when in cases of rebellion or invasion the public safety demands it," is held inoperative in every State of the Union, in case of a married woman against her husband—the marital rights of the husband being in all cases primary, and the rights of the wife secondary.

The right of trial by a jury of one's peers was so jealously guarded that States refused to ratify the original constitution until it was guaranteed by the sixth amendment. And yet the women of this nation have never been allowed a jury of their peers—being tried in all cases by men, native and foreign, educated and ignorant, virtuous and vicious. Young girls have been arraigned in our courts for the crime of infanticide; tried, convicted, hanged—victims, perchance, of judge, jurors, advocates—while no woman's voice could be heard in their defense. And not only are women denied a jury of their peers, but in some cases, jury trial altogether. During the war, a woman was tried and hanged by military law, in defiance of the fifth amendment, which specifically declares: "No person shall be held to answer for a capital or otherwise infamous crime, unless on a presentment or indictment of a grand jury, except in cases . . . . of persons in actual service in time of war." During the last presidential campaign, a woman, arrested for voting, was denied the protection of a jury, tried, convicted, and sentenced to a fine and costs of prosecution, by the absolute power of a judge of the Supreme Court of the United States.

Taxation without representation, the immediate cause of the rebellion of the colonies against Great Britain, is one of the grievous wrongs the women of this country have suffered during the century. Deploring war, with all the demoralization that follows in its train, we have been taxed to support standing armies, with their waste of life and wealth. Believing in temperance, we have been taxed to support the vice, crime and pauperism of the liquor traffic. While we suffer its wrongs and abuses infinitely more than man, we have no power to protect our sons against this giant evil. During the temperance crusade, mothers were arrested, fined, imprisoned, for even praying and singing in the streets, while men blockade the sidewalks with impunity, even on Sunday, with their military parades and political processions. Believing in honesty, we are taxed to support a dangerous army of civilians, buying and selling the offices of government and sacrificing the best interests of the people. And, moreover, we are taxed to support the very legislators and judges who make laws, and render decisions adverse to woman. And for refusing to pay such unjust taxation, the houses, lands, bonds, and stock of women have been seized and sold within the present year, thus proving Lord Coke's assertion, that " The very act of taxing a man's property without his consent is, in effect, disfranchising him of every civil right."

Unequal codes for men and women. Held by law a perpetual minor, deemed incapable of self-protection, even in the industries of the world, woman is denied equality of rights. The fact of sex, not the quantity or quality of work, in most cases, decides the pay and position ; and because of this injustice thousands of fatherless girls are compelled to choose between a life of shame and starvation. Laws catering to man's vices have created two codes of morals in which penalties are graded according to the political status of the offender. Under such laws, women are fined and imprisoned if found alone in the streets, or in public places of resort, at certain hours. Under the pretense of regulating public morals, police officers seizing the occupants of disreputable houses, march the women in platoons to prison, while the men, partners in their guilt, go free. While making a show of virtue in forbidding the importation of Chinese women on the Pacific coast for immoral purposes, our rulers, in many States, and even under the shadow of the national capitol, are now proposing to legalize the sale of American womanhood for the same vile purposes.

Special legislation for woman has placed us in a most anomalous position. Women invested with the rights of citizens in one section—voters, jurors, office-holders—crossing an imaginary line, are subjects in the next. In some States, a married woman may hold property and transact business in her own name ; in others, her earnings belong to her husband. In some States, a woman may testify against her husband, sue and be sued in the courts ; in others, she has no redress in case of damage to person, property, or character. In case of divorce on account of adultery in the husband, the innocent wife is held to possess no right to children or property, unless by special decree of the court. But in no State of the Union has the wife the right to her own person, or to any part of the joint earnings of the co-partnership during the life of her husband. In some States women may enter the law schools and practice in the courts ; in others they are forbidden. In some universities girls enjoy equal educational advantages with boys, while many of the proudest institutions in the land deny them admittance, though the sons of China, Japan and Africa are welcomed there. But the privileges already granted in the several States are by no means secure. The right of suffrage once exercised by women in certain States and territories has been denied by subsequent legislation. A bill is now pending in congress to disfranchise the women of Utah, thus interfering to deprive United States citizens of the same rights which the Supreme Court has declared the national government powerless to protect anywhere. Laws passed after years of untiring effort, guaranteeing married women certain rights of property, and mothers the custody of their children, have been repealed in States where we supposed all was safe. Thus have our most sacred rights been made the football of legislative caprice, proving that a power which grants as a privilege what by nature is a right, may withhold the same as a penalty when deeming it necessary for its own perpetuation.

Representation of woman has had no place in the nation's thought. Since the incorporation of the thirteen original States, twenty-four have been admitted to the Union, not one of which has recognized woman's right of self-government. On this birthday of our national liberties, July Fourth, 1876, Colorado, like all her elder sisters, comes into the Union with the invidious word "male" in her constitution.

Universal manhood suffrage, by establishing an aristocracy of sex, imposes upon the women of this nation a more absolute and cruel depotism than monarchy ; in that, woman finds a political master in her father, husband, brother, son. The aristocracies of the old world are based upon birth, wealth, refinement, education, nobility, brave deeds of chivalry ; in this nation, on sex alone ; exalting brute force above moral power, vice above virtue, ignorance above education, and the son above the mother who bore him.

The judiciary above the nation has proved itself but the echo of the party in power, by upholding and enforcing laws that are opposed to the spirit and letter of the constitution. When the slave power was dominant, the Supreme Court decided that a black man was not a citizen, because he had not the right to vote ; and when the constitution was so amended as to make all persons citizens, the same high tribunal decided that a woman, though a citizen, had not the right to vote. Such vacillating interpretations of constitutional law unsettle our faith in judicial authority, and undermine the liberties of the whole people.

These articles of impeachment against our rulers we now submit to the impartial judgment of the people. To all these wrongs and oppressions woman has not submitted in silence and resignation. From the beginning of the century, when Abigail Adams, the wife of one president and mother of another, said, " We will not hold ourselves bound to obey laws in which we have no voice or representation," until now, woman's discontent has been steadily increasing, culminating nearly thirty years ago in a simultaneous movement among the women of the nation, demanding the right of suffrage. In making our just demands, a higher motive than the pride of sex inspires us; we feel that national safety and stability depend on the complete recognition of the broad principles of our government. Woman's degraded, helpless position is the weak point in our institutions to-day; a disturbing force everywhere, severing family ties, filling our asylums with the deaf, the dumb, the blind; our prisons with criminals, our cities with drunkenness and prostitution; our homes with disease and death. It was the boast of the founders of the republic, that the rights for which they contended were the rights of human nature. If these rights are ignored in the case of one-half the people, the nation is surely preparing for its downfall. Governments try themselves. The recognition of a governing and a governed class is incompatible with the first principles of freedom. Woman has not been a heedless spectator of the events of this century, nor a dull listener to the grand arguments for the equal rights of humanity. From the earliest history of our country woman has shown equal devotion with man to the cause of freedom, and has stood firmly by his side in its defense. Together, they have made this country what it is. Woman's wealth, thought and labor have cemented the stones of every monument man has reared to liberty.

And now, at the close of a hundred years, as the hour-hand of the great clock that marks the centuries points to 1876, we declare our faith in the principles of self-government; our full equality with man in natural rights; that woman was made first for her own happiness, with the absolute right to herself—to all the opportunities and advantages life affords for her complete development; and we deny that dogma of the centuries, incorporated in the codes of all nations—that woman was made for man—her best interests, in all cases, to be sacrificed to his will. We ask of our rulers, at this hour, no special favors, no special privileges, no special legislation. We ask justice, we ask equality, we ask that all the civil and political rights that belong to citizens of the United States, be guaranteed to us and our daughters forever.

DOCUMENT 36 (III: 57–59): National Woman Suffrage
Association, Appeal and Petition for a Sixteenth
Amendment, November 10, 1876

WITH the close of the centennial year the new departure under
the fourteenth amendment ended.   Though defeated at the polls,
in the courts, in the national celebration, in securing a plank in
the platforms of the Republican and Democratic parties, and in
our own conventions—so far as the few were able to rouse the
many to simultaneous action—nevertheless a wide-spread agitation had been secured by the presentation of this phase of the
question.

Although the unanswerable arguments of statesmen and lawyers in the halls of congress and the Supreme Court of the United
States, had alike proved unavailing in establishing the civil and
political rights of women on a national basis, their efforts had not
been in vain.   The trials had brought the question before a new
order of minds, and secured able constitutional arguments which
were reviewed in many law journals.   The equally able congressional debates, reported verbatim, read by a large constituency
in every State of the Union, did an educational work on the

question of woman's enfranchisement that cannot be overestimated.

But when the final decision of the Supreme Court in the case of Virginia L. Minor made all agitation in that direction hopeless, the National Association returned to its former policy, demanding a sixteenth amendment. The women generally came to the conclusion that if in truth there was no protection for them in the original constitution nor the late amendments, the time had come for some clearly-defined recognition of their citizenship by a sixteenth amendment.

The following appeal and petition were extensively circulated :

To the Women of the United States:

Having celebrated our centennial birthday with a national jubilee, let us now dedicate the dawn of the second century to securing justice to women. For this purpose we ask you to circulate a petition to congress, just issued by the National Association, asking an amendment to the United States Constitution, that shall prohibit the several States from disfranchising citizens on account of sex. We have already sent this petition throughout the country for the signatures of those men and women who believe in the citizen's right to vote.

To see how large a petition each State rolls up, and to do the work as expeditiously as possible, it is necessary that some person in each county should take the matter in charge, urging upon all, thoroughness and haste. * * * The petitions should be returned before January 16, 17, 1877, when we shall hold our Eighth Annual Convention at the capital, and ask a hearing before congress.

Having petitioned our law-makers, State and national, for years, many from weariness have vowed to appeal no more; for our petitions, say they, by the tens of thousands, are piled up in the national archives, unheeded and ignored. Yet it is possible to roll up such a mammoth petition, borne into congress on the shoulders of stalwart men, that we can no longer be neglected or forgotten. Statesmen and politicians alike are conquered by majorities. We urge the women of this country to make now the same united effort for their own rights that they did for the slaves at the South when the thirteenth amendment was pending. Then a petition of over 300,000 was rolled up by the leaders of the suffrage movement, and presented in the Senate by the Hon. Charles Sumner. But the statesmen who welcomed woman's untiring efforts to secure the black man's freedom, frowned down the same demands when made for herself. Is not liberty as sweet to her as to him ? Are not the political disabilities of sex as grievous as those of color? Is not a civil-rights bill that shall open to woman the college doors, the trades and professions—that shall secure her personal and property rights, as necessary for her protection as for that of the colored man ? And yet the highest judicial authorities have decided that the spirit and letter of our national constitution are not broad enough to protect woman in her political rights; and for the redress of her wrongs they remand her to the State. If our *Magna Charta* of human rights can be thus narrowed by judicial interpretations in favor of class legislation, then must we demand an amendment that, in clear, unmistakable language, shall declare the equality of all citizens before the law.

Women are citizens, first of the United States, and second of the State wherein they reside; hence, if robbed by State authorities of any right founded in nature or secured by law, they have the same right to national protection against the State, as against the infringements of any foreign power. If the United States government can punish a woman for voting in one State, why has it not the same power to protect her in the exercise of that right in every State? The constitution declares it the duty of congress to guarantee to every State a republican form of government, to every citizen, equality of rights. This is not done in States where women, thoroughly qualified, are denied admission into colleges which their property is taxed to build and endow; where they are denied the right to practice law and are thus debarred from one of the most lucrative professions; where they are denied a voice in the government, and thus, while suffering all the ills that grow out of the giant evils of intemperance, prostitution, war, heavy taxation and political corruption, stand powerless to effect any reform. Prayers, tears, psalm-singing and expostulation are light in the balance compared with that power at the ballot-box that coins opinions into law. If women who are laboring for peace, temperance, social purity and the rights of labor, would take the speediest way to accomplish what they propose, let them demand the ballot in their own hands, that they may have a direct power in the government. Thus only can they improve the conditions of the outside world and purify the home. As political equality is the door to civil, religious and social liberty, here must our work begin.

Constituting, as we do one-half the people, bearing the burdens of one-half the national debt, equally responsible with man for the education, religion and morals of the rising generation, let us with united voice send forth a protest against the present political status of woman, that shall echo and reëcho through the land. In view of the numbers and character of those making the demand, this should be the largest petition ever yet rolled up in the old world or the new; a petition that shall settle forever the popular objection that "women do not want to vote."

ELIZABETH CADY STANTON, *President.*

MATILDA JOSLYN GAGE, *Chairman Executive Committee.*

SUSAN B. ANTHONY, *Corresponding Secretary.*

Tenafly, N. J., November 10, 1876.

To the Senate and House of Representatives in Congress assembled :

The undersigned citizens of the United States, residents of the State of————, earnestly pray your honorable bodies to adopt measures for so amending the constitution as to prohibit the several States from disfranchising United States citizens on account of sex.

DOCUMENT 37 (III: 75): "Susan B. Anthony Amendment," U. S. Congress, January 10, 1878

On January 10, 1878, our champion in the Senate, Hon. A. A. Sargent, of California, by unanimous consent, presented the following joint resolution, which was read twice and referred to the Committee on Privileges and Elections:

JOINT RESOLUTION *proposing an Amendment to the Constitution of the United States.*—

Resolved by the Senate and House of Representatives of the United States of America in congress assembled, two-thirds of each House concurring therein, That the following article be proposed to the legislatures of the several States as an amendment to the Constitution of the United States, which, when ratified by three-fourths of the said legislatures, shall be valid as part of the said constitution, namely :

ARTICLE 16, SEC. 1.—The right of citizens of the United States to vote shall not be denied or abridged by the United States or by any State on account of sex.

SEC. 2.—Congress shall have power to enforce this article by appropriate legislation.

DOCUMENT 38 (III: 104): American Woman Suffrage
Association, Response to NWSA's Petition for a
Sixteenth Amendment, February 4, 1878

Hon. George F. Hoar of Massachusetts, February 4, presented
in the Senate the 120 petitions with their 6,261 signatures, which,
by special request of its officers, had been returned to the headquarters of the American Association, in Boston.   In her appeal
to the friends to circulate the petitions, both State and national,
Lucy Stone, chairman of its executive committee, said:

The American Suffrage Association has always recommended petitions
to congress for a sixteenth amendment.   But it recognizes the far greater
importance of petitioning the State legislatures.   *First*—Because suffrage
is a subject referred by the constitution to the voters of each State.
Second—Because we cannot expect a congress composed solely of representatives of States which deny suffrage to women, to submit an amendment which their own States have not yet approved.   Just so it would
have been impossible to secure the submission of negro suffrage by a
congress composed solely of representatives from States which restricted
suffrage to white men.   While therefore we advise our friends to circulate
both petitions together for signature, we urge them to give special prominence to those which apply to their own State legislatures, and to see that
these are presented and urged by competent speakers next winter.

PART THREE: 1885 TO 1920

I. Old and New Leadership

THE FORMATION OF THE National American Woman Suffrage Association in 1890 followed more than a decade of slow drift toward common attitudes and several years of careful negotiations. The enthusiasm for unity among younger leaders in both NWSA and AWSA signaled a new period of activity and a shifting political outlook for the suffrage movement. Two elements were clearest in the plans of the emerging leadership. First, the movement was to be divested of its radical image, its ideas more closely approximating mainstream or middle-class views on such issues as race, religion, and immigration. Second, energies redirected from ideological boldness would be put to better use in strategic and tactical measures to put NAWSA on a fighting basis, prepared to utilize every advantageous situation for a major breakthrough. The intensity of this effort allowed little speculation about the losses sustained in the passing of old personalities and ideas.

No one reflected the old mood better than Elizabeth Cady Stanton, who in her later years became increasingly determined to strike at even the most sacred institutional and ideological barriers to women's freedom. In "Solitude of Self," a justly famous document, Stanton described her vision of an emancipation far greater than political rights. Liberation from all the artificialities of law and custom would allow women to determine their own destiny in a transformed society. But to achieve these ultimate ends, women had to guard their spirit of independence. Stanton therefore pressed a free-thought campaign even while the suffrage movement and the Protestant clergy moved toward an amiable relationship at the end of the nineteenth century. Stanton gathered a "revising committee" to create Part I of a *Woman's Bible*. Published in 1895 and denounced as heretical by the conservative clergy, the volume sufficiently encouraged fears among suffrage leaders to invite a public dissociation of the movement from it.

Disappointments in the outcome of state referenda during the 1890s deepened the drift toward conservatism. Initially, the Populist insurgence had stirred the optimism of suffrage leaders, especially for the prospects of women's vote in the western states. But the results were far from satisfying. Only in Colorado did principled Populist officials sustain the women's expectations, and only through the support of Republicans and Prohibitionists. In South Dakota in 1890 and Kansas in 1894, woman suffrage supporters felt betrayed by the inconsistency and partisan wrangling among reformers nominally pledged to woman's cause. The "wet vote" of the cities and the "ignorant vote" of the foreign-born added to the rancor of suffragists as the California and Oregon campaigns were turned back.

The emerging suffrage leaders, particularly Carrie Chapman Catt, drew the harsh conclusion that friendly reform movements could not be relied upon to carry through the struggle and that the existing NAWSA leadership was incompetent to succeed on its own. Her strategic alternative hinged ominously on "states rights," that is, to allow local attitudes on race, immigration, and other questions to determine local policy. By the eighties and nineties, the old suffrage leadership had grown more pessimistic about the possibility of a thoroughgoing democracy, and their successors lacked even the experience of the struggle for Black emancipation. At the NAWSA convention in 1899, a Black woman from Michigan proposed a censure of discrimination on southern Pullman trains, and after a heated debate, Anthony concluded that suffragists were too "helpless" to make any public statement on such questions. Albeit with a certain hesitancy, Catt and other NAWSA leaders condoned avowed racism and encouraged it by holding conventions in southern cities and supporting known racists for national NAWSA offices. Unguarded references to "foreigners," whether Oriental, Scandinavian, Slavic, or other, were less pointed only because Anglophilia was less coherent, either intellectually or organizationally, than race hatred outside the suffrage movement.

In their own eyes, however, the new suffrage strategists

had acted outside ideology, essentially bringing the steady drift within the movement to its logical conclusion. When woman suffrage advocates had been a small band of zealots, words and personalities counted most. But even by the eighties, the differences among the suffrage supporters were so small as to render nominal the principle of free expression, while Susan B. Anthony had made clear that in the name of suffrage all reform alliances could be jettisoned. When the suffrage movement revived in the 1890s, Catt and her co-workers determined to bar any expression of views which seemed threatening to the development of a tightly coordinated organization. Catt reportedly left a council with Stanton and Anthony at the time, filled with "pity for Miss Anthony and mingled exasperation and envy for Mrs. Stanton who had apparently managed to live eighty years without repressing any desires."[1] Catt had neither time nor patience for a Stanton-like ideologue; her sensibilities, and the spirit she injected into NAWSA, were more prosaic.

1. Mary Gray Peck, *Carrie Chapman Catt* (New York, 1934), 87.

DOCUMENT 39 (IV: 75–77): Debate on Woman
Suffrage and the Churches, NWSA Convention,
Washington, D.C., February 17-19, 1886

A letter from Mrs. Elizabeth Cady Stanton urged that the
question of woman suffrage should now be carried into the
churches and church conventions for their approval, and that
more enlightened teaching from the pulpit in regard to women
should be insisted upon. The letter was accompanied by a resolution to this effect, both expressed in very strong language. They
were read first in executive session. The following extracts are
taken from the stenographic report of the meeting:

Mrs. Helen M. Gougar (Ind.) moved that the resolution be laid
upon the table, saying: "A resolution something like this came into
the last convention, and it has done more to cripple my work and
that of other suffragists than anything which has happened in the
whole history of the woman suffrage movement. When you look
this country over you find the slums are opposed to us, while some
of the best leaders and advocates of woman suffrage are among the
Christian people. A bishop of the Roman Catholic Church stood
through my meeting in Peoria not long since. We can not afford to
antagonize the churches. Some of us are orthodox, and some of us

are unorthodox, but this association is for suffrage and not for the discussion of religious dogmas. I can not stay within these borders if that resolution is adopted, from the fact that my hands would be tied. I hope it will not go into open convention for debate.

Mrs. PERKINS (O.) : I think we ought to pay due consideration and respect to our beloved president. I have no objection to sending missionaries to the churches asking them to pay attention to woman suffrage; but I do not think the churches are our greatest enemies. They might have been so in Mrs. Stanton's early days, but to-day they are our best helpers. If it were not for their co-operation I could not get a hearing before the public. And now that they are coming to meet us half way, do not throw stones at them. I hope that resolution, as worded, will not go into the convention.

Mrs. MERIWETHER (Mo.) : I think the resolution could be amended so as to offend no one. The ministers falsely construe the Scriptures. We can overwhelm them with arguments for woman suffrage—with Biblical arguments. We can hurl them like shot and shell. Herbert Spencer once wrote an article on the different biases which distort the human mind, and among the first he reckoned the theological bias. In Christ's time and in the early Christian days there was no liberty, every one was under the despotism of the Roman Cæsars, but women were on an equality with men, and the religion that Christ taught included women equally with men. He made none of the invidious distinctions which the churches make to-day.

Mrs. SHATTUCK (Mass.) : We did not pass the resolution of last year, so it could not have harmed anybody. But I protest against this fling at masculine interpretation of the Scriptures.

Mrs. MINOR (Mo.) : I object to the whole thing—resolution and letter both. I believe in confining ourselves to woman suffrage.

Mrs. COLBY (Neb.) : I was on that committee of resolutions last year and wrote the modified one which was presented, and I am willing to stand by it. I have not found that it hurts the work, save with a few who do not know what the resolution was, or what was said about it. The discussion was reported word for word in the *Woman's Tribune* and I think no one who read it would say that it was irreligious or lacked respect for the teachings of Christ. I believe we must say something in the line of Mrs. Stanton's idea. She makes no fling at the church. She wants us to treat the Church as we have the State—viz., negotiate for more favorable action. We have this fact to deal with—that in no high orthodox body have women been accorded any privileges.

EDWARD M. DAVIS (Penn.) : I think we have never had a resolution offered here so important as this. We have never had a measure brought forward which would produce better results. I agree entirely with Mrs. Stanton on this thing, that the church is the greatest barrier to woman's progress. We do not want to proclaim ourselves an irreligious or a religious people. This question of religion does not touch us either way. We are neutral.

MADAME NEYMANN (N. Y.) :   Because the clergy has been one-sided, we do not want to be one-sided.   I know of no one for whom I have a greater admiration than for Mrs. Stanton.   Her resolution antagonizes no one.

MRS. BROOKS (Neb.) :   Let us do this work in such a way that it will not arouse the opposition of the most bigoted clergyman.   All this discussion only shows that the old superstitions have got to be banished.

MRS. SNOW (Me.) :   Mrs. Stanton wishes to convert the clergy.

MRS. DUNBAR (Md.) :   I don't want the resolution referred back to the committee, out of respect to Mrs. Stanton and the manner in which she has been treated by the clergy.   I do not want to lose the wording of the original resolution, and therefore move that it be taken up here.

MRS. GOUGAR :   I think it is quite enough to undertake to change the National Constitution without undertaking to change the Bible. I heartily agree with Mrs. Stanton in her idea of sending delegates to church councils and convocations, but I do not sanction this resolution which starts out—"The greatest barrier to woman's emancipation is found in the superstitions of the church."   That is enough in itself to turn the entire church, Catholic and Protestant, against us.

MRS. NELSON (Minn.) :   The resolution is directed against the superstitions of the church and not against the church, but I think it would be taken as against the church.

MISS ANTHONY (N. Y.) :   As the resolution contains the essence of the letter, I move that the whole subject go to the Plan of Work Committee.

The meeting adjourned without action, and on Friday morning the same subject was resumed.   A motion to table Mrs. Stanton's resolution was lost.   Miss Anthony then moved that both letter and resolution be placed in her hands, as the representative of the president of the association, to be read in open convention without indorsement.   "I do not want any one to say that we young folks strangle Mrs. Stanton's thought."

THE REV. DR. McMURDY (D. C.) :   I do not intend to oppose or favor the motion, but as a clergyman and a High Church Episcopalian, I can not see any particular objections to Mrs. Stanton's letter.   The Scriptures must be interpreted naturally.   Whenever Paul's remarks are brought up I explain them in the light of this nineteenth century as contrasted with the first.

It was finally voted that the letter be read without the resolution.

DOCUMENT 40 (IV: 145–46): Elizabeth Cady Stanton,
Letter, NWSA Convention, Washington, D.C.,
January 21-23, 1889

I notice that in some of our conventions resolutions of thanks are passed to senators, congressmen and legislators for advocating some minor privileges which have been conceded to women, such as admission to colleges and professions, limited forms of suffrage, etc. Now I do not see any occasion for gratitude to these honorable gentlemen who, after robbing us of all our fundamental rights as citizens, propose to restore a few minor privileges. There is not one impulse of gratitude in my soul for any of the fragmentary privileges which by slow degrees we have wrung out of our oppressors during the last half century, nor will there be so long as woman is robbed of all the essential rights of citizenship.

If strong appeals could induce the highway robber to return a modicum of what he had stolen, it might mitigate the miseries of his victim, but surely there would be no reason for gratitude, and an expression of thanks to him would be quite as much out of place as are complimentary resolutions passed in our conventions to legislators for their concessions to women. They deserve nothing at our hands until they make full restitution of all we possessed in the original compact under the colonial constitutions—rights over which in the nature of things men could have no lawful jurisdiction whatever. . . . . Woman has the same right to a voice in this government that man has, and it is based on the same natural desire and capacity for self-government and self-protection. . . . .

Until woman is recognized as an equal factor in civilization, and is possessed of her personal property, civil and political rights, all minor privileges and concessions are but so many added aggravations, and are insulting mockeries of that justice, liberty and equality which are the birthright of every citizen of a republic. "Universal suffrage," said Charles Sumner, "is the first proof and only basis of a genuine republic."

DOCUMENT 41 (IV: 148–49): Olympia Brown, "Foreign Rule," NWSA Convention, Washington, D.C., January 21-23, 1889

In Wisconsin we have by the census of 1880 a population of 910,-072 native-born, 405,425 foreign-born. Our last vote cast was 149,463 American, 189,469 foreign; thus you see nearly 1,000,000 native-born people are out-voted and out-governed by less than half their number of foreigners. Is that fair to Americans? Is it just to American men? Will they not, under this influence, in a little while be driven to the wall and obliged to step down and out? When the members of our Legislatures are the greater part foreigners, when they sit in the office of mayor and in all the offices of our city, and rule us with a rod of iron, it is time that American men should inquire if we have any rights that foreigners are bound to respect. . . . .

The last census shows, I think, that there are in the United States three times as many American-born women as the whole foreign population, men and women together, so that the votes of women will eventually be the only means of overcoming this foreign influence and maintaining our free institutions. There is no possible safety for our free school, our free church or our republican government, unless women are given the suffrage and that right speedily. . . . . The question in every political caucus, in every political convention, is not what great principles shall we announce, but what kind of a document can we draw up that will please the foreigners? . . . .

When we remember that the first foot to touch Plymouth Rock was a woman's—that in the first settlement of this country women endured trials and privations and stood bravely at the post of duty, even fighting in the ranks that we might have a republic—and that in our great Western world women came at an early day to make the wilderness blossom as the rose, and rocked their babies' cradles in the log cabins when the Indians' war-whoop was heard on the prairies and the wolves howled around their doors—when we re-

319

member that in the last war thousands of women in the Northwest bravely took upon themselves the work of the households and the fields that their husbands and sons might fight the battles of liberty—when we recollect all this, and then are told that loyal women, pioneer women, the descendants of the Pilgrim Fathers, are not even to ask for the right of suffrage lest the Scandinavians should be offended, it is time to rise in indignation and ask, Whose country is this? Who made it? Who have periled their lives for it?

Our American women are property holders and pay large taxes; but the foreigner who has lived only one year in the State, and ten days in the precinct, who does not own a foot of land, may vote away their property in the form of taxes in the most reckless manner, regardless of their interests and their rights. Women are well-educated; they are graduating from our colleges; they are reading and thinking and writing; and yet they are the political inferiors of all the riff-raff of Europe that is poured upon our shores. It is unbearable. There is no language that can express the enormous injustice done to women. . . . .

We can not separate subjects and say we will vote on temperance or on school matters. for all these questions are part of government. . . . . When women as well as men are voters, the church will get some recognition. I marvel that all ministers are not in favor of woman suffrage, when I consider that their audiences are almost entirely composed of women and that the church to-day is brought into disrepute because it is made up of disfranchised members. The minister would stand a hundred-fold higher than he does now if women had the suffrage. Everybody would want to know what the minister was saying to those women voters.

We are in danger in this country of Catholic domination, not because the Catholics are more numerous than we are, but because the Catholic church is represented at the polls and the Protestant church is not. The foreigners are Catholic—the greater portion of them; the foreigners are men—the greater part of them, and members of the Catholic church, and they work for it and vote for it. The Protestant church is composed of women. Men for the most part do not belong to it; they do not care much for it except as something to interest the women of their household. The consequence is the Protestant church is comparatively unrepresented at the ballot-box. . . . .

I urge upon you, women, that you put suffrage first and foremost, before every other consideration upon earth. Make it a religious duty and work for the enfranchisement of your sex, which means the growth and development of noble characters in your children; for you can not educate your children well surrounded by men and women who hold false doctrines of society, of politics, of morals. Leave minor issues, leave your differences of opinion about the Trinity, or the Holy Ghost, or endless misery; about high license and low license; or Dorcas Societies and Chautauqua Circles. Let them all go; they are of no consequence compared with the enfranchisement of women.

DOCUMENT 42 (IV: 554–57): South Dakota Campaign, 1890

The first of May Miss Anthony returned to South Dakota and established campaign headquarters in Huron. A mass convention of men and women was held and an active State organization formed with Mrs. Philena Everett Johnson, president, Mr. Wardall, vice-president, which co-operated with the national committee and inaugurated an active campaign. The new State had adopted as its motto, "Under God the People Rule," and the suffragists wrote upon their banners, "Under God the People Rule. Women Are People." A large number of national speakers came in the summer. Local workers would organize suffrage clubs in the schoolhouses and these efforts would culminate in large rallies at the county seats where some noted speakers would make addresses and perfect the organization.

Those from the outside who canvassed the State were Henry

B. Blackwell, editor *Woman's Journal,* Boston, the Rev. Anna
Howard Shaw, national lecturer, Mary Seymour Howell (N.
Y.), the Rev. Olympia Brown (Wis.), Matilda Hindman
(Penn.), Carrie Chapman Catt (Wash.), Laura M. Johns
(Kan.), Clara Bewick Colby (Neb.), the Rev. Helen G. Put-
nam (N. D.), Julia B. Nelson (Minn.) Miss Anthony was al-
ways and everywhere the moving spirit and contributed her serv-
ices the entire six months without pay. When $300 were lacking
to settle the final expenses she paid them out of her own pocket.
Mr. Blackwell also donated his services. Most effective State
work was done by Mrs. Emma Smith De Voe, and the home of
Mr. and Mrs. De Voe was a haven of rest for the toilers during
the campaign. Among the other valuable State workers were
Dr. Nettie C. Hall, Mrs. Helen M. Barker, and Mrs. Elizabeth
M. Wardall, superintendent of press. A large number of ministers indorsed the amendment. Two grand rallies of all the
speakers were held, one in Mitchell, August 26, 27, during which
time Miss Anthony, Mr. Blackwell, Miss Shaw and Mrs. Pick-
ler addressed the Republican State Convention; the other during
the State Fair in September. The 17th was "Woman's Day"
and the Fair Association invited the ladies to speak. Miss Anthony, Miss Shaw and Mrs. De Voe complied. The summing
up of the superintendent of press was as follows: Total number
of addresses by national speakers, 789; State speakers, 707; under
the auspices of the W. C. T. U., 104; total, 1,600; local clubs of
women organized, 400; literature sent to every voter.

It would be difficult to put into words the hardships of this
campaign of 1890 in a new State through the hottest and dryest
summer on record. Frequently the speakers had to drive twenty
miles between the afternoon and evening meetings and the audiences would come thirty miles. All of the political State conventions declined to indorse the amendment. The Republicans refused seats to the ladies on the floor of their convention although
Indians in blankets were welcomed. The Democrats invited
the ladies to seats where they listened to a speech against woman
suffrage by E. W. Miller, land receiver of the Huron district,
too indecent to print, which was received with cheers and applause by the convention. The minority committee report ask-

ing for an indorsement, presented by Judge Bangs of Rapid City, was overwhelmingly voted down. A big delegation of Russians came to this convention wearing huge yellow badges lettered, Against Woman Suffrage and Susan B. Anthony.

The greatest disappointment of the campaign was the forming of an Independent party by the Farmers' Alliance and the Knights of Labor. The Alliance at its convention the previous year, 478 delegates present, at the close of Miss Anthony's address, had declared that they would do all in their power to carry the suffrage amendment, and it was principally on account of their assurances of support and on the invitation of their leaders, that she undertook the work in South Dakota. The Knights of Labor at their convention in January of the present year had adopted a resolution which said: "We will support with all our strength the amendment to be voted on at the next general election giving women the ballot . . . . believing this to be the first step toward securing those reforms for which all true Knights of Labor are striving."

But the following June these two organizations formed a new party and absolutely refused to put a woman suffrage plank in their platform, although Miss Anthony addressed their convention and implored them to keep their promise, assuring them that their failure to support the amendment would be its death blow. The previous summer H. L. Loucks, president of the Farmers' Alliance, had made a special journey to the State suffrage convention at Minneapolis to invite her to come to South Dakota to conduct this canvass. He was a candidate for Governor on this new party ticket and in his speech of acceptance did not mention the pending amendment. Before adjourning the convention adopted a long resolution containing seven or eight declarations, among them one that "no citizen should be disfranchised on account of sex," but so far as any party advocacy was concerned the question was a dead issue.

A bitter contest was being made between Huron and Pierre for the location of the State capital, and the woman suffrage amendment was freely used as an article of barter. There were 30,000 Russians, Poles, Scandinavians and other foreigners in the State, most of whom opposed woman suffrage. The liquor dealers and gamblers worked vigorously against it, and they were reinforced by the women "remonstrants" of Massachusetts, who sent their literature into every corner of the State.

At the election, Nov. 4, 1890, the amendment received 22,072 ayes, 45,862 noes, majority opposed 23,790. The Republicans carried the State by 16,000 majority.

At this same election an amendment was submitted as to whether male Indians should be enfranchised. It received an affirmative vote of 45 per cent.; that for woman suffrage received 35 per cent. Of the two classes of voters it seemed the men preferred the Indians. It was claimed by many, however, that they did not understand the wording of the Indian amendment and thought they were voting against it.

As the School Suffrage possessed by women applied only to trustees and did not include the important offices of State and county superintendents, and as it was held that the franchise for this purpose could be secured only by a constitutional amendment, it was decided to ask for this. Through the efforts of Mrs. Anna R. Simmons and Mrs. Emma A. Cranmer, officers of the State Association, a bill for this purpose was secured from the Legislature of 1893. As there seemed to be no objection to women's voting for school trustees it was not supposed that there would be any to extending the privilege for the other school officers. It was submitted at the regular election in November, 1894, and defeated by 17,010 ayes, 22,682 noes, an opposing majority of 5,672.

In 1897 the above ladies made one more effort and secured from the Legislature the submission again of an amendment conferring the Full Suffrage on women. The campaign was managed almost entirely by Mrs. Simmons and Mrs. Cranmer. The National Association assisted to the extent of sending a lecturer, Miss Laura A. Gregg of Kansas, who remained for two months preceding the election; and $100 worth of literature also was furnished for distribution. The Dakota women raised about $1,500, and every possible influence was exerted upon the voters. The returns of the election in November, 1898, gave for the amendment 19,698; against, 22,983; adverse majority, 3,285.

DOCUMENT 43 (IV: 189–91): Elizabeth Cady Stanton, "Solitude of Self," Address before the U. S. Senate Committee on Woman Suffrage, February 20, 1892

The point I wish plainly to bring before you on this occasion is the individuality of each human soul—our Protestant idea, the right of individual conscience and judgment—our republican idea, individual citizenship. In discussing the rights of woman, we are to consider, first, what belongs to her as an individual, in a world of her own, the arbiter of her own destiny, an imaginary Robinson Crusoe with her woman Friday on a solitary island. Her rights under such circumstances are to use all her faculties for her own safety and happiness.

Secondly, if we consider her as a citizen, as a member of a great nation, she must have the same rights as all other members, according to the fundamental principles of our Government.

Thirdly, viewed as a woman, an equal factor in civilization, her rights and duties are still the same—individual happiness and development.

Fourthly, it is only the incidental relations of life, such as mother, wife, sister, daughter, which may involve some special duties and training. In the usual discussion in regard to woman's sphere, such men as Herbert Spencer, Frederick Harrison and Grant Allen uniformly subordinate her rights and duties as an individual, as a citizen, as a woman, to the necessities of these incidental relations, some of which a large class of women never assume. In discussing the sphere of man we do not decide his rights as an individual, as a citizen, as a man, by his duties as a father, a husband, a brother or a son, some of which he may never undertake. Moreover he would be better fitted for these very relations, and whatever special work he might choose to do to earn his bread, by the complete development of all his faculties as an individual. Just so with woman. The education which will fit her to discharge the duties in the largest sphere of human usefulness, will best fit her for whatever special work she may be compelled to do.

The isolation of every human soul and the necessity of self-dependence must give each individual the right to choose his own surroundings. The strongest reason for giving woman all the opportunities for higher education, for the full development of her faculties, her forces of mind and body; for giving her the most enlarged freedom of thought and action; a complete emancipation from all forms of bondage, of custom, dependence, superstition; from all the crippling influences of fear—is the solitude and personal responsibility of her own individual life. The strongest reason why we ask for woman a voice in the government under which she lives; in the religion she is asked to believe; equality in social life, where she is the chief factor; a place in the trades and professions, where she may earn her bread, is because of her birthright to self-sovereignty; because, as an individual, she must rely on herself. . . . . .

To throw obstacles in the way of a complete education is like putting out the eyes; to deny the rights of property is like cutting off the hands. To refuse political equality is to rob the ostracized of all self-respect, of credit in the market place, of recompense in the world of work, of a voice in choosing those who make and administer the law, a choice in the jury before whom they are tried, and in the judge who decides their punishment. Shakespeare's play of Titus and Andronicus contains a terrible satire on woman's position in the nineteenth century—"Rude men seized the king's daughter, cut out her tongue, cut off her hands, and then bade her go call for water and wash her hands." What a picture of woman's position! Robbed of her natural rights, handicapped by law and custom at every turn, yet compelled to fight her own battles, and in the emergencies of life to fall back on herself for protection. . . . . .

How the little courtesies of life on the surface of society, deemed so important from man towards woman, fade into utter insignificance in view of the deeper tragedies in which she must play her part alone, where no human aid is possible!

Nothing strengthens the judgment and quickens the conscience like individual responsibility. Nothing adds such dignity to character as the recognition of one's self-sovereignty; the right to an equal place, everywhere conceded—a place earned by personal merit, not an artificial attainment by inheritance, wealth, family and position. Conceding then that the responsibilities of life rest equally on man and woman, that their destiny is the same, they need the same preparation for time and eternity. The talk of sheltering woman from the fierce storms of life is the sheerest mockery, for they beat on her from every point of the compass, just as they do on man, and with more fatal results, for he has been trained to protect himself, to resist, to conquer. . . . .

In music women speak again the language of Mendelssohn, Beethoven, Chopin, Schumann, and are worthy interpreters of their great thoughts. The poetry and novels of the century are theirs, and they have touched the keynote of reform in religion, politics and social life. They fill the editor's and professor's chair, plead at the bar of justice, walk the wards of the hospital, speak from the pulpit and the platform. Such is the type of womanhood that an enlightened public sentiment welcomes to-day, and such the triumph of the facts of life over the false theories of the past.

Is it, then, consistent to hold the developed woman of this day within the same narrow political limits as the dame with the spinning wheel and knitting needle occupied in the past? No, no! Machinery has taken the labors of woman as well as man on its tireless shoulders; the loom and the spinning wheel are but dreams of the past; the pen, the brush, the easel, the chisel, have taken their places, while the hopes and ambitions of women are essentially changed.

We see reason sufficient in the outer conditions of human beings for individual liberty and development, but when we consider the self-dependence of every human soul, we see the need of courage, judgment and the exercise of every faculty of mind and body, strengthened and developed by use, in woman as well as man. . . . .

DOCUMENT 44 (IV: 216): Resolutions, NAWSA Convention, Washington, D.C., January 16-19, 1893

Resolved, That without expressing any opinion on the proper qualifications for voting, we call attention to the significant facts that in every State there are more women who can read and write than the whole number of illiterate male voters; more white women who can read and write than all negro voters; more American women who can read and write than all foreign voters; so that the enfranchisement of such women would settle the vexed question of rule by illiteracy, whether of home-grown or foreign-born production.

Resolved, That as all experience proves that the rights of the laboring man are best preserved in governments where he has possession of the ballot, we therefore demand on behalf of the laboring woman the same powerful instrument, that she may herself protect her own interests; and we urge all organized bodies of working women, whether in the field of philanthropy, education, trade, manufacture or general industry, to join our association in the endeavor to make woman legally and politically a free agent, as the best means for furthering any and every line of woman's work.

Resolved, That in all States possessing School Suffrage for women, suffragists are advised to organize in each representative district thereof, for the purpose of training and stimulating women voters to exercise regularly this right, using it as a preparatory school for the coming work of full-grown citizenship with an unlimited ballot. We also advise that women everywhere work for the election of an equal number of women and men upon school boards, that the State in taking upon itself the education of children may provide them with as many official mothers as fathers.

WHEREAS, Many forms of woman suffrage may be granted by State Legislatures without change in existing constitutions; therefore,

Resolved, That the suffragists in every State should petition for Municipal, School and Presidential Suffrage by statute, and take every practicable step toward securing such legislation.

Resolved, That we urge all women to enter protest, at the time of paying taxes, at being compelled to submit to taxation without representation.

DOCUMENT 45 (IV: 218-19): On National Conventions, NAWSA Convention, Washington, D.C., January 16-19, 1893

The motion of Miss Alice Stone Blackwell to amend the constitution so that it would not be obligatory to hold every annual convention in Washington, was amended by Mrs. Avery to the effect that "the annual delegate convention shall be held in Washington during the first session of each Congress, in order to influence national legislation; the meeting of the alternate conventions to be left an open question." Miss Anthony was greatly opposed to holding any of the national meetings outside of Washington, and in a forcible speech she said:

The sole object, it seems to me, of this organization is to bring the combined influence of all the States upon Congress to secure national legislation. The very moment you change the purpose of this great body from National to State work you have defeated its object. It is the business of the States to do the district work; to create public sentiment; to make a national organization possible;

329

and then to bring their united power to the capital and focus it on Congress. Our younger women naturally can not appreciate the vast amount of work done here in Washington by the National Association in the last twenty-five years. The delegates do not come here as individuals but as representatives of their entire States.

We have had these conventions here for a quarter of a century, and every Congress has given hearings to the ablest women we could bring from every section. In the olden times the States were not fully organized—they had not money enough to pay their delegates' expenses. We begged and worked and saved the money and the National Association paid the expenses of delegates from Oregon and California in order that they might come and bring the influence of their States to bear upon Congress.

Last winter we had twenty-three States represented by delegates. Think of those twenty-three women going before the Senate committee, each making her speech, and showing these Senators the interest in all these States. We have educated at least a part of three or four hundred men and their wives and daughters every two years to return as missionaries to their respective localities. I shall feel it a grave mistake if you vote in favor of a movable convention. It will lessen our influence and our power; but come what may, I shall abide by the decision of the majority.

Miss Anthony was strongly supported by Miss Shaw, Mrs. Colby, Mrs. Louisa Southworth, Mrs. Rosa L. Segur, Mrs. Olivia B. Hall, Mrs. Jean Brooks Greenleaf and others.

Mrs. Claudia Quigley Murphy (O.) expressed the sentiment of the other side in saying:

It seems better to sow the seed of suffrage throughout the country by means of our national conventions. We may give the people mass meetings and district and State conventions and various other things, but we can never give them anything as good as the national convention. We must get down to the unit of our civilization, which is the individual voter or person. We have worked for twenty-five years here among the legislators at Washington; we have gone to the halls of Congress and to the Legislatures, and we have found the average legislator to be but a reflex of the sentiment of his constituents. If we wish representation at Washington we can send our delegation to the halls of Congress this year and next year, the same as we have done in the past. This great convention does not go to Congress; it sends a committee. . . . . Let us get down to the people and sow the seed among them. It is the people we want to reach if we expect good results.

The amendment was warmly advocated by Mr. and Miss Blackwell, Miss Clay, Mrs. Dietrick, Mrs. Esther F. Boland and others. It was finally adopted by a vote of 37 yeas, 28 nays.

DOCUMENT 46 (IV: 513–18): Colorado Campaign, 1893

The women realized the conflict before them in the near future, and Mrs. Ellis Meredith volunteered to visit the Woman's Congress, which was to meet at Chicago in May, during the World's Fair, and appeal for aid to the representatives of the National Association who would be there. Miss Susan B. Anthony, Mrs. Lucy Stone and other notables were present and appointed a meeting to listen to appeals. These asked help for the Constitutional Convention Campaign in New York and the Kansas Amendment Campaign, which were both considered very hopeful compared to what was thought in the East to be the almost hopeless campaign in Colorado. Mrs. Lillie Devereux Blake presented the claims of New York, Mrs. Laura M. Johns of Kansas, and Mrs. Meredith of Colorado. "Why was your campaign precipitated when our hands are so full?" was one of the discouraging questions. "Are all those Mexicans dead?" asked Miss Anthony, referring to the heavy vote against equal suffrage in the first Colorado campaign of 1877. "No," said Mrs. Meredith, "the Mexicans are all there yet;" but she explained that there were favorable influences now which did not then exist. In the labor unions women members voted, and this fact inclined the men belonging to them to grant the full franchise. The W. C. T. U., now organized throughout the State, had become a firm friend and advocate, and the ruling political party was favorable. Clearly this was the time to strike.

A promise of consideration and such aid as the National Association was able to furnish was given. Later they decided to send Mrs. Carrie Chapman Catt and guarantee her expenses in case she was not able to raise them in the State. From her past record, they thought it likely she would not only do that but put money in the treasury, and the result justified their expectations. She was a financial help, but, much as money was needed, her eloquence and judgment were worth more, and she always will have a warm place in the hearts of Colorado women who were active in the campaign of 1893.

When that campaign opened, there were just $25 in the treasury. Lucy Stone sent a donation of $100. Iowa and California gave aid, and there were small contributions in money from members of the E. S. A. and from auxiliary clubs formed by Mrs. Chapman Catt in different parts of the State.

Besides these, others already had been organized. In Longmont a club was formed in the spring of 1893 by Mesdames Mary L. Carr, Orpha Bacon, Rosetta Webb and Jane Lincoln. They took up the study of laws relating to the property rights of women and endeavored to awaken interest in the question to be settled the following November. The majority which Longmont gave for suffrage is a testimony to the value of their work. In Colorado Springs Mrs. Mary C. C. Bradford was president of a large local society which afterward became auxiliary to the State association, with Mrs. Ella L. C. Dwinnell as president, and did excellent work in El Paso County. In Greeley many of the workers of 1877 were still active. Mrs. Lillian Hartman Johnson organized a club in Durango and spoke for the cause. Mrs.

A. Guthrie Brown formed one in Breckinridge of which Mesdames H. R. Steele, C. L. Westermann and E. G. Brown were active members.

All these clubs, large and small, scattered throughout the State, assisted in arousing public sentiment, but the situation in Denver was the one of most anxious interest. It is always in cities that reforms meet defeat, for there the opposing interests are better organized and more watchful. In no other State is the metropolis so much the center of its life as is Denver of Colorado. Through this modern Palmyra, which stands in the center of the continent and of the tide of commerce from East and West, flow all the veins and arteries of the State life. Arapahoe County, in which it is situated, contains more than one-fourth of the population of the entire State. Upon the women of Denver, therefore, was imposed a triple share of responsibility. Besides the importance of the large vote, there rested particularly upon the members of its suffrage club the burden of having invited this contest and made it a campaign issue.

In the early fall, the City League of Denver was organized with 100 members and Mrs. John L. Routt, wife of the ex-governor, as president. Mrs. Thomas M. Patterson and Mrs. N. P. Hill were prominent workers in this club. A Young Woman's League was formed by Misses Mary and Margaret Patterson and Miss Isabel Hill, and there were other leagues in various parts of the city. In all this work Mrs. Tyler was indefatigable.

Miss Minnie J. Reynolds, chairman of press work, enlisted the help of seventy-five per cent. of the newspapers. In some cases editorial approval and assistance were given, in others space was allowed for suffrage matter. In August Mrs. Elizabeth Tabor donated the use of two rooms in the opera house block, one large enough to seat several hundred persons, the other a suitable office for the corresponding secretary. Dr. Minnie C. T. Love had acted gratuitously in that capacity and opened communication with suffragists throughout the State, but it was now deemed necessary to employ some one who could devote her entire time to the work. Miss Helen M. Reynolds was chosen and added to unusual capability the most earnest zeal. The rooms were furnished through loans of rugs, desks, chairs, etc.

Equal suffrage was indorsed by the county conventions of the Republican, Prohibition and Populist parties, and also at a called meeting of the Democratic State Central Committee. Many ministers and lawyers spoke in its favor. Among the latter were Charles S. Thomas, since governor of the State, J. Warner Mills, Judge L. C. Rockwell, Charles Hartzell, Eugene Engley and Attorney-General I. N. Stevens, who was one of the most trusted advisers.

There were also women speakers of experience: Mrs. Therese Jenkins of Wyoming, Mrs. Susan S. Fessenden of Massachusetts; Mrs. Dora Phelps Buell, Mrs. Mary Jewett Telford, president of the Woman's Relief Corps in the Department of Colorado and Wyoming and also president for several terms of the State W. C. T. U., who made a five-months' speaking tour; Mrs. Leonora Barry Lake of St. Louis, who spoke efficiently under the auspices of the Knights of Labor. Mrs. Laura Ormiston Chant of England delivered an address on her way westward.

Some women made speeches who never had been on the platform before but have since developed much oratorical ability. When needed, women who did not dare risk an unwritten address read papers. Meetings were held all over the city and State. "I should think," said a banker, "from the campaign the women are running that they had a barrel of money;" but he was a contributor to the fund and knew it was very limited. In all about $2,000 were raised, over $300 of which were spent for literature. Some of the most efficient leaflets were written by members of the association and printed in Denver. Nearly 150,000 of these were issued.

In the city press Mrs. Patience Mapleton represented the cause in the *Republican;* Mrs. Ellis Meredith in the *Rocky Mountain News.* There were house to house canvassers, distributors of literature and others who rendered most valuable assistance and yet whose names must necessarily remain unrecorded. The most of this service was given freely, but some of the women who devoted all their time received moderate salaries, for most of the workers belonged to the wage-earning class. The speakers asked no compensation but their expenses were frequently borne. Halls and churches had to be paid for and on several occasions opera houses were rented. When in the final report the expenses of election day were given as $17 a murmur of amusement ran through the audience.

The women who "had all the rights they wanted" appeared late in the campaign. Some of them sent communications to the papers, complaining of the effort to thrust the ballot upon them and add to the already onerous duties of life. When told that they would not be compelled to vote and that if silent influence was in their opinion more potent than the ballot, it would not be necessary to cast it aside for the weaker weapon, they responded indignantly that if they had the franchise of course it would be their duty to use it. Let it be noted that many of them have voted regularly ever since they were enfranchised, though some have reconsidered and returned to their silent influence.

The liquor element slept in fancied security until almost the eve of election, as they did not believe the amendment would receive popular sanction. When they awoke to the danger they immediately proceeded to assess all saloon keepers and as many as possible of their prominent patrons. They got out a large number of dodgers, which were put into the hands of passers by. These were an attack upon equal suffrage and the women who advocated it, and at the bottom of the first issue was a brewer's advertisement. This dodger stated that "only some old maids like Lucy Stone, Susan Anthony, Frances Willard, Elizabeth Stanton and Mary Livermore wanted to vote." They also employed an attorney to juggle the ballots so that they might be thrown out on a technicality. There was consternation among the suffragists when the ballot was finally produced bearing the words "For the Amendment," "Against the Amendment," for it was well known that the measure was not an "amendment." The best legal talent in Denver was consulted and an opinion rendered that the ruse would prove of no avail, as the intention was still clear. The women, however, issued a leaflet instructing the voters just where to put the cross on the ticket if they wished to vote for equal suffrage.

The suffragists were divided in opinion as to the presence of women at the polls on the election day which was to decide their fate. Some thought it might be prejudicial, but the friends among the men strongly approved their presence in order to influence voters. What future election could be of more importance to women than this, and why should they hesitate to show their interest? Under directions from suffrage headquarters workers at the polls distributed the leaflets, often supplementing them by their own eloquence. No woman received any discourtesy.

The night of November 7 was an anxious one. Women went home and lay awake wondering whether they had done everything possible to insure success, or whether failure might be the result of some omission. When the returns published the next morning, although incomplete, showed that success really had crowned their efforts it seemed almost too good to be true. All day long and in the evening people were coming and going at suffrage headquarters with greetings and congratulations. Women of all classes seemed drawn together by the new tie of citizenship.

The full returns gave the result as follows: For suffrage, 35,798; against. 29,451; an affirmative majority of 6,347.

DOCUMENT 47 (IV: 246): Henry B. Blackwell, Address to NAWSA Convention, Atlanta, Georgia, January 31–February 5, 1895

Henry B. Blackwell urged the South to adopt woman suffrage as one solution of the negro problem:

Apply it to your own State of Georgia, where there are 149,895 white women who can read and write, and 143,471 negro voters, of whom 116,516 are illiterates.

The time has come when this question should be considered. An educational qualification for suffrage may or may not be wise, but it is not necessarily unjust. If each voter governed only himself, his intelligence would concern himself alone, but his vote helps to govern everybody else. Society in conceding his right has itself a right to require from him a suitable preparation. Ability to read and write is absolutely necessary as a means of obtaining accurate political information. Without it the voter is almost sure to become the tool of political demagogues. With free schools provided by the States, every citizen can qualify himself without money and without price. Under such circumstances there is no infringement of rights in requiring an educational qualification as a pre-requisite of voting. Indeed, without this, suffrage is often little more than a name. "Suffrage is the authoritative exercise of rational choice in regard to principles, measures and men." The comparison of an unintelligent voter to a "trained monkey," who goes through the motion of dropping a paper ballot into a box, has in it an element of truth. Society, therefore, has a right to prescribe, in the admission of any new class of voters, such a qualification as every one can attain and as will enable the voter to cast an intelligent and responsible vote.

In the development of our complex political society we have to-day two great bodies of illiterate citizens: In the North, people of foreign birth; in the South, people of the African race and a considerable portion of the native white population. Against foreigners and negroes, as such, we would not discriminate. But in every State, save one, there are more educated women than all the illiterate voters, white and black, native and foreign.

DOCUMENT 48 (IV: 248–49): Carrie Chapman Catt,
Report of the Plan of Work Committee, and comments
by Susan B. Anthony, NAWSA Convention, Atlanta,
Georgia, January 31–February 5, 1895

The report of the Plan of Work Committee, Mrs. Chapman
Catt, chairman, began by saying:

The great need of the hour is organization. There can be no
doubt that the advocates of woman suffrage in the United States
are to be numbered by millions, but it is a lamentable fact that our
organization can count its numbers only by thousands. There are
illustrious men and women in every State, and there are men and
women innumerable, who are not known to the public, who are
openly and avowedly woman suffragists, yet we do not possess the
benefit of their names on our membership lists or the financial help
of their dues. In other words, the size of our membership is not
at all commensurate with the sentiment for woman suffrage. The
reason for this condition is plain; the chief work of suffragists for
the past forty years has been education and agitation, and not organization. The time has come when the educational work has
borne its fruit, and there are States in which there is sentiment
enough to carry a woman suffrage amendment, but it is individual
and not organized sentiment, and is, therefore, ineffective.

The audience was greatly amused when Miss Anthony commented on this: "There never yet was a young woman who did
not feel that if she had had the management of the work from the
beginning the cause would have been carried long ago. I felt
just so when I was young."

DOCUMENT 49 (IV: 263–64): The Bible Resolution and Susan B. Anthony's comment, NAWSA Convention, Washington, D.C., January 23-28, 1896

This convention was long remembered on account of the vigorous contest over what was known as the Bible Resolution. Mrs. Elizabeth Cady Stanton recently had issued a commentary on the passages of Scripture referring to women, which she called "The Woman's Bible." Although this was done in her individual capacity, yet some of the members claimed that, as she was honorary president of the National Association, this body was held by the public as partly responsible for it and it injured their work for suffrage. A resolution was brought in by the committee declaring: "This association is non-sectarian, being composed of persons of all shades of religious opinion, and has no official connection with the so-called 'Woman's Bible' or any theological publication."

The debate was long and animated, but although there was intense feeling it was conducted in perfectly temperate and respectful language. Those participating were Rachel Foster Avery, Katie R. Addison, Henry B. Blackwell, Alice Stone Blackwell, Carrie Chapman Catt, Annie L. Diggs, Laura M. Johns, Helen Morris Lewis, Anna Howard Shaw, Frances A. Williamson and Elizabeth U. Yates speaking for the resolution; Lillie Devereux Blake, Clara B. Colby, Cornelia H. Cary, Lavina A. Hatch, Harriette A. Keyser, J. B. Merwin, Caroline Hallowell Miller, Althea B. Stryker, Charlotte Perkins Stetson, Mary Bentley Thomas and Victoria C. Whitney speaking against it.

Miss Anthony was thoroughly aroused and, leaving the chair, spoke against the resolution as follows:

The one distinct feature of our association has been the right of individual opinion for every member. We have been beset at each step with the cry that somebody was injuring the cause by the expression of sentiments which differed from those held by the majority. The religious persecution of the ages has been carried on under what was claimed to be the command of God. I distrust those people who know so well what God wants them to do, because I notice it always coincides with their own desires. All the way along the history of our movement there has been this same contest on account of religious theories. Forty years ago one of our noblest

339

men said to me: "You would better never hold another convention than allow Ernestine L. Rose on your platform;" because that eloquent woman, who ever stood for justice and freedom, did not believe in the plenary inspiration of the Bible. Did we banish Mrs. Rose? No, indeed!

Every new generation of converts threshes over the same old straw. The point is whether you will sit in judgment on one who questions the divine inspiration of certain passages in the Bible derogatory to women. If Mrs. Stanton had written approvingly of these passages you would not have brought in this resolution for fear the cause might be injured among the *liberals* in religion. In other words, if she had written *your* views, you would not have considered a resolution necessary. To pass this one is to set back the hands on the dial of reform.

What you should say to outsiders is that a Christian has neither more nor less rights in our association than an atheist. When our platform becomes too narrow for people of all creeds and of no creeds, I myself can not stand upon it. Many things have been said and done by our *orthodox* friends which I have felt to be extremely harmful to our cause; but I should no more consent to a resolution denouncing them than I shall consent to this. Who is to draw the line? Who can tell now whether these commentaries may not prove a great help to woman's emancipation from old superstitions which have barred its way?

Lucretia Mott at first thought Mrs. Stanton had injured the cause of all woman's other rights by insisting upon the demand for suffrage, but she had sense enough not to bring in a resolution against it. In 1860 when Mrs. Stanton made a speech before the New York Legislature in favor of a bill making drunkenness a ground for divorce, there was a general cry among the friends that she had killed the woman's cause. I shall be pained beyond expression if the delegates here are so narrow and illiberal as to adopt this resolution. You would better not begin resolving against individual action or you will find no limit. This year it is Mrs. Stanton; next year it may be I or one of yourselves who will be the victim.

If we do not inspire in women a broad and catholic spirit, they will fail, when enfranchised, to constitute that power for better government which we have always claimed for them. Ten women educated into the practice of liberal principles would be a stronger force than 10,000 organized on a platform of intolerance and bigotry. I pray you vote for religious liberty, without censorship or inquisition. This resolution adopted will be a vote of censure upon a woman who is without a peer in intellectual and statesmanlike ability; one who has stood for half a century the acknowledged leader of progressive thought and demand in regard to all matters pertaining to the absolute freedom of women.

Notwithstanding this eloquent appeal the original resolution was adopted by 53 yeas, 41 nays.

DOCUMENT 50 (IV: 373): Susan B. Anthony, Statement to NAWSA Convention, Washington, D.C., February 8-14, 1900

She began by saying: "In closing I would like to give a little object lesson of the two methods of gaining the suffrage. By one it is insisted that we shall carry our question to what is termed a popular vote of each State—that is, that its Legislature shall submit to the electors the proposition to strike the little adjective "male" from the suffrage clause. We have already made that experiment in fifteen different elections in ten different States. Five States have voted on it twice." She then summarized briefly the causes of the defeats in the various States, and continued:

Now here is all we ask of you, gentlemen, to save us women from any more tramps over the States, such as we have made now fifteen times. In nine of those campaigns I myself, made a canvass from county to county. In my own State of New York at the time of the constitutional convention in 1894, I visited every county of the sixty—I was not then 80 years of age, but 74. . . . .

There is an enemy of the homes of this nation and that enemy is drunkenness. Every one connected with the gambling house, the brothel and the saloon works and votes solidly against the enfranchisement of women, and, I say, if you believe in chastity, if you believe in honesty and integrity, then do what the enemy wants you not to do, which is to take the necessary steps to put the ballot in the hands of women. . . . .

I pray you to think of this question as you would if the one-half of the people who are disfranchised were men, if we women had absolute power to control every condition in this country and you were obliged to obey the laws and submit to whatever arrangements we made. I want you to report on this question exactly as if the masculine half of the people were the ones who were deprived of this right to a vote in governmental affairs. You would not be long in bringing in a favorable report if you were the ones who were disfranchised and denied a voice in your Government. If it were not women—if it were the farmers of this country, the manufacturers, or any class of men who were robbed of their inalienable rights, then we would see that class rising in rebellion, and the Government shaken to its very foundation; but being women, being only the mothers, daughters, wives and sisters of men who constitute the aristocracy, we have to submit.

DOCUMENT 51 (V: 8–12): Suffrage Strategy, NAWSA
Convention, Minneapolis, Minnesota, May 30–June 4,
1901

Mrs. Catt brought to the presidency a definite belief that Congress would not submit a Federal Suffrage Amendment nor would important States be gained on referendum until national and State officers and workers were better trained for the work required. The increasing evidence of a united and politically experienced opposition as manifested in legislative action and referendum results had convinced her that the cause would never be won unless its campaigns were equipped, guided and conducted by women fully aware of the nature of opposition tactics and prepared to meet every maneuver of the enemy by an equally telling counteraction. She had been appointed by Miss Anthony chairman of a Plan of Work Committee at the convention of 1895 and assembling the practical workers they agreed upon recommendations which proved a turning point in the association's policy. These were presented to that convention and adopted. A Committee on Organization was established with Mrs. Catt as chairman and contrary to the usual custom the convention voted that she be made a member of the National Board. For the last five years her committee had held conferences in connection with each convention which discussed and adopted plans for more efficient work. As president, she now determined to link more closely the work of national and State auxiliary organizations and in the pursuance of this aim and as ex-officio chairman of the convention program committee, she appointed the Executive Committee (consisting of the Board of Officers, the president and one member from each auxiliary State) to be the Committee on Plan of Work. For two entire days preceding this convention the Executive Committee had discussed methods of procedure, as presented by the Board of Officers, who had prepared these recommendations at a mid-year meeting held in Miss Anthony's home at Rochester in August.

The convention accepted the report which included the following: (1) Organization. That organization be continually the first aim of each State auxiliary as the certain key to success; that each State keep at least one organizer employed and endeavor to establish a county organization in each county or at least to form an organization in each county seat and at four other points; that organization work be done among women wage earners and that definite work be undertaken to win the endorsement and cooperation of other associations, chiefly the General Federation of Women's Clubs and the National Education Association. (2) Legislation. That each auxiliary State association appeal to Congress to submit to the Legislatures a 16th Amendment to the Federal constitution prohibiting the disfranchisement of U. S. citizens on account of sex; that the plan initiated by Miss Anthony be continued, namely, that all kinds of national and State conventions be asked to pass resolutions in favor of this amendment, to be sent to Congress; that State societies also ask their Legislatures to pass resolutions in favor of a 16th Amendment, these also to be sent to Congress; that auxiliaries whose States offer a reasonable possibility of a successful referendum try to secure the

submission of State suffrage amendments to the voters, with assurance of national cooperation; that auxiliaries whose State constitutions present obstacles to such procedure work to secure statutory suffrage, such as School, Municipal or Presidential; that
auxiliaries not strong enough to attempt a campaign work for the
removal of legal discriminations against women and attempt to
secure co-guardianship of children, equal property rights, the raising of the age of consent, the appointment of police matrons,
etc.; that a leaflet be prepared by Mrs. Laura M. Johns advising
best methods for successful legislative work. To carry out this
plan the Committees on Congressional Work, Presidential Suffrage and Civil Rights found their work for the year. (3) Press.
Recommendations were made for rendering this department of
work more efficient in the States; enrollment of persons believing
in woman suffrage to be continued in order to secure evidence of
the strength of general favorable sentiment; the literature of the
association to include a plan of work for local clubs.

Work conferences were interspersed during the convention;
one on Organization presided over by Miss Mary Garrett Hay;
one by Mrs. Priscilla D. Hackstaff, chairman Enrollment Committee; one by Mrs. Babcock, chairman Press Committee. A
chart showing the date of the opening of the Legislature in each
State; the provision for amending its constitution; the suffrage
and initiative and referendum laws and all other information
bearing upon the technical procedure of securing the vote State by
State was carefully drawn by the Organization Committee. With
this in hand each State was given its legislative task. It was
voted to urge the auxiliaries of Kansas, Indiana, New York,
Washington and South Dakota to ask for submission of State
constitutional amendments. It was voted that the corresponding
secretary be elected with the understanding that she would serve
at the national headquarters and be paid a salary.

The Executive Committee at a preliminary meeting repeated
the resolution of the preceding year against the official regulation
of vice in Manila, which was under United States control. It
closed: "We protest in the name of American womanhood and we
believe that this represents also the opinion of the best American

manhood.[1] This resolution was unanimously adopted by the delegates after strong addresses, and Miss Anthony, Dr. Shaw, Mrs. Catt, Mrs. Avery and Miss Blackwell were deputized to ask a hearing and present it to the American Medical Association meeting in St. Paul at this time. That body allowed them ten minutes to state their earnest wish that it would endorse the resolution but it took no action.

Miss Anthony had consented to act as chairman of the Congressional Committee and her report was heard with deep interest. Her work during the year was upon two distinct lines, the old familiar petition to Congress to pass the 16th Amendment granting full suffrage to women, and another brought about by new conditions—a petition that the word "male" should not be inserted in the electoral clause of the constitutions proposed by Congress for Hawaii and Porto Rico. These petitions were secured from every State and Territory, a tremendous work, and were laid before the members of Congress from each State. The most interesting petition for the amendment was from Wyoming, where one sheet was signed by every State officer, several U. S. officials and other prominent citizens. They had signed in duplicate several petitions and thus Miss Anthony had an autograph copy with her. The work of securing this petition was done chiefly by Mrs. Joseph M. Cary, wife of the Senator. Miss Anthony was chairman also of the Committee on Convention Resolutions and believed strongly that to present the question of woman suffrage to conventions of various kinds and secure resolutions from them was an efficacious means of propaganda. Her inter-

[1] WHEREAS, Judge William Howard Taft and the Philippine Commissioners in a telegram to Secretary Root dated January 17, 1901, affirm that ever since November, 1898, the military authorities in Manila have subjected women of bad character to "certified examination," and General MacArthur in his recent report does not deny this but defends it; and whereas the Hawaiian government has taken similar action; therefore

RESOLVED, That we earnestly protest against the introduction of the European system of State-regulated vice in the new possessions of the United States for the following reasons:

1. To subject women of bad character to regular examinations and furnish them with official health certificates is contrary to good morals and must impress both our soldiers and the natives as giving official sanction to vice.

2. It is a violation of justice to apply to vicious women compulsory medical measures that are not applied to vicious men.

3. Official regulation of vice, while it lowers the moral tone of the community, everywhere fails to protect the public health.

Examples were given from Paris, garrison towns of England and Switzerland, and St. Louis, the only city in the United States that had ever tried the system.

esting report for 1900 made at this time will be found in full in the History of Woman Suffrage, Volume IV, page 439.

In introducing Mr. Blackwell (Mass.), Mrs. Catt said: "The woman suffrage movement has known many women who have devoted their lives and energies to it. I know of only one man. Years ago when Lucy Stone was a sweet and beautiful girl he heard her speak and afterwards proposed to her to form a marriage partnership. When she said that this might prevent her from doing the large work she wanted to do for equal rights he promised to help her in it and loyally and faithfully all through their married life he did so, as constantly and earnestly as Lucy Stone herself; and even after her death he continues to give his time, his money and his effort to the same end. I am glad to introduce Henry B. Blackwell." Mr. Blackwell was the pioneer in urging the suffragists of every State to try to obtain from their Legislature a law giving them a vote for presidential electors. Their authority for this action was conferred by the National Constitution in Article 2, Section 2: "Each State shall appoint in such manner as the Legislature thereof may direct a number of electors equal to the whole number of Senators and Representatives to which the State may be entitled in the Congress." His comprehensive report made to this and other conventions was an unanswerable argument in favor of the right of a Legislature to confer this vote on women and eventually it was widely recognized.

DOCUMENT 52 (V: 32): Elizabeth Cady Stanton, "Educated Suffrage," NAWSA Convention, Washington, D.C., February 12-18, 1902

In this able and scholarly document Mrs. Stanton said:

The proposition to demand of immigrants a reading and writing qualification on landing strikes me as arbitrary and equally detrimental to our mutual interests. The danger is not in their landing and living in this country but in their speedy appearance at the ballot-box, there becoming an impoverished and ignorant balance of power in the hands of wily politicians. While we should not allow our country to be a dumping-ground for the refuse population of the old world, still we should welcome all hardy, common-sense laborers here, as we have plenty of room and work for them. . . . The one demand I would make for this class is that they should not become a part of our ruling power until they can read and write the English language intelligently and understand the principles of republican government. . . . To prevent the thousands of immigrants daily landing on our shores from marching from the steerage to the polls the national Government should prohibit the States from allowing them to vote in less than five years and not then unless the applicant can read and write the English language. . . . To this end, Congress should enact a law for "educated suffrage" for our native-born as well as foreign rulers, alike ignorant of our institutions. With free schools and compulsory education, no one has an excuse for not understanding the language of the country. As women are governed by a "male aristocracy" we are doubly interested in having our rulers able at least to read and write.

The popular objection to woman suffrage is that it would "double the ignorant vote." The patent answer to this is, abolish the ignorant vote. Our legislators have this power in their own hands. There have been various restrictions in the past for men. We are willing to abide by the same for women, provided the insurmountable qualification of sex be forever removed. . . . Surely, when we compel all classes to learn to read and write and thus open to themselves the door of knowledge not by force but by the promise of a privilege all intelligent citizens enjoy, we are benefactors, not tyrants. To stimulate them to climb the first rounds of the ladder that they may reach the divine heights where they shall be as gods, knowing good and evil, by withholding the citizen's right to vote for a few years will be a blessing to them as well as to the State. . . .

DOCUMENT 53 (V: 82–83): Belle Kearney, "The South and Woman Suffrage," NAWSA Convention, New Orleans, Louisiana, March 15-25, 1903

The address of Miss Belle Kearney, Mississippi's famous orator, was a leading feature of the last evening's program—The South and Woman Suffrage. It began with a comprehensive review of the part the South had had in the development of the nation from its earliest days. "During the seventy-one years reaching from Washington's administration to that of Lincoln," she said, "the United States was practically under the domination of southern thought and leadership." She showed the record southern leaders had made in the wars; she traced the progress of slavery, which began alike in the North and South but proved unnecessary in the former, and told of the enormous struggle for white supremacy which had been placed on the South by the enfranchisement of the negro. "The present suffrage laws in the southern States are only temporary measures for protection," she said. "The enfranchisement of women will have to be effected and an educational and property qualification for the ballot be made to apply without discrimination to both sexes and both races." The address closed as follows:

The enfranchisement of women would insure immediate and durable white supremacy, honestly attained, for upon unquestioned authority it is stated that in every southern State but one there are more educated women than all the illiterate voters, white and black, native and foreign, combined. As you probably know, of all the women in the South who can read and write, ten out of every eleven are white. When it comes to the proportion of property between the races, that of the white outweighs that of the black immeasurably. The South is slow to grasp the great fact that the enfranchisement of women would settle the race question in politics. The civilization of the North is threatened by the influx of foreigners with their imported customs; by the greed of monopolistic wealth and the unrest among the working classes; by the strength of the liquor traffic and encroachments upon religious belief. Some day the North will be compelled to look to the South for redemption from those evils on account of the purity of its Anglo-Saxon blood, the simplicity of its social and economic structure, the great advance in prohibitory law and the maintenance of the sanctity of its faith, which has been kept inviolate. Just as surely as the North will be forced to turn to the South for the nation's salvation, just so surely will the South be compelled to look to its Anglo-Saxon women as the medium through which to retain the supremacy of the white race over the African.

Miss Kearney's speech was enthusiastically received and at its end Mrs. Catt said she had been getting many letters from persons hesitating to join the association lest it should admit clubs of colored people. "We recognize States' rights," she said, "and Louisiana has the right to regulate the membership of its own association, but it has not the right to regulate that of Massachusetts or vice versa," and she continued: "We are all of us apt to be arrogant on the score of our Anglo-Saxon blood but we must remember that ages ago the ancestors of the Anglo-Saxons were regarded as so low and embruted that the Romans refused to have them for slaves. The Anglo-Saxon is the dominant race today but things may change. The race that will be dominant through the ages will be the one that proves itself the most worthy. . . . Miss Kearney is right in saying that the race problem is the problem of the whole country and not that of the South alone. The responsibility for it is partly ours but if the North shipped slaves to the South and sold them, remember that the North has sent some money since then into the South to help undo part of the wrong that it did to you and to them. Let us try to get nearer together and to understand each other's ideas on the race question and solve it together."

DOCUMENT 54 (V: 59–60): NAWSA Position on the
Race Question, Letter to the New Orleans
Times-Democrat, during March 1903 Convention

A discordant note in the harmony was struck by the *Times-Democrat,* which, in a long editorial, Woman Suffrage and the South, assailed the association because of its attitude on the race question.   The board of officers immediately prepared a signed statement which said in part:

The association as such has no view on this subject.   Like every other national association it is made up of persons of all shades of opinion on the race question and on all other questions except those relating to its particular object.   The northern and western members hold the views on the race question that are customary in their sections; the southern members hold the views that are customary in the South.   The doctrine of State's rights is recognized in the national body and each auxiliary State association arranges its own affairs in accordance with its own ideas and in harmony with the customs of its own section.   Individual members in addresses made outside of the National Association are of course free to express their views on all sorts of extraneous questions but they speak for themselves as individuals and not for the association. . . .
   The National American Woman Suffrage Association is seeking to do away with the requirement of a sex qualification for suffrage. What other qualifications shall be asked for it leaves to each State. The southern women most active in it have always in their own State emphasized the fact that granting suffrage to women who can read and write and who pay taxes would insure white supremacy without resorting to any methods of doubtful constitutionality.   The Louisiana association asks for the ballot for educated and taxpaying women only and its officers believe that in this lies "the only permanent and honorable solution of the race question." . . .
   The suffrage associations of the northern and western States ask for the ballot for all women, though Maine and several other States have lately asked for it with an educational or tax qualification.   To advise southern women to beware of lending "sympathy or support" to the National Association because its auxiliary so-

cieties in the northern States hold the usual views of northerners on the color question is as irrelevant as to advise them to beware of the National Woman's Christian Temperance Union because in the northern and western States it draws no color line; or to beware of the General Federation of Women's Clubs because the State Federations of the North and West do not draw it; or to beware of Christianity because the churches in the North and West do not draw it. . . .

II. The Convention as a Platform

BY THE 1890s, the suffrage convention had become a platform for views within the movement rather than a means for public agitation. In the NWSA-AWSA merger, the constituent system of delegates was adopted from AWSA, so that all in attendance were suffrage regulars and the convention process itself contained few surprises. Arguments were restricted to a few general points, usually organizational or at most tactical rather than ideological, and there was little interchange between opposing views. Rather naturally, then, delegates and guests read commonplace essays prepared beforehand. The ideas presented were by no means original: on the one hand, that women had special claims to virtue and a sphere to protect in the home; on the other hand, that women were inevitably part of a modern public life and engaged in economic activities, both with certain political responsibilities.

At closer range, the delegates' ideas often implied more than they stated about the real evolution of women in the larger society. There was a strength in the vision that women might soon be able to do whatever men now did but would learn from men's mistakes while retaining a closer touch with the human needs for peace and harmony. Equality was not only desirable but necessary for the self-protection of new groups of working women who suffered the double burden of wage-earning in the factories and sexual exploitation at home. The other urge, to maintain woman's sphere somehow, unfolded into a belief in a greater role for women in the evolving civilization. Like the Black impetus toward both integration and separation, women's desires for equality and for special advancement as women were not truly contradictory. Rather, both expressed the prospect of self-fulfillment and the reality of constrictions. Only as women gained more actual power could they sort out these two impulses and find in each a fulcrum for development. As Ruth Havens optimistically described the society of the future, the elevation of women would mark their new reintegration into a society transformed by them.

The political implications of these views were noticeably vague. Certainly racist and xenophobic attitudes were a constant, periodically reinforced by the mainstream suffrage interpretations of setbacks in gaining the vote. "Moral prophylaxis" was a typical slogan of women reformers' social vision in the last years of the nineteenth century and in the first years of the twentieth, provoked as much by a fear of "race suicide" as by a genuine concern for the lower classes. But alongside these atavisms grew a respect for working women, even those newly emigrated from eastern and southern Europe. Frequently socialists like Elsie Cole Phillips and Caroline Lowe became recognized as advocates of the working class within suffrage ranks, urging the solidarity of sex and class as more important than race or nativity. If they chose a label at all, leading suffrage campaigners would rightly call themselves "progressives." Afraid of revolutionary change and inclined to accept mainstream social and economic platitudes, they nevertheless determined that woman gain a place of dignity in an order less chaotic and corrupt than that inherited from the nineteenth century.

DOCUMENT 55 (IV: 116–17): Mary Seymour Howell,
"The Present and the Past," NWSA Convention,
Washington, D.C., January 25-27, 1887

The destiny of the world to-day lies in the hearts and brains of her
women. The world can not travel upward faster than the feet of
her women are climbing the paths of progress. Put us back if you
can; veil us in harems; make us beasts of burden; take from us all
knowledge; teach us we are only material; and humanity will go
back to the dark ages. The nineteenth century is closing over a
world arising from bondage. It is the grandest, sublimest spectacle ever beheld. The world has seen and is still looking at the lumi-
nous writing in the heavens—"The truth shall make you free"—and
for the first time is gathering to itself the true significance of liberty.
All the progress of these years has not come easily or from conservatism, but from the persistent efforts of enthusiastic radicals,
men and women with ideas in their heads and courage in their
hearts to make them practical.

Ever since woman took her life in her own hands, ever since she
began to think for herself, the dawning of a great light has flooded
the world. We are the mothers of men. Show me the mothers of
a country and I will tell you of the sons. If men would ever rise
above their sensuality and materialism, they must have mothers
whose pure souls, brave hearts and clear intellects have touched
them deeply before their birth and equipped them for the journey of
life. . . . .

It is the evening of the nineteenth century, but the starlight is
clearer than the morning of its existence. I look back and see in
each year improvement and advancement. I see woman gathering
up her soul and personality and claiming them as her own against
all odds and the world. I see her asking that this personality may

be impressed upon her nation. I see her speaking her soul from platforms, preaching in pulpits of a life of which this is the shadow. I see her pleading before courts, using her brains to solve the knotty questions of the law. Woman's sphere is the wide world, her sceptre the mind that God has given her, her kingdom the largest place that she has the brains to fill and the will to hold. So is woman influencing the world, and as her sphere widens the world grows better. With the freedom she now has, see how she is arousing the public conscience on all questions of right. . . .

What is conservatism? It is the dying faith of a closing century. What is fanaticism? It is the dawning light of a new era. Yes, a new era will dawn with the twentieth century. I look to that time and see woman the redeeming power of the world.

DOCUMENT 56 (IV: 151–52): Clara Bewick Colby,
"Woman in Marriage," NWSA Convention,
Washington, D.C., January 21-23, 1889

In her address on Woman in Marriage
Mrs. Clara Bewick Colby, editor of the *Woman's Tribune,* said:

It is customary to regard marriage as of even more importance
to woman than to man, since the maternal, social and household
duties involved in it consume the greater portion of the time and
thought of a large majority. Love, it is commonly said, is an incident in a man's life, but makes or mars a woman's whole existence. This, however, is one of the many popular delusions
crystallized into opinion by apt phraseology. To one who believes
in the divinely intended equality of the sexes it is impossible to consider that any mutual relation is an incident for the one and the
total of existence for the other. We may lay it down as a premise
upon which to base our whole reasoning that all mutual relations of
the sexes are not only divinely intended to, but actually do bring
equal joys, pains, pleasures and sacrifices to both. Whatever mistake one has made has acted upon the other, and reacted equally
upon the first.

The one great mistake of the ages—since woman lost her primal
independence and supremacy—to which is due all the sins and sorrows growing out of the association of the sexes, has been in making woman a passive agent instead of an equal factor in arranging
the laws, customs and conditions of this mutual state. Whether
marriage be a purely business partnership for the care and maintenance of children, or whether it be a sacrament to which the
benediction of the church gives peculiar sanctity and perpetuity and
makes the parties "no more twain but one flesh," in either case it
is an absurdity, which we only tolerate because of custom, for men
alone to make all the regulations and stipulations concerning it.

This unnatural and strained assumption by one sex of the control
of everything relating to marriage, and the equally unnatural and
mischievous passivity on the part of the other, have given birth to
the meek maiden waiting for her fate, to the typical disconsolate
and forlorn "superfluous woman," to the two standards of morality
for the sexes, to the mercenary marriage with all its attendant
miseries, to the selfish, exacting, querulous wife, to the disappointed
or tyrannical husband; and of late, with the wider possibilities of
individual pleasure and satisfaction, to the growing aversion of
young people to matrimony, and the rush of women to the divorce
courts for freedom from the galling bonds; all these and a thousand variations of each, until the nature of both sexes is so perverted that it is impossible to decide what is nature.

DOCUMENT 57 (IV: 209–11): Ruth C. D. Havens, "The Girl of the Future," NAWSA Convention, Washington, D.C., January 16-19, 1893

In the address of Mrs. Ruth C. D. Havens (D. C.) on The Girl of the Future, which was greatly enjoyed, she said:

The training and education of the girl of the present have seldom been discussed except from one standpoint—her suitable preparation for becoming an economical housekeeper, an inexpensive wife, a willing and self-forgetful mother, a cheap, unexacting, patient, unquestioning, unexpectant, ministering machine. The girl's usefulness to herself, to her sex and race, her preferences, tastes, happiness, social, intellectual or financial prosperity, hardly have entered into the thought upon this question. . . . .

If woman would be a student, a scientist, a lecturer, a physician; if she would be a pioneer in a wilderness of scoffers to make fair roads up which her sex might easily travel to equal educational and legal rights, equal privileges and pay in fields of labor, equal suffrage—she must divide her eager energies and give the larger half to superior homekeeping, wifehood and motherhood, in order that her new gospel shall be received with any respect or acceptance.

And probably no class of women have been such sticklers for the cultivation of all woman's modest, unassuming home duties as have been the great, ambitious teachers on this suffrage platform. . . .

But this will not be the training of the girl of the future. It is not the sort of preparation to which the boy of the present is urged. "Jack of all trades, good at none" is the old epithet bestowed upon a man who thus diffuses his energies. You do not expect a distinguished lawyer to clean his own clothes, a doctor to groom his horse, a teacher to take care of the schoolhouse furnace, a preacher to half-sole his shoes. This would be illogical, and men are nothing if not logical. Yet a woman who enters upon any line of achievement is invariably hampered, for at least the early years, with the inbred desire to add to the labor of her profession all the so-called feminine duties, which, fulfilled to-day, are yet to be done to-morrow, which bring to her neither comfort, gain nor reputation, and which by their perpetual demand diminish her powers for a higher quality of work. . . . .

Everywhere there is too much housekeeping. It is not economy of time or money for every little family of moderate means to undertake alone the expensive and wearing routine. The married woman of the future will be set free by co-operative methods, half the families on a square, perhaps, enjoying one luxurious, well-appointed dining-room with expenses divided *pro rata*. In many other ways housekeeping will be simplified. Homes have no longer room for people—they are consecrated to things. Parlors and bed-rooms are full of the cheap and incongruous or expensive and harmonious belongings of a junk shop. Plush gods hold the fort. All the average house needs to make it a museum is the sign, "Hands off." . . . .

The girl of the future will select her own avocation and take her own training for it. If she be a houseworker, and many will prefer to be, she will be so valuable in that line as to command much respect and good wages. If she be an architect, a jeweler, an electrical engineer, she will not rob a cook by mutilating a dinner, or a dressmaker by amateur cutting and sewing, or a milliner by creating her own bonnet. The house helper will not be incompetent, because the development and training of woman for her best and truest work will have extended to her also, and she will do housework because she loves it and is better adapted to it than to any other employment. She will preside in the kitchen with skill and science.

The service girl of the future will be paid perhaps double or treble her present wages, with wholesome food, a cheerful room, an opportunity to see an occasional cousin and some leisure for recreation. At present this would be ruinous, and why? Because too frequently the family has but one producer. The wife, herself a consumer, produces more consumers. Daughters grow up around a man like lilies of the field, which toil not, neither do they spin. Every member of every family in the future will be a producer of some kind and in some degree. The only one who will have the right of exemption will be the mother, for a child can hardly be born with cheerful views of living whose mother's life has been, for its sake, a double burden. From this root spring melancholy, insanity, suicide. The production of human souls is the highest production of all, the one which requires most preparation, truest worth, gravest care and holiest consecration. If the girl of the future recognizes this truth, she will have made an advance indeed. But apart from the mother every member of the family should be a material producer; and then there will be means sufficient for the producer in the kitchen to get such remuneration for her skill as will eliminate the incompetent, shirking, migratory creature of to-day. . . . .

I hardly need say to this audience that the girl of the future will vote. She will not plead for the privilege—she will be urged to exercise the right, and no one will admit that he ever opposed it, or remember that there was a time when woman's ballot was despised and rejected of men. She will not be told that she needs the suffrage for her own protection, but she will be urged to exercise it for the good of her country and of humanity. It will not be known that the Declaration of Independence was once a dead letter. No one will believe that it ever was declared that the Constitution did not protect this right. It will be incredible that women were once neither people nor citizens, *and yet were the mothers, and in so much the creators, of the men who governed them.*

DOCUMENT 58 (IV: 213–15): Carroll D. Wright, U. S. Commissioner of Labor, "The Industrial Emancipation of Women," NAWSA Convention, Washington, D.C., January 16-19, 1893

On the last evening, the Hon. Carroll D. Wright, U. S. Commissioner of Labor, delivered a valuable address on The Industrial Emancipation of Women, in which he said:

Until within a comparatively recent period, woman's subjection to man has been well-nigh complete in all respects, whether such subjection is considered from a social, political, intellectual or even a physical point of view. At first the property of man, she emerged under civilization from the sphere of a drudge to that of a social factor and, consequently, into the liberty of cultivating her mental faculties. . . . .

Industrial emancipation, using the term broadly, means the highest type of woman as the result, the word "industrial" comprehending in this sense all remunerative employment. The entrance of woman into the industrial field was assured when the factory system of labor displaced the domestic or hand labor system. The age of invention, with the wonderful ramifications which invention always has produced, must be held accountable for bringing woman into a field entirely unknown to her prior to that age. As an economic factor, either in art, literature or industry, she was before that time hardly recognizable. With the establishment of the factory system, the desire of woman to have something more than she could earn as a domestic or in agricultural labor, or to earn something where before she had earned nothing, resulted in her becoming an economic factor, and she was obliged to submit to all the conditions of this new position. It hardly can be said that in the lower forms of industrial pursuits she superseded man, but it is true that she supplemented his labors. . . . .

Each step in industrial progress has raised her in the scale of civilization rather than degraded her. As a result she has constantly gone up higher and gained intellectual advantages, such as the opening to her of the higher institutions of learning, which have in turn equipped her for the best professional employment. The moral plane of the so-called workingwoman certainly is higher than that of the woman engaged in domestic service, and is equal to that of any class of women in the community. . . . .

As women have occupied the positions of bookkeepers, telegraphers and many of what might be called semi-professional callings, men have entered engineering, electrical, mechanical and other spheres of work which were not known when women first stepped into the industrial field. As the latter have progressed from entire want of employment to that which pays a few dollars per week, men, too, have progressed in their employments, and occupied larger fields not existing before. . . . .

Woman is now stepping out of industrial subjection and coming into the industrial system of the present as an entirely new economic factor. If there were no other reasons, this alone would be sufficient to make her wages low and prevent their very rapid increase. . . . . The growing importance of woman's labor, her general equipment through technical education, her more positive dedication to the life-work she chooses, the growing sentiment that an educated and skilful woman is a better and truer companion in marriage than an ignorant and unskilful one, her appreciation of the value of organization, the general uplifting of the principle of integrity in business circles, woman's gradual approach to man's powers in mental achievement also, her possible and probable political influence—all these combined, working along general avenues of progress and evolution, will bring her industrial emancipation, by which she will stand on an equality with man in those callings in life for which she may be fitted. As she approaches this equality her remuneration will be increased and her economic importance acknowledged. . . . .

If woman's industrial emancipation leads to what many are pleased to call "political rights," we must not quarrel with it. It is not just that all other advantages which may come through this emancipation shall be withheld simply because one great privilege on which there is a division of sentiment may also come.

One of the greatest boons which will result from the industrial emancipation of woman will be the frank admission on the part of the true and chivalric man that she is the sole and rightful owner of her own being in every respect, and that whatever companionship may exist between her and man shall be as thoroughly honorable to her as to him.

DOCUMENT 59 (IV: 266–67): Charlotte Perkins Stetson [later Gilman], "The Ballot as an Improver of Motherhood," NAWSA Convention, Washington, D.C., January 23-28, 1896

The last number on the program was The Ballot as an Improver of Motherhood, by Mrs. Stetson. It was an address of wonderful power which thrilled the audience. Among other original statements were these:

We have heard much of the superior moral sense of woman. It is superior in spots but not as a whole. . . . . Here is an imaginary case which will show how undeveloped in some respects woman's moral sense still is: Suppose a train was coming with a children's picnic on board—three hundred merry, laughing children. Suppose you saw this train was about to go through an open switch and over an embankment, and your own child was playing on the track in front of it. You could turn the switch and save the train, or save your own child by pulling it off the track, but there was not time to do both. Which would you do? I have put that question to hundreds of women. I never have found one but said she would save her own child, and not one in a hundred but claimed this would be absolutely right. The maternal instinct is stronger in the hearts of most women than any moral sense. . . . .

What is the suffrage going to do for motherhood? Women enter upon this greatest function of life without any preparation, and their mothers permit them to do it because they do not recognize motherhood as a business. We do not let a man practice as a doctor or a druggist, or do anything else which involves issues of life and death, without training and certificates; but the life and death of the whole human race are placed in the hands of utterly untrained young girls. The suffrage draws the woman out of her purely personal relations and puts her in relations with her kind, and it broadens her intelligence. I am not disparaging the noble devotion of our present mothers—I know how they struggle and toil—but when that tremendous force of mother love is made intelligent, fifty per cent. of our children will not die before they are five years old, and those that grow up will be better men and women. A woman will no longer be attached solely to one little group, but will be also a member of the community. She will not neglect her own on that account, but will be better to them and of more worth as a mother.

DOCUMENT 60 (IV: 308–9): Rev. Anna Garlin Spencer, "Fitness of Women to Become Citizens from the Standpoint of Moral Development," NAWSA Convention, Washington, D.C., February 13-19, 1898

The Rev. Anna Garlin Spencer (R. I.) considered the Fitness of Women to Become Citizens from the Standpoint of Moral Development.

Government is not now merely the coarse and clumsy instrument by which military and police forces are directed; it is the flexible, changing and delicately adjusted instrument of many and varied educative, charitable and supervisory functions, and the tendency to increase the functions of government is a growing one. Prof. Lester F. Ward says: "Government is becoming more and more the organ of the social consciousness and more and more the servant of the social will." The truth of this is shown in the modern public school system; in the humane and educative care of dependent, defective and wayward children; in the increasingly discriminating and wise treatment of the insane, the pauper, the tramp and the poverty-bound; in the provisions for public parks, baths and amusement places; in the bureaus of investigation and control and the appointment of officers of inspection to secure better sanitary and moral conditions; in the board of arbitration for the settlement of political and labor difficulties; and in the almost innumerable committees and bills, national, State and local, to secure higher social welfare for all classes, especially for the weaker and more ignorant. Government can never again shrink and harden into a mere mechanism of military and penal control.

It is, moreover, increasingly apparent that for these wider and more delicate functions a higher order of electorate, ethically as well as intellectually advanced, is necessary. Democracy can succeed only by securing for its public service, through the rule of the majority, the best leadership and administration the State affords. Only a wise electorate will know how to select such leadership, and only a highly moral one will authoritatively choose such. . . . .

When the State took the place of family bonds and tribal relationships, and the social consciousness was born and began its long travel toward the doctrine of "equality of human rights" in government and the principle of human brotherhood in social organization, man, as the family and tribal organizer and ruler, of course took command of the march. It was inevitable, natural and beneficent so long as the State concerned itself with only the most external and mechanical of social interests. The instant, however, the State took upon itself any form of educative, charitable or personally helpful work, it entered the area of distinctive feminine training and power, and therefore became in need of the service of woman. Wherever the State touches the personal life of the infant, the child, the youth, or the aged, helpless, defective in mind, body or moral nature, there the State enters "woman's peculiar sphere," her sphere of motherly succor and training, her sphere of sympathetic and self-sacrificing ministration to individual lives. If the service of women is not won to such governmental action (not only through "influence or the shaping of public opinion," but through definite and authoritative exercise), the mother-office of the State, now so widely adopted, will be too often planned and administered as though it were an external, mechanical and abstract function, instead of the personal, organic and practical service which all right helping of individuals must be.

In so far as motherhood has given to women a distinctive ethical development, it is that of sympathetic personal insight respecting the needs of the weak and helpless, and of quick-witted, flexible adjustment of means to ends in the physical, mental and moral training of the undeveloped. And thus far has motherhood fitted women to give a service to the modern State which men can not altogether duplicate. . . . .

Whatever problems might have been involved in the question of woman's place in the State when government was purely military, legal and punitive have long since been antedated. Whatever problems might have inhered in that question when women were personally subject to their families or their husbands are well-nigh outgrown in all civilized countries, and entirely so in the most advanced. Woman's nonentity in the political department of the State is now an anachronism and inconsistent with the prevailing tendencies of social growth. . . . .

The earth is ready, the time is ripe, for the authoritative expression of the feminine as well as the masculine interpretation of that common social consciousness which is slowly writing justice in the State and fraternity in the social order.

DOCUMENT 61 (IV: 311): Harriot Stanton Blatch, "Woman as an Economic Factor," NAWSA Convention, Washington, D.C., February 13-19, 1898

The public demand for "proved worth" suggests what appears to me the chief and most convincing argument upon which our future claims must rest—the growing recognition of the economic value of the work of women. . . . . There has been a marked change in the estimate of our position as wealth producers. We have never been "supported" by men; for if all men labored hard every hour of the twenty-four, they could not do all the work of the world. A few worthless women there are, but even they are not so much supported by the men of their family as by the overwork of the "sweated" women at the other end of the social ladder. From creation's dawn our sex has done its full share of the world's work; sometimes we have been paid for it, but oftener not.

Unpaid work never commands respect; it is the paid worker who has brought to the public mind conviction of woman's worth. The spinning and weaving done by our great-grandmothers in their own homes was not reckoned as national wealth until the work was carried to the factory and organized there; and the women who followed their work were paid according to its commercial value. It is the women of the industrial class, the wage-earners, reckoned by the hundreds of thousands, and not by units, the women whose work has been submitted to a money test, who have been the means of bringing about the altered attitude of public opinion toward woman's work in every sphere of life.

If we would recognize the democratic side of our cause, and make an organized appeal to industrial women on the ground of their need of citizenship, and to the nation on the ground of its need that all wealth producers should form part of its body politic, the close of the century might witness the building up of a true republic in the United States.

DOCUMENT 62 (IV: 311–13): Florence Kelley, "Working Woman's Need of the Ballot," NAWSA Convention, Washington, D.C., February 13-19, 1898

Mrs. Florence Kelley, State Factory Inspector of Illinois, showed the Working Woman's Need of the Ballot.

No one needs all the powers of the fullest citizenship more urgently than the wage-earning woman, and from two different points of view—that of actual money wages and that of her wider needs as a human being and a member of the community.

The wages paid any body of working people are determined by many influences, chief among which is the position of the particular body of workers in question. Thus the printers, by their intelligence, their powerful organization, their solidarity and united action, keep up their wages in spite of the invasion of their domain by new and improved machinery. On the other hand, the garment-workers, the sweaters' victims, poor, unorganized, unintelligent, despised, remain forever on the verge of pauperism, irrespective of their endless toil. If, now, by some untoward fate the printers should suddenly find themselves disfranchised, placed in a position in which their members were politically inferior to the members of other trades, no effort of their own short of complete enfranchisement could restore to them that prestige, that good standing in the esteem of their fellow-craftsmen and the public at large which they now enjoy, and which contributes materially in support of their demand for high wages.

In the garment trades, on the other hand, the presence of a body of the disfranchised, of the weak and young, undoubtedly contributes to the economic weakness of these trades. Custom, habit, tradition, the regard of the public, both employing and employed, for the people who do certain kinds of labor, contribute to determine the price of that labor, and no disfranchised class of workers can permanently hold its own in competition with enfranchised rivals. But this works both ways. It is fatal for any body of workers to have forever hanging from the fringes of its skirts other bodies on a level just below its own; for that means continual pressure downward, additional difficulty to be overcome in the struggle to maintain reasonable rates of wages. Hence, within the space of two generations there has been a complete revolution in the attitude of the trades-unions toward the women working in their trades. Whereas forty years ago women might have knocked in vain at the doors of the most enlightened trade-union, to-day the Federation of Labor keeps in the field paid organizers whose duty it is to enlist in the unions as many women as possible. The workingmen have perceived that women are in the field of industry to stay; and they see, too, that there can not be two standards of work and wages for any trade without constant menace to the higher standard. Hence their effort to place the women upon the same industrial level with themselves in order that all may pull together in the effort to maintain reasonable conditions of life.

But this same menace holds with regard to the vote. The lack of the ballot places the wage-earning woman upon a level of irresponsibility compared with her enfranchised fellow workingman. By impairing her standing in the community the general rating of her value as a human being, and consequently as a worker, is lowered. In order to be rated as good as a good man in the field of her earnings, she must show herself better than he. She must be more steady, or more trustworthy, or more skilled, or more cheap in order to have the same chance of employment. Thus, while women are accused of lowering wages, might they not justly reply that it is only by conceding something from the pay which they would gladly claim, that they can hold their own in the market, so long as they labor under the disadvantage of disfranchisement? . . . .

Finally, the very fact that women now form about one-fifth of the employes in manufacture and commerce in this country has opened a vast field of industrial legislation directly affecting women as wage-earners. The courts in some of the States, notably in Illinois, are taking the position that women can not be treated as a class apart and legislated for by themselves, as has been done in the factory laws of England and on the continent of Europe, but must abide by that universal freedom of contract which characterizes labor in the United States. This renders the situation of the working woman absolutely anomalous. On the one hand, she is cut off from the protection awarded to her sisters abroad; on the other, she has no such power to defend her interests at the polls, as is the heritage of her brothers at home. This position is untenable, and there can be no pause in the agitation for full political power and responsibility until these are granted to all the women of the nation.

DOCUMENT 63 (IV: 357–58): Anna Barrows, "New Professions for Women Centering in the Home," NAWSA Convention, Washington, D.C., February 8-14, 1900

Anna Barrows (Mass.), literary editor of *The American Kitchen Magazine,* spoke on New Professions for Women Centering in the Home:

The main objection made by conservative people to definite occupations or professions for women has been that such callings would inevitably tend to destroy the home. Once let women prove that they can follow a trade or profession and yet make a home for themselves and others, and such objectors have no ground left. . . . . The fear is sometimes expressed that the club movement is drawing women away from home interests; but the general attention now given to household economics by all the women's clubs proves that women are realizing that knowledge of history, art and science is needed to give the broad culture necessary for the proper conduct of the home life. Although as yet few women's colleges offer adequate courses in home economics, nevertheless after marriage the college women begin to study household problems with all the energy brought out by the college training.

A very general comment on woman's desire for a share in municipal and national government is that the servant question is yet unsolved; that, since she has not succeeded in governing her own domain, she has no rights outside of it. By going outside of her home as an employe herself she is learning to deal with this problem. It has been necessary for women to have thorough business training in other directions before they could discover how unbusinesslike were the methods pursued in the average household. The more women have gone out of their homes into new occupations, the more they have realized that the home is dependent upon the same principles as the business world. The business woman understands human nature, and therefore can deal successfully with the butcher, the baker and other tradespeople. She has a power of adapting herself to new conditions which is impossible to her sister accustomed only to the narrow treadmill of housework.

Specialization is the tendency of the age, and by wise attention to this in the household, as elsewhere, enough time should be saved to each community for the world's work to be done in fewer hours, and for men and women to have time besides to be homemakers and good citizens. Little by little one art and craft after another has been evolved into the dignity of a profession, while housework as a whole has been left to untrained workers. Needle work, cookery and cleaning are dependent on the fundamental principles of all the natural sciences. . . . . There is need also of trained women to lead public sentiment to recognize the dignity of manual labor.

DOCUMENT 64 (V: 178–79): Jane Addams, "The Modern City and the Municipal Franchise for Women," NAWSA Convention, Baltimore, Maryland, February 7-13, 1906

It was at this meeting that Miss Jane Addams of Hull House, Chicago, made the address on The Modern City and the Municipal Franchise for Women, which was thenceforth a part of the standard suffrage literature. Quotations are wholly inadequate.

It has been well said that the modern city is a stronghold of industrialism quite as the feudal city was a stronghold of militarism, but the modern cities fear no enemies and rivals from without and their problems of government are solely internal. Affairs for the most part are going badly in these great new centres, in which the quickly-congregated population has not yet learned to arrange its affairs satisfactorily. Unsanitary housing, poisonous sewage, contaminated water, infant mortality, the spread of contagion, adulterated food, impure milk, smoke-laden air, ill-ventilated factories, dangerous occupations, juvenile crime, unwholesome crowding, prostitution and drunkenness are the enemies which the modern cities must face and overcome, would they survive. Logically their electorate should be made up of those who can bear a valiant part in this arduous contest, those who in the past have at least attempted to care for children, to clean houses, to prepare foods, to isolate the family from moral dangers; those who have traditionally taken care of that side of life which inevitably becomes the subject of municipal consideration and control as soon as the population is congested. To test the elector's fitness to deal with this situation by his ability to bear arms is absurd. These problems must be solved, if they are solved at all, not from the military point of view, not even from the industrial point of view, but from a third, which is rapidly developing in all the great cities of the world—the human-welfare point of view. . . .

City housekeeping has failed partly because women, the traditional housekeepers, have not been consulted as to its multiform activities. The men have been carelessly indifferent to much of this civic housekeeping, as they have always been indifferent to the details of the household. . . . The very multifariousness and complexity of a city government demand the help of minds accustomed to detail and variety of work, to a sense of obligation for the health and welfare of young children and to a responsibility for the cleanliness and comfort of other people. Because all these things have traditionally been in the hands of women, if they take no part in them now they are not only missing the education which the natural participation in civic life would bring to them but they are losing what they have always had.

DOCUMENT 65 (V: 225–26): Rev. Anna Garlin Spencer, Address to NAWSA Convention, Buffalo, New York, October 15-21, 1908

A principal feature of this important discussion was the strong, analytical address of the Rev. Anna Garlin Spencer, in the course of which she said:

The formation of the New York Society for Sanitary and Moral Prophylaxis marked an important era. For the first time the physicians as a whole assumed a social duty to promote purity. They had done it as individuals, but this was the first instance of their banding themselves together on a moral as well as a sanitary plane to enlighten the public as to the causes of social disease. . . . Dr. Prince Morrow should be everlastingly honored by every woman. . . . I consider no woman guiltless, whether she lives in a suffrage State or not, if she does not hold herself responsible for guarding less fortunate women. Corrupt custom has rent the sacred, seamless robe of womanhood and cast out part of the women, abandoning them to degradation. We must learn to recognize the responsibility of pure women for the fallen women, of the woman whose circumstances have enabled her to stand, for the woman whom adverse conditions have borne down. We should oppose the sacrifice of womanhood, whether of an innocent girl sacrificed with pomp and ceremony in church, or of a poor waif in the street; and the great protection is the ability of young girls to earn their living by congenial labor. All the social purity societies do not equal the trade schools as a preventive. . . .

We must not look at this matter from only one point of view or say that we can do nothing about it until we are armed with the ballot. I am a suffragist but not "high church," I am a suffragist and something else. We ought to have the ballot, we are at a disadvantage in our work while we are deprived of it, but even without it we have great power. We must stamp out the traffic in womanhood, it is a survival of barbarism. Womanhood is a unit; no one woman can be an outcast without dire evil to family life. What caused the doctors to come together in a Society for Sanitary and Moral Prophylaxis? It was because the evil done in dark places came back in injury to the family life. . . . We must make ourselves more terrible than an army with banners to despoilers of womanhood. . . . Men are no longer to be excused for writing in scarlet on their foreheads their incapacity for self-control. None of us is longer to be excused for cowardice and acquiescence in the sacrifice of womanhood. Not even that woman—vilest of all creatures on the face of the earth I do believe—the procuress, shall be beyond the pale of sympathy, for she is merely the product of the feeling on the part of men that they owe nothing to women or to themselves in the way of purity, and the feeling on the part of women that they have no right to demand of men what men demand of them. If women are going to amount to anything in government, they would better begin to practice here and now and band themselves together with noble men to bring about this reform.

DOCUMENT 66 (V: 304–5): Laura J. Graddick, Address to NAWSA Convention, Washington, D.C., April 14-19, 1910

Miss Laura J. Graddick, representing a labor union in the District of Columbia, said during an able and earnest address:

They say that politics is too corrupt for woman to enter the field as a voter but does she not live under a Government dominated by politics? Shame on the manhood of our country that our government housekeeping is so administered that woman can not come in contact with it and escape contamination. . . . If our Government is built on moral law it should be clean enough for a woman to have a voice in it. We assure you there are no better house-cleaners than women and the above statement certainly indicates the need of women in politics. There is no great cry on the part of men because of the contaminating influences which woman meets in the business and industrial world. They are not keeping her out of the various vocations of life because of the evil which she might encounter. Are not sweat-shop conditions and overwork and underpaid work evils far more destructive to the physical, mental and moral welfare of women than any condition in which suffrage might place them? Because of the great economic and political changes of the last century the working woman of to-day is entitled to the same rights accorded the working man in the political world. These changes have taken her from the home and brought her into business and industrial life, where she has become more and more man's equal and competitor, leaving behind those conditions which so long made her dependent upon him. This has not been of her choosing. Men, in their pursuit of wealth, have taken the work formerly done in the home, from the spinning and weaving even down to the baking and laundering, and massed it in great factories and shops. Instead of woman taking man's work, it is the reverse and he has appropriated to himself what was long supposed to be hers. Woman finds that what was formerly with her a work of love is now done under new conditions and strange environments.

This experience in the outside world is educating her, for she is studying conditions. She sees that she is forced to compete with those who have full political rights while she herself is a political nonentity. She finds that she must contend with and protect herself against conditions which are more often political than economic, thus forcing upon her the conviction that she too is entitled to be a voter. She sees that politics, business and industrial life generally are so united that one affects the other and that since she is a factor in two she should be granted the rights and privileges of the third. Think of the number of women wage-earners in this country who are without political representation, there being no men in the family, and at present laws all made without a woman's point of view! . . . The working woman does not ask for the ballot as a panacea for all her ills. She knows that it carries with it responsibilities but all that it is to man it will be and even more to woman. Let her remain man's inferior politically and unjust discriminations against her as a wage-earner will continue, but let her become his equal politically and she will then be in a position to demand equal pay for equal work.

DOCUMENT 67 (V: 348–49): Elsie Cole Phillips, Address
to NAWSA Convention, Philadelphia, Pennsylvania,
November 21-26, 1912

Mrs. Elsie Cole
Phillips of Wisconsin showed the standpoint of the so-called
working classes, saying in part:

The right to vote is based primarily on the democratic theory
of government. "The just powers of government are derived from
the consent of the governed." What does that mean? Does it
not mean that there is no class so wise, so benevolent that it is fitted
to govern any other class? Does it not mean that in order to have
a democratic government every adult in the community must have
an opportunity to express his opinion as to how he wishes to be
governed and to have that opinion counted? A vote is in the last
analysis an expression of a need—either a personal need known
to one as an individual as it can be known to no one else, or an
expression of a need of those in whom we are interested—sister-
women or children, for instance. The moment that one admits
this concept of the ballot that moment practically all of the anti-
suffrage argument is done away with. . . . Is it to strengthen
the hands of the strong? Oh, no; it is to put into the hands of
the weak a weapon of self-protection. And who are the weak?
Those who are economically handicapped—first of all the working
classes in their struggle for better conditions of life and labor. And
who among the workers are the weak? Wherever the men have
suffered, the women have suffered more.

But I would also like to point out to you how this affects the homekeeping woman, the wife and mother, of the working class, aside
from the wage-earning woman. Consider the woman at home who
must make both ends meet on a small income. Who better than she
knows whether or not the cost of living advances more rapidly than
the wage does? Is not that a true statement in the most practical
form of the problem of the tariff? And who better than she knows
what the needs of the workers are in the factories? Take the tene-
ment-house woman, the wife and mother who is struggling to bring
up a family under conditions which constantly make for evil. Who,
better than the mother who has tried to bring up six or seven children in one room in a dark tenement house, knows the needs of
a proper building? Who better than the mother who sees her boy
and her girl playing in the streets knows the need of playgrounds?
Who better than a mother knows what it means to a child's life—
which you men demand that she as a wife and a mother shall care

for especially—who, better than she, knows the cruel pressure that comes to that child from too early labor in what the U. S. census report calls "gainful occupations"?

There is a practical wisdom that comes out of the pressure of life and an educational force in life itself which very often is more efficient than that which comes through textbooks of college. . . . The ignorant vote that is going to come in when women are enfranchised is that of the leisure-class woman, who has no responsibilities and knows nothing of what life means to the rest of the world, who has absolutely no civic or social intelligence. But, fortunately for us, she is a small percentage of the women of this land, and fortunately for the land there is no such rapid means of education for her as to give her the ballot and let her for the first time feel responsibilities. . . .

Now the time has come when the home and the State are one. Every act, every duty of the mother in the home is affected by something the State does or does not do, and the only way in which we are ever going to have our national housekeeping and our national child-rearing done as it should be is by bringing into the councils of the State the wisdom of women.

DOCUMENT 68 (V: 350–51): Caroline A. Lowe, Address
to NAWSA Convention, Philadelphia, Pennsylvania,
November 21-26, 1912

Mrs. Caroline A. Lowe of Kansas City, Mo., spoke in behalf
of the 7,000,000 wage-earning women of the United States from
the standpoint of one who had earned her living since she was
eighteen and declared that to them the need of the ballot was a
vital one. She gave heart-breaking proofs of this fact and said:

From the standpoint of wages received we wage earners know
it to be almost universal that the men in the industries receive twice
the amount granted to us although we may be doing the same work.
We work side by side with our brothers; we are children of the
same parents, reared in the same homes, educated in the same schools,
ride to and fro on the same early morning and late evening cars,
work together the same number of hours in the same shops and we
have equal need of food, clothing and shelter. But at 21 years of

age our brothers are given a powerful weapon for self-defense, a larger means for growth and self-expression. We working women, because we find our sex not a source of strength but a source of weakness and a greater opportunity for exploitation, have even greater need of this weapon which is denied to us. Is there any justice underlying such a condition?

What of the working girl and her employer? Why is the ballot given to him while it is denied to us? Is it for the protection of his property that he may have a voice in the governing of his wealth, of his stocks and bonds and merchandise? The wealth of the working woman is far more precious to the welfare of the State. From nature's raw products the working class can readily replace all of the material wealth owned by the employing class but the wealth of the working woman is the wealth of flesh and blood, of all her physical, mental and spiritual powers. It is not only the wealth of today but that of future generations which is being bartered away so cheaply. Have we no right to a voice in the disposal of our wealth, the greatest that the world possesses, the priceless wealth of its womanhood? Is it not the cruelest injustice that the man whose material wealth is a source of strength and protection to him and of power over us should be given the additional advantage of an even greater weapon which he can use to perpetuate our condition of helpless subjection? . . . The industrial basis of the life of the woman has changed and the political superstructure must be adjusted to conform to it. This industrial change has given to woman a larger horizon, a greater freedom of action in the industrial world. Greater freedom and larger expression are at hand for her in the political life. The time is ripe for the extension of the franchise to women.

III. STATE VICTORIES AND DEFEATS

AS EARLY AS THE 1880S, state-level campaigners had taken the initiative in designing suffrage strategy. When the federal amendment appeared too distant, state victories provided both the momentum and the base upon which a successful national campaign would at last be built. After the turn of the century, a new verve was apparent at the state level, nurtured to a large extent by supporters from the Woman's Christian Temperance Union and local woman's clubs. In the south and particularly in the west, state campaigns demonstrated the growth in suffrage forces and the variety of tactics available to the new leadership.

The Washington campaign of 1910 was the bell-ringer for the new era. The support of progressives and labor and the lack of a coherent opposition were key elements for victory in a state where woman suffrage had always enjoyed considerable favor. In 1911 the California victory was cut from the same cloth, and was itself proof of the irreversible tide toward woman's vote. These advances served also to alarm antisuffrage forces, including conservatives and liquor dealers. In 1912 Arizona, Kansas, and Oregon voters granted suffrage to their women, while in Michigan suffrage efforts were turned back by bald-faced manipulation of ballots and in Wisconsin and Ohio substantial votes were rolled up against woman suffrage. Two years later Montana and Nevada were added to the suffrage column, but other attempts were beaten back. The 1915 results were even more revealing of national patterns. Suffrage lost in the heavily populated and therefore vital states of New York, Pennsylvania, New Jersey, and Massachusetts. In short, suffrage forces had managed to carry the day only west of the Mississippi and for the most part in sparsely populated areas. The urban centers with the masses of people and electoral votes were still beyond reach.

Several lessons could be drawn. In Illinois suffragists confronted with a governor who stubbornly refused even to submit the issue to referendum managed to turn away from mass agitation to lobbying among the state's politicians. Illinois suffragists therefore succeeded in gaining the right to vote in presidential elections and simultaneously rendered the doleful lesson that the "best men" could be reached easier than the ordinary voters. New York suffragists came to different conclusions. At every setback they forged ahead and continued to campaign in working-class neighborhoods, cooperate open-handedly with all progressive supporters, and sustain courageously their organizations beyond the hard-fought defeat of 1915 to the victory of 1917.

DOCUMENT 69 (VI: 675–82): Washington Campaign, 1910

CAMPAIGN. After the defeat of 1898 no amendment came before the Legislature for eleven years, nor was there any legislation on woman suffrage until a resolution to submit to the voters an amendment to the State constitution giving full suffrage was presented to the session of 1909. It was drafted by Senator George F. Cotterill of Seattle, a radical suffragist, after many conferences with Mrs. DeVoe, and was introduced, strangely enough, by Senator George U. Piper of Seattle, an able politician and a friend of the liquor interests, in honor of his dead mother, who had been ardently in favor of woman suffrage. It was presented in the House by Representative T. J. Bell of Tacoma. The State association rented a house in Olympia for headquarters and Mrs. DeVoe spent all her time at the Capitol, assisted by many of its members, who came at different times from over the State to interview their Representatives and Senators. The work was conducted so skilfully and quietly that no violent opposition of material strength was developed. The resolution passed the House January 29 by 70 ayes, 18 noes; the Senate February 23 by 30 ayes, 9 noes, and was approved by Governor Marion E. Hay on February 25.

The interests of the amendment were materially advanced later by Senator W. H. Paulhamus, then an anti-suffragist, who "in the interest of fair play" gave advance information as to the exact wording and position of the amendment on the ballot, which enabled the women to hold practice drills and to word their slogan, "Vote for Amendment to Article VI at the Top of the Ballot." The clause relating to the qualifications of voters was reproduced verbatim except for two changes: 1. "All persons" was substituted for "all male persons." 2. At the end was added "There shall be no denial of the elective franchise at any election on account of sex."

During the campaign of 1910 the State Equal Franchise Society, an offshoot from the regular organization, was formed, its members being largely recruited from the Seattle Suffrage Club, Mrs. Harvey L. Glenn, president, with which it cooperated. Headquarters were opened in Seattle July 5, with Mrs. Homer M. Hill, president, in charge and the organization was active during the last four months of the campaign.[1] The Political Equality League of Spokane, Mrs. May Arkwright Hutton, president, worked separately for fourteen months prior to the election, having been organized in July, 1909. The college women under the name of the College Suffrage League, with Miss Parker as president, cooperated with the regular State association.

Following the act of the Legislature twenty months were left to carry on the campaign destined to enfranchise the 175,000 women of the State. It was a favorable year for submission, as no other important political issue was before them and there was a reaction against the dominance of the political "machines."

The campaign was unique in its methods and was won through the tireless energy of nearly a hundred active, capable women who threw themselves into the work. The outstanding feature of the plan adopted by the State Equal Suffrage Association under the leadership of Mrs. DeVoe, was the absence of all spectacular methods and the emphasis placed upon personal intensive work on the part of the wives, mothers and sisters of the men who were to decide the issue at the polls. Big demonstrations, parades and large meetings of all kinds were avoided. Only repeated informal conferences of workers were held in different sections of the State on the call of the president. The result was that the real strength was never revealed to the enemy. The opposition was not antagonized and did not awake until

[1] Other officers of the Franchise Society were: Assistants, Mrs. Edward P. Fick and Mrs. D. L. Carmichael; corresponding secretary, Mrs. F. S. Bash; recording secretary, Mrs. W. T. Perkins; treasurer, Mrs. E. M. Rininger; financial secretary, Mrs. Phebe A. Ryan. Others who worked without pay were: Miss Martha Gruening of New York and Miss Jeannette Rankin of Montana. Mrs. George A. Smith, president of the Alki Point Suffrage Club of Seattle, worked independently but cooperated with the society in many ways. The society employed Mrs. Rose Aschermann, Mrs. Ethel Stalford, Charles E. Cline, Vaughn Ellis and John Gray of Washington.

election day, when it was too late. Although the women held
few suffrage meetings of their own, their speakers and organizers
constantly obtained the platform at those of granges, farmers'
unions, labor unions, churches and other organizations.

Each county was canvassed as seemed most expedient by in-
terviews, letters or return postals. Every woman personally solicited her neighbor, her doctor, her grocer, her laundrywagon
driver, the postman and even the man who collected the garbage.
It was essentially a womanly campaign, emphasizing the home
interests and engaging the cooperation of home makers. The
association published and sold 3,000 copies of The Washington
Women's Cook Book, compiled by the suffragists and edited by
Miss Linda Jennings of LaConner. Many a worker started out
into the field with a package of these cook books under her arm.
In the "suffrage department" of the Tacoma *News* a "kitchen
contest" was held, in which 250-word essays on household subjects were printed, $70 in prizes being given by the paper. Suf-
frage clubs gave programs on "pure food" and "model menus"
were exhibited and discussed.

Thousands of leaflets on the results of equal suffrage in other
States were distributed and original ones printed. A leaflet by
Mrs. Edith DeLong Jarmuth containing a dozen cogent reasons
Why Washington Women Want the Ballot was especially effective. A monthly paper, *Votes for Women,* was issued during
the last year of the campaign with Mrs. M. T. B. Hanna publisher and editor, Misses Parker, Mary G. O'Meara, Rose Glass
and others assistant editors. It carried a striking cartoon on
the front page and was full of suffrage news and arguments,
even the advertisements being written in suffrage terms.[1]

State and county fairs and Chautauquas were utilized by
securing a Woman's Day, with Mrs. DeVoe as president of the
day. Excellent programs were offered, prominent speakers secured and prizes given in contests between various women's
societies other than suffrage for symbolic "floats" and reports
of work during the year. Space was given for a suffrage booth,

[1] During the year following the winning of the franchise Mrs. Hanna published her
paper under the name of *The New Citizen*. Miss Parker published twelve numbers of
a monthly paper called *The Western Woman Voter*, from the files of which much
valuable data has been gleaned for this chapter.

from which active suffrage propaganda went on with the sale of Votes for Women pins, pennants and the cook book and the signing of enrollment cards. The great Alaska-Yukon-Pacific Exposition of 1909 at Seattle was utilized as a medium for publicity. A permanent suffrage exhibit was maintained, open air meetings were held and there was a special Suffrage Day, on which Judge Ben B. Lindsey of Denver spoke for the amendment. The dirigible balloon, a feature of the exposition, carried a large silken banner inscribed Votes for Women. Later a pennant with this motto was carried by a member of the Mountaineers' Club to the summit of Mt. Rainier, near Tacoma, said to be the loftiest point in the United States.[1] It was fastened to the staff of the larger pennant "A. Y. P." of the exposition and the staff was planted in the highest snows on the top of Columbia Crest, a huge white dome that rises above the crater.

The State association entertained the national suffrage convention at Seattle in 1909 and brought its guests from Spokane on·a special train secured by Mrs. DeVoe, as an effective method of advertising the cause and the convention.

The State Grange and the State Farmers' Union worked hard for the amendment. State Master C. B. Kegley wrote: "The Grange, numbering 15,000, is strongly in favor of woman suffrage. In fact every subordinate grange is an equal suffrage organization. . . . We have raised a fund with which to push the work. . . . Yours for victory." The State Federation of Labor, Charles R. Case, president, at its annual convention in January, 1910, unanimously adopted with cheers a strong resolution favoring woman suffrage and urged the local unions to "put forth their most strenuous efforts to carry the suffrage amendment . . . and make it the prominent feature of their work during the coming months."

Practically all the newspapers were friendly and featured the news of the campaign; no large daily paper was opposed. S. A. Perkins, publisher of eleven newspapers in the State, gave a standing order to his editors to support the amendment. The best publicity bureau in the State was employed and for a year its weekly news letter carried a readable paragraph on the sub-

[1] The member was Dr. Cora Smith King.—Ed.

ject to every local paper. Besides this, "suffrage columns" were printed regularly; there were "suffrage pages," "suffrage supplements" and even entire "suffrage editions"; many effective "cuts" were used, and all at the expense of the publishers.

The clergy was a great power. Nearly every minister observed Mrs. DeVoe's request to preach a special woman suffrage sermon on a Sunday in February, 1910. All the Protestant church organizations were favorable. The Methodist Ministerial Association unanimously declared for the amendment April 11 at the request of Miss Emily Inez Denney. The African Methodist Conference on August 10 passed a ringing resolution in favor, after addresses by Mrs. DeVoe and Miss Parker. The Rev. Harry Ferguson, Baptist, of Hoquiam was very active. In Seattle no one spoke more frequently or convincingly than the Rev. J. D. O. Powers of the First Unitarian Church and the Rev. Sidney Strong of Queen Anne Congregational Church. Other friends were the Rev. Joseph L. Garvin of the Christian Church, the Rev. F. O. Iverson among the Norwegians, and the Rev. Ling Hansen of the Swedish Baptist Church. Mrs. Martha Offerdahl and Mrs. Ida M. Abelset compiled a valuable campaign leaflet printed in Scandinavian with statements in favor by sixteen Swedish and Norwegian ministers. The Catholic priests said nothing against it and left their members free to work for it if they so desired. Among Catholic workers were the Misses Lucy and Helen Kangley of Seattle, who formed a Junior Suffrage League. Father F. X. Prefontaine gave a definite statement in favor of the amendment. Distinguished persons from outside the State who spoke for it were Miss Janet Richards of Washington, D. C., the well-known lecturer; Miss Jeannette Rankin of Montana, afterwards elected to Congress; Mrs. Clara Bewick Colby of Nebraska and Washington, D. C., and Mrs. Abigail Scott Duniway of Oregon.

None of the officers and workers connected with the State association received salaries except the stenographers. For four-and-a-half years Mrs. DeVoe, with rare consecration, gave her entire time without pay, save for actual expenses, and even these were at crucial times contributed by her husband, from whom she received constant encouragement and support. For the most part of the entire period she was necessarily absent from home, traveling over the State, keeping in constant personal touch with the leaders of all groups of women whether connected with her association or not, advising and helping them and on special days speaking on their programs. Her notable characteristics as a leader were that she laid personal responsibility on each friend and worker; from the first assumed success as certain and avoided arousing hostility by mixing suffrage with politics or with other reforms. She asked the voters everywhere merely for fair play for women and made no predictions as to what the women would do with the vote when obtained. It was her far-sighted general-ship and prodigious personal work that made success possible.

The Equal Franchise Society of Seattle planned to carry suf-frage into organizations already existing. It gave a series of luncheons at the New Washington Hotel and made converts among many who could not be met in any other way and was especially helpful in reaching society and professional people. Its workers spoke before improvement clubs, women's clubs, churches, labor unions, etc. A man was employed to travel and engage men in conversation on woman suffrage on trains, boats and in hotel lobbies and lumber camps. A good politician looked after the water front. The Political Equality League of Spokane worked in the eastern counties and placed in the field the effective worker, Mrs. Minnie J. Reynolds of Colorado.

The Franchise Department of the W. C. T. U. had done educational work for years under the leadership of Mrs. Mar-garet B. Platt, State president, and Mrs. Margaret C. Munns, State secretary, affectionately referred to as "the Margarets." Its speakers always made convincing pleas for suffrage and Mrs. Munns's drills in parliamentary usage were valuable in training the women for the campaign of 1910. Tribute must be paid to the fine, self-sacrificing work of this organization. In a pri-vate conference called by Mrs. DeVoe early in the campaign, the W. C. T. U. represented by these two, an agreement was reached that, in order not to antagonize the "whisky" vote, the temperance women would submerge their hard-earned honors and let the work of their unions go unheralded. They kept the faith.

A suffrage play, A Mock Legislative Session, written by Mrs.

S. L. W. Clark of Seattle, was given in the State House and repeated in other cities. Several hundred dollars' worth of suffrage literature was furnished to local unions. They placarded the bill boards throughout the State, cooperating with Dr. Fannie Leake Cummings, who managed this enterprise, assisted by the Seattle Suffrage Club, by Mrs. George A. Smith of the Alki Point Club and others who helped finance it to a cost of $535. The placard read: "Give the Women a Square Deal. Vote for the Amendment to Article VI," and proved to be an effective feature.

Mrs. Eliza Ferry Leary, among the highest taxpayers in the State, was chosen by the National Association Opposed to Woman Suffrage as their representative, but, having satisfied her sense of duty by accepting the office, she did nothing and thus endeared herself to the active campaigners for the vote. There were no other "anti" members in the State. The only meeting held was called by a brief newspaper notice at the residence of Mrs. Leary one afternoon on the occasion of a visit by a representative, Mrs. Frances E. Bailey of Oregon, at which six persons were present—the hostess, the guest of honor, three active members of the suffrage association and a casual guest. No business was transacted. With the "antis" should be classed the only minister who opposed suffrage, the Rev. Mark A. Mathews of the First Presbyterian Church, the largest in Seattle. He was born in Georgia but came to Seattle from Tennessee. His violent denunciations lent spice to the campaign by calling out cartoons and articles combating his point of view. When suffrage was obtained he harangued the women on their duty to use the vote, not forgetting to instruct them how to use it.

Election day was reported to the *Woman's Journal* of Boston by Miss Parker as follows: "It was a great victory. The women at the polls were wonderfully effective. Many young women, middle-aged women and white-haired grandmothers stood for hours handing out the little reminders. It rained—the usual gentle but very insistent kind of rain—and the men were so solicitous! They kept trying to drag us off to get our feet warm or bringing us chairs or offering to hand out our ballots while we took a rest, but the women would not leave their places until relieved by other women, even for lunch, for fear of losing a vote. The whole thing appealed to the men irresistibly. We are receiving praise from all quarters for the kind of campaign we made—no personalities, no boasting of what we would do, no promises, no meddling with other issues—just 'Votes for Women' straight through, because it is just and reasonable and everywhere when tried has been found expedient."

The amendment was adopted November 8, 1910, by the splendid majority of 22,623, nearly 2 to 1. The vote stood 52,299 ayes to 29,676 noes out of a total vote of 138,243 cast for congressmen. Every one of the 39 counties and every city was carried.

DOCUMENT 70 (VI: 148–56): Illinois Campaign,
1910-13

In the spring of 1910 the State Board decided to try suffrage
automobile tours. Mrs. Grace Wilbur Trout, president of the
Chicago Political Equality League, was appointed to take charge
of an experimental tour which required about six weeks of
preparatory work to insure its success. She visited the offices
of the newspapers and secured their co-operation. The tour
started on Monday, July 11, and the edition of the *Tribune* the
day before contained a full colored page of the women in the
autos and nearly a half page more of reading material about it.
The paper sent two reporters on the trip, who rode in the car
with the speakers. The *Examiner, Record Herald, Post* and
Journal sent reporters by railroad and trolley, who joined the
suffragists at their stopping places. The women spoke from the
automobile, which drove into some square or stopped on a prominent street corner, previously arranged for by the local committees. Mrs. McCulloch spoke from the legal standpoint; Miss
Nicholes from the laboring woman's view and Mrs. Stewart from
an international aspect. Mrs. Trout made the opening address,
covering the subject in a general way, and presented the speakers.
She herself was introduced by some prominent local woman and
on several occasions by the Mayor.

Sixteen towns were visited, and the *Tribune* said: "Suffrage tour ends in triumph. With mud bespattered 'Votes for Women' banners still flying, Mrs. Trout and her party of orators returned late yesterday afternoon. Men and women cheered them all the way in from their last stop at Wheaton to the Fine Arts Building headquarters." Similar tours in other parts of the State were conducted by Dr. Anna E. Blount, Mrs. Stewart, Miss Grim and Mrs. Jennie F. W. Johnson. Mrs. Trout took her same speakers and went to Lake Geneva, where meetings with speaking from automobiles were held under the auspices of Mrs. Willis S. McCrea, who entertained the suffragists in her spacious summer home. In the autumn at her house on Lincoln Parkway Mrs. McCrea organized the North Side Branch of the State association, afterwards (1913) renamed the Chicago Equal Suffrage Association.

In October the State convention was held at Elgin and Mrs. Stewart was re-elected. The Municipal and Presidential bills and the full suffrage amendment were introduced in the Legislature as usual. Miss Grim and Miss Ruth Harl were stationed at Springfield as permanent lobbyists and Mrs. McCulloch directed the work. At the time of the hearing a special suffrage train was run from Chicago to Springfield, with speaking from the rear platform at the principal places en route.

The State convention was held at Decatur in October, 1911, and Mrs. Stewart, wishing to retire from office after serving six strenuous years, Mrs. Elvira Downey was elected president. Organizing work was pushed throughout the State. Cook county clubs for political discussion were formed by Miss Mary Miller, a lawyer of Chicago. In the winter a suffrage bazaar lasting five days was held at the Hotel LaSalle, under the management of Mrs. Alice Bright Parker. Many of the younger suffragists took part in this social event. Every afternoon and evening there were suffrage speeches and several Grand Opera singers contributed their services. It was an excellent piece of propaganda work and aroused interest among people who had not been reached through other forms.

At the April primaries in Chicago in 1912, through the initiative of Mrs. McCulloch, a "preferential" ballot on the question of suffrage for women was taken.   This was merely an expression of opinion by the voters as to whether they favored it, which the Democratic Judge of Elections, John E. Owens, allowed to be taken, but it had no legal standing.   The State association conducted a whirlwind educational campaign immediately before the election.   Unfortunately, Prohibitionists, Socialists and many independent electors who favored it were not entitled to vote. The result was 135,410 noes, 71,354 ayes, every ward giving an adverse majority.   In October the State convention was held at Galesburg and Mrs. Grace Wilbur Trout was elected president. Mrs. Trout had been on the State board for two years and during this time had served also as president of the Chicago Political Equality League, which under her administration had increased its memberehip from 143 to over 1,000 members.   She began at once to strengthen the State organization for the legislative campaign of 1913.   There were still Senatorial districts in which there were no suffrage societies, and, as the time was short, competent women were immediately appointed in such districts to see that their legislators were interviewed and to make ready to have letters and telegrams sent to them at Springfield.

During the Legislature of 1911 Mrs. Trout had twice accompanied Mrs. McCulloch to Springfield and the antagonism manifested against woman suffrage made her realize that new tactics would have to be employed.   Mrs. McCulloch after many years of service had asked to be relieved and Mrs. Elizabeth K. Booth of Glencoe had been elected legislative chairman.   Mrs. Trout and she adopted a new plan without spectacular activities of any kind, believing that much publicity was likely to arouse the opponents.   It was decided to initiate a quiet, educational campaign and as the only possible way to secure sufficient votes to pass the measure, to convert some of the opponents into friends.   It was agreed also that a card index, giving data about every member of the Legislature, should be compiled at once to be used later for reference.   This plan was approved and adopted by the State board.

The members of the Board and suffrage friends throughout the State gathered information about the legislators and sent it to Mrs. Booth.   The cards when filled out stated the politics and

religion of the various Senators and Representatives, whether
they were married or single, whether their home relations were
harmonious, and tabulated any public service they had ever
rendered. This information made it easier to approach the different legislators in a way to overcome their individual prejudices. All effort was to be concentrated on the bill, which, with
variations, the State association had had before most of the
Legislatures since 1893. It read as follows:

> All women [naming usual qualifications] shall be allowed to vote
> for presidential electors, members of the State Board of Equaliza-
> tion, clerk of the appellate court, county collector, county surveyor,
> members of board of assessors, members of board of review, sanitary
> district trustees, and for all officers of cities, villages and towns
> (except police magistrates), and upon all questions or propositions
> submitted to a vote of the electors of such municipalities or other
> political division of this State.
> All such women may also vote for the following township officers:
> supervisor, town clerk, assessor, collector and highway commissioner,
> and may also participate and vote in all annual and special town
> meetings in the township in which such election district shall be.
> Separate ballot boxes and ballots shall be provided. . . .

As soon as the Legislature convened in 1913 a struggle developed over the Speakership, and there was a long and bitter
deadlock before William McKinley, a young Democrat from
Chicago, was finally elected. Then another struggle ensued over
a United States Senator. During these weeks of turmoil little
could be accomplished for the suffrage bill, but February 10
Mrs. Booth went to Springfield and from then attended the
sessions regularly. She sat in the galleries of the Senate and
House and soon learned to recognize each member and rounded
up and checked off friendly legislators.

The Progressives had a large representation and had made
plans to introduce as a party measure a carefully drafted Woman
Suffrage bill. Mrs. Trout and Mrs. Booth suggested to the
leaders that it would be far better to let the State association
sponsor this measure than to have it presented by any political
party. They finally agreed, but Mrs. McCulloch had accompanied
Mrs. Booth to Springfield taking the bill which she herself had
drafted and which she insisted upon having substituted. Out of
deference to her long years of service her bill was taken instead

of the Progressives'. It named the officers for which women should be allowed to vote instead of being worded like the Progressive draft, which said: "Women shall be allowed to vote for all officers and upon all propositions submitted except where the Constitution provides that the elector shall be a male citizen." In Mrs. Booth's official report to the State convention, held in the fall of 1913 at Peoria, she said: "As we failed to introduce the form of bill approved by the Progressives' constitutional lawyers they introduced it, and it required considerable tact to allay their displeasure and induce them to support our bill." Medill McCormick, one of the leading Progressives in the Legislature, helped greatly in straightening out this tangle. He was a faithful ally of the suffrage lobby and rendered invaluable assistance. Other Progressives who gave important service were John M. Curran and Emil N. Zolla of Chicago; J. H. Jayne of Monmouth; Charles H. Carmon of Forrest, and Fayette S. Munro of Highland Park.[1]

On March 10 Mrs. Trout went to Springfield to secure if possible the support of the Democratic Governor, Edward F. Dunne, for the bill. Mrs. Booth said in her official report: "The Governor told us that he would not support any suffrage measure which provided for a constitutional amendment, as this might interfere with the Initiative and Referendum Amendment, upon which the administration was concentrating its efforts. We assured him that we would not introduce a resolution for an amendment and that we desired the support of the administration for our statutory bill, as we realized that no suffrage measure could pass if it opposed. He then acquiesced." The work at Springfield became more and more complicated and at times seemed almost hopeless. No politicians believed the suffragists had the slightest chance of success. From April 7 Mrs. Trout went down every week. The women had the strong support of the Chicago press and editorials were published whenever

[1] The State association always did everything possible to cooperate with the National Suffrage Association. On March 1, headed by Mrs. Trout, 83 women left Chicago by special train for Washington. In the big suffrage parade there on the 3rd they wore a uniform regalia of cap and baldric and were headed by a large band led by Mrs. George S. Wells, a member of the State Board, as drum major. There was a woman out-rider, Mrs. W. H. Stewart, on a spirited horse. Mrs. Trout led, carrying an American flag, and the Illinois banner was carried by Royal N. Allen, a prominent member of the Progressive party and the railroad official who had charge of the special train.

they were especially needed during the six months' struggle. After considerable educational work the Springfield newspapers also became friendly and published suffrage editorials at opportune times. The papers were refolded so that these editorials, blue penciled, came on the outside, and placed on the desks of the legislators.

The bill was introduced in the House by Charles L. Scott (Dem.) and in the Senate by Hugh S. Magill (Rep.). All efforts were centered on its passage first through the Senate. After nearly three months of strenuous effort this was finally accomplished on May 7, 1913, by a vote of 29 ayes (three more than the required majority) and 15 noes. It is doubtful whether this action could have been secured without the skilful tactics of Senator Magill, but he could not have succeeded without the unfailing co-operation of Lieutenant Governor Barratt O'Hara. Among other Senators who helped were Martin B. Bailey, Albert C. Clark, Edward C. Curtis, Samuel A. Ettelson, Logan Hay and Thomas B. Stewart, Republicans; Michael H. Cleary, William A. Compton, Kent E. Keller, Walter I. Manny and W. Duff Piercy, Democrats; George W. Harris and Walter Clyde Jones, Progressives.

The day the bill passed Mrs. Trout left Springfield to address a suffrage meeting to be held in Galesburg that evening and the next day one at Monmouth. In each place resided a member of the House who was marked on the card index as "doubtful," but both, through the influence of their constituents, voted for the bill. Mrs. Booth remained in Springfield to see that it got safely over to the House. The two women wished the bill to go into the friendly Elections Committee and the opponents were planning to put it into the Judiciary Committee, where it would remain during the rest of the session. The suffrage lobby worked into the small hours of the night making plans to frustrate this scheme. Arrangements were made with Speaker McKinley to turn it over to the Elections Committee, and when the morning session opened this was done before the opponents realized that their plot had failed.

The women were indebted to David R. Shanahan, for many years an influential Republican member, who, representing a "wet" district in Chicago, felt that he could not vote for the bill, but without his counsel it would have been still more difficult to pass it. To overcome the pitfalls, Mrs. Trout appealed to the enemies to give the women of Illinois a square deal, especially to Lee O'Neil Browne, a powerful Democratic leader. He had always opposed suffrage legislation, but he finally consented to let the bill, so far as he was concerned, be voted up or down on its merits. It was this spirit of fair play among its opponents as well as the loyalty of its friends that made possible the final victory.

Up to this time Mrs. Trout and Mrs. Booth had worked alone, but now Mrs. Trout asked Mrs. Antoinette Funk, a lawyer, of Chicago, who had done active work for the Progressive party, to come to Springfield, and she arrived on May 13. A week later Mrs. Medill McCormick came to reside in the capital and her services were immediately enlisted. She was a daughter of the late Senator Mark Hanna, who had inherited much of her father's ability in politics and was an important addition to the suffrage lobby. On May 14 the bill had its first reading and was referred to the Elections Committee. On the 21st it was reported with a recommendation that it "do pass." The opponents were now thoroughly alarmed. Anton J. Cermak of Chicago, president of the United Societies, a powerful organization of liquor interests, directed the fight against it. Leaflets were circulated giving the "preferential" suffrage vote taken in Chicago the year before, with a list of the negative votes cast in each ward to show the Chicago members how badly it had been beaten by their constituents. The bill was called up for second reading June 3 and there was a desperate attempt to amend and if possible kill it, but it finally passed in just the form it had come over from the Senate.

The hope of the opposition now was to keep Speaker McKinley from allowing the bill to come up for third reading. He told Mrs. Trout that hundreds of men from Chicago as well as from other parts of the State had come to Springfield and begged him to prevent it from coming to a vote. The young Speaker looked haggard and worn during those days, and he asked her to let him know it if there was any suffrage sentiment in the

State. She immediately telephoned to Mrs. Harriette Taylor
Treadwell, president of the Chicago Political Equality League,
to have letters and telegrams sent at once to Springfield and to
have people communicate by telephone with the Speaker when he
returned to Chicago for the week end. Mrs. Treadwell called
upon the suffragists and thousands of letters and telegrams were
sent. She also organized a telephone brigade by means of which
he was called up every fifteen minutes by men as well as women,
both at his home and his office, from early Saturday morning
until late Monday night the days he spent in Chicago. She was
assisted in this work by Mrs. James W. Morrisson, secretary of
the Chicago Equal Suffrage Association; Mrs. George Bass,
president of the Chicago Woman's Club; Mrs. Jean Wallace
Butler, a well-known business woman; Mrs. Edward L. Stillman,
an active suffragist in the Rogers Park Woman's Club; Miss
Florence King, a prominent patent lawyer and president of the
Chicago Woman's Association of Commerce; Miss Mary Miller,
another Chicago lawyer and president of the Chicago Human
Rights Association; Mrs. Charlotte Rhodus, president of the
Woman Suffrage Party of Cook County and other influential
women. Mrs. Trout telephoned Miss Margaret Dobyne, press
chairman of the association, to send out the call for help over
the State, which she did with the assistance of Miss Jennie F. W.
Johnson, the treasurer, and Mrs. J. W. McGraw, the auditor.

A deluge of letters and telegrams from every section of Illinois
awaited the Speaker when he arrived in Springfield Tuesday
morning. He needed no further proof and announced that the
bill would be called up for final action June 11. The women
in charge of it immediately began to marshal their forces for
the last struggle. Messages were sent to each friend of the
measure in the House, urging him to be present without fail.[1]
On the eventful morning there was much excitement at the
Capitol. The "captains," previously requested to be on hand

[1] "Captains" had been appointed among the members and each furnished with a list
and it was his duty to see that the men on it were in their seats whenever the bill
was up for discussion. The following Representatives served as "captains" and rendered
important service: William F. Burres, Norman G. Flagg, Edward D. Shurtleff, Homer
J. Tice and George H. Wilson, Republicans; John P. Devine, Frank Gillespie, William
A. Hubbard, W. C. Kane, Charles L. Scott and Francis E. Williamson, Democrats; Roy
D. Hunt, J. H. Jayne, Medill McCormick and Emil N. Zolla, Progressives; Seymour
Stedman, Socialist.

early, reported if any of their men were missing, these were at once called up by telephone and when necessary a cab was sent for them. The four women lobbyists were stationed as follows: Mrs. Booth and Mrs. McCormick in the gallery; Mrs. Trout at the only entrance of the House left open that day, and Mrs. Funk to carry messages and instructions between these points. Mrs. Booth checked off the votes and Mrs. Trout stood guard to see that no friendly members left the House during roll calls and also to prevent the violation of the law which forbade any lobbyist to enter the floor of the House after the session had convened. The burly doorkeeper, who was against the suffrage bill, could not be trusted to enforce the law if its enemies chose to enter.

Events proved the wisdom of this precaution. A number of favoring legislators who started to leave the House during the fight were persuaded to return and the doorkeeper soon told Mrs. Trout she would have to go into the gallery. As she did not move he came back presently and said that Benjamin Mitchell, one of the members of the House leading the opposition, had instructed him that if she did not immediately go to the gallery he would put a resolution through the House forcing her to do so. She politely but firmly said it was her right as a citizen of Illinois to stay in the corridor and remained at her post. As a consequence no one entered the House that day who was not legally entitled to do so. During the five hours' debate all known parliamentary tactics were used to defeat the bill. When Speaker McKinley finally announced the vote—ayes 83 (six more than the required majority), noes 58—a hush fell for an instant before the wild outburst of applause. It seemed as if there had passed through those legislative halls the spirit of eternal justice and truth and the eyes of strong men filled with tears.

DOCUMENT 71 (VI: 459–64): New York City Campaign, 1915

The story of the growth of the woman suffrage movement in Greater New York is one of the most interesting chapters in the history of this cause, for while it advanced slowly for many years, it rose in 1915 and 1917 to a height never attained elsewhere and culminated in two campaigns that in number of adherents and comprehensive work were never equaled.

The Brooklyn Woman Suffrage Association was formed May 13, 1869, and the New York City Society in 1870. From this time various organizations came into permanent existence until in 1903 there were fifteen devoted to suffrage propaganda. In Manhattan (New York City) and Brooklyn these were bound together by county organizations but in order to unite all the suffragists in cooperative work the Interurban Woman Suffrage Council was formed in 1903 at the Brooklyn home of a pioneer, Mrs. Priscilla D. Hackstaff, with the President of the Kings County Political Equality League, Mrs. Martha Williams, presiding. The Interurban began with a roster of five which gradually increased to twenty affiliated societies, with an associate membership besides of 150 women. Under the able leadership of Mrs. Carrie Chapman Catt, chairman, it established headquarters in the Martha Washington Hotel, New York City, Feb.

The History is indebted for this part of the chapter to Mrs. Oreola Williams Haskell, former president of the Kings County Political Equality League; head of the Press Bureau of the New York City Woman Suffrage Party through the two campaigns, 1915-1917, and of the League of Women Voters from its beginning until the present time.

15, 1907, with a secretary, Miss Fannie Chafin, in charge, and maintained committees on organization, literature, legislative work, press and lectures; formed clubs, held mass meetings and systematically distributed literature. The Council was the first suffrage organization in New York City to interview Assemblymen and Senators on woman suffrage and it called the first representative convention held in the big metropolis.

The Woman Suffrage Party of Greater New York was launched by this Council at Carnegie Hall, October 29, 1909, modelled after that of the two dominant political parties. Its first convention with 804 delegates and 200 alternates constituted the largest delegate suffrage body ever assembled in New York State. The new party announced that it would have a leader for each of the 63 assembly districts of the city and a captain for each of the 2,127 election districts, these and their assistant officers to be supervised by a borough chairman and other officers in each borough, the entire force to be directed by a city chairman assisted by city officers and a board of directors. Mrs. Catt, with whom the idea of the Party originated, and her co-workers believed that by reaching into every election district to influence its voters, they would bring suffrage close to the people and eventually influence parties and legislators through public opinion.

The population of Greater New York was 4,700,000 and the new party had a task of colossal proportions. It had to appeal to native Americans of all classes and conditions and to thousands of foreign born. It sent its forces to local political conventions; held mass meetings; issued thousands of leaflets in many languages; conducted street meetings, parades, plays, lectures, suffrage schools; gave entertainments and teas; sent appeals to churches and all kinds of organizations and to individual leaders; brought pressure on legislators through their constituents and obtained wide publicity in newspapers and magazines. It succeeded in all its efforts and increased its membership from 20,000 in 1910 to over 500,000 in 1917.

In 1915, at the beginning of the great campaign for a suffrage amendment to the State constitution, which had been submitted by the Legislature, the State was divided into twelve campaign districts. Greater New York was made the first and under the leadership of Miss Mary Garrett Hay, who since 1912 had served as chairman, the City Woman Suffrage Party plunged into strenuous work, holding conventions, sending out organizers, raising $50,000 as a campaign fund, setting a specific task for each month of 1915 up to Election Day, and forming its own committees with chairmen as follows: Industrial, Miss Leonora O'Reilly; The Woman Voter, Mrs. Thomas B. Wells; Speakers' Bureau, Mrs. Mabel Russell; Congressional, Mrs. Lillian Griffin; the French, Mrs. Anna Ross Weeks; the German, Miss Catherine Dreier; the Press, Mrs. Oreola Williams Haskell; Ways and Means, Mrs. John B. McCutcheon.

The City Party began the intensive work of the campaign in January, 1915, when a swift pace was set for the succeeding months by having 60 district conventions, 170 canvassing suppers, four mass meetings, 27 canvassing conferences and a convention in Carnegie Hall. It was decided to canvass all of the 661,164 registered voters and hundreds of women spent long hours toiling up and down tenement stairs, going from shop to shop, visiting innumerable factories, calling at hundreds of city and suburban homes, covering the rural districts, the big department stores and the immense office buildings with their thousands of occupants. It was estimated that 60 per cent of the enrolled voters received these personal appeals. The membership of the party was increased by 60,535 women secured as members by canvassers.

The following is a brief summing up of the activities of the ten months' campaign.[1]

Voters canvassed (60 per cent of those enrolled)......... 396,698
Women canvassed   60,535
Voters circularized 826,796
Party membership increased from 151,688 to........... 212,223
Watchers and pickets furnished for the polls.............   3,151
Numbers of leaflets printed and distributed.............2,883,264
Money expended from the City treasury................. $25,579
Number of outdoor meetings.......................5,225
Number of indoor meetings (district)............. 660
Number of mass meetings........................   93
Political meetings addressed by Congressmen, Assem-
    blymen and Constitutional Convention delegates...   25
    Total number of meetings......................   6,003

[1] Extended space is given to the two New York campaigns because they were the largest ever made and were used as a model by a number of States in later years.—ED.

Night speaking in theaters............................ 60
Theater Week (Miner's and Keith's).................... 2
Speeches and suffrage slides in movie theaters.......... 150
Concerts (indoor, 10, outdoor, 3).................... 13
Suffrage booths in bazaars............................ 6
Number of Headquarters (Borough 4, Districts, 20)..... 24
Campaign vans (drawn by horses 6, decorated autos 6, district autos 4), vehicles in constant use................ 16
Papers served regularly with news (English and foreign) 80
Suffrage editions of papers prepared.................... 2
Special articles on suffrage........................... 150
Sermons preached by request just before election........ 64

A *Weekly News Bulletin* (for papers and workers) and the *Woman Voter* (a weekly magazine) issued; many unique features like stories, verses, etc.; hundreds of ministers circularized and speakers sent to address congregations; the endorsements of all city officials and of many prominent people and big organizations secured.

In order to accomplish the work indicated by this table a large number of expert canvassers, speakers, executives and clerical workers were required. Mrs. Catt as State Campaign chairman was a great driving force and an inspiration that never failed, and Miss Hay in directing the party forces and raising the money showed remarkable ability. Associated with her were capable officials—Mrs. Margaret Chandler Aldrich, Mrs. Wells, Mrs. Martha Wentworth Suffren, Mrs. Robert McGregor, Mrs. Cornelia K. Hood, Mrs. Marie Jenney Howe, Mrs. Joseph Fitch, Mrs. A. J. Newbury, and the tireless borough chairmen, Mrs. James Lees Laidlaw, Manhattan; Mrs. H. Edward Dreier, Brooklyn; Mrs. Henrietta Speke Seeley, Bronx; Mrs. Alfred J. Eno, Queens, and Mrs. William G. Willcox, Richmond.

The spectacular activities of the campaign caught and held public attention. Various classes of men were complimented by giving them "suffrage days." The appeal to the firemen took the form of an automobile demonstration, open air speaking along the line of march of their annual parade and a ten dollar gold piece given to one of their number who made a daring rescue of a yellow-sashed dummy—a suffrage lady. A circular letter was sent to 800 firemen requesting their help for all suffragists. "Barbers' Day" produced ten columns of copy in leading New York dailies. Letters were sent in advance to 400 barbers informing them that on a certain day the suffragists would call upon

them.   The visits were made in autos decorated with barbers'
poles and laden with maps and posters to hang up in the shops
and then open air meetings were held out in front.   Street cleaners
on the day of the "White Wings" parade were given souvenirs of
tiny brooms and suffrage leaflets and addressed from automobiles.
A whole week was given to the street car men who numbered
240,000.   Suffrage speeches were given at the car barns and
leaflets and a "car barn" poster distributed.

Forty-five banks and trust companies were treated to a "raid"
made by suffrage depositors, who gave out literature and held
open meetings afterward.   Brokers were reached through two
days in Wall Street where the suffragists entered in triumphal
style, flags flying, bugles playing.   Speeches were made, souvenirs
distributed and a luncheon held in a "suffrage" restaurant.   The
second day hundreds of colored balloons were sent up to typify
"the suffragists' hopes ascending."   Workers in the subway
excavations were visited with Irish banners and shamrock fliers;
Turkish, Armenian, French, German and Italian restaurants were
canvassed as were the laborers on the docks, in vessels and in
public markets.

A conspicuous occasion was the Night of the Interurban
Council Fires, when on high bluffs in the different boroughs huge
bonfires were lighted, fireworks and balloons sent up, while music,
speeches and transparencies emphasized the fact that woman's
evolution from the campfire of the savage into a new era was
commemorated.   Twenty-eight parades were a feature of the open
air demonstrations.   There were besides numbers of torchlight
rallies; street dances on the lower East Side; Irish, Syrian, Italian
and Polish block parties; outdoor concerts, among them a big one
in Madison Square, where a full orchestra played, opera singers
sang and eminent orators spoke; open air religious services with
the moral and religious aspects of suffrage discussed; a fête held
in beautiful Dyckman Glen; flying squadrons of speakers whirling
in autos from the Battery to the Bronx; an "interstate meet" on
the streets where suffragists of Massachusetts, New Jersey and
New York participated.   Ninety original features arranged on
a big scale with many minor ones brought great publicity to the
cause and the suffragists ended their campaign valiantly with sixty

speakers talking continuously in Columbus Circle for twenty-six hours.

On the night of November 2, election day, officers, leaders, workers, members of the Party and many prominent men and women gathered at City headquarters in East 34th Street to receive the returns, Mrs. Catt and Miss Hay at either end of a long table. At first optimism prevailed as the early returns seemed to indicate victory but as adverse reports came in by the hundreds all hopes were destroyed. The fighting spirits of the leaders then rose high. Speeches were made by Dr. Anna Howard Shaw, Mrs. Catt, Miss Hay, Dr. Katherine Bement Davis, Mrs. Laidlaw and others, and, though many workers wept openly, the gathering took on the character of an embattled host ready for the next conflict. After midnight many of the women joined a group from the State headquarters and in a public square held an outdoor rally which they called the beginning of the new campaign.

The vote was as follows:

	For	Against	Lost by
Manhattan Borough	88,886	117,610	28,724
Brooklyn Borough	87,402	121,679	34,277
Bronx Borough	34,307	40,991	6,684
Richmond Borough	6,108	7,469	1,361
Queens Borough	21,395	33,104	11,709

Total opposed, 320,853; in favor, 238,098; adverse majority, 82,755.

Two days after the election the City Party united with the National Association in a mass meeting at Cooper Union, where speeches were made and $100,000 pledged for a new campaign fund. The spirit of the members was shown in the words of a leader who wrote: "We know that we have gained over half a million voters in the State, that we have many new workers, have learned valuable lessons and with the knowledge obtained and undiminished courage we are again in the field of action." In December and January the usual district and borough conventions for the election of officers and then the city convention were held. At the latter the resolution adopted showed a change from the oldtime pleading: "We demand the re-submission of the woman suffrage amendment in 1917. We insist that the Judiciary Committee shall present a favorable report without delay and that the bill shall come to an early vote." Much legislative work was necessary to obtain re-submission, for which the City Party worked incessantly until the amendment was re-submitted by the Legislatures of 1916 and 1917 and preparations were again made for a great campaign.

DOCUMENT 72 (VI: 512–17): Ohio Campaign, 1913-17

The campaign opened in Toledo, April 14, 15, was hectic. Everything possible was done to bring the amendment to the attention of the voters. Cleveland suffragists put on a beautiful pageant, A Dream of Freedom. A pilgrimage was made to the Friends' Meeting House in Salem where the suffrage convention of 1850 was held and the resolutions of those pioneers were re-adopted by a large, enthusiastic audience. Women followed party speakers, taking their audiences before and after the political meeting. State conventions of all sorts were appealed to and many gave endorsement, those of the Republicans and the Democrats refusing. Groups of workers would visit a county, separate and canvass all the towns and then keep up their courage by returning to the county seat at night and comparing notes. Street meetings and noon meetings for working people were held. Everything which had been tried out in any campaign was done.

From the beginning of 1913 to the election in November, 1914, there was constant work done for the amendment. The total number of votes cast on it was 853,685; against, 518,295; for 335,390; lost by 182,905 votes. There were gains in every county but only 14 were carried, where there had been 24 in 1912.

That the liquor interests and the anti-suffragists worked together was clearly established. The Saturday preceding the election the president of the State Suffrage association saw in her own city of Warren a man distributing literature from door to door and accompanied by a witness she followed him and picked up several packages in different parts of the city. They contained two leaflets, one giving information on how to vote on the Home Rule or "wet" amendment, the other giving instructions how to vote against the suffrage amendment. The latter had a facsimile ballot marked against it and was signed by five women. The *Liberal Advocate* of Oct. 21, 1914, (official organ of the liquor interests), published at Columbus, had a picture and a write-up of Mrs. A. J. George of Brookline, a speaker from the Massachusetts Anti-Suffrage Association, with a headline saying that she would be present at a luncheon of anti-suffragists on the 27th in that city and also speak elsewhere in the State.

After the defeats of 1912 and 1914 the suffragists abandoned the idea of carrying an amendment. The revised constitution provided for "home rule" for cities, which allowed them to adopt their own charters instead of going to the Legislature. Suffragists believed that these charters could provide for woman suffrage in municipal affairs. In 1916 East Cleveland decided to frame a charter and they saw a chance to make a test. This campaign was the work of the Woman Suffrage Party of Greater

Cleveland. On June 6 a city charter was submitted to the voters and adopted including woman suffrage. A suit was brought to test its constitutionality and it was argued in the Supreme Court, one of the lawyers being a woman, Miss Florence E. Allen.[1] By agreement between the court and election officials women voted at the regular municipal election in November. The court upheld its validity April 3, 1917, and the constitutionality of Municipal woman suffrage in charter cities was established.

In the fall of 1917 the women of Lakewood, a city adjoining Cleveland on the west, gave municipal suffrage to its women by charter after a vigorous campaign. Columbus undertook to put this in its charter and a bitter campaign took place. It was the house to house canvass and the courageous work of the Columbus women and State suffrage officers which brought the victory when it was voted on at the election in August, 1917. Sandusky was not successful.

A partial poll of the Legislature on the subject of Presidential suffrage for women in 1915 had shown that it would be futile to attempt it but after endorsements of woman suffrage by the national party conventions in 1916 it was determined to try.

The Legislature of 1917 was Democratic and Representative James A. Reynolds (Cleveland) met the State suffrage workers upon their arrival in Columbus for the opening of the session and informed them that he was going to sponsor their bill. On January 16 Representative Pratt, Republican, of Ashtabula and Mr. Reynolds, Democrat, each introduced a measure for Presidential suffrage. By agreement the Reynolds bill was chosen and he fought the battle for it against great odds. He was the one anti-prohibitionist who worked for it, considering it his duty and his privilege, and, because of his standing and because his party was in power, he was the only one perhaps who could have carried it through. He stood by the suffragists until Tennessee had ratified and the contest was over.

On Jan. 30, 1917, the bill to give women a vote for Presidential electors was reported favorably from the House Committee on Elections, and on February 1 it passed the House by 72 ayes,

[1] Miss Allen was counsel in all court cases of the Ohio suffragists from 1916 to 1920. In 1920 she was elected Judge in the Common Pleas Court of Cuyahoga county (Cleveland), the first woman in the United States to fill such an office.

50 noes, fifty-five per cent. of the Democratic members voting for it and sixty-nine per cent of the Republicans. In the Senate the leader of the "wets" introduced a resolution for the submission of a full suffrage amendment in the hope of sidetracking the Reynolds bill but the latter reached the Senate February 2, before the Holden bill could be considered. The suffragists, wishing to expedite matters, did not ask for a hearing but the "antis" did and at Mr. Reynolds' request the former were present. At this hearing the women leaders of the "antis" and the liquor men occupied seats together on the floor of the Senate. The next morning the bill was reported favorably from the Federal Relations Committee and passed on February 14, by 19 ayes, 17 noes. Immediately the leader of the opposition changed his vote to yes in order to move a reconsideration. This he was not permitted to do because a friend of the measure forced the reconsideration the next day, and as this was lost by a vote of 24 to 10, the bill itself went on record as having received the vote of the "wet" leader and having passed by 20 to 16. Governor James M. Cox signed it Feb. 21.

Very soon the opponents opened headquarters in Columbus and circulated petitions to have the Presidential suffrage bill referred to the voters for repeal. The story of these petitions is a disgraceful one. Four-fifths of the signatures were gathered in saloons, the petitions kept on the back and front bars. Hundreds of names were certified to by men who declared they saw them signed, an impossibility unless they stood by the bar eighteen hours each day for some weeks and watched every signature. Some petitions, according to the dates they bore, were circulated by the same men in different counties on the same day. Some of them had whole pages of signatures written in the same hand and some had names only, no addresses. The suffragists copied some of these petitions after they were filed in Columbus and although the time was short brought suit to prove them fraudulent in six counties. In four the court ordered all but a few names thrown out. In Scioto all the names were rejected and in Cuyahoga county (Cleveland), 7,000 names were thrown out. The petitions in Franklin county (Columbus), Lucas (Toledo) and Montgomery (Dayton) were unquestionably fraudulent but the election boards were hostile to woman suffrage and powerful with the courts and refused to bring cases. When suffrage leaders attempted to intervene the courts declared they had no jurisdiction.

The suffragists were on duty in Columbus from January to October,—long, weary, exciting months. It was clearly proved in the cases brought that the petitions were fraudulently circulated, signed, attested and certified. In the course of an attempt to bring a case against Franklin county a ruling of the Common Pleas Court was that the Secretary of State should be restrained from counting the signatures from seventeen counties because the Board of Elections had not properly certified them. The Secretary of State telegraphed these boards and they certified again, although there is no constitutional or statutory provision for recertification. Nevertheless when these corrected certifications were made the Judge dissolved the injunction and 17,000 names were restored to the petition. U. S. Senator Warren G. Harding in a Decoration Day speech at Columbus declared himself decidedly opposed to accepting this referendum.

Cases were brought to the Supreme Court via the Court of Appeals, one a general suit demanding that petitions from certain counties be rejected because they were fraudulent and insufficient, the other to mandamus the Secretary of State to give the suffragists a hearing to prove their charges. The first was dismissed, the Supreme Court saying it had no jurisdiction over a case which had not been finished in the court from which the appeal had been taken. They returned to the Court of Appeals and tried one case on the constitutionality of the law of 1915, which gives the Board of Elections and Common Pleas Judges the right to examine the petitions and pass upon their validity, instead of the Secretary of State. The court decided to give no decision as election was so near at hand.

The law made no provision to meet the expenses of petition suits and the suffragists had to bear the cost, no small undertaking. The election boards which were dominated by politicians who had been notorious for their opposition to suffrage, interposed every possible obstacle to the attempt of the suffragists to uncover fraud. In some counties it was impossible to bring cases. Women were absorbed in war work and thousands of them bitterly resented the fact that at such a time their right to vote should be questioned. The referendum was submitted with the proposal so worded on the ballot that it was extremely difficult to know whether to vote yes or no.

At the election in November, 1917, the majority voted in favor of taking away from women the Presidential suffrage. The vote for retaining it was 422,262; against, 568,382; the law repealed by a majority of 146,120. More votes were polled in 1917 than in 1914. The law was upheld in 15 counties, in 11 of which suffrage had then carried three times.

Ohio suffragists now turned their attention entirely towards national work. It was apparent that while the liquor interests continued their fight, women with a few thousand dollars, working for principle, could never overcome men with hundreds of thousands of dollars working for their own political and financial interests. Intensive organized congressional work was carried on henceforth for the Federal Suffrage Amendment.

IV. THE FEDERAL AMENDMENT

THE FINAL VICTORY of woman suffrage in the United States was due both to effective national leadership of the suffrage forces and to favorable historical circumstances. The political momentum of the state campaigns added authority to NAWSA's pleas for congressional support and raised the possibility of a sweeping national campaign. But the successful coordination of the now huge suffrage resources was nevertheless a feat of will and expertise. Carrie Chapman Catt almost personally drove the organization forward, toward its political potential. Even then the recalcitrant forces of opposition might have delayed suffrage another decade. Woodrow Wilson's grudging support, the democratic-collectivist tone of his administration's domestic and foreign policies, and above all World War I provided Catt and her colleagues with the opportunity NAWSA had heretofore lacked. Never free of strategic miscalculation and personality clash, ridden with the contradictions of the very respectability woman suffrage had attained, NAWSA went forward in the face of all organized opposition toward ever-greater campaigns for victory.

The internal life of NAWSA, however, remained at least until 1916 only a little short of chaotic. The Reverend Anna Howard Shaw lacked perhaps the opportunity but certainly the capacity to overcome differences in the suffrage ranks. The most serious rift grew out of NAWSA's endorsement of a proposed federal amendment sponsored by John Shafroth of Colorado and A. Mitchell Palmer of Pennsylvania, which would guarantee referenda in any state where 8 percent of the voters from the last election signed an initiative petition. The intent of the Shafroth-Palmer measure was to mitigate the resistance of congressmen opposing federal dictation and to make the referenda universal. But the effect was to further splinter NAWSA over national strategy. The unwillingness of Shaw and her officers to lead became a self-fulfilling

413

prophecy in the impossibility of effective coordination that Shafroth-Palmer offered.

NAWSA's own Congressional Committee stepped into the breach, claiming the Stanton-Anthony tradition for itself. Its leader, Alice Paul, was like a young Carrie Chapman Catt, gifted with a superb sense of organizational dynamics. But Paul came of age in a suffrage movement so vast and confused that only an experienced leader with a national following could provide decisive direction. Paul was game for the effort, nevertheless. The shifting title of her own group, from Congressional Committee, to Congressional Union, and finally to National Woman's Party, suggested her escalating sense of self-importance and her continual search for new forms of agitation. As Catt later remarked, only NAWSA's abandonment of the Shafroth-Palmer Amendment prevented a serious split, from which Paul's group would doubtless have been the primary beneficiary.

Catt, once the advocate of states' autonomy, now found herself the champion of a national discipline calculated to avert the twin dangers of Paul's competition and of NAWSA's own lethargy and internal fractiousness. Fresh from her organizational triumphs in the New York Woman Suffrage party, Catt assumed the NAWSA presidency in 1915 with precise notions of leadership and tactics. She quickly organized a group of full-time functionaries absolutely loyal to her perspectives. And by the 1916 national convention, she was prepared to put her program across to the membership as the "Winning Plan."

NAWSA, in Catt's vision, was to use the leverage gained through state victories to persuade the major parties to commit themselves fully to a national amendment, thereby bringing hostile congressmen into line. The most dramatic activities of 1916 reflected this scheme. At the Republican convention in Chicago, more than five thousand women marched in a blinding rainstorm to the convention hall, arriving just as delegates were arguing that women did not want the ballot. After an extended debate on the floor, the G.O.P. adopted a compromise resolution favoring the extension of suffrage state by state. This emphasis on states' rights was disappointing, but the acceptance of essentially the same position by the heretofore hostile Democrats was considered a victory. Some six thousand women, carrying yellow parasols and wearing yellow sashes, lined both sides of the Democratic convention hall entrance in St. Louis, while a tableau was enacted with enfranchised states represented by women in red, white, and blue; partial suffrage in gray; and no suffrage in black. Inside the hall, women in the galleries contributed to the atmosphere with their cheering, hissing, and waving. Delegates bemoaned the "Reign of Terror" but at last they complied.

Woodrow Wilson's address to the NAWSA convention later that year confirmed the direction of events. Only a few years earlier, Taft had paternalistically warned suffragists that the nation was not ready. Now Wilson gave a philosophical interpretation of suffrage history close to NAWSA's own, ridden with natural rights archaisms, void of any deep or social comprehension, but nevertheless brimming with idealistic phraseology about the final triumph of a long crusade. As Wilson's public assent gradually turned into pressure upon reluctant elements of his party, the passage of suffrage became more certain.

American entry into World War I provided a decisive impetus. Suffrage was now touted as a war measure. This ideological slant helped melt opposition of conservatives, and in turn the state victories in New York and elsewhere in 1917 convinced many eastern urban bosses that continued resistance was useless. The same year, legislatures in Ohio, Indiana, Rhode Island, Nebraska, and Michigan enacted presidential suffrage, and Arkansas granted suffrage in party primaries. State agitation was now virtually eclipsed, with the political powers of women voters in the enfranchised states providing the measure of persuasion that generations of agitators had lacked. The passage of the Volstead Act was a final fillip, eradicating most of the remnants of opposition.

After the passage of the Susan B. Anthony Amendment in the House and the near miss by two votes in the Senate, the suffrage campaign showed new electoral strength. In 1918, suffrage supporters could claim defeat of at least two senatorial opponents. Yet the decisive vote the following year yielded more relief than joy. The ratification campaign that followed further taxed the patience and energies of loyalists, but at last sufficient numbers of the state legislatures acted favorably for women to vote in the 1920 national elections.

The final NAWSA convention and the formation of the League of Women Voters voiced a premature optimism. But Catt's rhetoric reflected a deserved pride in the distance traversed by the organized movement for women's participation in political democracy.

DOCUMENT 73 (V: 377–81): Congressional Committee Activities, NAWSA Convention, Washington, D.C., November 29–December 5, 1913

An excellent report was presented at this time by Miss Alice Paul, chairman of the Congressional Committee. From the founding of the National Association in 1869 prominent representatives had appeared before committees of every Congress and during many winters Miss Susan B. Anthony had remained in Washington until she obtained a report from these committees, but after she ceased to do this, although the hearings were still granted, nobody made it an especial business to see that the committees made reports and so none was made and action by Congress seemed very remote. In 1910, when the movement entered a new era, the association appointed a special Congressional Committee to look after this matter. By the time of the convention of 1911 the two great victories in Washington and California had been gained and the prospect of a Federal Amendment began to grow brighter. A large committee was appointed consisting chiefly of the wives of Senators and Representatives with Mrs. William Kent (Calif.) chairman. No busier women could have been selected and beyond making excellent arrangements for the hearings, the committee was not active. In 1912, when Kansas, Oregon and Arizona enfranchised women, the whole country awoke to the fact that the turning point had been reached and universal woman suffrage through an amendment to the Federal Constitution was inevitable.

At this time Miss Paul and Miss Burns returned from England, where they had been studying and doing social welfare work and had been caught in the maelstrom of the "militant" suffrage movement, then at its height. Both had taken part in demonstra-

tions before the House of Commons and been sent to prison
and they came back to the United States filled with zeal to inaugurate a campaign of "militancy" here. The idea was coldly received
by the suffrage leaders and they modified it to the extent of asking
the National Association to cooperate in organizing a great suffrage parade to take place in Washington the day before the
inauguration of Woodrow Wilson. Dr. Shaw had seen and
taken part in such parades in London and was favorably inclined
to the project. She put Miss Paul at the head of the Congressional Committee with power to choose the other members to organize the parade, with the proviso that they must themselves
raise all the money for it but they could have the authority of
the National Association letterheads. Headquarters were opened
in a basement on F Street near the New Willard Hotel in Washington. They displayed astonishing executive ability, gathered
about them a small army of women and during the next twelve
months raised $27,378, the larger part of it in Washington and
most of the remainder in Philadelphia. The parade was long,
beautiful and impressive, women from many States participating.
The report of the Congressional Committee presented to the convention by Miss Paul slightly condensed, read as follows:

Work for Federal Amendment:

Headquarters were opened in Washington, Jan. 2, 1913.
Hearings were arranged before the Woman Suffrage Committee
of the Senate; before the Rules Committee of the House, when members of the National Council of Women Voters were the speakers;
before the Rules Committee during the present convention.
Processions: March 3, when from 8,000 to 10,000 women participated; April 7, when women from congressional districts went
to Congress with petitions and resolutions; July 31, when an automobile procession met the "pilgrims" at the end of their "hike" and
escorted them through the streets of Washington to the Senate.
This procession was headed by an automobile in which rode several
of the Suffrage Committee of the Senate.
Pilgrimages coming from all parts of the country and extending
over the month of July were organized, about twelve. These all
ended in Washington on July 31, when approximately 200,000 signatures to petitions were presented to the Senate.
Deputations: Three deputations to the President were organized
immediately preceding the calling of the special session of Congress in order to ask him to give the administration support to the
suffrage amendment during the special session. One of these was

from the National Association, one from the College Suffrage League and one from the National Council of Women Voters. On November 17 a fourth deputation, composed of seventy-three women from New Jersey, was sent to the President to urge him to take up the amendment during the regular session of Congress.

Local arrangements were made for the conventions of the National Council of Women Voters and the convention of the National American Woman Suffrage Association.

A campaign under a salaried organizer was conducted through the resort regions of New Jersey, Long Island and Rhode Island during July, August and September; and one through New Jersey, Delaware and Maryland during July. A month's campaign was carried on in North Carolina. On September 1 permanent headquarters were opened in Wilmington in charge of a salaried organizer and since that time a vigorous campaign has been carried on in Delaware in the attempt to influence the attitude of the Senators and Representatives from that State.

A salaried press chairman has been employed throughout the year, who has furnished daily press copy to the local papers, to the Washington correspondents of the various papers throughout the country and to all of the telegraphic bureaus in Washington. Approximately 120,000 pieces of literature have been printed and distributed. A weekly paper under the editorship of Mrs. Rheta Childe Dorr was established on November 15. This now has a paid circulation of about 1,200 and is self-supporting from its advertisements.

A Men's League was organized, General Anson Mills, U. S. A., being the temporary and Dr. Harvey W. Wiley the permanent chairman. A large number of Congressmen are members.

Eight theater meetings, exclusive of those during this convention, have been held in Washington. Smaller meetings both indoor and out have been held almost daily and frequently as many as five or ten a day. A tableau was presented on the Treasury steps at the time of the suffrage procession of March 3 under the direction of Miss Hazel Mackaye. A suffrage play was given, also two banquets, a reception and a luncheon, and a benefit and a luncheon were given for the purpose of raising funds.

A delegation in two special cars went to New York for the procession of May 3. An even larger delegation went to Baltimore for the procession of May 31. The play given in Washington was reproduced in Baltimore for the benefit of one of the suffrage societies there. A week's campaign was conducted in the four southern counties of Maryland prior to the primary election, at the request of one of the State's societies.

The Congressional Union was formed during the latter part of April and now numbers over a thousand members.

Congressional Work.

Senate and House Joint Resolution Number One for Federal Amendment introduced in Congress April 7, 1913.

Woman Suffrage Committee of Senate voted on May 14 to report the resolution favorably and did so unanimously, one not voting. On July 31 twenty-two Senators spoke in favor of the resolution and three against it. On September 18 Senator Andrieus Jones (N. M.) spoke in favor and asked for immediate action. On the same day Senator Henry F. Ashurst (Ariz.) announced on the floor of the Senate that he would press the measure to a vote at the earliest possible moment.

Three resolutions were introduced in the House for the creation of a Woman Suffrage Committee and referred to the Rules Committee and are still before it.

The amendment resolution is awaiting third reading in the Senate and is before the Judiciary Committee of the House.

The action of the Senate was due to the fact that under the new administration a committee had been appointed which was favorable to woman suffrage instead of one opposed as heretofore, with a chairman, Senator Charles S. Thomas of Colorado, who had helped the women of his own State to secure the suffrage twenty years before. The resolutions in the Lower House were introduced by old and tried friends and the association's new Congressional Committee had arranged hearings, brought pressure to bear on members and not permitted them to forget or ignore the question. Miss Agnes E. Ryan, business manager of the *Woman's Journal*, said in her account: "The convention received the report with enthusiastic applause, giving three cheers and rising to its feet to show its appreciation."

This report was signed by Miss Paul as "chairman of the Congressional Committee and president of the Congressional Union" and she said at the beginning that it was impossible to separate the work of the two. At its conclusion Mrs. Catt moved that the part of the report as from the Congressional Committee be accepted, which was done by the convention. She then asked what was the relation between the two and why, if this was a regular committee of the National American Association, no appropriation had been made for its work during the coming year and why there was no statement in the treasurer's report of its expenditures during the past year. It developed that the committee had raised and expended its own funds, which had not passed through the national treasury, and that the Congressional Union was a society formed the preceding April to assist the work of the committee. It was moved by Mrs. Catt and carried that the convention request the Official Board to continue the Congressional Committee and to cooperate with it in such a way as to remove further causes of embarrassment to the association. The motion was amended that the board should appropriate what money could be spared for the work of this committee.[1]

The movement for woman suffrage was now so plainly centering in Congress, which had been the goal for over forty years, that there was a widespread feeling that the national headquarters should be established in Washington. Mrs. Oliver H. P. Belmont, a delegate from New York, through whose generosity it had been possible to take them to that city in 1909, offered a motion that they now be removed to Washington. She had given notice of this action the preceding day and the opponents were prepared. A motion to lay it on the table was quickly made and all discussion cut off. The opposition of the national officers was so apparent that many delegates hesitated to express their convictions for the affirmative but nevertheless the vote stood 134 ayes, and 169 noes.

[1] When the board met after the convention it was disclosed that the Congressional Union, instead of being merely a local society to assist the committee in its efforts with Congress, as Miss Paul had said, was a national organization to work for the Federal Amendment. That is, it was to duplicate the work which the National Association had been formed to do in 1869 and had brought to its present advanced stage. The association's letterheads had been used for this purpose and persons from all parts of the country had sent their names and money, many supposing they were assisting the National Association. Miss Paul had been obtaining names for membership in the Union during all the sessions of the convention. The board decided that there must be complete separation of the work of the committee and the Union; that the same person could not be at the head of both and that the plans of the Union must be regularly submitted to the Board. Miss Paul refused to accept these conditions and she was at once relieved from the chairmanship of the Congressional Committee and the other members resigned. The Union was continued as a separate organization. Another committee was appointed by the National American Association consisting of Mrs. Ruth Hanna McCormick, chairman; Mrs. Antoinette Funk, Mrs. Sherman Booth, all of Illinois, Mrs. Desha Breckinridge (Ky.), Mrs. Helen H. Gardener (D. C.), Mrs. H. Edward Dreier (N. Y.), Mrs. James Tucker (Calif.). Headquarters were opened in the Munsey Building, Washington, with the Illinois women in charge.

DOCUMENT 74 (V: 416–17): Shafroth-Palmer
Amendment and "Brief," NAWSA Convention,
Nashville, Tennessee, November 12-17, 1914

Mrs. McCormick then called on Mrs. Funk to present the Shafroth-Palmer Amendment, which had been introduced in the House by A. Mitchell Palmer (Penn.), and the argument for it. The amendment read as follows:

Whenever any number of legal voters of any State to a number exceeding 8 per cent. of the number of legal voters at the last preceding general election held in such State, shall petition for the submission to the legal voters of said State of the question whether women shall have equal rights with men in respect to voting at all elections to be held in such State, such question shall be so submitted, and if a majority of the legal voters of the State voting on the question shall vote in favor of granting to women such equal rights, the same shall thereupon be deemed established, anything in the constitution or laws of such State to the contrary notwithstanding.

In beginning her carefully prepared "brief" Mrs. Funk said:

This amendment to the U. S. Constitution must pass both branches of the national Congress by a two-thirds vote and be ratified by a majority vote of three-fourths of the State Legislatures before it becomes a law. So far it is identical with the Bristow-Mondell amendment. The difference between the two is that after the latter amendment has passed three-fourths of the State Legislatures it completely enfranchises the women. The Shafroth-Palmer amendment, after it has passed three-fourths of the State Legislatures, enables 8 per cent. of the voters of a State to bring the suffrage question up for the consideration of the voters at the next general election. Such a petition may be filed at any time, not only once but indefinitely, until suffrage is won, and a majority of those voting on the question is sufficient to carry the measure. In other words, every State where the women are not at present enfranchised may be a campaign State every year. If the male voters are obliged to hear the woman suffrage question agitated and discussed at a perennial campaign, how long will it be before, in desperation and self-defense, they will vote in favor of it?

Now, why is the Shafroth-Palmer amendment easier to pass Congress than the Bristow-Mondell amendment? First of all it shifts the responsibility of actually enfranchising the women from the Senators and Representatives to the people of their respective States.   Second, the State's rights doctrine is the one objection raised to every federal issue that comes before Congress. It is primarily the greatest obstacle to federal legislation on any subject and is recognized as a valid objection by the members of Congress and particularly those from the North, who feel that they owe to the members of the South the justice of refraining from interference in matters vital to the South. . . .

Third, the Democratic party is committed to the initiative and referendum but not to woman suffrage. . . . The President has endorsed the initiative and referendum and has fully convinced himself of its merit. . . . We are asking the Democratic party to give us, the women of the country, the initiative and referendum on the question of whether or not we shall be allowed to vote, and no State can have this question forced upon it or even settled until a majority of the voters of the State cast their ballots in favor of it.

DOCUMENT 75 (V: 453–55): The Congressional Union,
NAWSA Convention, Washington, D.C.,
December 14-19, 1915

Another problem came before this convention—the policy of
the recently formed Congressional Union to adopt the method
of the "militant" branch of the English suffragists and hold the
party in power responsible for the failure to submit the Federal
Suffrage Amendment. They had gone into the equal suffrage
States during the congressional campaign of 1914 and fought
the re-election of some of the staunchest friends of this amendment, Senator Thomas of Colorado, for instance, chairman of
the Senate Committee which had reported it favorably and a
lifelong suffragist. The press and public not knowing the difference between the two organizations were holding the National
American Association responsible and protests were coming from
all over the country. Some of the younger members, who did
not know the history and traditions of the old association, thought
that there should be cooperation between the two bodies. Both
had lobbyists actively working at the Capitol, members of Congress were confused and there was a considerable feeling that
some plan for united action should be found. Miss Zona Gale,
the writer, offered the following motion, which was carried without objection: "Realizing that all suffragists have a common
cause at heart and that difference of methods is inevitable, it is
moved that an efficiency commission consisting of five members
be appointed by the Chair to confer with representatives of the
Congressional Union in order to bring about cooperation with the
maximum of efficiency for the successful passage of the Susan
B. Anthony Amendment at this session of Congress." The
Handbook of the convention (page 155) has the following:

In accordance with the action of the convention, on the motion of Miss Zona Gale, the president of the National American Woman Suffrage Association appointed a committee of five consisting of Mrs. Carrie Chapman Catt of New York; Mrs. Medill McCormick of Illinois; Mrs. Stanley McCormick of Massachusetts; Mrs. Antoinette Funk of Illinois and Miss Hannah J. Patterson of Pennsylvania, to confer with a similar committee from the Congressional Union on the question of cooperation in congressional action. These committees met at the New Willard on December 17, Miss Alice Paul, Miss Lucy Burns, Mrs. Lawrence Lewis, Miss Anne Martin and Mrs. Gilson Gardner being present as representatives of the Congressional Union, all but Mrs. Lewis (Penn.) of the District of Columbia.

Its representatives made two suggestions: (1) That the Congressional Union should affiliate with the National American Woman Suffrage Association. (2) That in any event frequent meetings for consultation should be held between the legislative committees of the two in order to secure more united action.

In the discussion of these suggestions it developed that at this time the Congressional Union has no election policy and that its future policy must depend on political situations. The Union declares itself to be non-partisan according to its constitution, which pledges its members to support suffrage regardless of the interests of any national political parties. At this point the report of the joint conference ends.

The committee of five representing the National American Association recommends that no affiliation shall take place because it was made quite clear that the Congressional Union does not denounce nor pledge itself not to resume what we term its anti-party policy and what they designate as their election policy; also because it is their intention, as announced by them, to organize in all States in the Union for congressional work, thus duplicating organizations already existing. Your committee further recommends that the incoming board of officers give their serious consideration to the suggestion of conferences with a view to securing more united action in the lobby work in Washington.

At the conference Mrs. Catt explained to Miss Paul that the association could not accept as an affiliated society one which was likely to defy its policy held since its foundation in 1869, which was neither to support nor oppose any political party, nor to work for or against any candidate except as to his attitude toward woman suffrage. Miss Paul would give no guarantee that the Congressional Union would observe this policy. It was thought that some way of dividing the lobby work might be found but in a short time the Union announced its program of fighting the candidates of the Democratic party without any reference to their position on the Federal Amendment or their record on woman suffrage. They offered as a reason that as the Democratic party was in control of the Government it should have the Federal Amendment submitted. There never was a time when the Democrats had the necessary two-thirds of the members of each house of Congress, but enough of them favored it so that it could have been carried if enough of the Republicans had voted for it. It was plainly evident that it would require the support of both parties. The policy of the Congressional Union, put into action throughout the presidential campaign of 1916, made any co-operation impossible.

DOCUMENT 76 (V: 675–77): The National Woman's Party, 1913-17

The National Woman's Party was organized in the spring of 1913 under the name of the Congressional Union for Woman Suffrage. Its original purpose was to support the work of the Congressional Committee of the National American Woman Suffrage Association and its officers were the members of that committee: Miss Alice Paul (N. J.); Miss Crystal Eastman (Wis.); Miss Lucy Burns (N. Y.); Mrs. Lawrence Lewis (Penn.); Mrs. Mary Beard (N. Y.). In successive years names added to its executive committee were those of Mesdames Oliver H. P. Belmont, William Kent, Gilson Gardner, Donald R. Hooker, John Winters Brannan, Harriot Stanton Blatch, Florence Bayard Hilles, J. A. H. Hopkins, Thomas N. Hepburn, Richard Wainwright; Miss Elsie Hill, Miss Anne Martin and others. A large advisory committee was formed.

The object of the Union was the same as that of the National Association—to secure an amendment to the Federal Constitution which would give universal woman suffrage. At the annual convention of the association in December, 1913, a new Congressional Committee was appointed and the Congressional Union became an independent organization. Its headquarters were in Washington, D. C. It never was regularly organized by States, districts, etc., although there were branches in various States. The work was centralized in the Washington headquarters and the forces were easily mobilized. The exact membership probably was never known by anybody. It was a small but very active organization and Miss Paul was the supreme head with no restrictions. A great deal of initiative was allowed to the workers in other parts of the country who were often governed by the exigencies of the situation. After the first few years annual conventions were held in Washington.

While the principal object of the National Association always was a Federal Amendment, for which it worked unceasingly, it realized that Congress would not submit one until a number of States had made the experiment and their enfranchised women could bring political pressure to bear on the members. Therefore the association campaigned in the States for amendments to their constitutions. The Union did no work of this kind but when it was organized nine States had granted full suffrage to women, the time was ripe for a big "drive" for a Federal Amendment and it could utilize this tremendous backing. Within the next five years six more States were added to the list, including the powerful one of New York. In addition the National Association, cooperating with the women in the States, had secured in fourteen others the right for their women to vote for Presidential electors. The Federal Amendment was a certainty of a not distant future but there was yet a great deal of work to do.

In carrying on this work, while the two organizations followed similar lines in many respects there were some marked differences. The National Association was strictly non-partisan, made no distinction of parties, and followed only constitutional methods. The Congressional Union held the majority party in Congress wholly responsible for the success or failure of the Federal Amendment and undertook to prevent the re-election of its members. In the Congressional elections of 1914 its representatives toured the States where women could vote and urged them to defeat all Democratic candidates regardless of their attitude toward woman suffrage. This policy was followed in subsequent campaigns.

In 1915 the Union held a convention in San Francisco during the Panama-Pacific Exposition and sent envoys across the country with a petition to President Wilson and Congress collected at its headquarters during the exposition. In 1916 it held a three days' convention in Chicago during the National Republican convention and at this time organized the National Woman's Party with the Federal Suffrage Amendment as the only plank in its platform and a Campaign Committee was formed with Miss Anne Martin of Nevada as chairman. At a meeting in Washington in March, 1917, the name Congressional Union was officially changed to National Woman's Party and Miss Paul was elected chairman.

On Jan. 10, 1917, the Union began the "picketing" of the White House, delegations of women with banners standing at the gates all day "as a perpetual reminder to President Wilson that they held him responsible for their disfranchisement." They stood there unmolested for three months and then the United States entered the war. Conditions were no longer normal, feeling was intense and there were protests from all parts of the country against this demonstration in front of the home of the President. In June the police began arresting them for "obstructing the traffic" and during the next six months over 200 were arrested representing many States. They refused to pay their fines in the police court and were sent to the jail and workhouse for from three days to seven months. These were unsanitary, they were roughly treated, "hunger strikes" and forcible feeding followed, there was public indignation and on November 28 President Wilson pardoned all of them and the "picketing" was resumed. Congress delayed action on the Federal Amendment and members of the Union held meetings in Lafayette Square and burned the President's speeches. Later they burned them and a paper effigy of the President on the sidewalk in front of the White House. Arrests and imprisonments followed.

While these violent tactics were being followed the Union worked also along legitimate lines, organized parades, lobbied in Congress, attended committee hearings, went to political conventions, interviewed candidates and worked unceasingly. When the amendment was submitted for ratification it transferred its activities to the Legislatures and the Presidential candidates.

DOCUMENT 77 (V: 488–89): Carrie Chapman Catt,
"The Crisis," NAWSA Emergency Convention, Atlantic
City, New Jersey, September 4-10, 1916

At 3:30 Mrs. Catt began her president's address before an
audience that filled the large theater and listened with intense
interest until the last word was spoken at five o'clock. It was a
masterly review of the movement for woman suffrage and a program for the work now necessary to bring it to a successful end.
The opening sentences were as follows:

I have taken for my subject, "The Crisis," because I believe that
a crisis has come in our movement which, if recognized and the
opportunity seized with vigor, enthusiasm and will, means the final
victory of our great cause in the very near future. I am aware that
some suffragists do not share in this belief; they see no signs nor
symptoms today which were not present yesterday; no manifestations in the year 1916 which differ significantly from those in the
year 1910. To them, the movement has been a steady, normal growth
from the beginning and must so continue until the end. I can only
defend my claim with the plea that it is better to imagine a crisis
where none exists than to fail to recognize one when it comes, for
a crisis is a culmination of events which calls for new considerations and new decisions. A failure to answer the call may mean
an opportunity lost, a possible victory postponed. . . .

This address, coming at the moment when woman suffrage
was accepted as inevitable by the President of the United States
and all the political parties, was regarded as the key-note of the
beginning of a campaign which would end in victory. In pamph-
let form it was used as a highly valued campaign document.

Mrs. Catt showed the impossibility of securing suffrage for all
the women of the country by the State method and pointed out

that the Federal Amendment was the one and only way. "Our cause has been caught in a snarl of constitutional obstructions and inadequate election laws," she said, after drawing upon her own experience to show the hazards of State referenda, and we have a right to appeal to our Congress to extricate it from this tangle. If there is any chivalry left this is the time for it to come forward and do an act of simple justice. In my judgment the women of this land not only have the right to sit on the steps of Congress until it acts but it is their self-respecting duty to insist upon their enfranchisement by that route. . . . Were there never another convert made there are suffragists enough in this country, if combined, to make so irresistible a driving force that victory might be seized at once. How can it be done? By a simple change of mental attitude. If you are to seize the victory, that change must take place in this hall, here and now. The crisis is here, but if the call goes unheeded, if our women think it means the vote without a struggle, if they think other women can and will pay the price of their emancipation, the hour may pass and our political liberty may not be won. . . . The character of a man is measured by his will. The same is true of a movement. Then *will* to be free." The address made a deep impression and was accepted as a call to arms.

DOCUMENT 78 (V: 496–98): Woodrow Wilson's
Address, NAWSA Convention, Atlantic City, New
Jersey, September 4-10, 1916

As he came from the street to the stage with Mrs. Wilson, also gowned in white, he passed through a lane of suffragists, one from each State, designated by banners, with broad sashes of blue and gold across their breasts. He was accompanied by Private Secretary Tumulty and several distinguished men and the entire stage behind the decorations of palms and other plants was surrounded by a cordon of the secret service. Forty-three large newspapers throughout the country were represented at the reporters' table.

The President had asked to speak last and he listened with much interest to a program of noted public workers as follows: Why Women Need the Vote. The Call of the Working Woman for the Protection of the Woman's Vote—Mrs. Raymond Robins, president of National Women's Trades Union League. Mothers in Politics—Miss Julia Lathrop, chief of National Children's Bureau. A Necessary Safeguard to Public Morals—Dr. Katharine Bement Davis, Chief of Parole Commission, New York City. Working Children—Dr. Owen R. Lovejoy, general secretary of National Child Labor Committee. Each speaker emphasized the necessity for the enfranchisement of women as a means for the nation's highest welfare. Mrs. Catt was in the chair and introduced the President, who said with much earnestness and sincerity:

Madam President, Ladies of the Association: I have found it a real privilege to be here tonight and to listen to the addresses which you have heard. Though you may not all of you believe it, I would a great deal rather hear somebody else speak than speak myself, but I would feel that I was omitting a duty if I did not address you tonight and say some of the things that have been in my thoughts as I realized the approach of this evening and the duty that would fall upon me.

The astonishing thing about the movement which you represent is not that it has grown so slowly but that it has grown so rapidly. No doubt for those who have been a long time in the struggle, like your honored president, it seems a long and arduous path that has been trodden, but when you think of the cumulating force of the movement in recent decades you must agree with me that it is one of the most astonishing tides in modern history. Two generations ago—no doubt Madam President will agree with me in saying this—it was a handful of women who were fighting for this cause; now it is a great multitude of women who are fighting for it. There are some interesting historical connections which I should like to attempt to point out to you.

One of the most striking facts about the history of the United States is that at the outset it was a lawyers' history. Almost all of the questions to which America addressed itself, say a hundred years ago, were legal questions; were questions of methods, not questions of what you were going to do with your government but questions of how you were going to constitute your government; how you were going to balance the powers of the State and the Federal government; how you were going to balance the claims of property against the processes of liberty; how you were going to make up your government so as to balance the parts against each other, so that the Legislature would check the Executive and the Executive the Legislature. The idea of government when the United States became a nation was a mechanical conception and the mechanical conception which underlay it was the Newtonian theory of the universe. If you take up the Federalist you see that some parts of it read like a treatise on government. They speak of the centrifugal and centripetal forces and locate the President somewhere in a rotating system. The whole thing is a calculation of power and adjustment of parts. There was a time when nobody but a lawyer could know enough to run the government of the United States. . . .

And then something happened. A great question arose in this country which, though complicated with legal elements, was at bottom a human question and nothing but a question of humanity. That was the slavery question, and is it not significant that it was then, and then for the first time, that women became prominent in politics in America? Not many women—those prominent in that day are so few that you can almost name them over in a brief catalogue—but, nevertheless, they then began to play a part not only in writing but in public speech, which was a very novel part for women to play in America; and after the Civil War had settled some of what seemed to be the most difficult legal questions of our system the life of the nation began not only to unfold but to accumulate.

Life in the United States was a comparatively simple matter at the time of the Civil War. There was none of that underground struggle which is now so manifest to those who look only a little way beneath the surface. Stories such as Dr. Davis has told tonight were uncommon in those simpler days. The pressure of low wages, the agony of obscure and unremunerated toil did not exist in America in anything like the same proportions as they exist now. And as our life has unfolded and accumulated, as the contacts of it have become hot, as the populations have assembled in the cities and the cool spaces of the country have been supplemented by feverish urban areas, the whole nature of our political questions has been altered. They have ceased to be legal questions. They have more and more become social questions, questions with regard to the relations of human beings to one another, not merely their legal relations but their moral and spiritual relations to one another.

This has been most characteristic of American life in the last few decades, and as these questions have assumed greater and greater prominence the movement which this association represents has gathered cumulative force, so that when anybody asks himself, What does this gathering force mean? if he knows anything about the history of the country he knows that it means something *which has not only come to stay but has come with conquering power.*

I get a little impatient sometimes about the discussion of the channels and methods by which it is to prevail. *It is going to prevail* and that is a very superficial and ignorant view of it which attributes it to mere social unrest. It is not merely because women are discontented, it is because they have seen visions of duty, and that is something that we not only can not resist but if we be true Americans we do not wish to resist. Because America took its origin in visions of the human spirit, in aspirations for the deepest sort of liberty of the mind and heart, and, as visions of that sort come to the sight of those who are spiritually minded America comes more and more into its birthright and into the perfection of its development; so that what we have to realize is that in dealing with forces of this sort we are dealing with the substance of life itself.

I have felt as I sat here tonight the wholesome contagion of the occasion. Almost every other time that I ever visited Atlantic City I came to fight somebody. I hardly know how to conduct myself when *I have not come to fight anybody but with somebody.*

I have come to suggest among other things that when the forces of nature are working steadily and the tide is rising to meet the moon, you need not be afraid that it will not come to its flood. We feel the tide; we rejoice in the strength of it, and *we shall not quarrel in the long run as to the method of it,* because, when you are working with masses of men and organized bodies of opinion, you have got to carry the organized body along. The whole art and practice of government consist not in moving individuals but in moving masses. It is all very well to run ahead and beckon, but, after all, you have got to wait for them to follow. I have not come to ask you to be patient, because you have been, but I have come to congratulate you that there has been a force behind you that will beyond any peradventure be triumphant and for which you can afford a little while to wait.

DOCUMENT 79 (V: 513–15): NAWSA Convention,
Washington, D.C., December 12-15, 1917

The Forty-ninth National Suffrage Convention, which met in
Poli's Theater at Washington Dec. 12-15, 1917, was held under
the most difficult conditions that ever had been faced in the long
history of these annual gatherings. Always heretofore they
had been comfortable, happy times, when the delegates came from
far and wide to exchange greetings, report progress and plan the
future work for a cause to which many of them were giving
their entire time and effort. Now great changes had taken place,
as the Call for the convention indicated.

Since last we met the all-engulfing World War has drawn our own
country into its maelstrom and ominous clouds rest over the earth,
obscuring the vision and oppressing the souls of mankind, yet out
of the confusion and chaos of strife there has developed a stronger
promise of the triumph of democracy than the world has ever known.
Every allied nation has announced that it is fighting for this and our
own President has declared that "we are fighting for democracy, for
the right of those who submit to authority to have a voice in their
own government." New Russia has answered the call; Great Britain
has pledged full suffrage for women and the measure has already
passed the House of Commons by the enormous majority of seven
to one. Canada, too, has responded with five newly enfranchised
provinces; France is waiting only to drive the foe from her soil to
give her women political liberty.

Such an array of victories gives us faith to believe that our own
Government will soon follow the example of other allied nations
and will also pledge votes to its women citizens as an earnest of its
sincerity that in truth we do fight for democracy. This is our first
national convention since our country entered the war. We are
faced with new problems and new issues and the nation is realizing
its dependence upon women as never before. It must be made to
realize also that, willingly as women are now serving, they can serve
still more efficiently when they shall have received the full measure
of citizenship. These facts must be urged upon Congress and our
Government must be convinced that the time has come for the
enfranchisement of women by means of an amendment to the Federal Constitution.

Men and women who believe that the great question of world

democracy includes government of the people, by the people and for the people in our country, are invited to attend our convention and counsel with us on ways and means to attain this object at the earliest possible moment.[1]

On account of the large rush of soldiers to the eastern coast and the many other problems of transportation travelling had become very hard and expensive but so greatly had the interest in suffrage increased among women that nearly 600 delegates were present, the highest number that had ever attended one of the conventions. They came through weather below zero, snow-storms and washouts; trains from the far West were thirty-six hours late; delegates from the South were in two railroad wrecks. It was one of the coldest Decembers ever known and the eastern part of the country had never before faced such a coal famine, from various reasons. Washington was inundated with people, the vast number who had suddenly been called into the service of the Government, the soldiers and the members of their families who had come to be with them to the last, and this city of only a few hundred thousand inhabitants had neither sleeping nor eating accommodations for all of them. The suffrage convention had been called before these conditions were fully known and because of the necessity of bringing pressure at once on Congress. The national suffrage headquarters were now occupying a large private house and the officers were cared for there but the delegates were obliged to scatter over the city wherever they could find shelter, were always cold and some of the time not far from hungry and prices were double what was expected. Notwithstanding all these drawbacks the convention program was carried out and a large amount of valuable work accomplished, tried and loyal suffragists being accustomed to hardships and self-sacrifice.

The victory in New York State the preceding month had marked the beginning of the end and the universal enfranchisement of women seemed almost in sight. Even the intense excite-

[1] Signed: Dr. Anna Howard Shaw, honorary president; Mrs. Carrie Chapman Catt, president; Mrs. Walter McNab Miller, Mrs. Stanley McCormick and Miss Esther G. Ogden, vice-presidents; Mrs. Frank J. Shuler, corresponding secretary; Mrs. Thomas Jefferson Smith, recording secretary; Mrs. Henry Wade Rogers, treasurer; Mrs. Pattie Ruffner Jacobs, auditor; Mrs. Maud Wood Park, chairman Congressional Committee; Miss Rose Young, chairman of Press; Mrs. Arthur L. Livermore, chairman of Literature.

ment of the war had not entirely overshadowed what had now became a national issue. Under the auspices of Mrs. Helen H. Gardener, resident in Washington, an Advisory Council was formed to act in an honorary capacity and extend official recognition to the convention, Senators, Representatives, Cabinet officers, Judges, clergymen and others prominent in the life of the capital, with their wives and other women of their family, cheerfully giving their names for this purpose.

The evening before the convention opened a reception by invitation was given in the ball room of the New Willard Hotel to Dr. Shaw, Mrs. Catt and the other officers and the delegates, the following acting as hostesses: Mrs. William Gibbs McAdoo, Mrs. Newton D. Baker, Mrs. Thomas W. Gregory, Mrs. Albert Sidney Burleson, Mrs. Josephus Daniels, Mrs. Franklin K. Lane, Mrs. David F. Houston, Miss Agnes Hart Wilson, Mrs. James R. Mann, Mrs. Philip Pitt Campbell. The first seven were the wives and the eighth the daughter of the members of President Wilson's Cabinet, only Mrs. Robert Lansing being absent, who, like her husband, was an anti-suffragist.

DOCUMENT 80 (V: 534–36): Anna Howard Shaw,
NAWSA Convention, Washington, D.C.,
December 12-15, 1917

In a stirring address Dr. Shaw showed
what the country expected of women at this critical time, saying:

We talk of the army in the field as one and the army at home
as another. We are not two armies; we are one—absolutely one
army—and we must work together. Unless the army at home does
its duty faithfully, the army in the field will be unable to carry to a
victorious end this war which you and I believe is the great war
that shall bring to the world the thing that is nearest our hearts—
democracy, that "those who submit to authority shall have a voice
in the government" and that when they have that voice peace shall
reign among the nations of men.

The United States Government, learning from the weaknesses
and the mistakes of the governments across the sea, immediately
after declaring war on Germany knew that it was wise to mobilize
not only the man power of the nation but the woman power. It took
Great Britain a long time to learn that—more than a year—and it
was not until 50,000 women paraded the streets of London with
banners saying, "Put us to work," that it dawned upon the British
government that women could be mobilized and made serviceable
in the war. And what is the result? It has been discovered that
men and women alike have within them great reserve power, great
forces which are called out by emergencies and the demands of a
time like this.

Dr. Shaw described the forming of the Woman's Committee
of the Council of National Defense by the Government and her
selection as its chairman. She said she had no idea what the
committee was expected to do, so she went to the Secretary of
the Navy to find out, and continued: "I learned that the Woman's Committee was to be the channel through which the orders
of the various departments of the Government concerning women's war work were to reach the womanhood of the country;
that it was to conserve and coordinate all the women's societies in
the United States which were doing war work in order to prevent
duplication and useless effort. This was very necessary, not because our women are not patriotic but because they are so patriotic
that every blessed woman in the country was writing Washington,
or her organization was writing for her, asking the Government
what she could do for the war and of course the Government

did not know; it has not yet the least idea of what women can do."

An amusing picture was given of men supervising a department of the Red Cross where women were knitting, making comfort bags, etc. She showed how for the past forty years women in their clubs and societies had been going through the necessary evolution, "until today," she said, "they are a mobilized army ready to serve the country in whatever capacity they are needed. So when the Council of National Defense laid upon the Woman's Committee the responsibility of calling them together to mobilize women's war work, we knew exactly how to do it. . . . It is not a question of whether we will act or not, the Government has said we *must* act; it is an order as much as it is an order that men shall go and fight in the trenches. It is an order of the Government that the women's war work of the country shall be coordinated, that women shall keep their organizations intact, that they shall get together under directed heads. I said to the gentlemen here in Washington, when at first they feared our women might not be willing to cooperate: 'If you put before them an incentive big enough, if you appeal to them as a part of the Government's life, not as a by-product of creation or a kindergarten but as a great human, living energy, ready to serve the country, they will respond as readily as the men.' "

We must remember that more and more sacrifices are going to be demanded but I want to say to you women, do not meekly sit down and make all the sacrifices and demand nothing in return. It is not that you want pay but we all want an equally balanced sacrifice. The Government is asking us to conserve food while it is allowing carload after carload to rot on the side tracks of railroad stations and great elevators of grain to be consumed by fire for lack of proper protection. If we must eat Indian meal in order to save wheat, then the men must protect the grain elevators and see that the wheat is saved. We must demand that there shall be conservation all along the line. I had a letter the other day giving me a fearful scorching because of a speech I made in which I said that we women have Mr. Hoover looking into our refrigerators, examining our bread to see what kind of materials we are using, telling us what extravagant creatures we are, that we waste millions of money every year, waste food and all that sort of thing, and yet while we are asked to have meatless days and wheatless days, I have never yet seen a demand for a smokeless day! They are asking through the newspapers that we women shall dance, play bridge, have charades, sing and do everything under the sun to raise money to buy tobacco for the men in the trenches, while the men who want us to do this have a cigar in their mouth at the time they are asking it! I said that if men want the soldiers to have tobacco, let them have smokeless days and furnish it! If they would conserve one single cigar a day and send it to the men in the trenches the soldiers would have all they would need and the men at home would be a great deal better off. If we have to eat rye flour to send wheat across the sea they must stop smoking to send smokes across the sea.

There is no end to the things that women are asked to do. I know this is true because I have read the newspapers for the last six months to get my duty before me. The first thing we are asked to do is to provide the enthusiasm, inspiration and patriotism to make men want to fight, and we are to send them away with a smile! That is not much to ask of a mother! We are to maintain a perfect calm after we have furnished all this inspiration and enthusiasm, "keep the home fires burning," keep the home sweet and peaceful and happy, keep society on a level, look after business, buy enough but not too much and wear some of our old clothes but not all of them or what would happen to the merchants? . . . We are going to rise as women always have risen to the supreme height of patriotic service. . . .

The Woman's Committee of the Council of National Defense now asks for your cooperation, that we may be what the Government would have us be, soldiers at home, defending the interests of the home, while the men are fighting with the gallant Allies who are laying down their lives that this world may be a safe place and that men and women may know the meaning of democracy, which is that we are one great family of God. That, and that only, is the ideal of democracy for which our flag stands.

DOCUMENT 81 (V: 550–51): NAWSA Convention,
St. Louis, Missouri, March 24-29, 1919

For the first time since it was founded in 1869 the National American Woman Suffrage Association in 1918 omitted its annual convention. Suffragists were accustomed to strenuous effort but this year strained to the last ounce the strength of all engaged in national work. The Congressional Committee could not secure the respite of a single day and were summoning women from all parts of the country for service in Washington and demanding extra work from them at home, telegrams, letters, influence from the constituencies, etc. There was a vote Jan. 10, 1918, in the Lower House and a continual pressure from that moment to get a vote in the Senate, which did not come till October and was adverse. Then the committee pushed on without stopping. Mrs. Shuler, the corresponding secretary, had been in the Michigan, South Dakota and Oklahoma campaigns all summer and was exhausted. The three States were carried for suffrage and when the election was over all the forces were used to obtain Presidential suffrage in the big legislative year beginning January, 1919. It was a question of pressing forward to victory or stopping to prepare for and hold a convention and lose the opportunities for gains in Congress.

During the first ten months of 1918 the vast conflict in Europe had gone steadily on; the United States had sent over millions of soldiers and other millions were in training camps on this side of the ocean; transportation was blocked; the advanced cost of living had brought distress to many households; thousands of families were in mourning, and everywhere suffragists were devoting time and strength to those heavy burdens of war which always fall on women. By November 1, when it would have been necessary to issue the call for a convention, there was no prospect of a change in these hard conditions, and when on

November 11 the Armistice was suddenly declared no one was interested in anything but the end of the war and its world-wide aftermath.   During the dark days of 1918, however, there had come a tremendous advance in the status of woman suffrage. The magnificent way in which women had met the demands of war, their patriotic service, their loyalty to the Government, had swept away the old-time objections to their enfranchisement and fully established their right to full equality in all the privileges of citizenship.   Early in the winter the Lower House of Congress by a two-thirds vote declared in favor of submitting to the Legislatures an amendment to the Federal Constitution, the object for which the National Suffrage Association had been formed, and the Parliament of Great Britain had fully enfranchised the majority of its women.   In the spring the Canadian Parliament conferred full Dominion suffrage on women.   Before and after the Armistice the nations of Europe that had overthrown their Emperors and Kings gave women equal voting rights with men.   In November at their State elections, Michigan, South Dakota and Oklahoma gave complete suffrage to women. The U. S. Senate was still holding out by a majority of two against submitting the Federal Amendment but it was almost universally recognized that the seventy years' struggle for woman suffrage in this country was nearing the end.

DOCUMENT 82 (V: 684): Carrie Chapman Catt, "The
Nation Calls," League of Women Voters National
Convention, St. Louis, Missouri, March 24-29, 1919

Every suffragist will hope for a memorial dedicated to the memory of our brave departed leaders, to the sacrifices they made for
our cause, to the scores of victories won. . . . I venture to propose
one whose benefits will bless our entire nation and bring happiness
to the humblest of our citizens—the most natural, the most appropriate and the most patriotic memorial that could be suggested—a
League of Women Voters to "finish the fight" and to aid in the
reconstruction of the nation. What could be more natural than
that women having attained their political independence should
desire to give service in token of their gratitude? What could be
more appropriate than that such women should do for the coming
generation what those of a preceding did for them? What could
be more patriotic than that these women should use their new freedom to make the country safer for their children and their children's children?

Let us then raise up a League of Women Voters, the name and
form of organization to be determined by the members themselves;
a league that shall be non-partisan and non-sectarian and consecrated
to three chief aims: 1. To use its influence to obtain the full enfranchisement of the women of every State in our own republic
and to reach out across the seas in aid of the woman's struggle for
her own in every land. 2. To remove the remaining legal discriminations against women in the codes and constitutions of the several States in order that the feet of coming women may find these
stumbling blocks removed. 3. To make our democracy so safe for
the nation and so safe for the world that every citizen may feel secure and great men will acknowledge the worthiness of the American
republic to lead.

DOCUMENT 83 (V: 594–95): Call to the Victory
Convention of the National American Woman Suffrage
Association and the First Congress of the League of
Women Voters, Chicago, Illinois, February 12-18, 1920

The official report of the Fifty-first convention, in 1920, was
entitled Victory Convention of the National American Woman
Suffrage Association and First Congress of the League of Women
Voters and the Call was as follows:

"Suffragists, hear this last call to a suffrage convention!

"The officers of the National American Woman Suffrage Association hereby call the State auxiliaries, through their elected delegates, to meet in annual convention at Chicago, Congress Hotel,
February 12th to 18th, inclusive. In other days our members and
friends have been summoned to annual conventions to disseminate
the propaganda for their common cause, to cheer and encourage
each other, to strengthen their organized influence, to counsel as
to ways and means of insuring further progress. At this time
they are called to rejoice that the struggle is over, the aim achieved
and the women of the nation about to enter into the enjoyment
of their hard-earned political liberty. Of all the conventions held
within the past fifty-one years, this will prove the most momentous. Few people live to see the actual and final realization of
hopes to which they have devoted their lives. That privilege
is ours.

"Turning to the past let us review the incidents of our long
struggle together before they are laid away with other buried
memories. Let us honor our pioneers. Let us tell the world of
the ever-buoyant hope, born of the assurance of the justice and
inevitability of our cause, which has given our army of workers
the unswerving courage and determination that at last have overcome every obstacle and attained their aim. Come and let us
together express the joy which only those can feel who have suffered for a cause.

"Turning to the future, let us inquire together how best we can
now serve our beloved nation. Let us ask what political parties

want of us and we of them.   Come one and all and unitedly make
this last suffrage convention a glad memory to you, a heritage
for your children and your children's children and a benefaction
to our nation. "

INDEX OF PROPER NAMES

SUBJECT INDEX

Abolitionism: basis of suffrage activities, 4–6; heritage in Civil War, 205

Abolitionists: women as, 79; role in woman's rights, 115; indifferent to women's petitions, 219

Advocate of Moral Reform, 4

AERA. *See* American Equal Rights Association

Agriculture: women's role in, 168

Akron, Ohio: woman's rights convention in, 103–5

Albany, N.Y.: temperance convention in, 141–42; Stanton's oration in, 153; woman's rights convention, 161

Alaska-Yukon-Pacific Exposition, 386

American Anti-Slavery Society: participation of women in, 5–6 *passim*; formation of, 69

American democracy: reformers' faith in, 43

American Equal Rights Association (AERA): importance of, 16–20 *passim*; formed, 224, 230–31; conventions, 235–44; 257–74

American Federation of Labor, 367

American liberty: women's contribution to, 228–29

American Medical Association, 345

American Revolution: ideology for suffragists, 1, 3; milestone in freedom, 49; related to British traditions, 56; women's activities in, 57–59 *passim*

American Woman Suffrage Association (AWSA): limited documentation in *History of Woman Suffrage*, xix-xx *passim*; founded, 20; drift toward political isolation, 22; strategy of supporting partial suffrage, 25; leaders seek state referenda victories, 282, 308

"Americanization": NAWSA campaign in World War I, 40

An Appeal in Favor of that Class of Americans Called Africans: antislavery tract, 5

Anglo-Saxons: superiority refuted, 349

Anglo-Saxon women: as salvation of South, 349

Antioch College, 158

Antislavery movement: women's activities in, 65–67, 69, 71–72, 77–79 *passim*

Antislavery societies: women's role in challenged, 79–82 *passim*

Arizona: woman suffrage victory, 381

Arkansas: legislature grants woman suffrage in primary, 415

Art: women's participation in, 166

Atlanta, Ga.: woman suffrage convention in, 337–38

Atlantic City, N.J.: woman suffrage convention in, 430–34

Auto tours: for woman suffrage in Illinois, 391

AWSA. *See* American Woman Suffrage Association

Baltimore, Md.: woman suffrage convention in, 371

"Barber's Day," 403

Beatrice, Nebr.: publication place of *Woman's Tribune*, 26

Bible: implications for women discussed, 13, 100, 131–32, 135, 148

Bible Resolution: debated at woman suffrage convention, 339–40

Bills of Attainder: demand none for women, 300–301

Black male suffrage: relation to woman suffrage discussed, 231, 238–44 *passim*, 254–56, 328, 337

Blacks: emancipation of, related to woman's rights, 200–208 *passim*, 305

Black women: need for suffrage, 103–4, 235–36, 263, 267

Bloomer costume, 9

Boarding House Bill: to aid women, 161

Boston: woman's rights convention in, 157